This collection of essays, attuned to pertinent issues and controversies surrounding classic Reformed covenant theology, beckons readers to enter the rich field of Reformed thought on the covenants. This book explores covenant theology in both its rudimentary formulations and its broad applications. As a leading Reformed theologian of our generation, Venema takes up debates that center on the covenant of works, assessing with care the case for the so-called republication of that covenant. He also tackles the important topic of the relationship between divine election and the covenant of grace; and not to be missed is his careful analysis of the election and salvation of believers' children who die before coming to faith. Likewise of relevance is Venema's engagement with advocates of the Federal Vision, in which their misapprehension of covenant theology is fairly explained and soundly debunked. This volume shows that covenant theology is still a lively topic, and integral to explaining the gospel of Jesus Christ.

—**J. Mark Beach**, Mid-America Reformed Seminary

Contemporary debate in covenant theology, particularly on the covenant of works, often pits biblical scholar against systematic theologian and both against historians. Not only is this not the way it should be, this valuable collection of essays models the integration of Scripture, history, and dogmatics, and sets forth a clear statement of the classic Reformed understanding of *covenant*. Along the way, we are treated to a thorough, accessible, and incisive critical overview of twentieth-century scholarship on the covenant, including the significant roles played by the neo-orthodoxy of Karl Barth and the more recent New Perspectives on Paul. Venema correctly points out that accepting or rejecting the Augustinian (!) distinction between humanity's pre-fall fellowship with God and the post-fall renewed fellowship with God in Christ is a key issue in the debate. On a subject as contentious as *covenant*, no one work will settle matters finally and satisfy everyone. While legitimate debates should continue (on *republication*, for example), Venema's even-tempered treatment provides a high standard of both form and content for this discussion.

—**John Bolt**, Jean and Kenneth Baker Professor of Systematic Theology, Calvin Theological Seminary

I have given the better part of thirty years of my academic attention to the formulation and development of covenant theology. A lot of voices out there are speaking on this subject—some very good, others very bad; some useful critics and interlocutors, others less so; some advocates with views worth entertaining, others with opinions best not given a second thought. Sorting those things out (which is which?) requires significant knowledge and judgment, even for rather advanced students of covenant theology. Cornel Venema possesses both, so he is an expert to whom I have often looked for analysis and assessment of important issues relating to classic covenant theology. In particular, matters relating to the Mosaic administration have long been acknowledged to be among the most difficult in articulating the unified covenant of grace, and have prompted the most substantial disagreements within the orthodox Reformed tradition. Venema is superb in his synopsis of and engagement with these kinds of issues. For these reasons and more, I warmly commend this book to all students of covenant theology, and I look forward to returning to it again and again as I seek to think biblically about the covenants.

—**J. Ligon Duncan**, Chancellor/CEO, Reformed Theological Seminary; John E. Richards Professor of Systematic Theology, RTS Jackson

No one today is better qualified to address the perennially important issues of covenant theology than Cornel Venema. In this volume he considers some of these issues in the context of current discussions and debates, doing so in a particularly instructive and helpful manner. I commend it highly.

—**Richard B. Gaffin Jr.**, Professor of Biblical and Systematic Theology, Emeritus, Westminster Theological Seminary

This is a book full of insightful commentary from Professor Venema. In places I rejoiced to see him correct some misunderstandings with his usual clarity and incisiveness. Even those who might disagree with him will have to be at their best. I commend this wide-ranging study to all students of the Scriptures, and Reformed theology in particular.

—**Mark Jones**, Minister, Faith Vancouver, Vancouver, British Columbia

A number of significant contemporary controversies within the Reformed church are rooted in various understandings (and misunderstandings) of covenant theology. In this helpful and instructive collection of essays, Dr. Cornelis Venema sheds much-needed light on issues ranging from the doctrine of republication to the Federal Vision theology. Regardless of whether one agrees with all of Venema's specific conclusions, his arguments cannot be ignored. A must-read for those interested in the debates associated with covenant theology.

—**Keith A. Mathison**, Professor of Systematic Theology, Reformation Bible College

Covenant theology lies at the heart of Reformed theology. It often lies at the heart of controversies among theologians as well. Cornel Venema addresses key debates surrounding covenant theology with patience, gentleness, respect, and charity. His work is valuable for its tone, as much as for its content. If read prayerfully, this book has the potential to promote greater unity in Reformed churches, protect people from error, and increase our love for God in Christ.

—**Ryan M. McGraw**, Professor of Systematic Theology, Greenville Presbyterian Theological Seminary

Reformed theologian Cornelis Venema's book *Christ and Covenant Theology* examines the comprehensive theme of God's eternal purpose to fellowship with his people. Stressing that God's covenant can be rightly understood only by keeping the person and work of Christ central, Dr. Venema clearly portrays the doctrine of the covenant as synthesizing the biblical understanding of God's purpose in creation and new creation. While addressing perennial issues in the Reformed understanding of covenant theology, Dr. Venema does not neglect recent debates swirling around a proper view of the covenant. Especially noteworthy is his refutation of the Federal Vision as well as N. T. Wright's harmful denial of the Reformation's biblical view of justification. *Christ and Covenant Theology* is compelling, comprehensive, and replete with pastoral implications. Here is a book to make the reader think, but also a book leading the reader to worship Christ, the origin and the end of God's loving and gracious purpose to dwell in everlasting communion with his covenant people.

—**David B. McWilliams**, Senior Minister, Covenant Presbyterian Church, Lakeland, Florida

Christ and Covenant Theology is necessary reading on the currently debated issues of covenant theology. Venema provides an excellent survey of the various modern critiques of covenant theology and of the current debates concerning the doctrine of the covenants in Reformed circles. He follows this with a carefully honed analysis and critique that respects both the biblical foundations of covenantal thought and the foundational arguments of the orthodox Reformed confessional and theological tradition. The volume also contains an exposition of related topics that serves to underline the importance of a well-formed understanding of covenant to the Reformed faith and to clarify the central core of traditional Reformed covenantal thought.

—**Richard A. Muller**, Senior Fellow, Junius Institute for Digital Reformation Research; P. J. Zondervan Professor of Historical Theology, Emeritus, Calvin Theological Seminary

No part of Scripture, either in its detail or overall perspective, can be rightly understood without the key of covenant theology. And, as the title suggests (and as Sinclair Ferguson's preface underlines), the focus of covenant theology is in its essence Christ himself. The title itself, therefore, is a compendium of theology! We have come to expect great things from Dr. Venema's writings and this volume does not disappoint. Treatments of three major issues currently troubling Reformed churches are done with masterful analysis. Quite frankly, these pages are necessary reading from one finest theologians of our time.

—**Derek W. H. Thomas**, Chancellor's Professor, Reformed Theological Seminary; Senior Minister, First Presbyterian Church, Columbia, South Carolina; Teaching Fellow, Ligonier Ministries

Dr. Venema offers helpful reflection on issues ranging from the Adamic covenant of works to the so-called republication of the covenant of works in the Mosaic economy. Many readers will find especially instructive his critical interaction with the Federal Vision and N. T. Wright, particularly from the perspective of classic Reformed covenant theology. Wide ranging and thoughtful, *Christ and Covenant Theology* explores a number of important theological topics with admirable clarity and makes a distinctive contribution to the subjects it addresses.

—**Lane G. Tipton**, Charles Krahe Associate Professor of Systematic Theology, Westminster Theological Seminary

Covenant theology is alive and well in the contemporary Reformed world. Recent discussions and controversies about *covenant*, while important, can be difficult to follow. Venema has produced a clear and helpful work that will navigate readers through these issues and will point them to the rich resources that are available in historical Reformed writings on covenant. *Christ and Covenant Theology* will amply repay careful reading and reflection.

—**Guy Prentiss Waters**, James M. Baird Jr. Professor of New Testament, Reformed Theological Seminary, Jackson

CHRIST + COVENANT THEOLOGY

CHRIST + COVENANT THEOLOGY

Essays on Election, Republication, and the Covenants

CORNELIS P. VENEMA

P&R PUBLISHING
P.O. BOX 817 • PHILLIPSBURG • NEW JERSEY 08865-0817

Italics within Scripture quotations indicate emphasis added.

Printed in the United States of America

ISBN 978-1-62995-251-2 (pbk)
ISBN 978-1-62995-252-9 (ePub)
ISBN 978-1-62995-253-6 (Mobi)

Library of Congress Cataloging-in-Publication Data

Names: Venema, Cornelis P., author.
Title: Christ and covenant theology : essays on election, republication, and the covenants / Cornelis P. Venema.
Description: Phillipsburg : P&R Publishing, 2017. | Includes bibliographical references and index.
Identifiers: LCCN 2016039116| ISBN 9781629952512 (pbk.) | ISBN 9781629952529 (epub) | ISBN 9781629952536 (mobi)
Subjects: LCSH: Covenants--Religious aspects--Reformed Church. | Covenant theology. | Election (Theology) | Reformed Church--Doctrines.
Classification: LCC BT155 .V38 2017 | DDC 231.7/6--dc23
LC record available at https://lccn.loc.gov/2016039116

To all of my former and present students at Mid-America
Reformed Seminary, with the hope that their teaching ministries
will focus upon the glory of Christ's person and work
as the Mediator of the covenant of grace.

Contents

Foreword

Our God is a covenant-making and covenant-keeping God. That is who he is; it is how he reveals himself; it is how we are invited to come to know him in Jesus Christ. So whenever there is a rediscovery of biblical theology, the importance of God's covenant relationship with his people is also restored to its place of prominence in both systematic and practical theology. This, in turn, filters into the life of the people of God and anchors them in place in the unfolding of God's purposes. As it goes with the appreciation of God's covenant dealings with his people, so it goes with the church's perspective on Scripture, on history, and on the providence of God in the life of both the family of God and the individual Christian believer, and, ultimately, on the consummation of all things. This is so because the Bible is covenant oriented from beginning to end.

Not infrequently such a claim has been regarded as exaggerated on the one hand or demeaned as a systematic or dogmatic construction on the other—seen as not a reality rooted in the exegesis of Scripture. Thus, it is said, the term *covenant* is absent from the opening chapters of Scripture (not appearing before the Noah narrative in Genesis 6:18); and by the time of the New Testament it has almost entirely disappeared except when reference is being made to passages in the Old Testament. But this, it should be said, is in part to miss the fact that the promise to Noah is of covenant *recovery*, made by the Lord who is known from Genesis 2:4 as Yahweh, his quintessentially covenantal name. It is the God of exodus and redemption, the Lord of history, the *covenant* God who was active in creation and present with his people from the very beginning. And then the whole new epoch inaugurated by Christ falls under the rubric of the words

"I will make a new covenant." Thus just as B. B. Warfield noted that covenant is the architectonic principle of the Westminster Confession, so also the same may be said of Scripture. It is not its *only* governing theme, but it is fundamental to it. Indeed it is the framework within which God sets the scene for the coming of Christ and for the bringing in of his kingdom. Elsewhere, in connection with the deity of Christ, Warfield also shrewdly pointed out that it is not simply in "the big texts" that the strongest evidence is to be found. It is all-pervasive, it is the presupposition, the *sine qua non* of everything that is recorded of Jesus in the Gospels and all that is expounded about him in the Epistles.

The same is true of God's covenant—it is ubiquitous. True, it often goes unmentioned and the term does not constantly appear; but this is so only because it is the lens through which everything is to be seen clearly. For in one sense there is no such "thing" as a covenant. It is not an abstract *res* or commodity we can take out and examine. For it is not a reality that can somehow be separated from the person of the Lord himself—any more than a marriage covenant is an objectifiable *res*, a "thing" that can be abstracted from the man and the woman who are bound together in an unreserved commitment of love for and to one another. *Covenant* describes the relationship itself in all its multiple dimensions, both legal and existential. For that reason, it is present in their lives even when—perhaps for weeks, months, or even years—no verbal reference is made to the covenant into which they have entered. In this sense the covenant is much more than a "thing" that is somehow part of their relationship; it is the foundation and presupposition of the whole. In one sense it simply is the whole—one person binding himself or herself to another unreservedly "for better, for worse, for richer, for poorer . . . ." The marriage covenant is therefore not so much something that the couple looks at but the lenses through which they view the whole of their life together. They do not look at their marriage to find their covenant so much as look through that covenant at the privileges of their married life. It is no wonder then that marriage serves as such a prominent metaphor for God's covenant with his people.

At the end of the day this helps us understand why, when we turn over the blank page that separates the "Old Testament or Covenant" from the "New Testament or Covenant of our Lord Jesus Christ," we discover something that may at first surprise but on deeper reflection is seen to be inevitable. In the New Testament the term *covenant* virtually drops out of use. Indeed, apart from references to God's ancient covenant promises pointing forward to the Messiah, Jesus Christ, it could be argued that—apart from its use in Hebrews—it seems to disappear from circulation.

But this is to misunderstand. For ultimately God's covenant with his people is not only *found in* Jesus Christ; it is Jesus Christ. The new covenant, the final covenant, the covenant in which is experienced the fullness of God's promise "I will be your God and you will be my people" is made in him. In him all the (covenant) promises of God find their "yes!" So when we rightly speak of "Christ and the covenant," this is ultimately the same as speaking of the "Christ who *is* the covenant." In him we are given the final disclosure of the true inner nature of the covenant that God made with his people and unfolded in the succession and progression of covenants that punctuate the narrative of the whole Old Testament. The new covenant is "in my blood," he said. Now to be in covenant with God is to be "in Christ" who is himself the covenant of God. Indeed, Paul's staggeringly pervasive use of the *en Christō* phrase and its variants—peppering the pages of his letters—is simply another way of expressing the new covenant relationship. This is surely why the language employed in the former outworking of his earlier covenant promises in relation to faith and obedience or unbelief and disobedience *now* is employed to describe the effects of the responses of faith or unbelief in relationship to Jesus Christ. So to those who trust Yahweh the covenant Lord, blessings flow; to those who turn away, only curses remain. This is the covenant dynamic. These terms *blessing* and *cursing* represent covenant language and constitute a vocabulary inseparable from it. So for those who are in Christ, all spiritual blessings become their inheritance. From this point of view a passage like Ephesians 1:1–14, which describes these blessings without mentioning the word *covenant*, is nevertheless covenantal through and through. Unless we appreciate this relationship between covenant and Christ, we will have a shallower view of what these blessings mean—in fact of what *blessing* itself means.

In this way, while it is a helpful analogy to say that covenant is like Old Testament scaffolding that, when taken down, leaves Christ fully revealed, it may also be said that the covenant revelation of the Old Testament provides us with the skeleton of which Jesus Christ is the body and soul. His coming does not involve jettisoning covenantal thinking but discovering its fullness embodied in him. For in his affirmation that he came not to destroy the Law and the Prophets but to fulfill them it is implicit that he did the same with the covenant. So just as the fulfilment of the former (Law and Prophets) means that we are to understand Jesus in terms of them, so too in order to appreciate the magnitude of his work we need a clear and full understanding of covenant.

All this being so, it should be clear that our covenant theology as such is bound to impact every aspect of our theology. Naturally that will be true of theology proper, the doctrine of God, since he is *Yahweh*, the Covenant Lord. But it will also be true of the nature of sin, since it makes us covenant-breakers (*asunthetoi*, Rom. 1:31); of the work of Christ, since in his blood the new covenant is constituted; and of the application and consummation of redemption, in which God becomes our God and we become his people; not to mention the covenantal import of baptism and the Lord's Supper and the final consummation in which covenantal language is employed to describe its ultimate reality: "I will be his God and he will be my son" (Rev. 21:7).

In the history of the church, the rediscovery of this whole-Bible, Christocentric, covenantal perspective—which is what biblical theology really is—leads, it seems inevitably, to questions about the nature and role of the law of God. This was true already in the days of Jesus and the apostles. Our Lord himself had to explain how the new covenant related to the nature and function of the law (Matt. 5:17–48). The apostle Paul was accused of demeaning it, and therefore in the context of his biblical-theological exposition in Galatians 3 himself raises the question, "Why then the law?" (Gal. 3:19).

It should not surprise us, then, that whenever there is an awakening to the importance of covenant theology, Paul's question follows, and on occasion is compelled by the rejection of any ongoing role for the law for those who are *in Christ*. In turn this question may well lead on to serious discussion and debate about the nature of justification and also of the corporate and familial implications of the new covenant.

Proof of this is found in at least three of the centuries that have passed since the church fractured and fragmented in the sixteenth century. The recovery of a biblical covenant theology raised these questions for the magisterial Reformers of the sixteenth century. Similar "hot button" topics reemerged in the context of the covenant theology of the seventeenth century. Those familiar with this connection are therefore little surprised that, following the resurgence of interest in the idea of the covenant in scholarly writing some seventy years or so ago, these same old questions are being revisited: What is the function of the law of God? What does justification mean? What are the corporate implications of covenant-oriented theology?

For anyone abreast of the controversies of the day, it is altogether unnecessary for me to say all this. But it may be helpful for readers who casually pick up *Christ and Covenant Theology* and wonder whether it is an important book to read. In fact, its importance lies first in the cardinal importance of covenant theology; and then, in the importance of getting it right. This is a serious piece of work, for serious readers. But anyone willing to wrestle with the issues presented here will undoubtedly be informed but also will grow in understanding how the gospel works.

Professor Cornelis Venema needs no commendation from me, either personally or academically. He has served for many years now as the President of Mid-America Reformed Seminary. In addition to the gifts with which he fulfills a multitude of administrative responsibilities, he has also been able to find time and energy to devote his formidable intellect to some of the most important doctrinal and pastoral issues of the day. In particular—as will become clear in these pages—he has given the good part of a lifetime to reflecting on the issues involved in both the development and the articulation of covenant theology. From time to time he has given us the fruits of his own rich reservoir of knowledge and scholarly understanding of this great theme in a variety of valuable articles that have helped to inform, challenge, and at times correct our thinking about God's covenants. Now in *Christ and Covenant Theology* many of these reflections are brought together into a coherent single volume in which he takes up a number of important issues that have arisen in the development of covenant theology from the Reformation period right through to the contemporary church. His contribution is both knowledgeable and incisive and should be welcomed on all sides.

In particular Dr. Venema treats three major issues. The first is the long-standing question of the nature of the relationship between God and man established in creation—which is coupled with the further question of the nature of the Mosaic covenant. The second is an issue that has perhaps surfaced most frequently in the Continental Reformed theological tradition, namely the relationship of God's election to his covenant, and then in the light of that the much-discussed and deeply sensitive question of the election, baptism, and salvation of children. The third question involves the relationship between covenant and justification, and indeed the very nature of justification itself—an issue that has surfaced in North America in relationship to what has been denominated "Federal Vision" theology, and in the broader theological world has been an important point of debate in the rise of what (following James D. G. Dunn) has come to be known as "the new perspective." This, for American evangelicals, has probably been most associated with the writing and teaching of N. T. Wright.

The issues Professor Venema discusses, then, are by no means simple, nor is the scholarly debate that surrounds them always straightforward or for that matter dispassionate. He deals with all this in a gracious but candid way. To some readers these issues may at first seem recondite, "in-house" scholastic discussions among learned theologians with little relevance to the theology or life of the ordinary Christian. It is true that the issues themselves have often arisen in the formulations of learned theologians—and, admittedly, these formulations come and go. But underneath and behind the issues discussed here, concerning covenant, law, and justification, lies the biggest and most important question of all—the question of God. More pointedly, the double-edged question, "Who is God, really—and what is he actually like in his nature and character? Who *is* the God of the covenant?" For it is a fundamental axiom of all coherent theology that as God reveals himself to be, so he is in himself. And so while Dr. Venema conducts his side of the discussions in a scholarly, reasoned, learned, and footnoted manner, no one should doubt that the issues he discusses are of major personal, pastoral, and real-life theological significance.

Christ and Covenant Theology therefore deals with elements in Reformed theology that are both fundamental and pressing. Cornelis Venema is to be welcomed as a guide here, for he possesses enviable expertise in both Calvin and the Reformed theological tradition, as well as a detailed understanding of Scripture. His knowledge of the subject, his grasp of the literature, and his understanding of its ramifications and repercussions both in theological thinking and practical living well qualify him to help us. The material he handles is demanding. But since he deals with a great theme in a serious and responsible way, joining him to wrestle through these questions cannot fail to instruct our minds and illumine our understanding. In addition, it should help us to think more clearly about God, about Christ, about the ministry of the Spirit, about the nature of the gospel, about the life of the church, and, very near to home doubtless for many readers, the way in which the character and covenant of God relate to our children.

So *Christ and Covenant Theology* digs out a rich vein of gold from the mine of Scripture, seeking to understand it "together with all the saints" and to follow through on the implications and ramifications of the new covenant for the whole of the Christian life.

What is promised here, then, is a vigorous and exhilarating theological workout as well as an adventure in biblical theology for every reader. No further comment is needed, except perhaps to reiterate the exhortation heard so long ago by Augustine (himself a covenant theologian) and to which he responded with such profound implications for the history of the whole church: *Tolle lege!* So, pick up this book, and read it.

Sinclair B. Ferguson
Teaching Fellow
Ligonier Ministries

Acknowledgments

I would be remiss if I were not to acknowledge a number of people who contributed in various ways to the preparation and completion of this book. I am deeply grateful for helpful discussions through the years with my faculty colleagues at Mid-America regarding many of the issues in covenant theology that have arisen recently among Reformed theologians and churches. I am especially thankful for the insights of my colleague, J. Mark Beach, whose dissertation offers a fine analysis of the covenant theology of Francis Turretin.[1] In Turretin's classic formulation of the doctrine of the covenants, we find a model of biblical exposition and systematic formulation that offers a consensus opinion on a number of issues long disputed among Reformed theologians. I am grateful as well for the assistance of Glenda Mathes and Ruben Zartman, who willingly edited the manuscript; Rachel Luttjeboer, who worked readily and patiently on the preparation of the select bibliography; and Daniel Ragusa, who helped with the preparation of the indexes. I am also grateful to P&R Publishing for agreeing to publish the volume, and for all the help John Hughes provided along the way. I am especially delighted and grateful that Sinclair Ferguson agreed to write the foreword.

1. *CCT.*

Introduction

> "He who has an ear, let him hear what the Spirit says to the churches. To the one who conquers I will grant to eat of the tree of life, which is in the paradise of God." (Rev. 2:7)

> "Then the angel showed me the river of the water of life, bright as crystal, flowing from the throne of God and of the Lamb through the middle of the street of the city; also, on either side of the river, the tree of life with its twelve kinds of fruit, yielding its fruit each month. The leaves of the tree were for the healing of the nations. No longer will there be anything accursed, but the throne of God and of the Lamb will be in it, and his servants will worship him. They will see his face, and his name will be on their foreheads. And night will be no more. They will need no light of lamp or sun, for the Lord God will be their light, and they will reign forever and ever." (Rev. 22:1–5)

In the biblical drama of the living God's works in creation and redemption, no theme is more lustrous than that of God's gracious intention to enjoy communion with humans who bear his image and whose lives have been broken through sin. The biblical story of creation and redemption, like a musical oratorio that has four distinct movements, begins with God's great work of creation, moves quickly to the fall into sin, then choruses God's gracious purpose of redemption, and crescendos in anticipation of the day when God's creative and redemptive purposes will reach their consummation in the new heavens and earth. Before and underneath the grand symphony recounted in Scripture, lies God's surprising, undeserved, and invincible purpose to initiate and ultimately to consummate a relationship of mutual love and commitment between himself and those who belong to him through the work of his Son, Jesus Christ. At every note, the Scriptures represent the triune God as the sovereign Lord of history, who graciously condescends to enjoy fellowship with us. Despite the disruption and loss of the original fellowship with God that the human race once enjoyed in Adam before the fall into sin, God intends to grant the fullness of unbreakable fellowship with his people through the work of the "last" Adam, Jesus Christ (Rom. 5:12–21; 1 Cor. 15:42–49).

The beautiful imagery of the book of Revelation, which concludes the biblical story of redemption, offers a rich portrait of the fullness of human life when God's aim to enjoy fellowship with his people reaches its goal. Paradise lost has now become paradise regained. The "tree of life" in the garden of Eden, which was a kind of sacramental sign and seal of the fullness of human life in eternal communion with God, represents the fulfillment of God's work of redemption in Christ. Christian believers who overcome in the course of their earthly pilgrimage will one day "eat of the tree of life" in the world to come. Though Adam, and the fallen human race in union with him, forfeited the right to access the tree of life in the prefall state, believers are promised the fullness of life in the presence of the living God through union with Christ after his return. The imagery that Genesis uses to describe the original human privilege of fellowship with God and service under his lordship in the first creation, now portrays the renewal of creation in the consummation of God's kingdom. Through the triumph of the Lamb of God, believers anticipate a day when God's intention to dwell with his people is realized.

In that day, all of the people of God, drawn from among all the nations and people of the earth, will enjoy the promised rest of unbreakable fellowship with and service to God and others in his name. All the brokenness and trouble wrought by human sin and disobedience will be reversed. The curse of God upon the human race, and even upon the creation itself as it groans in expectation of the revelation of the sons of God (Rom. 8:18–25), will be redressed.

Life in communion with God will be an unending delight. To glorify God and to enjoy him forever will no longer be a wistful hope, but a blessed reality. Every way in which human sin has marred God's creation and handiwork will be undone. Human life in fellowship with God will finally be "the way it is supposed to be," an offering of unending worship and praise to God through Christ. The original calling of God—to subdue all of human life, even the creation itself, under his royal reign—will be achieved.

This grand narrative of the biblical history of redemption provides a framework for this book's essays. Though I deliberately avoided the term *covenant*, Scripture's main themes find their biblical-theological, even systematic coherence, in the idea of covenant. In the history of Reformed theology especially, the gracious condescension of God to enter into fellowship with human beings as his image-bearers has been expressed confessionally and theologically by means of the doctrine of the covenant. While it has been suggested, even by theologians within the Reformed tradition, that Reformed theology suffers from a kind of "covenant overload,"[1] a distinctive feature of this theology is its insistence that the doctrine of the covenant offers an appropriate synthesis of the biblical understanding of God's purposes in the creation of human beings according to his image in Adam before the fall and the re-creation of the new humanity according to the image of the last Adam, Christ, after the fall.

Though the emphasis upon covenant always needs to meet the test of scriptural examination, Reformed theology has historically met this test. Even the structure of the biblical canon, consisting as it does of an "old testament" and a "new testament," witnesses to the centrality of covenant in the biblical story of creation and redemption. Throughout the biblical story of redemption, language descriptive of the original relationship between the triune God and the human race in Adam is often present, explicitly or implicitly, in the way the work of redemption is characterized. The imagery of Revelation evidences that the original goal for human life in communion with

1. See, e.g., John H. Stek, "Covenant Overload in Reformed Theology," *CTJ* 29, 1 (1994): 12–41.

God, foreshadowed in the biblical account of creation in Genesis 1–2, finds its fruition in the renewed communion with God believers will enjoy in the fullness of life in God's new creation. While it is not my purpose in this volume to offer a biblical-theological exposition and defense of the centrality of covenant to the biblical story of redemption, these pages evidence my conviction that the inclinations of Reformed covenant theology are fundamentally correct and biblically defensible.

As will become additionally obvious throughout this book's chapters, the doctrine of the covenant has elicited considerable ongoing discussion, even controversy, within the North American Reformed and Presbyterian community. Some of these debates recall those in the period of Reformed orthodoxy during the late sixteenth and seventeenth centuries. In contemporary discussions of the doctrine of the covenant, however, several issues have received special attention. These issues, which are addressed at various points throughout the chapters of this book, include: (1) whether we may speak of the original, prefall relationship between God and the human race in Adam as a covenant relationship, even though the express language of "covenant" is not ordinarily used to characterize it; (2) whether the original covenant relationship should be described as a "covenant of works" in distinction from the postfall "covenant of grace"; (3) whether in all of the distinct administrations of the covenant, before and after the fall into sin, the source of the covenant relationship lies in God's unmerited favor toward his image-bearers, who may never be regarded as strictly deserving God's promised blessing; (4) whether the covenant of grace, particularly during the Mosaic administration, includes the republication of the prefall covenant of works; (5) whether the doctrines of covenant and election, though intimately related, need to be distinguished in order to acknowledge the presence of nonelect persons within the covenant in its historical administration; (6) whether in all of the administrations of the covenant before and after the fall, the law of God remains a perpetual rule of righteousness and gratitude whose obligations must be met in order for human beings to enjoy the blessedness of unbreakable fellowship with God; (7) whether in the covenant of grace, Christ, the "last" Adam, discharges all of the obligations of the law on behalf of his people in order to secure their inheritance of eternal life; and (8) whether the destiny of the new humanity in Christ includes not only the grace of free justification with God, but also the grace of sanctification in renewed obedience to the law of God. Throughout the course of the book, the significance of these issues will be addressed in respect to a number of contemporary debates regarding the doctrine of the covenant.

While it would be tempting to preview the resolution of these issues, doing so in an introduction would be premature. At this point, I will offer only this summary of the book's argument: the chapters, individually and in concert, aim to defend what might be termed a consensus opinion on these issues. The subtext of my treatment of older and newer debates in the history of covenant theology is that many of the controversies regarding them in the Reformed community would be diminished by avoiding one-sided, exaggerated formulations that do not enjoy the sanction of better reflection throughout the history of confessional Reformed theology. Although I am not interested in an approach to the doctrine of the covenant that merely aims at a repristination of older formulations, it is important to know enough about the history of Reformed covenant thinking to avoid repeating old missteps or detours along the way. While there is considerable room for diversity of formulation and emphasis within the boundaries of the historic Reformed confessions, it is important to remain adequately tethered to the consensus that is expressed in them.

The title of the book, *Christ and Covenant Theology*, captures the burden of my argument throughout. In the biblical story of God's fellowship with his people, the person and work of Christ are always central. The destiny of human life in unbroken fellowship with God, which was first promised to Adam before the fall into sin, was ultimately to be fulfilled within God's gracious purpose through the work of the eschatological or "last" Adam. The beginnings of life in communion with God, which human beings enjoyed in Adam before the fall, were unable to reach the fullness of unbroken communion with God apart from the work of Christ, in whom all the promises of God, including eternal life, are fulfilled (Rom. 6:23; 2 Cor. 1:20). The story of creation and redemption that Scripture tells is a story leading to Christ. God's gracious purposes for covenant communion with his people are always fulfilled in Christ, through whom believers find their life and blessedness in fellowship with God. Though I argue at various points that it is necessary to distinguish the prefall covenant in Adam from the postfall covenant in Christ, these covenants, each in their own way, testify to the glory and blessing of human fellowship with God through Christ. The burden of my argument throughout is that Christ, and Christ alone, is always the One through whom God's gracious intention to enjoy fellowship with his people finds its beginning and end.

The subtitle of the book, *Essays on Election, Republication, and the Covenants*, hints at its genesis. In the last two decades, I have written a number of essays on these topics. Many of these essays were first published in the *Mid-America Journal of Theology*, a publication of the faculty of Mid-America Reformed Seminary in Dyer, Indiana. Several chapters had their beginnings in essays written for a volume on the topic of covenant theology and baptism or as a draft document for a denominational study committee report on the so-called "Federal Vision," a revisionist form of covenant theology that has disturbed the peace of several Presbyterian and Reformed denominations in North America. Most of the essays have been significantly revised—and, I hope, improved—for inclusion in this volume. Since the book represents a collection of essays originally written to stand alone, the reader will find, as is often true of anthologies, that there is some overlapping in content of the chapters. At the same time, since many of the chapters discuss distinct issues in covenant theology, they can be read independently by readers with a specific interest. Though the chapters are ordered by theological and historical factors, they may be read in a different sequence that is governed by the readers' interests.

The first part of the book begins with three essays focusing upon a dominant feature of classic Reformed covenant theology, the bi-covenantalism that is codified in the WCF. Though the early writers of the Reformed tradition during the sixteenth-century Reformation do not expressly speak of the prefall relationship between God and the human race in Adam as a covenant relationship, by the time of the writing of the WCF in the mid-seventeenth century the distinction between a prefall covenant of works and a postfall covenant of grace was common. In the opening chapter, I offer a defense of the WCF's bi-covenantalism, and respond to recent criticisms against the doctrine of a prefall covenant of works. The second and third chapters offer a lengthy review of a recent book-length defense of the idea that the Mosaic administration, though an administration of the covenant of grace, included the republication in some sense of the covenant of works. Though the republication thesis has been advanced with considerable vigor by some in the Reformed community as an important emphasis in the Reformed theological tradition, I argue that it was a minority viewpoint among writers of the orthodox period, and that in its modern expression reflects the revisions of covenant theology associated with the name of Meredith Kline.

The second part of the book consists of five chapters addressing various dimensions of the relationship between the doctrines of the covenant and of election in Reformed theology. Though it is commonly acknowledged that Reformed theology is marked by a special emphasis upon each of these doctrines, there is considerable debate regarding how they are related. Do covenant and election represent two distinct, even incompatible, "central dogmas" in the history of Reformed theology? In recent years, a number of interpreters of the Reformed tradition have advanced the thesis that the doctrine of election served as a kind of organizing principle for Reformed theology in the orthodox period, and that all of its doctrinal themes were subordinated to an abstract and austere doctrine of divine sovereignty. According to this thesis, the doctrine of the covenant emerged in the Reformed theological tradition in two different forms. In one form, the doctrine of the covenant was articulated on the basis of the doctrine of election, diminishing the mutuality and conditionality of the covenants in their administration. In this trajectory of Reformed theology, a "monoplcuric" or unilateral view of the covenant predominated. In the second form, the doctrine of covenant was stressed in order to give greater emphasis to history and the mutuality of the covenant relationship between God and his people. Two of the chapters in this part of the book focus upon the treatment of covenant and election in the theology of Herman Bavinck. In my estimation, Bavinck's treatment of these doctrines and their interrelation represents well the classic Reformed view of the coherence and harmony between these two aspects of God's purpose and work in Jesus Christ. The subsequent two chapters treat an important article in the CD that addresses the confidence believing parents may have in the election and salvation of their children whom God calls to himself in their infancy. The last of the chapters in this part of the book examines the relation between covenant theology and the baptism of children of believing parents. All the chapters in this part of my book aim to illustrate the intimate interplay in Reformed theology between covenant and election.

The third part of the book enters more directly into the arena of recent controversies regarding the doctrine of the covenant. Three chapters summarize and assess what has come to be termed the "Federal Vision." These chapters are based upon a draft document originally written on behalf of a study committee commissioned by a synod of the United Reformed Churches in North America. Although the controversy regarding the "Federal Vision" has its roots in discussions within the Presbyterian churches in North America that subscribe to the Westminster Standards, my evaluation of the "Federal Vision" appeals especially to the Three Forms of Unity (BC, HC, and CD). In my assessment of the "Federal Vision," I show how some controversial formulations are as much at odds with the Three Forms of Unity as they are with the Westminster Standards. After these three chapters on the "Federal Vision," I address one further controversial reformulation of the doctrine of the covenant, especially in terms of its implications for the doctrine of justification by grace alone through faith alone on the basis of Christ's work alone. This reformulation is associated with the writings of N. T. Wright, who redefines the meaning of justification from the vantage point of the so-called "new perspectives on Paul."

In order to identify the main themes of the essays throughout the book, and also to provide a synopsis of their conclusions with respect to the doctrine of Christ and the covenants, I conclude the book with a summary chapter. In this chapter, I return to the principal issues that have emerged in recent discussions of the doctrine of the covenant in the Reformed community in North America and offer a synthesis of the implications of the book's essays for addressing them in a systematic fashion.

Abbreviations

ARC	Cornelis P. Venema, *Accepted and Renewed in Christ: The "Twofold Grace of God" and the Interpretation of Calvin's Theology*. Göttingen: Vandenhoeck & Ruprecht, 2007
BC	Belgic Confession (note that this and other confessional standards are cited from *ERCC*, referenced below)
CCT	J. Mark Beach, *Christ and the Covenant: Francis Turretin's Federal Theology as a Defense of the Doctrine of Grace*. Göttingen: Vandenhoeck & Ruprecht, 2007
CD	Canons of Dort
CNTC	*Calvin's New Testament Commentaries*. Edited by David W. Torrance and Thomas F. Torrance. 12 vols. Grand Rapids, MI: Eerdmans, 1960
CO	John Calvin, *Ioannis Calvini opera quae supersunt omnia*. Edited by G. Baum, E. Cunitz, E. Reuss, et al. 59 vols. *Corpus Reformata*. Brunsvigae, Ger.: Schwetschke, 1862–1900
CTJ	*Calvin Theological Journal*
ERCC	*Ecumenical and Reformed Creeds and Confessions*, Classroom Edition. Orange City, IA: Mid-America Reformed Seminary, 1991
ESV	English Standard Version

GFA	Cornelis P. Venema, *The Gospel of Free Acceptance in Christ: An Assessment of the Reformation and New Perspectives on Paul.* Carlisle, PA: Banner of Truth, 2006
HBP	Cornelis P. Venema, *Heinrich Bullinger and the Doctrine of Predestination: Author of "the Other Reformed Tradition"?* Texts and Studies in Reformation and Post-Reformation Thought, edited by Richard A. Muller. Grand Rapids, MI: Baker Academic, 2002
HC	Heidelberg Catechism
IET	Francis Turretin, *Institutes of Elenctic Theology.* Edited by James T. Dennison Jr. Translated by George M. Giger. 3 vols. Phillipsburg, NJ: P&R Publishing, 1992, 1994, 1997
ICC	International Critical Commentary
Institutes	John Calvin, *Institutes of the Christian Religion.* Edited by John T. McNeill. Translated by Ford Lewis Battles. 2 vols. Library of Christian Classics. Philadelphia: Westminster, 1960
JETS	*Journal of the Evangelical Theological Society*
JVN1	*Justification and Variegated Nomism*, vol. 1, *The Complexities of Second Temple Judaism*, ed. D. A. Carson, Peter T. O'Brien, and Mark A. Seifrid. Grand Rapids, MI: Baker Academic, 2001
JVN2	*Justification and Variegated Nomism*, vol. 2, *The Paradoxes of Paul*, ed. D. A. Carson, Peter O'Brien, and Mark A. Seifrid. Grand Rapids, MI: Baker Academic, 2004
KJV	King James Version
MAJT	*Mid-America Journal of Theology*
NICNT	New International Commentary on the New Testament

NIV	New International Version
NT	New Testament
ORF	Herman Bavinck, *Our Reasonable Faith: A Survey of Christian Doctrine*. Translated by Henry Zylstra. 1960. Reprint, Grand Rapids, MI: Baker, 1977
OS	John Calvin, *Opera Selecta*. Edited by P. Barth and G. Niesel. 5 vols. München: Kaiser, 1926–52
OT	Old Testament
R&R	*Reformation and Revival*
RD	Herman Bavinck, *Reformed Dogmatics*. Edited by John Bolt. Translated by John Vriend. 4 vols. Grand Rapids, MI: Baker Academic, 2003, 2004, 2006, 2008
Romans	N. T. Wright, *The Letter to the Romans*. Vol. 10 of *The New Interpreter's Bible*. Nashville: Abingdon, 2002
ST	L. Berkhof, *Systematic Theology*. 4th ed. Grand Rapids, MI: Eerdmans, 1939, 1941
TAAT	E. Calvin Beisner, ed. *The Auburn Avenue Theology, Pros and Cons: Debating the Federal Vision. The Knox Theological Seminary Colloquium on the Federal Vision, August 11–13, 2003*. Ft. Lauderdale, FL: Knox Theological Seminary, 2004
TFV	Steve Wilkins and Duane Garner, eds. *The Federal Vision*. Monroe, LA: Athanasius, 2004
TLNF	Bryan D. Estelle, J. V. Fesko, and David VanDrunen, eds. *The Law Is Not of Faith: Essays on Works and Grace in the Mosaic Covenant*. Phillipsburg, NJ: P&R Publishing, 2009
WCF	Westminster Confession of Faith

WLC	Westminster Larger Catechism
WSC	Westminster Shorter Catechism
WTJ	*Westminster Theological Journal*

Part I

The Covenant of Works and the Covenant of Grace

1

The Covenant of Works in the Westminster Confession of Faith

> "1. The distance between God and the creature is so great, that although reasonable creatures do owe obedience unto him as their Creator, yet they could never have any fruition of him as their blessedness and reward, but by some voluntary condescension on God's part, which he hath been pleased to express by way of covenant. 2. The first covenant made with man was a covenant of works, wherein life was promised to Adam; and in him to his posterity, upon condition of perfect and personal obedience." WCF 7.1–2.

In his extensive study of the WCF, *The Westminster Assembly and Its Work*, Benjamin Breckinridge Warfield remarked that "[t]he architectonic principle of the Westminster Confession is supplied by the schematization of the Federal theology, which had obtained by this time in Britain, as on the Continent, a dominant position as the most commodious mode of presenting the *corpus* of Reformed doctrine."[1] Certainly, when the WCF is compared and contrasted with earlier Reformed confessions of the sixteenth century, it distinguishes itself by its full expression of federal or covenant theology, including this theology's characteristic distinction between the covenant of works and the covenant of grace. No one reading the WCF can fail to detect the fruit of developments in the doctrine of

1. Benjamin Breckinridge Warfield, *The Westminster Assembly and Its Work* (New York: Oxford University Press, 1931), 56.

the covenant that occurred within the earliest period of Reformed theology in the first half of the sixteenth century. For example, the WCF's distinction between a prefall covenant of works and a postfall covenant of grace—a distinction which plays such a foundational role in covenant theology—is not found in the writings of John Calvin, and was only first expressed among the Reformed in the writings of Zacharias Ursinus, an author of the HC.

The development of covenant theology in the period between the early Reformation and the writing of the WCF has been much discussed in recent literature.[2] One of the disputed issues that has surfaced is the degree to which the later covenant theology is consistent with the earlier views of John Calvin. Those who maintain a divergence of viewpoints between Calvin and the later covenant theologians frequently note that Calvin nowhere mentions or develops a specific doctrine of a covenant of works. Calvin, these writers repeatedly point out, only knew a covenant of grace. It has also been argued that a significant divergence emerged within Reformed theology between, on the one hand, a "testamentary" or monopleuric view of the covenant shaped by the doctrine of election, and

2. See, e.g., Mark W. Karlberg, "The Mosaic Covenant and the Concept of Works in Reformed Hermeneutics: A Historical-Critical Analysis with Particular Attention to Early Covenant Eschatology" (Th.D. diss., Westminster Theological Seminary, 1980); Karlberg, "Reformed Interpretation of the Mosaic Covenant," *WTJ* 43, 1 (1980): 1–57; Karlberg, "The Original State of Adam: Tensions in Reformed Theology," *Evangelical Quarterly* 59, 4 (1987): 291–309; Ernest F. Kevan, *The Grace of Law: A Study in Puritan Theology* (1964; repr. Grand Rapids, MI: Baker, 1976); Peter Alan Lillback, "Ursinus' Development of the Covenant of Creation: A Debt to Melanchthon or Calvin?," *WTJ* 43, 1 (1981): 247–88; Lillback, *The Binding of God: Calvin's Role in the Development of Covenant Theology* (Grand Rapids, MI: Baker Academic, 2001); Michael McGiffert, "From Moses to Adam: The Making of the Covenant of Works," *Sixteenth Century Journal* 19, 2 (1988): 131–55; Geerhardus Vos, "The Doctrine of the Covenant in Reformed Theology," in *Redemptive History and Biblical Interpretation*, ed. Richard B. Gaffin Jr. (Phillipsburg, NJ: Presbyterian and Reformed, 1980), 234–67; David A. Weir, *The Origins of the Federal Theology in Sixteenth-Century Reformation Thought* (Oxford: Clarendon, 1990); *CCT*, esp. 13–77; Richard A. Muller, "The Covenant of Works and the Stability of Divine Law in Seventeenth-Century Reformed Orthodoxy: A Study in the Theology of Herman Witsius and Wilhelmus à Brakel," *CTJ* 29, 1 (1994): 75–100; Rowland S. Ward, *God & Adam: Reformed Theology and the Creation Covenant* (Wantirna, Australia: New Melbourne Press, 2003); and Andrew A. Woolsey, *Unity and Continuity in Covenantal Thought: A Study in the Reformed Tradition to the Westminster Assembly* (Grand Rapids, MI: Reformation Heritage, 2012).

on the other hand, a full or dipleuric covenant doctrine.[3] Reams of paper have been printed in evaluating these developments on the doctrine of the covenant in early and post-Reformation Reformed theology.

Rather than reviewing the history of the development of covenant theology or answering the questions that have arisen in the literature on this subject, I want to consider some criticisms that have more recently been registered against the formulation of the doctrine of the covenant of works in the WCF. Since this formulation expresses the dominant position of the covenant theology of the period in which the Confession was written (and indeed of subsequent Reformed covenant theology), these criticisms raise important questions regarding this doctrine's warrant or biblical propriety. My aim is to evaluate the validity of these criticisms and answer some of the objections that have been pressed against the WCF's understanding of the covenant of works.

It will become evident in what follows that there are two broad sources for such criticisms of the WCF. The first arises primarily within the framework of neoorthodoxy, that revision of classical Reformed theology associated with the theology of Karl Barth. The second arises within the quite different framework of Reformed orthodoxy, though it represents something of an adjustment and refinement of the classical Reformed doctrine of the covenant of works. After briefly summarizing the main lines of these criticisms of the WCF, I will conclude with a brief defense of the Westminster doctrine of the covenant of works.

3. Cf. Leonard Trinterud, "The Origins of Puritanism," *Church History* 20, 1 (1951): 37–57; Richard Greaves, "The Origins and Early Development of English Covenant Thought," *Historian* 31, 1 (1968): 21–35; J. Wayne Baker, *Heinrich Bullinger and the Covenant: The Other Reformed Tradition* (Athens, OH: Ohio University Press, 1980). This thesis of a twofold development in Reformed theology, or a divergence between two incompatible views of the covenant, has been subjected to vigorous criticism. See Lyle D. Bierma, "Federal Theology in the Sixteenth Century: Two Traditions?," *WTJ* 45, 2 (1983): 304–21; Bierma, "Covenant or Covenants in the Theology of Olevianus," *CTJ* 22, 2 (1987): 228–50; Bierma, "The Role of Covenant Theology in Early Reformed Orthodoxy," *Sixteenth Century Journal* 21, 3 (1990): 453–62; Woolsey, *Unity and Continuity*, esp. 336–43; and *HBP*.

Criticisms of the Westminster Confession of Faith

Before considering two writers who have expressed the gist of the Barthian criticism of the WCF's view of the covenant of works, it will be helpful to consider a few important themes in the theology of Karl Barth which find their echo in this criticism.

Karl Barth

To understand Karl Barth's antipathy to the distinction between a prefall covenant of works and a postfall covenant of grace, it is essential to grasp what he means by speaking of the creation as the "external basis of the covenant" and the covenant as the "internal basis of creation." Speaking of the former, Barth argues that

> [t]he existence and being of the creature willed and constituted by God are the object and to that extent the presupposition of His love. Thus the covenant is the goal of creation and creation the way to the covenant. Nor is creation the inner basis of the covenant. . . . The inner basis of the covenant is simply the free love of God, or more precisely the eternal covenant which God has decreed in Himself as the covenant of the Father with His Son as the Lord and Bearer of human nature, and to that extent the Representative of all creation. Creation is the external—and only the external—basis of the covenant.[4]

In Barth's theology of the covenant, God's free act of calling the creation into existence provides a context for him to enter into covenant with the creature. The creation constitutes the sphere within which God's gracious care for the creature in Jesus Christ can be expressed and realized. It is in this sense, then, that the creation constitutes the external basis of the covenant, the arena within which God's saving purpose toward humanity in Christ can be realized and effected.

However, Barth also insists that the creation has no independent

4. Karl Barth, *The Doctrine of Creation*, vol. 3.1 of *Church Dogmatics* (Edinburgh: T. & T. Clark, 1958), 97.

existence or meaning apart from the covenant of grace. The covenant of grace, eternally purposed in Christ and realized in all of God's dealings with the creation, is the "internal basis of creation."

> The covenant whose history had still to commence was the covenant which, as the goal appointed for creation and the creature, made creation necessary and possible, and determined and limited the creature. If creation was the external basis of the covenant, the latter was the internal basis of the former. If creation was the formal presupposition of the covenant, the latter was the material presupposition of the former. If creation takes precedence historically, the covenant does so in substance. If the proclamation and foundation of the covenant is the beginning of the history which commences after creation, the history of creation already contains, as the history of the being of all creatures, all the elements which will subsequently meet and be unified in this event and the whole series of events which follow; in the history of Israel, and finally and supremely in the history of the incarnation of the Son of God.[5]

For Barth the whole purpose of God's work of creation is the realization of communion and fellowship between God and his people in Christ. In the free bestowal of his favor and mercy upon the creature in Christ, God shows his glory and realizes his purposes of self-revelation and self-communication to the creature. In the covenant of grace, the triumphant "yes" of God to the creature of his favor resounds, and the essential purpose of creation is realized.

It is evident that Barth can find no place for a covenant of works in distinction from the covenant of grace, which precedes *in history* the fall into sin and that does not express the saving grace exhibited in the gospel. Not only does Barth regard the biblical account of creation and fall to be nonhistorical *saga*, but he also resists any suggestion of a *transition in history from wrath to grace subsequent to the fall into sin*. From the beginning, God's dealings with the creature

5. Ibid., 231–32.

are preeminently and exclusively *gracious*. There is no change that occurs in history in the relationship between God and the creature because of the fall into sin. Furthermore, consistent with his view of the covenant of grace as the internal basis of creation, Barth rejects any ordering of law and gospel in which the gospel does not have the first (as well as the last) word. At no point in God's dealings with the creature does the law precede the gospel. Not only in eternity, but also in history, the triumphant "yes" of God's grace is the first and definitive word. To suggest that, prior to God's gracious dealings with his covenant people in the history of redemption, there existed another covenant relationship, a covenant of works, is to introduce a concept that betrays the most fundamental feature of all of God's dealings with humanity—the free turning of God toward humanity in Christ.

From Barth's perspective, a doctrine of the covenant of works like that enunciated in the WCF threatens the gospel of God's grace in Christ. It rests upon a precritical view of biblical history, viewing the biblical account of the creation and fall of man as though it were a straightforward historical account and transition from favor to disfavor with God.[6] But more important, it permits the suggestion that humanity's covenant relationship with God, prior to the fall, might be construed as one contingent upon obedience to a probationary command of God. The latter idea would entail placing law before grace in God's prefall dealings with humanity. It would suggest that man's relationship to God, at least in the primal circumstances before the fall into sin, was founded upon and sustained by meritorious works done in obedience to the law.

Many of the objections to the WCF's understanding of the covenant of works stem from the influence of these themes in Barth's theology. Though there are other sources for similar criticisms, it is the theology of Barth that informs many of the arguments against

6. In this chapter and throughout, I will frequently use the term "man" rather than "human being/s" in order to express the generic and covenant unity of the human race in Adam, the representative and organic head of the human race. Though this terminology may not conform to contemporary sensitivities regarding inclusive language, it remains unavoidable for this purpose.

the *legalism* of the WCF's doctrine of the covenant, especially its formulation of the covenant of works. To illustrate the influence of Barth and the nature of this criticism, it will be useful to turn to the arguments of two critics of the WCF who follow this approach.

Holmes Rolston III

One of the most vigorous advocates that the WCF's doctrine of the covenant of works leads to legalism, is Holmes Rolston III.[7] Rolston believes that the Westminster's formulation represents a substantial betrayal of the original Reformation insight that man's standing before God is always founded upon *grace alone*. When the WCF describes the covenant of works as a covenant in which "life was promised to Adam; and in him to his posterity, upon condition of perfect and personal obedience," Rolston thinks it introduces into Reformed theology a concept of *merit* that militates against the genius of the Reformation rediscovery of the gospel of grace.

In Rolston's summary of the classic view of the covenant of works, he maintains that it begins with and always insists upon the "merit and ability of man."[8] In this first covenant, the Mosaic law's teaching that the promise of life is conditional upon man's obedience to the law (cf. Lev. 18:5) is read back into the original state described in Genesis 1 and 2. The condition of this covenant is not faith, but works, and the reward of life is earned by law-keeping. Thus, man's standing before God, his covenant fellowship with God, is founded upon and maintained by meritorious good works. Furthermore, there is a tendency in this older covenant theology, Rolston insists, to identify the obligation of obedience with the *natural law* which binds man's conscience perpetually as a creature and which is sharply

7. Holmes Rolston III, *John Calvin versus the Westminster Confession* (Richmond, VA: John Knox, 1972); Rolston, "Responsible Man in Reformed Theology: Calvin versus the Westminster Confession," *Scottish Journal of Theology* 23, 2 (1970):129–56. Rolston's argument is most succinctly stated in the second of these sources, from which I will draw primarily for my summary of his criticism. The former source is an expanded version of the earlier article. Rolston clearly writes from a revisionist perspective, even regarding the Confession of 1967 of the United Presbyterian Church as marking the end of Presbyterianism's venture in covenant theology.

8. Rolston, "Responsible Man," 133.

distinguished from the sphere of God's grace toward his people in Christ. The extent to which this doctrine of the covenant is ruled by the idea of merit is evident also in its insistence that the saving work of Christ, the Mediator, involves a work of obedience, as the second Adam, in which the law is fulfilled on our behalf. This is a doctrine, accordingly, that is wholly colored by the themes of obedience and merit and that mutes the gospel testimony of God's prevenient grace in all of his dealings with his people.

Rolston finds all this in marked contrast with the *order of grace* that predominates and pervades the theology of John Calvin, and from which the WCF and its covenant theology is an obvious declension. Calvin knew nothing, Rolston argues, of the two-covenant doctrine of the WCF; in fact, he was not a covenant theologian at all, at least not in the normal use of these terms. For Calvin, "[a]ll things are ordered according to the movement of God's grace in creation and purpose in redemption."[9] All of God's dealings with the creature, whether before or after the fall, express this order of grace.

> Although Calvin does not use just that term, he speaks often of both the order and of the divine grace first instituted. The part given to man is reflexive of grace. From the start Calvin transcends the concept of order as primarily moral and legal and places this under the higher order of grace. What is paramount is that God is gracious and requires acknowledgement of his grace.[10]

Rolston believes that Calvin does not speak, therefore, of two covenants, a covenant of works and a covenant of grace, but of one order of grace, an order that may be either "inverted" through the fall into sin or "reestablished" through redemption. There are not two distinct covenants but one, the covenant of grace being a "reflection of and . . . restoration of . . . the original order."[11]

For Rolston there is no indication in Calvin's theology that man's relationship before God is sustained or maintained on the

9. Ibid., 137.
10. Ibid., 139.
11. Ibid., 141.

basis of meritorious good works. For Calvin, *grace always precedes the law*, even in paradise, and man's obedience never merits God's acceptance but only expresses man's grateful and responsible answer to God's gracious dealings with him. Life is always God's gift, never the achievement of the obedient creature. What man ought to do is always reflexive of grace, unlike in later covenant theology wherein what man ought to do is fundamentally reflexive of law. This also accounts for the superficial doctrine of sin in covenant theology. Whereas covenant theology identifies sin primarily with disobedience to the law, Calvin identified sin with "man's faithless rejection of the goodness of God in favour of his own self-willed efforts to seek his own happiness elsewhere."[12] Rolston finds the WCF, therefore, to depart seriously in its covenant doctrine from the theology of John Calvin and the Reformers. In this doctrine the grace of God in Christ is no longer the first or primary word. In its place has come an emphasis upon man's legal obligation to his Creator by virtue of the covenant of works.

James B. Torrance

A second critic of the WCF who follows a similar line to Barth is James B. Torrance.[13] Torrance also regards the federal theology of the seventeenth century, especially as this is set forth in the WCF, to be a "rationalistic" departure from the early Scottish tradition of Knox, the Scots Confession, the pre-Westminster confessions, and the theology of John Calvin. It is evident that Torrance believes the source for a growing legalism in Scottish theology and practice, confirmed in the so-called "Marrow Controversy,"[14] lay in an increasing

12. Ibid., 150.

13. James B. Torrance, "Covenant or Contract? A Study of the Theological Background of Worship in Seventeenth-Century Scotland," *Scottish Journal of Theology* 23, 1 (1970): 51–76; Torrance, "Calvin and Puritanism in England and Scotland—Some Basic Concepts in the Development of 'Federal Theology,'" in *Calvinus Reformator: His Contribution to Theology, Church and Society* (Potchefstroom, South Africa: Potchefstroom University for Christian Higher Education, 1982): 264–77; Torrance, "Strengths and Weaknesses of the Westminster Theology," in *The Westminster Confession*, ed. Alisdair Heron (Edinburgh: St. Andrews, 1982), 40–53. In what follows I will trace Torrance's argument primarily as it is found in the first of these articles.

14. The "Marrow Controversy" refers to an ecclesiastical dispute within the Scottish

emphasis upon the federal scheme and the *conditional* character of the covenant between God and his people. According to Torrance, the idea of "conditional grace" was introduced into Scottish theology through the route of federal theology.

Torrance claims that while the original, biblical idea of covenant expresses an *unconditional binding* of two parties in covenant loyalty and faithfulness, the federal theology shifted the emphasis from this concept of covenant to that of a *legal contract.* Whereas a covenant is rooted in mutual promises and commitments, freely given and received, the federal theology, by distinguishing between a covenant of works and a covenant of grace, reconfigured the covenant as a contractual relationship. This theology "is built upon a deep seated *confusion* between a covenant and a contract, a failure to recognise that the God and Father of our Lord Jesus Christ is a Covenant-God and not a contract-God."[15] In this understanding, God appears as a Sovereign Employer and man as a servant-vassal. No longer is the covenant relationship rooted in the gracious condescension of God to the creature, in which the creature stands as a beloved child or graciously embraced friend. Everything in the covenant of works has the color of a contractual relationship between employer and employee, master and servant.

Torrance claims that a number of deleterious consequences follow from this reconceptualization of the covenant. In the federal theology there is the reemergence, for example, of the older, medieval view that

---

Presbyterian church in the early eighteenth century. In 1718 James Hog of Carnock republished *The Marrow of Modern Divinity*, thought to be a work of Edward Fisher, an English Calvinist of the seventeenth century (E[dward] F[isher], *The Marrow of Modern Divinity, with a Recommendatory Preface by James Hog*, 9th ed., corrected [Edinburgh: John Mosman and William Brown, 1718]). This two-volume work criticized "neo-nomianism," the reintroduction of an inappropriate understanding of the believer's obligation to fulfill the law's demands in order to obtain or be maintained in the way of salvation. Though the book pleased such notables as Thomas Boston, it met with considerable hostility within the Scottish Presbyterian church. Torrance regards this chapter in the church's history to be an instance of the growing influence of a legalism, earlier introduced by means of the WCF's doctrine of the covenant of works. On the Marrow Controversy, see Joseph H. Hall, "The Marrow Controversy: A Defense of Grace and the Free Offer of the Gospel," *MAJT* 10 (1999): 239–57; and Sinclair Ferguson, *The Whole Christ: Legalism, Antinomianism, & Gospel Assurance—Why the Marrow Controversy Still Matters* (Wheaton, IL: Crossway, 2016).

15. Torrance, "Covenant or Contract?," 66.

grace presupposes nature and *grace perfects nature.*[16] Contrary to the Reformation insight that nothing precedes God's gracious turning to the creature, this theology treats grace as a remedial measure, secondary to the original circumstance in which man stood before God under the obligation of the law of nature in a covenant of nature. The priority of God's grace in all his dealings with the creature is thereby imperiled. Furthermore, in a criticism especially reminiscent of the theology of Karl Barth, Torrance regards the doctrine of *limited atonement* to be an extension of this covenant scheme. The federal theology knows only one solidarity of all human beings and that is their solidarity with the first Adam, whose fall into sin alienated the whole human race from God. It does not know of that fundamental solidarity taught in the Scriptures in which all human beings are united in Christ, whose headship extends over all creation and whose solidarity is inclusive of all human beings since he is the head of the human race. This means that you cannot say to all human beings, "Christ died for you," though you may and even must say to all, "You are all guilty and under judgment." But according to Torrance, this betrays the triumphant note of joy that must resound in all gospel preaching—"you are what you are by God's grace in Christ!"[17] All of this moves the accent from what God has done for us already in Christ to what we have to do for ourselves, if we would benefit from his saving work.

For these and other reasons, Torrance insists that the federal theology of the WCF is the primary culprit in stimulating—even reintroducing—a doctrine of meritorious good works into Reformed theology. The grand themes of the Reformation, *sola gratia, solo Christo, sola fide*, find in this theology their demise.

S. G. De Graaf and G. C. Berkouwer

The two previous critics of the federal theology whom we have considered generally express a Barthian rejection of any distinction between a prefall covenant of works and a postfall covenant of grace. In their theological conception, there is ultimately but *one order of*

16. Ibid., 67.

17. Ibid., 69. In this aspect of his argument, Torrance is also following Barth's lead in denying a transition from wrath to grace in history, subsequent to the fall into sin.

grace that defines *all* of the triune God's dealings with his covenant creature, whether before or after the fall (assuming that this distinction has historical significance). This is not true, however, of the position of S. G. De Graaf and G. C. Berkouwer, two Dutch theologians who criticize the WCF's formulation of a covenant of works, but nonetheless admit a prefall covenant of "creation" or of "favor," as they prefer to term it, that must be carefully distinguished from the postfall covenant of grace. Consequently, though they criticize the WCF's formulation for its alleged "legalistic" implication, they do not deny the fundamentals of covenant theology or the distinction between two covenants, the one before, the other after the fall into sin.

The concern expressed by De Graaf and Berkouwer is that "[m]an's original life under God's rule cannot be regarded, for even a moment, apart from God's love and communion."[18] The covenant of works formulation suggests that there is a legal order above or before the order of grace in God's dealings with his covenant creature. In this understanding, the law and its obligation are easily separated from the life and fellowship with God that precede it. Thus, the relationship between God and his covenant partner is misconstrued in the original circumstance before the fall into sin; it becomes the relationship between a servant and his master, not that, for instance, between a child and his father or between a wife and her husband. The bond of communion and fellowship, within which the law has its rightful place as a rule of life, is made secondary to the obligation or demand of obedience, on the basis of which God's favor is obtained. As Berkouwer puts it,

> [w]e err if we interpret this distinction as though God's original covenant had to do with *our* work or *our* achievement or *our* fulfillment of his law, while the later covenant of grace has reference to the pure gift of his *mercy* apart from all *our works*. If we assume this we are compelled to say that God's original relation to man was strictly "legal," or that the structure of that relation was determined by man's merit.[19]

18. G. C. Berkouwer, *Sin*, trans. Philip C. Holtrop, Studies in Dogmatics (Grand Rapids, MI: Eerdmans, 1971), 206.

19. Ibid., 207.

De Graaf likewise finds the idea of a covenant of works inimical to understanding the original covenant relation between God and man as one which was founded upon God's favor and goodness. According to De Graaf, the idea of a covenant of works suggests that God's favor comes at the *end* of man's relationship with God rather than at the *beginning*, as its source and foundation. This intimates that the covenant life man enjoys in fellowship with God comes only as a reward for obedience, as something merited or bestowed because man has made himself worthy of it. Contrary to this suggestion, De Graaf maintains

> [t]here is never any speaking of merit or reward in the covenant of God, even in the so-called covenant of works. God in his covenant is always the first who gives his love. Through his love he must teach us to love; and our love can never be anything other than a response to his love. Through the law God rules the fellowship of love we have with him, a fellowship which has no norm in itself, but for which God himself has established a norm. And so it is that we by our responsibility to the norm grow in the communion of the love of God. Thus the law is covenant law. In the place of a "covenant of works," then, it is better to speak of a "covenant of God's favor."[20]

De Graaf believes that in the terminology of a "covenant of works," there lurks the tendency to abstract the law from its setting within God's original favor to the creature, which gives the creature his place as a child and friend of God, called to obedience within the communion he already enjoys with the Creator. This conception conjures up the possibility of an absolute antithesis between works and grace,

20. S. G. De Graaf, *Het Ware Geloof* (Kampen: J. H. Kok, 1954), 31–32 (translation mine). De Graaf makes the same point, suggesting that we speak of a "covenant of favor," in his article, "De Genade Gods en de Structuur Der Gansche Schepping," *Philosophia Reformata* 1 (1936): 20–21: "Het is daarom m.i. beter, niet meer te spreken van 'werken verbond', waardoor we onwillekeurig de gedachte aan verdienen en loon, en dan ook aan een voorloopig Zich terughouden van God in het Paradijs indragen. De term 'verbond van Gods gunst' drukt beter uit de wekelijke verhouding. Voor het verbond na den zondeval blijft dan de term 'verbond van Gods genade', dat is van Gods schuldvergevende gunst."

merit and favor, in which man's standing before God is thought, at least in its original and primary form, to be founded upon meritorious works. Indeed, Berkouwer even goes so far as to argue that this language raises once more the specter of meritorious good works within the orbit of Reformed doctrine, a specter that threatens the Reformation criticism of the Catholic doctrine of justification by grace.

> Therefore whoever burdens the so-called "covenant of works" with the notion of achievement and presumes that we gain God's favor in this way, must endorse the idea of a "nomological" ur-existence of man and must cut asunder the law of God from the fellowship of God. In that way he isolates and hypostasizes the law. It is not clear how this infusion of *meritum* can leave room for a genuine criticism of Rome concerning the meritoriousness of works.[21]

What is clear from Berkouwer and De Graaf's criticisms is that they are concerned about a formulation of the "covenant of works" that places man's standing before God, in the original circumstance before the fall into sin, upon the foundation of merit and reward. This kind of formulation threatens not only to *distinguish* the prefall and the postfall covenants, but ultimately to *oppose* them: the first would

21. Berkouwer, *Sin*, 208. For similar criticisms of the doctrine of the covenant of works, see C. Van der Waal, *The Covenantal Gospel* (Neerlandia, AB: Inheritance, 1990), 47–56; Norman Shepherd, *The Call of Grace: How the Covenant Illuminates Salvation and Evangelism* (Phillipsburg, NJ: P&R Publishing, 2000), 23–41; and Clarence Stam, *The Covenant of Love: Exploring Our Relationship with God* (Winnipeg, MB: Premier, 1999), 47–54. Van der Waal expresses the common opinion of these authors, when he argues that Adam "was not created to be a legitimate pharisee, pelagian, or remonstrant" (54), as the doctrine of a covenant of works suggests. Though this criticism does not represent the best of the Continental (Dutch) tradition on the doctrine of the prefall covenant, it does reflect in part the absence of any express formulation of a "covenant of works" in the Three Forms of Unity (the HC, BC, and CD). I will have occasion to revisit this criticism of the covenant of works in subsequent chapters, especially chaps. 9–12, which treat the covenant views of the so-called "Federal Vision" movement and Norman Shepherd. These criticisms often betray one trajectory of thought within the Continental tradition, namely, the alleged contrast between the covenant theology of Continental Reformed theology and that of the Westminster Standards. One of my principal claims throughout this volume is that there is no substantive difference between the Westminster Standards and the Three Forms of Unity on the doctrine of Christ and the covenants.

be founded upon a principle of works; the second would be founded upon a principle of grace. Therefore, though they both acknowledge a real difference between these covenants—this is in part the reason for De Graaf's suggestion that we speak of a "covenant of favor" for the first covenant, and of a "covenant of grace" for the covenant after the fall into sin—they do not wish to acknowledge that man's covenant fellowship with God is ever founded upon something other than the love and goodness of God in granting it as his gift.[22] In this respect, their criticism of the formulation of a "covenant of works," though bearing some similarity to that of Karl Barth and those who follow in a Barthian line, should not be confused with it.

John Murray

The last critic of the WCF's formulation of the doctrine of the covenant of works whom I wish to consider is John Murray. Murray, though a faithful exponent of the system of doctrine contained in the WCF, was perhaps more critical of this aspect of the WCF than he was of any other. Based upon his own biblical-theological reflection, Murray offered several of what he believed were necessary correctives to the traditional formulations of federal theology, including the classical form found in the WCF.

Murray's original objection to the idea of a covenant of works stems from his reformulation of the doctrine of the covenant. According to Murray, "covenant" in the biblical writings always expresses a gracious disposition of God toward the partner with whom he covenants; the notion of a "covenant of works," accordingly, is contrary to the ordinary meaning of covenant in the Scriptures, at least when they speak of God's covenanting with man. In an encyclopedia

22. See Daniel P. Fuller, *Gospel and Law: Contrast or Continuum? The Hermeneutics of Dispensationalism and Covenant Theology* (Grand Rapids, MI: Eerdmans, 1980), 18–64; Fuller, *The Unity of the Bible* (Grand Rapids, MI: Zondervan, 1992), who argues that covenant theology shares with dispensationalism an unfortunate and unbiblical *disjoining* of grace and law, as well as a *disordering* of the relation as one of law first and then grace. Though I will address this criticism in the second part of this chapter, Fuller's criticism, like that of Barth and others, fails to do justice to the biblical history of creation, fall, and redemption, treating the prefall circumstance of man as though it were in almost every particular the same as the postfall circumstance.

article in which he traced briefly the history of covenant theology, Murray voiced this reservation about the older federal theology's doctrine of a covenant of works.[23] However, he provided a more complete statement of his revision of the doctrine of the covenant works in his important article, "The Adamic Administration."[24] As the title of this article suggests, Murray objected to the language of a covenant of works, not only in that it militated against the gracious character of God's covenanting with man, but also in that it speaks of a prefall "covenant," whereas the Scriptures reserve the language of covenant to God's postfall dealings with the sinful creature.

Murray opens his treatment of the Adamic administration, his preferred terminology for the prefall arrangement between God and Adam (as representative head of the human race), by noting that, prior to the special arrangement described in Genesis 2, man (who was created in God's image) existed in a relationship with God of "perfect legal reciprocity."[25] By this language, Murray refers to man's original obligation to live before God in accordance with the demand of God's law, the demand that he love and serve God with all his heart, soul, strength, and mind. This obligation to love God, the original demand of God's law of nature, constitutes the perpetual obligation of man as a creature formed for free and responsible service to God, his Creator. Were man to have fulfilled this law and preserved his original state of integrity, he would have continued righteous and holy before God, and "[i]n this righteousness he would be justified, that is, approved and accepted by God, and he would have life."[26]

However, in addition to this original circumstance of providence, a circumstance which Murray describes as "mutable" and absent

23. John Murray, "Covenant Theology," in *The Encyclopedia of Christianity* (Marshallton, DE: National Foundation for Christian Education, 1972), 3:199–216.

24. John Murray, "The Adamic Administration," in *Select Lectures in Systematic Theology*, vol. 2 of *Collected Writings of John Murray* (Carlisle, PA: Banner of Truth, 1977), 47–59. For a comprehensive study of Murray's doctrine of the covenant that compares it to that of Meredith Kline and the original formulations of the orthodox period, see Jeong Koo Jeon, *Covenant Theology: John Murray's and Meredith G. Kline's Response to the Historical Development of Federal Theology in Reformed Thought* (Lanham, MD: University Press of America, 1999).

25. Murray, *Select Lectures*, 47.

26. Ibid.

"full-orbed communion with God in the assurance of permanent possession and increasing knowledge,"[27] Murray notes that the account in Genesis describes an additional "arrangement" or "administration" of God's providence, ordinarily termed the covenant of works. In addition to the perpetual obligation of obedience under which Adam stood from creation, God also "gave to Adam a specific command or, more accurately, a specific prohibition."[28] By means of a special prohibition (Gen. 2:17), to which was attached a particular threat of death, God entered into a peculiar relationship with Adam. This relationship or administration threatened death and carried within itself the implicit promise of life, though this promise is only indirectly suggested by the reference in Genesis 3:22, 24 to the "tree of life."

> The Adamic administration is, therefore, construed as an administration in which God, by a special act of providence, established for man the provision whereby he might pass from the status of contingency to one of confirmed and indefectible holiness and blessedness, that is, from *posse peccare* and *posse non peccare* to *non posse peccare*. The way instituted was that of "an intensified and concentrated probation," the alternative issues being dependent upon the issues of obedience or disobedience (cf. G. Vos: *Biblical Theology*, 22f.).[29]

27. Ibid.

28. Ibid., 48.

29. Ibid., 49. Cf. Karlberg, "Reformed Interpretation," 48–53, who criticizes Murray at this point for contrasting the obligations of obedience to the law, under which Adam stood at creation, from the specific obligations of the Adamic administration. He suggests that thereby Murray improperly separates the specific obligations of the "Adamic administration" from the obligations of obedience to the law which Christ, the second Adam, fulfilled in the covenant of grace (Rom. 5:12–21). However, it seems clear from Murray's statement (including his quotation from Vos) that he views the special obligation of obedience in the Adamic arrangement to be simply an intensification or concentration of the original obedience owed God by Adam by virtue of creation. For Murray, the key point is that God also graciously (undeservedly) attaches to this obligation, by a special providence, the promise of eternal life. Therefore, though it may be true that Murray treats the "Adamic arrangement" as a special providence that is not inherent within the original state of creation *simpliciter*, Murray does not posit a *dichotomy* between the prefall state of *nature* (with the obedience to law required of man as creature) and of *grace* (with the probationary command and an attached promise of eternal life as component of a gracious and sovereign administration, a special providence). The point Murray is anxious to preserve is that the promise of life,

There are several respects in which Murray's treatment of this Adamic administration differs from traditional covenant theology. As we have already noted, this difference is partially terminological. Rather than speak of a "covenant of works" or a "covenant of life" (the language of the WSC),[30] Murray prefers to speak of an "Adamic administration," noting that the language of covenant is not used explicitly in the Bible to describe this relationship. But the divergence is far more than terminological. Murray also avoids the terminology of "works" because he wants to underscore the fact that, though the relationship of this arrangement includes within itself a concentrated probation, this administration is "sovereignly dispensed by God," and is "not a contract or compact. Sovereign disposition is its patent characteristic."[31] Accordingly, this arrangement, though non-soteric or non-redemptive, is consonant with the essential characteristic of the biblical understanding of a covenant as a "sovereign, divine administration . . . [that] continues without any modification or retraction of its benefits by the immutable promise and faithfulness of God."[32]

which was attached to the particular stipulation of the probationary command, was freely (undeservedly) extended to Adam by a special act of divine providence. God does not owe this promise to Adam, as creature, but freely extends it to Adam in the "Adamic administration" as an undeserved favor.

30. WSC 12 reads: "What special act of providence did God exercise towards man in the estate wherein he was created? When God had created man, he entered into a covenant of life with him, upon condition of perfect obedience; forbidding him to eat of the tree of the knowledge of good and evil, upon pain of death."

31. Murray, *Select Lectures*, 50.

32. John Murray, *The Covenant of Grace: A Biblico-Theological Study* (London: Tyndale, 1954), 14. This language is taken from Murray's summary of what is essential to the biblical view of the covenant of grace. It is noteworthy to what extent Murray fashions his definition of the Adamic administration along lines that parallel his definition of the covenant of grace. This allows him to show a similarity in the covenant relation before and after the fall: each expresses a sovereign and gracious, because undeserved, favor toward man as creature (whether in the state of integrity or in the state of fallenness). However, because his generic definition of covenant emphasizes sovereign promise and disposition, the obligations of obedience in the Adamic administration may not seem to be as integral to the prefall covenant as the WCF represents them. This is the burden of Karlberg's criticism of Murray's reformulation of the prefall covenant relationship: it does not permit the obedience of Christ, the second Adam, to the law of God as Creator to be understood as a fulfillment of man's original obligations as creature under the covenant of works. Cf. Karlberg, "Reformed Interpretation," 52–53; Karlberg, "Original State," 297–300. Karlberg's criticisms of Murray's formulation of the prefall "Adamic administration" reflect

In Murray's estimation, the language, "covenant of works," fails to do justice to the elements of grace entering into the administration. Despite the fact that the condition of obedience is essential to the probation which comprises such an important component of the Adamic administration, Murray regards the gracious origin and sovereign disposition of this arrangement as sufficient to prevent our legitimately terming it a "covenant of works." By means of this Adamic administration, God promised Adam—were he to fulfill the terms of the probation—an entrance into immutable and perpetual life in communion with himself, a state of glory that would exceed the mutability and contingency of his original state. This promise, according to Murray, is an instance of gracious condescension and kindness which God did not owe the creature, but which he was pleased to grant to him. This promise would not be granted upon the principle of *strict justice or merit*—God's justice does not require that Adam should ever be granted the status of immutability in fellowship with God—but would be an expression of God's undeserved favor.

Consistent with his aversion to the language of "covenant of works" and parallel insistence that God's grace and sovereign disposition are basic to the Adamic administration, Murray also challenged another feature of the older federal theology, namely, that the Mosaic economy or covenant included within itself a repetition of the obligation of obedience, first enunciated in the covenant of works.

> The view that in the Mosaic covenant there was a repetition of the so-called covenant of works, current among covenant theologians, is a grave misconception and involves an erroneous construction of the Mosaic covenant, as well as fails to assess the uniqueness of the Adamic administration. The Mosaic covenant was distinctly redemptive in character and was continuous with and extensive of the Abrahamic covenants.[33]

---

the influence of the covenant theology of Meredith Kline. See n39 below for further comment on Kline's view that the prefall covenant was a covenant of "strict justice," which operated on the basis of what Kline terms a "works-inheritance" or merit principle.

33. Murray, *Select Lectures*, 50. In the following two chapters of this volume, I will offer an extensive assessment of the claim of some recent writers that the Mosaic economy

Because Murray desires to emphasize the gracious and sovereign disposition of the Adamic arrangement, as well as the essential graciousness of the biblical covenant of grace, he does not want to admit the legal requirement of obedience to be as integral to this arrangement or the postfall covenant of grace as was typically the case in the history of covenant theology. Although the older covenant theology regarded this legal requirement to be integral to the covenant of works, and even to the covenant of grace, Murray distinguishes sharply between the natural obligation of obedience and the probationary obedience of the Adamic administration. In treating the work of Christ as the second Adam, therefore, Murray also resists the usual understanding that it included, in an important sense, the fulfillment of the legal obedience required by the covenant of works. Although the obedience Christ rendered fulfilled the obedience in which Adam failed, Murray notes that it

> would not be correct to say, however, that Christ's obedience was the same in content or demand. Christ was called on to obey in radically different conditions, and required to fulfill radically different demands.[34]

Murray's treatment of the WCF's doctrine of the covenant of works, then, is not so much a repudiation of any of its essential teaching as a revision and refinement of some aspects of the WCF's formulation that he finds objectionable or misleading. Without denying the important sense in which Christ's mediatorial work involved an act of obedience as the second Adam, fulfilling Adam's original obligation of obedience, intensified and concentrated in the probationary command, Murray accents the elements of grace in the "Adamic administration." In Murray's judgment, the WCF's language of a "covenant of works" inadequately accounts for these aspects of the first covenant. Furthermore, the WCF does not fully indicate that this first covenant or "Adamic administration" was a

---

included "in some sense" the republication of the prefall covenant of works.

34. Murray, *Select Lectures*, 58.

divinely initiated and sovereignly administered disposition of God toward his image-bearers.

In Defense of the Westminster Confession of Faith

A careful evaluation of the preceding criticisms of the WCF's formulation of the doctrine of the covenant of works shows that there are several outstanding issues. Particularly within the orbit of neoorthodoxy and Barthian theology, the distinction between a prefall and a postfall covenant is emphatically rejected. Following the lead of Barth, critics of the WCF like Rolston and Torrance do not distinguish between a covenant of works and a covenant of grace, since they regard this as an illegitimate denial of the *one order of grace* which characterizes all of the triune God's dealings with his covenant creature. Furthermore, though the other critics we have considered do not share the Barthian theologians' denial of a distinction between a prefall and postfall covenant, they object to the WCF's designation of the first covenant as a covenant of *works*. It is frequently argued, as we have seen, that this terminology introduces the idea that man's standing before God, at least in the prefall circumstance, was founded upon "meritorious" good works. This, it is argued, threatens to make the creature's fellowship and communion with God, not so much a gift of God's grace, but a reward for good works. It also threatens to so distinguish man's covenant communion with God before and after the fall that the essential meaning of the covenant relationship is altered. In the first instance, God becomes man's debtor; in the second instance, man becomes God's debtor. The issues in these criticisms deal not only with the terminology of a covenant of *works*, but also the underlying doctrine of the covenant and the alleged intrusion of the idea of *merit* into the relationship between creature and Creator.

Admittedly, these criticisms and the issues they raise cannot be answered completely in this chapter. That would call for an examination of the whole doctrine of the covenant, in biblical, historical, and theological terms. However, there are several points that can be made in defense of the WCF. These points need to be borne in mind, especially in order to avoid placing an unwarranted construction on the WCF's doctrine of the covenant of works.[35]

Two Covenants or One?

The first consideration has to do with the question whether we should confess, on the basis of scriptural teaching, the reality of two covenants, one before and the other after the fall, or one. Though this may appear to be an unnecessary question, since the answer may seem so obvious, it is one raised by recent criticisms of the WCF.

It must be clearly understood that one of the most profound differences between the older covenant theology and much—though by no means all—modern theology, lies just at this point. The theology of Karl Barth and his epigones has ultimately no place for the biblical revelation of the *history* of creation, fall, and redemption. In the criticisms of Barth, Rolston, and Torrance, the difference between man's situation before the face of God prior to and after the fall into sin is flattened out, even obliterated. These theologians do not clearly echo the scriptural teaching that man was originally created good, after God's own image, and placed in a covenant relationship of fellowship with God. This covenant communion with God, before the fall into sin, included promises and demands. It was, moreover, a mutable relationship, liable to being broken and lost through sin and disobedience. This original covenant communion, however the difference is articulated, cannot be identified with the postfall situation in which God's covenant people through the covenant of grace are restored once more to communion with God. This latter covenant, the covenant of grace, is a covenant with the new humanity in Christ, the Mediator, and involves the calling out of a people for God's own possession from among the whole, fallen human race.

When the WCF, therefore, speaks of a prefall covenant of works between the triune God and all of humanity in Adam, and then distinguishes this prefall covenant from a postfall covenant of grace, made with a new people, the new humanity, those who

35. As noted previously, I will have occasion at several points throughout the course of this book to return to the question of the nature of the "works" required in the prefall covenant of works. My resolution of the question here will only be provisional.

are in restored communion with God through Christ, it echoes the basic structure of the biblical story of creation, fall, and subsequent redemption. The structure of biblical history, which constituted the foundation of the older covenant theology (and of orthodox Christian theology generally), is often missing in modern theological revisions of the covenant, of which Karl Barth's is a notable example. In this revision there is no longer any place for a historical fall from favor with God through the sin and disobedience of our covenant representative, Adam. Nor is there any place for a subsequent covenanting between God and his people in the covenant of grace, by means of which fallen man is *restored to renewed covenant fellowship with God in Christ, the second Adam*. In this revisionist theology of the covenant, there is only one covenant between God and the creature, a gracious covenant in Christ, which spans—perhaps it would be better to say, which obliterates—the difference between man's state of original sinless integrity in communion with God and his subsequent reintroduction to communion in the covenant of grace (cf. Rom. 5:12–21; 1 Cor. 15:42–49).

Consequently, it is absolutely critical to a biblical theology of the covenant that we recognize the basic correctness of the WCF's distinction between man's fellowship with God before the fall and his renewed fellowship with God through the gracious work of Christ after the fall. Even though some may choose not to speak of "covenant" in the prefall state (for example, Murray), this does not alter the fact that a theology faithful to biblical teaching must reckon with the difference in man's standing before God in the pre- and postfall states. The WCF accomplishes this by means of its formulation of a covenant of works and a covenant of grace.

A "Voluntary Condescension"

This brings us to what may be a more difficult issue, which has to do with the nature of the prefall relationship between the triune Creator and his sinless image-bearers. We have seen that the WCF has been frequently charged with a misconstrual of this relationship that rests man's communion with God on the foundation of meritorious works. Implicit in this criticism is the fear that the formulation of the WCF, though rightly distinguishing the pre- and postfall states, so distinguishes man's communion with God before the fall from his communion with God by grace after the fall, that there is almost an *antithesis* in the meaning of covenant before and after the fall. Or, to state it somewhat differently, the language of the WCF suggests a kind of *equivocation* on the meaning of covenant: in the one instance, it describes the relationship and communion of an Employer and employee, a Master and a servant (the prefall covenant of works), and in the other instance it describes the relationship of a Father and a child, or of a Husband and a wife (the postfall covenant of grace). The former covenant is merited; the latter is freely and graciously given. The former covenant is a matter of justice; the latter is a matter of grace.

This construction of the meaning and significance of the WCF's doctrine of the covenant of works, however, is open to serious objection. It trades too much upon the explicit language of a covenant of *works* and neglects to notice other aspects of the WCF's understanding of the covenant. Specifically, it fails to note that the WCF also speaks of God's *condescending favor* in the covenant of works and of God's *freely granted justice* in the covenant of grace. The full statement of the doctrine of the covenant in the WCF includes *promise and demand as essential constituents of both the covenant of works and the covenant of grace*. It is imperative to notice that the WCF, before defining the covenant of works in chapter 7.2 begins with a statement of the way all of the Creator's dealings with the creature are ordered covenantally (7.1). In this statement, we read that

> [t]he distance between God and the creature is so great, that although reasonable creatures do owe obedience unto him as their Creator, yet they could never have any fruition of him as their blessedness and reward, but by some voluntary condescension on God's part, which he hath been pleased to express by way of covenant.

By employing the language of *voluntary condescension*, the WCF makes it clear that the original covenant relationship was a sovereignly administered bestowal of God's favor to his image-bearers. In this covenant relationship, it is God who takes the initiative and condescends to the creature. He enters into a communion with Adam as his "son" (Luke 3:38) and not simply as a servant, in which a promise is made and an obligation stipulated. This language, accordingly, expresses something of what Murray and others mean when they speak of the "gracious elements" in the covenant of works, or when they insist that this covenant was not based upon a principle of "strict" justice, namely, the principle that man receives from God in this covenant only that which he in the strictest sense deserves. Adam is granted and established in a communion of life with his Creator in the covenant of works. And though he is obligated by the terms of his probation to offer a free obedience to his Creator, this obligation does not stand at the foreground or as the *foundation* of the covenant relationship, but rather it serves to express the manner and requirement of its administration.[36]

The WCF's emphasis upon all of God's covenants as voluntary condescensions exonerates the Confession from the charge of depriving the original covenant of the elements of God's favor and goodness, as though it were only a matter of strict justice between a master

36. Cf. De Graaf, "Genade Gods," who argues that, in the covenant of works, God's favor stands at the *end* rather than at the *beginning* of the covenant relationship. This is not necessarily the case, at least not in the statement of the doctrine in the WCF. Though it is true that the promise of life is upon condition of obedience, it is not true that Adam possessed nothing of that life, as a bestowal of God's condescending favor, at the beginning of the covenant relationship. Part of the difficulty here is that Murray, following a hallowed tradition of Reformed theology, properly regards the promise of life in the covenant of works to include an eventual *transition in Adam's standing before God from a state of mutability and contingency to one of irrevocable life in communion with God*. Because the obligation of obedience is regarded as a *probationary* obligation, it presumes some point of termination, at which time the promise of life would be irrevocably fulfilled. This latter promise, though conditioned upon Adam's obedience to his probation, grants much more than strict justice would require and is, therefore, an instance or element of grace in the sense of *unmerited favor* (though not of grace in the sense of *demerited* or *forfeited favor*). However, De Graaf makes the legitimate observation here, that God *threatens* death in the event of Adam's disobedience, implying that Adam enjoyed life-communion (albeit in a mutable state) with God from the beginning. The account in Genesis 2 does not teach that Adam was promised life *only after*, or at the successful completion of, a period of probation. Though Adam did not yet experience indefectible life in communion with God, as Murray properly emphasizes, he did experience the beginnings of life.

and his servant. Moreover, by its apparent distinction between the original natural state in which "reasonable creatures do owe obedience unto him [God] as their Creator" and the covenant of works, the WCF preserves the element of unmerited bestowal in this original covenant.[37] It simply cannot be argued convincingly that the WCF neglects this component of the original covenant relationship between God and the creature before the fall into sin and the institution of the covenant of grace. Though it may be helpful to reserve the term "grace" for God's unmerited favor toward undeserving sinners, there can be no objection to the claim that the Confession's language of "voluntary condescension" refers to the *undeserved favor* God as Creator shows to his sinless creatures and image-bearers.

The Terminology of "Covenant of Works"

No consideration of the criticisms often brought against the WCF on the covenant of works can avoid dealing with the question of terminology. Does the language of a covenant of *works* present,

37. I have already mentioned in a preceding footnote (n29) Mark Karlberg's criticism of the WCF for introducing a "speculative element" with this distinction between man's natural state and the subsequent introduction of a covenant of works. In both the WCF and in the reformulation of John Murray, there is (allegedly) present a disjunction between the original state of nature and the subsequent covenant of works that parallels the older, medieval distinction between *nature* and *grace*. Since it is not clear that the covenant of works is native to man's circumstance as creature, a state of nature is posited that antedates the state of "super-added" favor in the doctrine of the WCF and of John Murray. In my judgment, this criticism may have limited validity in respect to Murray's revision of the doctrine of the covenant of works, but less so in respect to the teaching of the WCF. The language of the WCF suggests that *the nature of the difference between Creator and creature requires covenant as the medium of communion or fellowship*. If this is the case, then the WCF ultimately does not separate between a state of nature and a state of covenant before the fall, but suggests that the covenant of works is a kind of administration or particularizing of that covenant relationship in and for which man was originally created. For a recent argument showing that man's original circumstance at creation was that of being in covenant with God, see Mark Vander Hart, "Creation and Covenant Part One: A Survey of the Dominion Mandate in the Noahic and Abrahamic Covenants," *MAJT* 6, 1 (1990): 3–18. The parallels between the language used to describe the terms of man's original created state and calling, and that used to describe the reestablishment of man in communion with God in the covenant of grace, suggest that, biblically, man is be understood as from the beginning a creature created for *covenant* with God. However, the prefall covenant must not be identified with creation *simpliciter*, since WSC 12 and WLC 20 do place the "covenant of life," as a work of God's providence, subsequent to creation.

especially in view of what we argued in the preceding section, something of a *one-sided* understanding of the original covenant? Perhaps it would be better to speak in terms of a "covenant of life," the language used for this covenant relationship in WSC 12. This language, or language like that of "covenant of creation" or "covenant of favor," does not diminish or belie the fact that God's original covenant with man was a bestowal of his favor, an act of undeserved and sovereign goodness in which the Creator took man into communion with himself as a friend and son. By contrast, the language of a covenant of "works," when exclusively employed as a description of the prefall covenant, may seem to convey that man's standing in this covenant was founded solely upon his own achievements or accomplishments.

One aspect of terminology with which I am not directly concerned here has to do with the absence of the language of "covenant" in the Bible to describe the prefall state. It is certainly true, as John Murray has argued, that the Scriptures do not clearly describe the original relationship between God and his image-bearers as a "covenant," and therefore the use of this language is not expressly biblical. However, the arguments in the history of theology for terming this relationship a "covenant" remain compelling. These arguments openly acknowledge that the doctrine is not expressly set down in the Scriptures, but nonetheless there are a number of biblical teachings or *sedes doctrinae* that cumulatively warrant the designation of this relationship as a covenant, the normal biblical designation for God's communion with his redeemed people in the covenant of grace.[38] When

38. The only instance in which the Bible speaks of a "covenant" in connection with Adam is Hosea 6:7 ("But like Adam they transgressed the covenant"). The meaning of the expression כְּאָדָם has always been disputed, some taking it to be a reference to a place name, not Adam, the head of the human race. For a defense of the claim that this phrase refers, among other things, to Adam's transgression of the covenant, see Benjamin Breckinridge Warfield, "Hosea 6.7: Adam or Man?," in *Selected Shorter Writings of Benjamin B. Warfield*, ed. John E. Meeter, 2 vols. (Nutley, NJ: Presbyterian and Reformed, 1970), 1:116–29; Duane Garrett, *Hosea, Joel*, New American Commentary 19A (Nashville: Broadman and Holman, 1997), 162–63; and Byron G. Curtis, "Hosea 6:7 and Covenant-Breaking like/at Adam," in *TLNF*, 170–209. However, the *sedes doctrinae* for the traditional description of the Creator's relationship with Adam before the fall are many. Among them are the following: the explicit use of God's peculiar covenant name, יְהוָה, throughout Genesis 2 and 3; the presence of a variety of covenantal elements in the description of God's dealings with Adam in Genesis 2 and 3 (the sovereign administration of a peculiar bond or communion

the constituent elements of a covenant are present, and when the normal biblical term for a divinely instituted and administered communion between God and his creature is "covenant," there should be no substantial objection to the use of this language. John Murray, who highlights the lack of an express biblical reference, prefers the terminology of an "Adamic administration." This terminology is not only alien to the biblical descriptions of the prefall state, however, but also to the biblical descriptions of God's communion with man in general.

On the matter of terminology, two points need to be made. First, the terminology of "covenant of works" needs to be complemented by the alternative terminology of "covenant of life" or "covenant of favor" (or even "covenant of creation"). There is a one-sidedness in the language of a covenant of *works* that demands the use of these complementary designations. It is especially helpful to speak of the prefall covenant as a "covenant of favor" since this language reminds us that this covenant was initiated and established by God, placed man in an undeserved position of special favor, and granted him life in communion with God which his obedience would maintain, unfold, and perfect. Even the obligation of obedience to the law, concentrated and intensified in the so-called probationary command, was an invitation to man to respond to his covenant Creator in heartfelt, thankful service. These dimensions of the first covenant can easily be diminished, when the exclusive terminology for this covenant is that of a "covenant of works."

A second consideration counterbalances this one. The language of a "covenant of works" helps to emphasize what was integral to the first covenant, namely, the obligation of obedience *on condition of*

between the Lord and Adam, the stipulation of a particular obligation, the pronouncement of a sanction or curse, the implicit promise or "sacramental sign" of life in the "tree of life" mentioned in Genesis 3:22, 24); the parallels in the language employed in Genesis to describe the prefall and postfall relationship between God and his people; and the apparent reminiscences of the covenant of grace in its earlier administrations, as well as the prefall covenant communion of God with man, in the descriptions of the eschatological covenant communion in Revelation 21–22. One hesitates here to apply the well-known words of Shakespeare, "a rose by any other name would smell as sweet," but it does seem appropriate. Why not term something a "covenant," though the express term is not employed in the Bible, when the thing being described has all the earmarks of a covenant?

which man would be perfected in immutable covenant communion with God. In the account in Genesis 2 of the stipulation of obedience, this dimension of the first covenant is most prominent. The language of the WCF, accordingly, keeps clearly before us the fact that no communion with God is possible for man, certainly no communion in which man might enjoy the fullness of life, short of one in which he offers to his Creator a glad-hearted obedience. Furthermore, this language clearly distinguishes the first covenant from the covenant of grace on precisely that matter which is most decisive. Though the first covenant was indeed an undeserved bestowal of divine favor, it was a favor shown to a sinless creature who had not yet forfeited through sin any further claim upon God's goodness. Moreover, the promise of the prefall covenant, eternal life in unbreakable communion with God, was granted upon "condition of personal and perfect obedience," to use the language of the WCF. There is a real difference between *undeserved favor* shown a sinless creature, obliged to perfect obedience by the terms of the prefall covenant of works, and the *undeserved grace* granted the disobedient covenant breaker in the postfall covenant of grace. The language of the WCF helps keep the difference between man's status before and after the fall clearly in perspective. God's dealings with man before the fall were not gracious in the strict sense of favor toward a fallen creature, as in the covenant of grace. In the covenant of grace, the demand and obligation of obedience remain, but God graciously gives a Mediator through whom that demand and obligation are met. What was promised man in the first covenant, on condition of "perfect and personal obedience," is given to the believer in the covenant of grace through the work of obedience of the second Adam. Only through the free gift of that righteousness which belongs to Christ, the second Adam, does the believer who receives this gift by faith become acceptable to God and again find himself received into his favor as a redeemed son (Rom. 5:18–21).

Therefore, the real difference between the first and second covenants is maintained by and reflected in the WCF's distinction between a covenant of *works* and a covenant of *grace*. Though this language may not be complete or altogether satisfactory, it preserves well the difference between a communion which, *to be maintained and perfected*, requires free and heartfelt obedience, and a communion which, *to be restored and regained*, requires the gracious and merciful granting of eternal life through the work of a Savior. It echoes the scriptural truth that the life promised man in the first covenant is only restored to man and ultimately realized in eschatological glory in the covenant of grace (cf. Rom. 6:23; Rev. 2:7).

What about "Merit?"

In order not to leave one further loose end among the common objections to the WCF's doctrine of the covenant of works, it is necessary at this point to consider whether it is ever permissible to speak of "merit" in the relationship between God and his covenant creature. One of the difficulties that emerges from a review of the criticisms of the WCF is the ambiguity of the language of "condition" and "merit" in many treatments of the covenant of works.

It should be evident from the foregoing that there is one obvious sense in which the language of "merit" has no place in a biblical theology of the covenant: *at no point in God's dealings with man as covenant creature may we say that God, in the strict sense of justice, owes the creature anything.*[39] Everything God bestows upon the creature,

39. For a contrary view, which argues that the covenant of works enunciated a doctrine of merit or strict justice, see Meredith Kline, *Kingdom Prologue: Genesis Foundations for a Covenantal Worldview* (Eugene, OR: Wipf & Stock, 2006), 107–17. Kline argues for a sharp distinction between "law covenant" and "promise covenant" that elucidates the difference between the covenant of works and the covenant of grace. According to Kline, the covenant of works is the original and basic type of covenant administration in Scripture. It is a law covenant in which obedience is stipulated, and a promise and sanction are attached. Such a law covenant operates according to a "law-inheritance" principle; obedience to what is stipulated "merits" the inheritance in the sense of strict justice. The inheritance granted in the covenant of works is based upon covenanted justice and is in no respect an instance of divine grace or unmerited favor. By comparison, the covenant of grace continues to recognize the foundational place of law or the stipulation of obedience, but there is now *added* the promise that God will mercifully fulfill this stipulation through Christ. Accordingly, the covenant of grace continues to uphold the "law-inheritance" principle, so powerfully enunciated in the covenant of works, but it does so by way of the addition of an alternative "faith-inheritance" principle, in which the covenant member receives life through faith in Christ, the Mediator of the covenant of grace. Christ's obedience to the law and his suffering of the law's curse obtain life for the believer. Though there are features of Kline's formulations that are acceptable, especially his insistence that the stipulation of obedience, first made in the covenant of works, remains operative in the covenant of grace,

whether in creation or redemption, is an undeserved benefit of his goodness and kindness. This holds true as much for man in his original state as in his redeemed state, though there is a difference between the favor shown sinless man and the grace shown the sinner, the covenant breaker who has forfeited any claim upon God's continued favor. At no point in God's dealings with man may we say that man gets what he deserves, strictly speaking, from God.[40]

The fact is that God, by entering into covenant with man, has bound himself by the promises as well as the demands of that covenant. This means that Adam's obedience to the stipulated obedience, though it were an outworking and development within the covenant communion in which he was placed by God's prevenient favor, would nonetheless "merit" or "deserve" the reward of righteousness God himself had promised. In the covenant itself God bound himself to grant, as in some sense a reward well-deserved, the fullness of covenant fellowship into which Adam was called. The terms of the stipulation of obedience—the explicit threat of death in the case of disobedience, the implicit promise of life in the case of obedience—warrant a qualified use of the language of "merit" or "reward."[41]

---

he tends to diminish the aspect of God's *favor*, as I prefer to speak of it, in God's original condescension to Adam, his image-bearer, in the covenant before the fall into sin. See also Lee Irons, "Redefining Merit: An Examination of Medieval Presuppositions in Covenant Theology," in *Creator, Redeemer, Consummator: A Festschrift for Meredith G. Kline*, ed. Howard Griffith and John R. Muether (Greenville, SC: Reformed Academic Press, 2000), 253–69. Irons defends Kline's view that the covenant of works was administered according to a "law-inheritance" principle of "strict" justice or merit. He also rejects the idea that God "favored" Adam by promising him a reward that was disproportionate to what he strictly deserved as a mere creature, arguing that this notion assumes the medieval distinction between "condign" and "congruent" merit. It is not surprising, therefore, that Irons concludes that the WCF's language of "voluntary condescension" reflects an unbiblical nominalism in its view of God's will.

40. For a similar view of the language of "voluntary condescension" in the WCF, see Robert Letham, *The Westminster Assembly: Reading Its Theology in Historical Context* (Phillipsburg, NJ: P&R Publishing, 2009), 231–32. Letham correctly criticizes Meredith Kline's insistence that the covenant of works enunciated a principle of "strict justice." According to Letham, "the Confession stresses condescension as underlying all God's covenants, including the prefall one. Whatever the place of law may be, it is in harmony with God's free and sovereign stooping down to do us a favor" (231).

41. Consequently, in the history of Reformed theology, the language of "covenanted merit"(*meritum ex pacto*) has been employed to emphasize that God grants Adam the "right" to the reward of eternal life by virtue of the promise of the covenant of works, even

This becomes especially significant when we consider the work of Christ, the covenant Mediator and second Adam. Christ, by his obedient fulfillment of all that the law required, can legitimately be said to have *merited* or *earned* the Father's favor toward his people, those for whom he actively obeyed the law and on whose behalf he suffered its curse (his so-called "active" and "passive" obedience). Christ met the conditions of the first covenant and obtained for his people a favor previously lost through the disobedience of their first federal head, Adam.

In this connection, it is instructive to note that Calvin, to whom many appeal when criticizing the WCF's language of "works" and of "condition" in describing the first covenant, explicitly defends the practice of speaking of Christ's work in the covenant of grace as "meritorious." Admittedly, Calvin readily acknowledges that Christ's work is not meritorious in the sense that our salvation finds its ultimate source in God's justice. Christ himself, in his person and his work as Mediator, is wholly the gracious gift of the Father on behalf of his people. In that sense, all of Christ's work finds its source in the grace, the unmerited favor, of God toward undeserving sinners. Nonetheless, integral to the gracious work of Christ is an obedience, after the pattern of Adam's disobedience, which remedies our circumstance as sinners by *meriting* God's favor and restoring us to a state of acceptance with God.[42] Christ's work as Mediator, including

---

though, as a creature, Adam's obedience could never earn in the sense of "strict merit" (the reward is commensurate with the work performed). See, e.g., *IET*, 2:710–23; *RD*, 2:569–71; and Richard A. Muller, *Dictionary of Latin and Greek Theological Terms Drawn Principally from Protestant Scholastic Theology* (Grand Rapids, MI: Baker, 1985), s.v. *ex pacto*, 108–9. Turretin's treatment of the meaning of the language of "merit," whether "properly" in the sense of "strict justice" or "improperly" in the sense of the covenanted promise of life upon condition of personal and perfect obedience, offers the most satisfying theological resolution of this question.

42. *Institutes*, 3.17.1: "In discussing Christ's merit, we do not consider the beginning of merit to be in him, but we go back to God's ordinance, the first cause. For God solely of his own good pleasure appointed him Mediator to obtain salvation for us. Hence it is absurd to set Christ's merit against God's mercy. For it is a common rule that a thing subordinate to another is not in conflict with it. For this reason nothing hinders us from asserting that men are freely justified by God's mercy alone, and at the same time that Christ's merit, subordinate to God's mercy, also intervenes on our behalf. Both God's free favor and Christ's obedience, each in its degree, are fitly opposed to our works. Apart from

both his perfect obedience to the demands of God's law and his suffering the penalty due the lawbreaker, earns salvation for his people. Though all stems from God's undeserved grace or favor, this does not mean that the actual work accomplished by Christ in no respect can be described as "meriting" salvation for his people. In the work of Christ as Mediator, God's "exact justice and rich grace" are demonstrated and maintained.[43]

Therefore, whether or not one is fully satisfied with the WCF's choice of words when it speaks of a "covenant of works," it remains true that the biblical teaching which the covenant doctrine of this confession expresses is the common inheritance of the Reformed churches historically. This inheritance has always understood the work of Christ, in the context of redemption and the covenant of grace, to be one which restores fallen man to that original favor and communion with God in and for which he was first created. The covenant of grace is a postfall remedy for the rupture in the covenant relationship between God and man brought about by the failure of Adam to live happily in terms of the first covenant. And it is a remedy that fulfills the covenant creature's obligations to his Creator, thereby restoring him to, and perfecting him in, fellowship with God.

Conclusion

Though not exhaustive, the preceding defense against many recent criticisms of the WCF's doctrine of the covenant of works

---

God's good pleasure Christ could not merit anything; but did so because he had been appointed to appease God's wrath with his sacrifice, and to blot out our transgressions with his obedience. To sum up: inasmuch as Christ's merit depends upon God's grace alone, which has ordained this manner of salvation for us, it is just as properly opposed to all human righteousness as God's grace is." Though Calvin is speaking here in the context of redemption, and not creation, it is not difficult to see that his reasoning would equally well apply to the circumstance of Adam in the covenant of works. Though Adam by virtue of God's favor and goodness was placed in fellowship with God from the beginning, his blessedness and continuance within this fellowship *depended upon* his grateful obedience to the stipulations of this communion. In this latter, subordinate sense, you might say Adam would have "merited" or "deserved" the fellowship his obedience maintained.

43. The language "exact justice and rich grace of God" is found in WCF 11.3, which describes the work of Christ whose "obedience and satisfaction" satisfy the just demands of God's holy law on behalf of his people.

should caution against jettisoning its formulations too quickly. It is especially important that critics of the WCF, especially those who write from within the framework of a commitment to historic Reformed orthodoxy, not unwittingly join their voices to those who do not share this commitment and whose criticisms arise out of a radically unbiblical framework.

The WCF's formulation of the doctrine of the covenant of works rightly preserves the difference between the covenant of favor which man enjoyed before the fall into sin and the covenant of grace by which this favor, once forfeited, is restored. It preserves the real historical difference between sinless man's fellowship and communion with God, a fellowship to be expressed and fulfilled in the way of obedience, and the sinner's restoration to fellowship through the work of Another, the second Adam. Furthermore, the WCF reminds us in its covenant doctrine that the saving work of Christ, the Mediator of the covenant of grace, involved not only an atoning death which satisfied the truth and justice of the first covenant, but also a saving life of obedience by which man's creaturely/covenantal obligation to his Creator was fulfilled. In so doing, the WCF helps us to see more clearly the glory of our covenant Mediator, by whose life, death, and resurrection the believer is restored to covenantal life and fellowship with God.

2

The Covenant of Works and the Mosaic Economy (1): *The Case for "Republication"*

If Reformed theology is known for any particular theological leitmotif or fundamental theme, it is the doctrine of the covenant(s). In the historical development of Reformed theology in the period subsequent to the reformatory labors of the early Reformers, the doctrine of the covenant became the primary idiom within which Reformed theologians of the orthodox period (late sixteenth and seventeenth centuries) articulated the relationship between the triune God and human beings whom he created after his own image for fellowship with himself. In the orthodox formulation of Reformed covenant theology, which is classically codified in the Westminster Standards at the midpoint of the seventeenth century, human beings obtain their blessedness only within the framework of the covenant relationship that God established with the human race in the first Adam before the fall and that he graciously reestablishes and brings to fruition in the "last" Adam, the promised "seed" of the woman, after the fall.

In the period of Reformed orthodoxy, the doctrine of the covenant was commonly articulated in the form of a bi-covenantalism that distinguished a prelapsarian "covenant of works" from a postlapsarian "covenant of grace." In this two-covenant scheme, the covenant of works, as its common name intimates, included the promise of life to Adam and his posterity "upon condition of personal and perfect obedience," and the curse-sanction of condemnation and death in the event of Adam's disobedience to its stipulations.[1] Because the first Adam was appointed the covenant "head" of the human race—a "public person" in the traditional language of covenant theology—his disobedience under the covenant of works demerited God's favor and brought the entire human race under God's just displeasure and condemnation. Though abrogated as a means to inherit life in perfected and indefectible communion with God, this covenant of works constitutes the framework for the biblical story of God's work of redemption through Christ, the last Adam.

After the fall into sin, the covenant of grace represents the means whereby the triune God, now as Redeemer of a new humanity in Christ, restores fallen sinners to fellowship with himself and freely grants them eternal life. Within the overarching and sovereign purposes of God, the covenant of grace is the appointed means whereby the eschatological life forfeited through Adam's sin and disobedience would be graciously granted to his elect posterity. Furthermore, in the work of Christ, the Mediator of the covenant of grace, the truth and justice of God which were manifest in the prelapsarian covenant of works, are upheld, since Christ fulfilled all the obligations of the law in the place and on behalf of his people. Life and blessing in communion with the triune God are only possible through the work of Christ in whom God's grace superabounds and the just demands of God's law are fully satisfied. Though there are a number of important differences between the covenant of works and the covenant of grace, there is a fundamental sense in which the work of Christ remedies graciously and justly the consequences of Adam's sin and obtains eternal life for those who are united to him by faith. In the work of redemption, the justice and mercy of God are simultaneously demonstrated, and the promise of blessedness originally made to Adam before the fall is granted to those for whom Christ was appointed as covenant head.

In the classic period of Reformed covenant theology, accordingly, the doctrine of the covenants of works and of grace provided a

1. In this paragraph, I am summarizing the main elements of WCF 7, which treats the doctrine of the covenants of works and of grace. The prelapsarian covenant relationship is variously denominated by covenant theologians. Sometimes it is termed a "covenant of nature" or a "covenant of creation."

comprehensive biblical-theological account of the way human beings, created in God's image, obtain life and blessing in communion with the living God. The covenant theology of the Reformed tradition also provided a coherent account of the unity within the diversity of the various administrations of the covenant of grace throughout the history of redemption. From the moment of the first "mother promise" (*protevangelium*) in Genesis 3:15 until the coming of Christ in the fullness of time to fulfill all the types and shadows of the OT economy, the triune Redeemer was progressively revealing the one way of salvation and blessing for fallen sinners, which is by grace alone through faith alone in Jesus Christ alone.

In language that was already employed by John Calvin in the sixteenth century, a standard feature of Reformed covenant theology was the insistence that the covenant of grace throughout redemptive history was one in substance though diverse in mode of administration.[2] Through the various administrations of the covenant of grace from Adam to Abraham to Moses to the time of the so-called latter prophets, the promise of restored communion with God through the promised "seed" was progressively adumbrated and foreshadowed. With the coming of Christ in the fullness of time, all of the promises of the OT economy were fulfilled and God's redemptive purposes were accomplished. A principal theme, therefore, of the covenant theology in the period of Reformed orthodoxy was that of the basic unity of the gospel throughout the course of the history of redemption. Whereas OT believers trusted in the Christ who was to come, NT believers trust in the Christ who has come and in whom the blessing of restored communion with God the Redeemer will be consummated.

While this summary of the main tenets of classic Reformed covenant theology is in some respects inadequate, it does provide a background for the focus of this and the next chapter, which is to offer a critical evaluation of a recent, important study in Reformed covenant theology, *The Law Is Not of Faith: Essays on Works and Grace in the*

2. *Institutes*, 2.10.2. WCF 7.6 expresses well the consensus on this point: "There are not therefore two covenants of grace, differing in substance, but one and the same, under various dispensations."

Mosaic Covenant.[3] The authors of this volume, several of whom are professors at Westminster Seminary in California, offer a historical, biblical, and theological defense of the idea that the Mosaic covenant included "in some sense" a *republication* of the covenant of works.[4] While the authors of this volume maintain their general adherence to the main lines of historic Reformed covenant theology, they are anxious to defend the claim that the Mosaic covenant plays a distinctive role in the history of the covenant by reiterating the "works principle" of the covenant of works as the basis for Israel's inheritance of and continuance within the land of Canaan. According to the authors of this volume, Israel's disobedience to the legal requirements of the Mosaic administration represented a kind of repetition of Adam's prelapsarian disobedience and failure to obtain life in communion with God. By means of the republication of the works principle of the covenant of works under the Mosaic administration, Israel and all who are members of the covenant of grace were taught to look for a covenant mediator who would satisfy all the obligations of the law on behalf of his people and secure for them the inheritance of eternal life in communion with God. Israel's disobedience under the law of the Mosaic administration becomes, therefore, an "antitype" of the obedience of the true Israel in the person of God's own Son who became incarnate in order to accomplish the redemption of his people. The title of the book, *The Law Is Not of Faith*, derives from the language of the apostle Paul in Galatians 3:12, and is intended to capture this contrast between the Mosaic administration, which in some sense required perfect obedience as the ground of Israel's inheritance, and the new covenant in Christ, which reveals that faith is the exclusive means of obtaining the free promise of justification and life.

I will have occasion in this chapter to unpack further the sense in which the authors of this volume view the Mosaic administration as a

3. *TLNF.* Throughout this chapter and the next, whenever reference is made to this volume, the page number will be given in the text within parentheses.

4. I place the phrase "in some sense" within quotation marks because this is an expression that is frequently used by various authors throughout the book. As we shall see, one of the principal challenges to any reader of the book is to determine precisely *in what sense* the Mosaic administration republishes the covenant of works.

republication of the covenant of works. However, it should be noted that the question of the distinctive nature and role of the Mosaic covenant in the history of redemption was much discussed by the principal Reformed authors in the course of the formulation of the doctrine of the covenant in the period of Reformed orthodoxy. There is ample precedent in the history of Reformed theology on the doctrine of the covenant for a careful reflection upon the peculiar features of the Mosaic administration within the history of redemption. However, the distinctive thesis of the authors of this book is that classic Reformed covenant theology commonly viewed the Mosaic administration as in some sense a republication of the prelapsarian covenant of works. According to the authors, the doctrine of *republication* was a predominant position within Reformed orthodoxy and can be defended on historical, exegetical, and theological grounds as integral to a biblical-theological doctrine of the covenant that preserves the radical contrast between the law and faith (in Christ) as antithetical means of obtaining justification and life in communion with God.

Before I offer a critical evaluation of the republication view in a subsequent chapter, I will begin with a survey of the principal arguments of the various authors of *TLNF*. Since there is a considerable diversity of opinion between the authors, I will focus upon the primary arguments and, where possible, the consensus that emerges throughout the volume. In the next chapter, I will examine whether these arguments and the consensus opinion of the authors are consistent with the writings of several key figures in the development of Reformed covenant theology and the codification of the doctrine of the covenant in the Reformed confessions. Though my critical assessment will also include a consideration of some of the exegetical and theological features of the claim that the Mosaic covenant republished the covenant of works, this consideration will not be the primary focus of my assessment of this claim.

The Editors' Introduction

In their introduction to *TLNF*, the editors begin with a case study, which represents an imaginary presbytery examination of a candidate for the gospel ministry who opines that the Mosaic covenant taught a "works principle" that represented a republication of the covenant of works. In response to the candidate's interpretation of the Mosaic covenant, the presbytery queries him at some length regarding the compatibility of this claim with the WCF's insistence that the Mosaic covenant was an administration of the covenant of grace. If the Mosaic covenant republishes the covenant of works, how can it be in substance an administration of the covenant of grace? Doesn't this view of the Mosaic covenant smack of a kind of dispensational contrast between the OT "legal" economy and the NT "grace" economy?

To these queries, the candidate responds by noting the "typological" function of the Mosaic law. The Mosaic law's demand for perfect obedience in a passage like Leviticus 18:5 (cf. Luke 10:28, "do this and you will live") ultimately served to teach Israel the impossibility of inheriting the promise through obedience and pointed her to Christ, whose perfect obedience "under the law" is the only basis for securing the promise of eternal life. By means of this typological republication of the covenant of works, the Mosaic covenant taught Israel that blessings or curses in the land of Canaan depended upon her perfect obedience to the law. In this sense, the Mosaic covenant repeated Adam's "probation" under the covenant of works and taught a "works principle" that grounded Israel's land inheritance upon her obedience to the law's requirements. Furthermore, the candidate observes that this view of the peculiar function of the Mosaic covenant is reflected in the WCF's appeal to passages like Romans 10:5 and Galatians 3:12, both of which cite Leviticus 18:5 to support the doctrine of a covenant of works.

The intention of the editors in their description of this imaginary candidacy examination at presbytery is to introduce the main focus and claim of the various authors of *TLNF.* Whereas the view of the candidate might appear novel and unsettling to a contemporary presbytery, the doctrine of the republication of the covenant of works under the Mosaic administration is actually "part of the warp and woof of Scripture and sound doctrine" (6). Far from being a "theological novelty," the doctrine of republication represents a sound biblical-theological perspective upon Israel's "probation and exile" as it is recorded throughout the OT narrative of the covenant Lord's dealings with his people, Israel. Both of "God's sons, Adam and Israel, lived under *nomos*-governed circumstances" (9), and both failed the terms of their probation in a way that called for the coming of God's true Son, Christ, who fulfilled all the obligations of the law and thereby secured the inheritance of eternal life for those who are united to him by faith. While acknowledging a diversity of opinion and formulation regarding the uniqueness of the Mosaic covenant in the history of the covenant, the editors insist that the idea of republication belongs to the mainstream of historic Reformed covenant theology and is embedded, for example, in the way the Westminster divines treat the Mosaic covenant in WCF 19 (10). According to the editors, "the divines saw that the law given to Adam was of a piece with that given to Israel at Sinai. In other words, in some sense, the covenant of works was republished at Sinai. It was not republished, however, as the covenant of works per se, but as part of the covenant of grace, which pointed to the person and work of Christ" (11). However, despite the common teaching of the doctrine of republication by Reformed stalwarts such as Amandus Polanus, Francis Turretin, and Charles Hodge, contemporary Reformed theology, influenced by such disparate figures as John Murray, Norman Shepherd, and even Karl Barth, has come to regard the idea with suspicion and even hostility (11–13).[5]

The purpose of the editor's introduction, therefore, is to impress upon the reader that the doctrine of republication under the Mosaic administration belongs to the historic view of Reformed orthodoxy and that it constitutes an important, if not essential, feature of a sound biblical-theological interpretation of the covenant. Indeed, in the opinion of the editors, the historic Reformed view of the contrast

5. On p. 11 the editors quote Polanus to say "[t]he repetition of the covenant of works is made by God," and footnote volume 1:44 (*Prolegomena to Theology*) of Richard Muller's *Post-Reformation Reformed Dogmatics* (Grand Rapids, MI: Baker, 2003). This reference should be to the first edition of Muller's work (1987) where Muller offers a brief description of Polanus's identity and major works. However, the quotation does come from Amandus Polanus, *The Substance of the Christian Religion* (London: W. Apsley, 1608), which is cited by the editors in the following footnote.

between the law and the gospel, which represent two antagonistic principles for obtaining the promise of eternal life in fellowship with God, is closely linked with this view of the Mosaic covenant. By means of their introduction, the editors aim to alert the reader to the importance of a proper view of the Mosaic covenant for an understanding of the work of Christ, especially his obedience "under the law" as the basis for the believer's justification before God. In the estimation of the editors, the doctrine of republication is a critical component of a biblical and Reformed doctrine of the covenant of grace, and the loss of an understanding of this doctrine represents a serious declension in Reformed theology. The purpose of the book is to demonstrate upon historical, exegetical, and theological grounds that more recent Reformed theology has failed to appreciate the importance of this view of the Mosaic covenant. In the opinion of the editors, the stakes in the debate regarding the peculiar nature of the Mosaic covenant in contrast to other administrations of the covenant of grace could not be higher.

In order to prepare for my critical assessment of the republication thesis and the claims made on its behalf, I will now offer a summary of the arguments of the three major parts of the volume.

The Historical Arguments

The first part of *TLNF* consists of three chapters that defend the assertion that the doctrine of republication was a standard feature of the historic Reformed doctrine of the covenant. In the first of these historical studies ("Calvin and Witsius on the Mosaic Covenant"), J. V. Fesko treats the writings of two architects of the classic Reformed doctrine of the covenant, John Calvin and Herman Witsius. In the second ("Princeton and the Law: Enlightened and Reformed"), D. G. Hart considers the doctrine of the natural law in the theology of "old" Princeton and its significance so far as the republication thesis is concerned. In the third and last chapter in this part of the book ("Works in the Mosaic Covenant: A Reformed Taxonomy"), Brenton C. Ferry endeavors to articulate a taxonomy of viewpoints on the role of the law in the Mosaic covenant that are present in the history of Reformed theology. For the purposes of my review, the first and third of these studies are the most important to an evaluation of the claims of the book's authors.

In his chapter on Calvin and Witsius, Fesko begins with an acknowledgment that Reformed orthodox theologians, including the Westminster divines, adopted a variety of viewpoints on the Mosaic covenant (25).[6] Whereas some viewed the Mosaic covenant as a covenant of works, others viewed it as a kind of admixture of a covenant of works and of grace, and still others viewed it as simply a covenant of grace. Rather than attempt to sort out all of the diversity of position represented in the orthodox Reformed tradition, Fesko singles out John Calvin and Herman Witsius, the one an early Reformer of the sixteenth century, the other a mediating theologian of the late seventeenth century, in order to offer what he terms a "comparative historical-theological snapshot . . . on this challenging issue" (26). Since Calvin and Witsius are generally regarded as key figures in the early and later period of Reformed orthodox reflection on the covenant, their views on the peculiar nature of the Mosaic administration are of special importance to an understanding of classic Reformed theology on the question.

Fesko introduces his treatment of Calvin's doctrine of the covenant by noting Calvin's emphasis upon the *substantial unity* of the covenant of grace throughout the course of the history of redemption. Employing the traditional Aristotelian categorical distinction between *substance* (that which makes something what it is) and *accident* (that which is only adventitious or a matter of appearance or circumstance), Calvin insisted that the covenant of grace, whether in the Mosaic administration of the old covenant economy or in the Christian administration of the new covenant economy, was one in

6. Subsequent to the writing of this chapter, I was asked by the editors of the *Confessional Presbyterian* to engage the republication doctrine in a two-part exchange with Fesko. For this exchange, see J. V. Fesko, "The Republication of the Covenant of Works," *Confessional Presbyterian* 8 (2012): 197–212; Cornelis P. Venema, "The Law of Moses: Not a Disguised Covenant of Works," *Confessional Presbyterian* 8 (2012): 212–27; Fesko, "The Accommodated Scriptures: A Response to Cornelis Venema," *Confessional Presbyterian* 9 (2013): 178–87; and Venema, "The Mosaic Economy and the Covenant of Grace," *Confessional Presbyterian* 9 (2013): 157–78.

"substance and reality" though different in "mode of administration."[7] Though the Mosaic covenant represented salvation through faith in Christ in shadows and ceremonies, and though this administration typified the spiritual blessings of communion with God in earthly and temporal forms, the doctrine of salvation was the same in the old economy as in the new.

However, Fesko maintains that Calvin also distinguished "two separate covenants" within the Mosaic administration: a "legal covenant" (*foedus legale*) and an "evangelical covenant" (*foedus evangelicum*) (30). On the one hand, the Mosaic administration "set forth a covenant governed by a works principle, namely, eternal life through obedience." On the other hand, the Mosaic administration set forth antithetically a gracious covenant, which promised eternal life to Israel, not through obedience to the requirements of the law but through faith in Christ. According to Fesko, Calvin viewed the Mosaic administration as in substance a covenant of grace, though in the particular "accidents" of its administration it was a legal covenant (31). By enunciating a legal covenant, which promised Israel an inheritance through obedience to the requirements of the law, the Mosaic administration demonstrated "man's sinfulness" and "inability to merit eternal life by his obedience" (32). In this way, the Mosaic covenant served to drive sinners to seek salvation, not in the works of the law, but in the way of faith in Christ who alone fulfilled all the obligations of the law on behalf of his people.

The second Reformed theologian whom Fesko considers, Herman Witsius, was a theologian of the later orthodox period. Between the time of Calvin's early reformatory labor and that of Witsius, considerable development had occurred in the Reformed understanding of the covenant. Witsius's treatment of the doctrine of the covenant presupposes, for example, the explicit bi-covenantalism of the WCF, which draws a careful and clear distinction between the prelapsarian covenant of works and the postlapsarian covenant of grace. Witsius also writes as a mediating theologian who sought to find consensus

7. *Institutes*, 2.10.2 (*OS* 3:404): "Patrum omnium foedus adeo substantia et re ipsa nihil a nostro differet, ut unum prorsus atque idem sit: administration tamen variat."

within the differing formulations of his contemporaries on a number of disputed questions of covenant theology, including the question of the distinctive nature of the Mosaic administration. In Fesko's assessment of Witsius's position on the Mosaic administration, he observes that his formulations, though in harmony with those of Calvin, are more articulate and precise on what distinguishes the Mosaic economy (40–41).

In his consideration of Witsius's view, Fesko notes that Witsius embraces Calvin's distinction between the "substance" and the "circumstances" of the covenant of grace in its various administrations. In substance, the old and new economies of the covenant are the same. However, they differ in their circumstances. Witsius also followed Calvin's lead in observing that what distinguishes the Mosaic administration in the history of redemption is its "legal" nature (36). Where Witsius advances upon Calvin is in his emphasis upon the *typological* function of the law within the framework of the Mosaic administration. According to Fesko, Witsius viewed the law within the Mosaic administration as a republication of the covenant of works, which served a "pedagogical" purpose to drive Israel to Christ and to demonstrate that there is no possibility of obtaining life in communion with God through obedience to the law's demands. However, in addition to this pedagogical function of the law as a republication of the covenant of works, Witsius ascribes a special role to the law within the Mosaic administration in the economy of redemption (*historia salutis*). In Witsius's theology, the Mosaic administration was a "national" covenant between God and Israel, "one by which they [*sic*] could earn their salvation through their obedience" (37). Even though Israel proved incapable of fulfilling the law's requirements and thereby attaining life in the Promised Land, at this level the Mosaic administration replicated Adam's probation in the garden of Eden. Just as Adam forfeited the promise of life through his disobedience, so Israel forfeited the inheritance of the land through disobedience to the demands of the law mediated through Moses (37). Combining elements of the covenants of works and of grace, the Mosaic covenant functioned typologically to foreshadow the person and work of Christ, the last

Adam and true Israel, whose obedience secured the inheritance of life for believers.

Upon the basis of his treatment of the views of Calvin and Witsius, Fesko concludes that both of these theologians posited the presence of a "works principle" in the Mosaic administration. For Calvin, this works principle operated at the level of the individual Israelite's procurement of the promise of life (*ordo salutis*), and served only "hypothetically" as a means of demonstrating the impossibility of life upon the basis of obedience to the law. For Witsius, this works principle operated also at the level of Israel's corporate or national life (*historia salutis*) and demanded not a perfect but a "sincere" obedience as the means of life and blessing in the Promised Land (39). Consequently, both theologians represented the Mosaic covenant as a kind of "republication of the covenant of works," whose legal requirements for Israel's inheritance of life served ultimately to expose Israel's sinfulness and the futility of obtaining life in fellowship with God through obedience to the law.

If the purpose of Fesko's contribution to this volume is to illustrate the way two leading theologians of the Reformed tradition interpreted the Mosaic administration as "in some sense" a republication of the covenant of works, Brenton C. Ferry's contribution aims to offer a comprehensive taxonomy of representative Reformed views on the role of works in the Mosaic economy. Expressing his dissatisfaction with previous attempts to sort out the various viewpoints on the distinctiveness of the Mosaic administration,[8] Ferry seeks to

8. Ferry refers especially to three studies on the history of Reformed covenant theology, but expresses reservations regarding their reading of the sources: Peter Golding, *Covenant Theology: The Key of Theology in Reformed Thought and Tradition* (Fearn, Ross-shire: Christian Focus Publications, 2004); Rowland S. Ward, *God & Adam: Reformed Theology and the Creation Covenant* (Wantirna, Australia: New Melbourne Press, 2003); and Mark Karlberg, *Covenant Theology in Reformed Perspective: Collected Essays and Book Reviews in Historical, Biblical, and Systematic Theology* (Eugene, OR: Wipf and Stock, 2000). In my judgment, Ward's book is the most useful of these studies. Karlberg's interpretation of the history of Reformed covenant theology suffers from an undue attachment to the formulations of Meredith Kline. It is noteworthy that the authors of *TLNF* do not refer to the fine study of my colleague, *CCT*. Beach's study fills some of the gaps in the literature on the history of Reformed covenant theology, and provides a comprehensive treatment of Turretin's position on the kinds of questions the authors of *TLNF* address.

organize the rich and diverse formulations of the leading Reformed theologians of the orthodox period on the question of the uniqueness of the Mosaic administration. In doing so, Ferry attempts to fortify the historical argument for the presence, if not the predominance, of the "republication" thesis among Reformed theologians in the formative period of the development of covenant theology.

In order to achieve his purpose, Ferry distinguishes three key questions on the relation between the Mosaic administration and the covenant of grace: (1) "how does the Mosaic covenant relate forward to the new covenant?"; (2) "how does the Mosaic covenant relate backward to the covenant of works?"; and (3) "how does the Mosaic covenant relate to the covenant of grace?" (77–78). Though we will not offer a summary of Ferry's answer to each of these three questions, the second, which directly focuses upon the relation of the Mosaic administration to the covenant of works, is clearly the most pertinent to the overall thesis of the volume under review and requires our special attention.

On the specific question as to whether the Mosaic administration was in some sense a republication of the covenant of works, Ferry distinguishes two broad types of views: "material republication" and "formal republication." By the first type of view, material republication, Ferry means to identify a "soft" form of the republication thesis. Theologians who favored the idea of material republication simply emphasized the continuity in the *material content* of the moral law given through Moses to Israel and the moral law as it was engraved upon Adam's conscience and known by nature in the prelapsarian covenant relationship. This view does not regard the law as it was mediated through Moses as in any substantial sense a covenant of works, but as merely a reiteration of the moral obligations that belong to the moral law of God in any of its distinct promulgations throughout the course of history (91–92). Regarding this type of view, Ferry observes that "it extracts any sense of a covenantal function or intent from the likeness between Adam and Moses, admitting only a moral continuity, which can be said about every historical dispensation of time from the probation to the eschaton" (92). In this broad type of view, the Mosaic administration doesn't republish the covenant of works as such, but only republishes the moral obligations of obedience that are intrinsic to any historical revelation of God's will for his moral creatures.

After a brief description of the first type of republication view, Ferry offers a more extensive taxonomy of distinct versions of the second type of view, which regards the Mosaic administration to have in some way reintroduced the original prelapsarian covenant of works. In this "hard" republication type of view, various Reformed theologians affirmed that the Mosaic administration reiterated not only the moral content of the law's demands for perfect obedience, but also did so in the form of a covenant. Though Ferry hastens to add that these theologians rejected the inference that the Lord ever intended the law "to be used as a mechanism for actually earning eternal life" (92), he nonetheless maintains that the majority of Reformed theologians affirmed that the covenant of works was republished through Moses.

In his effort to offer a more nuanced taxonomy of diverse formulations among Reformed theologians, Ferry distinguishes no less than five versions of the formal republication type: (1) a "relative, formal covenant of works" view that distinguishes the Mosaic economy as a covenant of grace for believers, who acknowledge Christ as the One who alone fulfilled all that the law requires on behalf of his people, and as a covenant of works for unbelievers, who find themselves condemned and without excuse by the law's demands (93); (2) a "pedagogical, formal republication" view that interprets the Mosaic law as a "tutor" that leads believers to Christ (94); (3) a "hypothetical, formal republication" view that was commonly represented by Reformed theologians who argued that the Mosaic law made a hypothetical promise of salvation and life to all who keep the law perfectly, but that served by God's design to break down Israel's pride and expose human inability (93);[9] (4) a "typological, formal republication" view

9. Though Ferry cites Calvin as an example of this kind of formal republication view, I will argue in the following chapter that Calvin does not conceive of the Mosaic administration as a republication of the covenant of works. Calvin's view is much closer to what Ferry terms a "material" republication view, since Calvin only affirms that the Mosaic law reiterates the requirements of the natural (moral) law that was the rule of Adam's obedience

that emphasized the typological nature of the law's demands, which illustrated and pointed forward to Christ by emphasizing Israel's obligation to inherit the land by "the national principle of works" (97); and (5) a "complex, formal republication" view that regarded the Mosaic administration as a complex republication of both the covenant of grace and the covenant of works (97). Ferry concludes, upon the basis of his survey and distinctions between various versions of the republication thesis, that some version of the doctrine of a republication of the covenant of works was a commonplace in the history of Reformed covenant theology. Rather than interpreting these versions of the republication thesis as incompatible, he also maintains that they were largely "complementary" in character.

Together with Fesko's chapter on the views of Calvin and Witsius, Ferry's chapter endeavors to offer a general historical argument for the principal thesis of *TLNF*, namely, that the special function of the Mosaic administration within the framework of the economy of the covenant of grace throughout history was its republication of the works principle of the prelapsarian covenant of works. Though the formulation of how this works principle functioned in the Mosaic administration might differ among Reformed theologians, its presence was commonly acknowledged among Reformed theologians of the formative period in the history of Reformed theology. By means of its enunciation of this works principle, the Mosaic covenant promised Israel an inheritance of life and blessing in the Promised Land and simultaneously threatened the curse of exclusion and exile in the event of disobedience. Israel's probation under the Mosaic law was a kind of repetition of Adam's probation in the prelapsarian covenant of works and served ultimately within God's purposes to direct believers to Christ, the obedient Adam and faithful Israel, who procured for his people a covenant inheritance and blessing through his perfect obedience to the law's demands and substitutionary endurance of its curse-sanctions.

---

before the fall. The position Ferry terms a "material" republication view is, as I shall also argue below, the most common view in the Reformed tradition and hardly warrants being termed a "republication" of the covenant of works in any significant sense. Ferry's taxonomy here and throughout is rather confusing and, for that reason, unhelpful.

The Biblical Arguments

In the second and most extensive section of *TLNF*, six authors contribute chapters offering a variety of biblical studies that cumulatively support the thesis of a republication of the covenant of works in the Mosaic economy. To summarize the exegetical arguments of these authors represents a more formidable (if not impossible) challenge than the one we faced in treating the first and historical section of the volume. Here our summary of the arguments of *TLNF* will have to be even more selective and impressionistic than in the preceding. For our purposes, we will largely omit a treatment of three of the chapters in this section, since they are not as directly relevant to the principal claims of the book. These chapters treat such disparate biblical subjects as: the way the Psalms point forward to Christ, the truly righteous King, who secures entrance into fellowship and life with God for his people (chap. 5, "The King, the Law, and Righteousness in the Psalms: A Foundation for Understanding the Work of Christ," by Richard P. Belcher, Jr.); whether Hosea 6:7 teaches that Israel's violation of the covenant repeated the violation of the covenant through Adam's disobedience (chap. 6, "Hosea 6:7 and Covenant-Breaking like/at Adam," by Byron G. Curtis); and the interpretation of Paul's appeal to Leviticus 18:5 in Romans 10:5 (chap. 7, "Romans 10:5 and the Covenant of Works," by Guy P. Waters). Although these chapters offer a number of suggestive and intriguing exegetical insights, they do not have as direct a bearing upon the principal claims of the authors of *TLNF* as do the others.[10]

The first chapter in this section of *TLNF* that directly supports the republication thesis is a study by Bryan D. Estelle on Leviticus 18:5 and Deuteronomy 30:1–14. Estelle's chapter is extensive and offers a complex case for a form of the republication thesis. Estelle interprets these two OT passages within their broad canonical

10. Curtis's chapter, "Hosea 6:7 and Covenant-Breaking like/at Adam," offers an interesting and rather compelling case for an interpretation of Hosea 6:7 that implies the idea of a prelapsarian covenant with Adam. Waters's chapter, "Romans 10:5 and the Covenant of Works," does not advance the kind of republication thesis that is present in the majority of the chapters of *TLNF*. Waters's interpretation of Romans 10:5 and Paul's appeal to Leviticus 18:5 is not substantially different from the view that I will argue in the next section was common in the Reformed tradition.

context, and argues that the apostle Paul appropriately adduces them as illustrative of two antithetical inheritance principles that were enunciated in the Mosaic covenant. According to Estelle, these two passages "paradoxically" communicate what is required in order for believers to obtain entitlement to heaven or eternal life, though they set forth principles that are antithetical: a works principle that requires perfect obedience to the law in order for Israel to obtain life and a grace principle that reveals that eternal life can only be obtained through the perfect work and obedience of Jesus Christ. In Estelle's summary of the thesis of his chapter, he observes that "these passages in their canonical development and context teach that God initiated and definitively obtained the goal of entitlement to heaven through the work of Christ which man may now possess by faith and not through his own works" (110).

In order to make his case, Estelle first treats the meaning of Leviticus 18:5, one of only two passages from Leviticus that the apostle cites in his epistles: "You must keep my statutes and my ordinances, which, if one does them, he shall live by them: I am the Lord" (Estelle's translation). In its original setting (Lev. 18:1–5), this passage especially urges the Israelites to avoid the sexual practices of the Egyptians and Canaanites. In his treatment of the passage, Estelle argues that there are two particularly important questions that it raises: (1) how far the demands and promises of Leviticus 18:5 extend; and (2) what is meant by the "life" promised to those who do what the law requires (114). To the first of these questions, Estelle responds by noting that in its original setting the requirements of the law extended to all of the children of Israel, including the sojourners in the land (115). In this respect, there is a kind of "democratization" of the law's obligations; everyone is obliged to keep the Lord's statutes and ordinances. The extension of the law's obligations to all the Israelites and inhabitants of the land anticipates in an "inchoate" fashion the "universal tenor" of the apostle Paul's appeal to this passage in Romans 10:5 (116). In the broader canonical framework of Paul's interpretation of this OT text, the obligations of obedience to the law in order to obtain life in fellowship with the Lord are addressed to all human beings without exception.

To the second of these questions, Estelle acknowledges that the "life" proffered to those who do what the law requires originally focused on what might be termed "temporal" or "mundane" blessings in the Land of Promise. However, it would be a mistake to restrict the "life" promised in this passage to such blessings, since these blessings were—again in the broader canonical framework of interpretation—a typological prefigurement of the fullness of life in communion with the Lord. They pointed forward to Christ in whom all the blessings of life, including entitlement to heaven, the true Promised Land, are obtained for those who belong to him by faith. This does not mean that the promise of life in Leviticus 18:5 was merely hypothetical, pointing forward to Christ and his obedience, which obtains entitlement to heaven for his people. So far as Israel's tenure in the Land of Promise was concerned, Leviticus 18:5 posits a "real connection" between obedience to the law and the maintenance of her land inheritance and well-being (119). By virtue of this connection between obedience and blessing, Israel's right to the promised inheritance could only be established through obedience, though this right should not be regarded as the "meritorious grounds of life in the eternal sense" (119).

The second passage Estelle treats is Deuteronomy 30:1–14, a passage that makes a remarkable promise regarding Israel's restoration from exile and the initiative of God's grace in enabling the people to live in obedience, however imperfect, to the requirements of God's law. Unlike Leviticus 18:5, which requires an obedience that Israel was ultimately unable to fulfill and whose promise was "conditional," the promise of future restoration and life in covenant with the Lord that is given in Deuteronomy 30 is an "unconditional" promise of blessing (130). Whereas "the principle of works was republished at Sinai" and summarized in the language of Leviticus 18:5 ("do this and live"), the principle of the Lord's gracious initiative and provision is starkly revealed in the promise of Deuteronomy 30:1–14 (131). In Estelle's summary, "this amazing passage anticipates ahead of time the plight in which the Israelite nation will find itself, destitute and unable to fulfill the stipulations of the covenant *on its own*. It also describes the new measure of obedience—accomplished *by divine initiative*—in which they will satisfy the conditions hanging over them" (124, emphasis original). When this passage is interpreted in conjunction with its "echoes" in the prophecies of Jeremiah (cf. chap. 31) and Ezekiel, as well as the NT's language of the fulfillment of the promise in Christ and by his outpoured Spirit, it must be viewed as standing in marked contrast to the works principle set forth in the Mosaic economy. What the Israelites were not able to obtain through obedience to the demands of the law, the Lord will graciously grant by his sovereign initiative and working, namely, the circumcision of the hearts of his people and the gracious enablement to live in obedience before the Lord. Consequently, the promise of Deuteronomy 30 reminds Israel "that the whole old covenant order will be annihilated, it will be wiped out, and it will go down in judgment as a *modus operandi*. The new covenant is not like that: it is not subject to breaking because it is built upon God's initiative to complete it and Christ's satisfaction in his penalty-paying substitution and his probation keeping" (130).

The most important section of Estelle's chapter addresses the way the apostle Paul appeals to Leviticus 18:5 and Deuteronomy 30:1–14 in Romans 10:5–6, and to Leviticus 18:5 in Galatians 3. The apostle Paul adduces these passages from the Mosaic economy in a way that goes "beyond what is recoverable when these texts are taken in isolation from one another in the context of their immediate environment" (132). However, the apostle Paul's use of these passages is consonant with their original meaning within the Mosaic administration, and makes special use of the antithesis that they express between two inheritance principles, the one a principle of works and the other a principle of grace. In both Romans 10:5–6 and Galatians 3 (where the apostle contrasts Leviticus 18:5 with Habakkuk 2:4), Paul draws a stark contrast between a righteousness that is by the law and a righteousness that is by faith in Christ alone. In so doing, the apostle understands the Mosaic administration to include a "works principle," which posits a real connection between Israel's obligations of obedience to the law and inheritance of life. "Although the substance of the covenant of grace is the same in both testaments, in the old covenant there was the need for compliance so that this would be *the meritorious grounds* for Israel's continuance in the land, the typological kingdom" (136, emphasis added). When the Lord summoned Israel to obedience in Leviticus 18:5, he communicated a works principle that is no longer operative in the new economy with the coming of Christ. Consequently, we may conclude that "the new covenant context has essentially changed matters here" (136).

In the Mosaic administration, the requirement of obedience to the law functioned at two levels: at one level, this requirement set forth a works principle of inheritance that Israel was unable to meet and that only "antitypically" is met in the perfect obedience of Christ; and at another level, this requirement set forth the need for a grateful or "sincere" though imperfect obedience. The latter requirement remains an integral part of the new covenant in Christ, though the former has now been "eclipsed" (137). Paul's appeal to these two passages, therefore, can only be properly interpreted in terms of an "antithetical" reading of Leviticus 18:5 and Deuteronomy 30:1–14. In the Pauline appeal to this passage, the Mosaic administration is treated at one level as a republication of the works principle of the prelapsarian covenant of works, though Israel's probation, unlike Adam's, is articulated in "positive terms (temporal blessings)" rather than primarily in terms of the negative curse-sanction of the Adamic covenant administration (145).

The second essay that we consider in the biblical studies section of *TLNF* is authored by T. David Gordon and offers an interpretation of the apostle Paul's contrast of the Abrahamic and Sinaitic covenants in Galatians 3:6–14. Gordon's essay sets forth the most provocative and forceful version of the republication thesis that governs the essays in this volume. In his essay, Gordon treats the way the apostle Paul sharply contrasts the two covenant administrations made with Abraham and with the Israelites at Sinai some 430 years later and insists that the Pauline contrast is incompatible with the way some Reformed theologians, especially John Murray, have argued for the coherence between these covenant administrations. In particular, Gordon identifies five key contrasts in Paul's argument in Galatians 3:6–14 that are "fatal" to Murray's thesis and that of other Reformed theologians who maintain that the "condition of obedience" in the Mosaic covenant was essentially the same as in the Abrahamic (240–41).[11]

The first contrast Gordon notes between the Abrahamic and Mosaic covenants relates to the extensiveness of those with whom the covenant is made. In the case of the Abrahamic covenant, the promise to Abraham includes that of a "seed" in whom all the families of the earth will be blessed. The Abrahamic covenant, therefore, promises blessings that will include all the peoples of the earth, Gentiles as well as the people of Israel. In the case of the Mosaic covenant, however, the Gentiles are excluded through the distinguishing requirements of circumcision, feast day observances, and dietary laws. Though the Sinaitic covenant was restrictive in terms of its recipients, it did serve to preserve the "integrity" of Abraham's seed and thereby facilitate the promise of the Abrahamic covenant (242–43).

The second contrast or difference between these two covenants is more germane to Gordon's basic thesis. In Galatians 3:10–13, the apostle Paul sharply distinguishes these two covenants in terms of their outcome: the Abrahamic covenant blesses; the Sinaitic covenant curses. Whereas the Abrahamic covenant is "largely promissory" of what the Lord will do in graciously granting the blessing of life-communion to his people, the Sinaitic covenant especially emphasizes "the threat of curse-sanctions" in the event of Israel's failure to do all that the law requires (245). Gordon observes that the threat of curse-sanctions, which is such an integral part of the Sinai covenant, is "entirely absent from the Abrahamic administration" and constitutes a substantial difference that sharply differentiates its unique character. Though a number of Reformed theologians have

11. Gordon cites the following statement of Murray as an example of the position to which his essay is a "counterpart": "What needs to be emphasized now is that the Mosaic covenant in respect of the condition of obedience is not in a different category from the Abrahamic. It is too frequently assumed that the conditions prescribed in connection with the Mosaic covenant place the Mosaic dispensation in a totally different category as respects grace, on the one hand, and demand or obligation, on the other. In reality there is nothing that is principally different in the necessity of keeping the covenant and of obedience to God's voice, which proceeds from the Mosaic covenant, from that which is involved in the keeping required in the Abrahamic" (John Murray, *The Covenant of Grace: A Biblico-Theological Study* [1954; repr., Phillipsburg, NJ: Presbyterian and Reformed, 1988], 22).

endeavored to mitigate this contrast by arguing that the apostle Paul is addressing "an alleged abuse of the Sinai covenant," Paul is actually addressing a problem that belongs inherently to the Sinai covenant. Since the Sinai covenant placed its recipients "covenantally under the law" and its curse-sanction, it could only condemn and curse, and not bless.

The third difference that Gordon discerns in Paul's argument in Galatians 3:6–14 is that the Abrahamic covenant is "characterized by faith, the Sinai covenant is characterized by works of the law" (246). In Paul's description of the Abrahamic and Sinai covenants, there is a repeated emphasis upon the sharp contrast between faith/belief in the promise and doing what the law requires. When God promised Abraham a seed, this promise was not contingent or based upon Abraham's obedience. However, when God required Israel's obedience to the law at Sinai, the blessings of the covenant were contingent or based upon Israel's doing what the law requires. Again, Gordon insists that this contrast is not between the Abrahamic covenant and an alleged "abuse" of the covenant on the part of the Israelites who sought to obtain the covenant's blessings through meritorious obedience. The contrast is between what "characterizes" or belongs to the nature of these two, radically distinct covenant administrations (247).

In Gordon's essay, the fourth and fifth contrasts that surface in Paul's argument in Galatians 3:6–14 are most important. Each of these contrasts serves to underscore the far-reaching and insuperable contrast between the two covenants, the promissory covenant with Abraham and the legal covenant with Israel at Sinai. The fourth contrast is between an Abrahamic covenant that justifies through faith alone in the promise and a Sinai covenant that is not able to justify since it requires perfect obedience to the law in order for Israel to receive blessing and not cursing (248). In the apostle Paul's argument, it is "incontrovertible" that no one is able to be justified before God by the law and that the only possible way of justification is through faith in Christ. This is the precise meaning of Paul's phrase, "the law is not of faith," in Galatians 3:12. The fifth contrast between these two covenants confirms the contrast between Abraham and

Moses, when the apostle Paul "by synecdoche" denominates the first by the term "promise" and the second by the term "law." Though these terms do not capture all the elements that belong to these two respective covenants, they do capture what is distinctive and antithetical about them. The dominating and characteristic feature of the Abrahamic covenant is that of promise. The dominating and characteristic feature of the Sinai covenant is that of law. According to Gordon's summary, "[t]his consistent use of the synecdoche 'promise' to refer to the Abrahamic administration, and the equally consistent use of the synecdoche 'law' to refer to the Sinai administration, demonstrate convincingly that Paul did not conceive these two covenants as similar in kind, but rather as dissimilar in kind; one is characteristically promissory; the other is characteristically legal" (250).

At the conclusion of his essay, Gordon, having offered his interpretation of the marked contrast between the Abrahamic covenant and the Mosaic covenant in Paul's argument in Galatians 3:6–14, raises the question why John Murray failed to recognize this contrast and adopted what Gordon terms a "monocovenantal" reading of the history of redemption. In Gordon's estimation, Murray's (and others') failure here was likely due to his focus upon the error of dispensationalism with its radical separation between the dispensations of law and grace and between Israel and the church. Furthermore, Murray, as a systematic theologian, was more intent upon a coherent and systematic formulation of the doctrine of the covenant and in the process failed to give priority to a careful exegesis of the argument of Paul in Galatians. The problem with Murray's attempt to treat these two covenants as essentially one in their promise and demand is that it does not comport with the "plain teaching" of Galatians 3. "What we must not do," Gordon argues, "is evade the plain teaching of Paul that the Sinai covenant itself, as it was delivered by the hand of Moses 430 years after the Abrahamic covenant, was a different covenant, different in kind, characteristically legal, Gentile-excluding, non-justifying because it was characterized by works, and therefore cursing its recipients and bearing children for slavery" (251). Indeed, so different in kind were these covenants that Gordon goes so far as to say that, were he among the children of Israel at Sinai, he would also have "resisted" this covenant as a "legal covenant" that could only "fail" due to the sin of the people of Israel.

The last essay that we consider in this section of *TLNF* deals particularly with the apostle Paul's argument in Galatians 5:1–6. In this essay, S. M. Baugh offers a more nuanced view of the republication thesis than that of Gordon, but nonetheless argues that the "works principle" of the covenant of works is a feature of the Mosaic administration to which Paul appeals in this passage against his opponents in Galatia.

At the outset of his chapter, Baugh appeals to Charles Hodge, who observed that the apostle Paul often speaks of the Mosaic law as though it were a kind of reiteration of the covenant of works, promising life on condition of perfect obedience. In Baugh's estimation, it is remarkable that many contemporary Reformed theologians no longer acknowledge this fact. Since the "precise character of a covenant of works resides in the imposition of an obligation to personal and perfect (or entire) obedience to its stipulated conditions," the key question is whether the Mosaic covenant includes such an obligation (259–60). To this question, Baugh answers by asserting that indeed the Mosaic covenant does disclose such an obligation or "works principle within its broader covenantal administration" (260). Even though the Mosaic covenant includes what Baugh terms a "typological priestly embodiment of mediation (the ceremonial Law)" and must therefore be regarded as essentially a covenant of grace, it also includes a works principle. What is peculiar to the Mosaic administration is that it republishes the covenant of works and its works principle, while at the same time revealing the gospel of salvation through Christ who fulfilled all the types and ceremonies of the law. When the Mosaic law is "narrowly considered," it reveals the works principle of the original prelapsarian covenant in a typological manner, representing Israel's blessedness and tenure in the land as based upon perfect obedience to the demands of the law (260). In order to confirm his thesis, Baugh treats Paul's argument in Galatians 5:1–6 and seeks to show how the apostle understood the Mosaic law to require personal and perfect obedience on the part of its recipients in order for them to obtain the Lord's blessing and favor.

Baugh begins his treatment of Galatians 5:1–6 by noting the importance of verse 1 in which the apostle Paul warns his readers to remain in the freedom that Christ won for them and not to submit "again to a yoke of slavery." In this verse, the apostle links his warning with his preceding argument against those who would seek to be justified before God by their obedience to the law. Anyone who seeks to be justified before God on the basis of obedience to the requirements of the law, particularly the requirement of circumcision, assumes a personal obligation that he will not be able to meet. For this reason, the apostle supports his warning in verses 3–4 by reminding his opponents of the implication of seeking to be justified by doing what the law requires.

In Baugh's opinion, the language of Galatians 5:1–6, especially the apostle's insistence that anyone who seeks to be justified by obedience to the law's requirement of circumcision will thereby obligate himself to the "whole law," confirms that Paul understood the law to enunciate a fundamental "works principle," namely, that the law requires personal and perfect obedience to all of its demands. Only those who are able to fulfill or to do everything that is demanded in the entire law of God will be able, upon the basis of such perfect obedience, to obtain favor and life in fellowship with God. By reminding his opponents of this principle, Paul assumes that no one is able to do or to "finish" off and "complete" all the requirements of the law. For this reason, no one is able to obtain blessing and life through the law (274–75). When Paul's opponents insist upon circumcision in obedience to the law as a basis for justification before God, they assume thereby an obligation to obey the entire law that they cannot meet. Furthermore, by seeking to be justified upon the basis of their obedience to the law, they not only undertake an exercise in futility but also "sever" or "cut themselves off" from Christ (v. 4). Either a person is justified by his own personal obedience to the whole law, which is an impossibility for human beings who cannot do all that the law requires, or a person is justified by faith in Jesus Christ alone. The antithesis or contrast in these verses is between two ways of obtaining the promise of salvation and life: by works of the law or by grace through faith.

Theological Implications

The third part of *TLNF* consists of two chapters that address some of the broader theological implications of the republication thesis. The first of these chapters, "Natural Law and the Works Principle under Adam and Moses" by David VanDrunen, addresses the manner in which the Mosaic law reiterates the moral obligations of the natural law that governed Adam's relationship to God in the prelapsarian state. The second, "Obedience Is Better than Sacrifice" by Michael Horton, provides an exposition of Psalm 40, arguing that Christ obtained the right to enter into God's presence and enjoy fellowship with him on the basis of his active and passive obedience. Horton argues that Christ thereby achieved what was promised to Adam and then to Israel, and in a manner that upheld the just requirements of the holy law of God. While Horton's essay makes its own contribution to the principal argument of the volume, we will only summarize VanDrunen's essay, which presents a more fulsome and provocative statement of the republication thesis.[12]

VanDrunen introduces his essay with a helpful statement of his basic argument and thesis. In his judgment, one of the important reasons for the lack of attention to the presence of a "works principle" in the Mosaic economy among contemporary Reformed theologians stems from the neglect of the natural law (283). Since these two ideas, the works principle in the Mosaic administration and the doctrine of natural law, are systematically related, neglect of the one will inevitably lead to a neglect of the other.

VanDrunen defines natural law as the "content of God's moral law" that is "made known to every human being through natural revelation" (284). The natural law is written or engraved upon the heart of human beings as God's image-bearers and is "perceived through the judgments of conscience." Negatively, the natural law

12. For a fuller treatment of the doctrine of the covenant by Michael Horton, and one that regards the Mosaic economy as in some sense a republication of the covenant of works, see Michael Horton, *God of Promise: Introducing Covenant Theology* (Grand Rapids, MI: Baker, 2006). Horton follows closely the formulations of Meredith Kline, and speaks of "structural" differences (47) between the Abrahamic covenant, which was unconditional in its promise, and the Mosaic covenant, which was conditional upon Israel's obedience to the law as the basis for its tenure in the land of Canaan (35–50).

reminds all people of their sin and just condemnation before God, including their need of a Savior. Positively, the natural law serves as a "standard for the development of civil law" (284). Rather than being a "philosophical ethical theory of Roman Catholicism," which diminishes the noetic effects of sin upon human awareness of the moral obligations of the divine law, the doctrine of natural law is a commonplace in historic Reformed theology. By the "works principle," VanDrunen means to refer to "the law's demand for perfect, personal obedience, with sanctions of blessing and curse to follow obedience and disobedience respectively to this demand" (284). In VanDrunen's opinion, the predominant view of the Reformed tradition is that the works principle was present, not only in the prelapsarian covenant of works between God and Adam but also in the postlapsarian Mosaic covenant. The republication of the works principle in the Mosaic covenant, however, was not to offer Israel "a way of attaining everlasting life (impossible for sinners) but for redemptive-historical, typological purposes such as reminding sinners of their fall and judgment under Adam, their inability to provide perfect obedience to God themselves, and their hope of a coming Messiah who would himself be born under this works principle and satisfy its requirements on behalf of his people" (284–85).

Recognizing that his thesis may seem "somewhat complex," VanDrunen argues for it in three successive stages. First, he presents a case for the correctness of the Reformed tradition's teaching that the natural law proclaims the works principle. Second, he shows that the Reformed tradition also properly viewed the law of Moses as a reiteration or "application" of the natural law to the unique circumstances of Israel in the history of redemption. And third, he maintains that the presence of the works principle, both in the covenant of works and in the Mosaic covenant, serves a divinely intended purpose, namely, to teach Israel to understand the "basic predicament of the *whole human race*" (285, emphasis original). By means of the republication of the works principle, the Lord taught his people that all human beings stand condemned by the law and are unable to extricate themselves from this predicament through their own moral efforts or works. Though the arguments for each of these points in VanDrunen's chapter are at times dense, we will present a summary of each of them in as simple and accurate a manner as possible.[13]

The first stage in VanDrunen's argument is pivotal to all that he maintains in the second and third stages. The fundamental claim VanDrunen makes is that the natural law contains inherently the works principle that is an essential feature of the Adamic covenant. The natural law not only discloses the moral will of God for all human beings who bear his image, but it also discloses the consequences of human failure to do what the law requires. In VanDrunen's judgment, "the law of nature not only imparts knowledge of and obligation to God's basic moral will but also makes known the *sanctions* that attach to this obligation: life and blessing for obedience and death and curse for disobedience" (286). In the history of Reformed reflection upon the natural law, it is commonly acknowledged that the natural law discloses God's moral will, and that this law is known by all human beings as image-bearers of God. However, VanDrunen observes that there is some "ambiguity" among Reformed theologians regarding the relation between the disclosure of the natural law and the prelapsarian covenant relationship (290).

On the one hand, some Reformed theologians affirm that God created human beings with a natural knowledge of the moral law and an awareness of the reward or punishment that follows upon obedience or disobedience to its requirements. But at the same time, these theologians are unwilling to *identify* the creation of human beings after God's image and under the moral obligations of the natural law with the prelapsarian covenant of works. For these theologians, the promise of "eschatological life," which was implicit in the prelapsarian covenant relationship, is something "added on to creation in the divine image" (290). Because the promise of eschatological life is presumably a covenanted promise that exceeds what human beings as creatures could justly obtain through their obedience to the natural law, these theologians distinguish between man's state as a moral

13. For a further statement and defense of his understanding of the republication thesis, see David VanDrunen, "Israel's Recapitulation of Adam's Probation under the Law of Moses," *WTJ* 73, 2 (2011): 303–24.

creature and image-bearer and his state as a covenant creature to whom God binds himself by covenantal promises and sanctions. On the other hand, some Reformed theologians expressed themselves in a way that implies an intrinsic connection between God's creation of man in his image and God's covenant with him through the law with its rewards and punishments.[14] For VanDrunen, the "ambiguity" of Reformed theologians at this point is helpfully resolved in the theology of a more recent biblical theologian, Meredith Kline, who maintains that the essence of the covenant of works is given with the creation of man in God's image and with an awareness of the works principle embedded in the moral law (291). When God discloses the natural law to his image-bearers, that disclosure is itself the covenant of works, since it includes the communication of the promise of life and the sanction of death.[15]

After offering a case for the connection between the doctrine of natural law and the works principle, which together constitute the elements of the original prelapsarian covenant of works, VanDrunen turns to the subject of the natural law and the Mosaic covenant. Though VanDrunen does not take up explicitly the thesis of republication in the second stage of his argument, the implications of this feature of his argument for the republication thesis are clear. If the Mosaic law represents a particular promulgation in the history of redemption of the original requirements of the moral law,

14. VanDrunen cites Francis Turretin and Herman Bavinck as examples of the former view, and Wilhelmus à Brakel as an example of the latter view. I will offer an evaluation of this reading of the sources in my treatment of some of the theological implications of the arguments of the authors of *TLNF*.

15. VanDrunen appeals to Meredith Kline's description of the covenant of works to support the thesis that the prelapsarian covenant of works was inherent in the creation of Adam in God's image, and that the so-called probationary command of Genesis 2:17 added nothing to what Adam already knew through natural revelation. See Meredith G. Kline, *Kingdom Prologue: Genesis Foundations for a Covenantal Worldview* (Overland Park, KS: Two Age Press, 2000), 92: "Man's creation as image of God meant, as we have seen, that the creating of the world was a covenant-making process. There was no original non-covenantal order of mere nature on which the covenant was superimposed. Covenantal commitments were given by the Creator in the very act of endowing the man-creature with the mantle of the divine likeness. And those commitments were eschatological." In my assessment of the theological arguments of *TLNF*, I will offer an evaluation of VanDrunen and Kline's rather novel view of the prelapsarian covenant.

then it must also include a republication of what belongs intrinsically to the nature of the law with its obligations and corresponding sanctions. The presence of the natural law in the Mosaic covenant, now in the form of a particular application of the moral obligations of God's will, requires the inference that the Mosaic covenant includes a republication of the covenant of works at some level. As VanDrunen puts it, "if the Reformed tradition is correct in seeing the Mosaic law as a particular application of the natural law for theocratic Israel, and if the natural law proclaims the works principle, then there is at least an initial presumption for recognizing the works principle as *one of* the constitutive aspects of the Mosaic covenant" (301, emphasis original). In his defense of this inference, VanDrunen appeals to historical and biblical evidences for the identification of the natural law and the moral law as it was communicated through the Mosaic administration to Israel. Once it is acknowledged that the law of Moses is rooted in and reiterates the fundamental requirements of the natural law, especially in its moral and civil aspects, it should be apparent that the works principle is also reiterated in the Mosaic law.

In the last stage of his argument, VanDrunen takes up the question of the purpose of the republication of the works principle in the Mosaic covenant through the moral law. In VanDrunen's assessment of this purpose, he suggests that in a "general" way this republication was given "for the historical purpose of serving as a pedagogue unto Christ (Gal. 3:24), who alone brings salvation" (309). The law served within God's purpose as a means of exposing Israel's sinful inability to procure life and favor with the Lord on the basis of obedience to the strict demands of God's law. Furthermore, the exposure of Israel's inability was itself a microcosm of the exposure through the law of the inability of all human beings without exception to obtain the blessing of God's covenant favor through works of the law. In comparison to the natural law, the revelation of the obligations of the moral law through Moses represents a "perfectly lucid" manifestation of human sinfulness that surpasses the more obscure knowledge able to be obtained through natural revelation (309). According to VanDrunen, the teaching of the apostle Paul in Galatians 4:3, 9 confirms this purpose of the Mosaic law's republication of the works principle of the Adamic covenant. In this passage, Paul "identifies slavery under the *stoicheia* ['elementary principles,' ESV] as something that life under the Mosaic law and life under paganism had in common" (311). VanDrunen, who favors the translation of *stoicheia* as "elementary principles" or "basic teachings," interprets Paul's language in this passage to confirm the essential unity of the natural and the Mosaic law in their revelation of a works principle that can only leave its recipients in a state of slavery or bondage. The contrast that Paul draws between freedom from the law through faith in Christ alone and slavery under the law is a radical contrast between two principles of inheritance, the one by grace and the other by works. In drawing this contrast, the apostle does not represent the works principle in the Mosaic law as a kind of "legalistic Jewish perversion of the law" but as an inherent feature of the Mosaic economy (311).

Though this completes our summary of the main stages of VanDrunen's argument, there is one question prompted by his argument at the close of the chapter that requires brief notice. VanDrunen poses the question this way: "If the natural law written on the heart proclaims the works principle, and if in Christ we are no longer under the works principle . . . then are New Testament Christians in fact not under the natural law, though it seems to be constitutive of the very image of God in which we are being re-created?" (313). The reason VanDrunen is compelled to raise this rather provocative question is patent. If the obligations of the moral law, whether in the prelapsarian or the postlapsarian circumstances, necessarily place their recipients under the promises and sanctions of the covenant of works with its works-inheritance principle, then how can believers in the covenant of grace be subject to the law's demands? Does not the freedom from the law that believers enjoy through Christ include a freedom from the moral law as well? VanDrunen does not shy away from this question, but answers it with the provocative claim that believers are not subject to the moral law *as believers, so far as their conduct in relation to fellow believers within the "spiritual" kingdom of Christ is concerned.* Though believers, so far as their conduct in the "natural" or "civil" kingdom is concerned, may be subject to the natural law, they are not subject to the natural law as Christians. Due to the provocative nature of this conclusion, we need to quote at length VanDrunen's own statement of it:

> First, in regard to the question whether New Testament Christians are under the natural law the answer is yes and no, and this answer depends upon the historic Reformed "two kingdoms" doctrine. Insofar as they are called to live in common with the world in the civil kingdom, Christians still exist under the authority of the natural law. . . . But insofar as they are called out of the world into the kingdom of Christ, Christians do not operate according to the natural law (though their basic moral obligations remain the same), for they are not under the works principle, either in regard to their justification before God or in regard to their conduct toward one another (313).[16]

If someone were to object to this position by citing Jeremiah 31:33, which speaks of God's promise to write the law upon the hearts of his people, VanDrunen claims that this does not refer to the natural law but to the law of freedom that belongs to the covenant of grace.

With this summary of VanDrunen's essay, I conclude my survey of the main arguments of *TLNF.* Though my survey does not fully present the detailed arguments of the various authors, it will suffice as a basis for the critical evaluation of their most important claims in the next chapter.

16. VanDrunen's separation between the two kingdoms, the civil kingdom and the spiritual kingdom (the church), is a subject that goes beyond the limits of my review of *TLNF.* His suggestion that the moral law as such governs only the conduct of believers within the civil kingdom is consistent with the strict separation that he wishes to maintain between these two kingdoms. For a further elaboration and defense of VanDrunen's two-kingdom construction, see David VanDrunen, *A Biblical Case for Natural Law* (Grand Rapids, MI: Acton Institute, 2006); and VanDrunen, *Natural Law and the Two Kingdoms: A Study in the Development of Reformed Social Thought* (Grand Rapids, MI: Eerdmans, 2010). For a critical assessment of the two kingdoms perspective, see Ryan C. McIlhenny, ed., *Kingdoms Apart: Engaging the Two Kingdoms Perspective* (Phillipsburg, NJ: P&R Publishing, 2012); and Cornelis P. Venema, "One Kingdom or Two? An Evaluation of the 'Two Kingdoms' Doctrine as an Alternative to Neo-Calvinism," *MAJT* 23 (2012): 77–129.

A Summary of the Principal Claims of *The Law Is Not of Faith*

One of the difficulties that a reviewer faces when considering a volume that consists of a series of essays by individual authors is the challenge of determining whether it sets forth any common themes or whether it only sets forth the individual viewpoints of the different contributors. The obvious challenge to a reviewer of a book like *TLNF* is to avoid ascribing specific views to all the authors, when they may only be the peculiar views of one or more contributors. I have already acknowledged that some of the essays in *TLNF* are not as relevant to the main arguments of the book as others. The principal thesis of the book is undoubtedly the claim that the Mosaic administration "in some sense" republished the prelapsarian covenant of works. However, the authors of this volume offer a variety of formulations of the republication thesis, and it would be unfair to ascribe the views of one author to all of the others. For this reason, I would like, in preparation for the critical evaluation that follows, to conclude this section of my review of *TLNF* with a summary of what I judge to be the principal claims of the authors, particularly in respect to the republication thesis. In doing so, I will also identify the contributors of the volume who most directly argue for these claims, acknowledging thereby that not all the contributors agree with every one of them.

Upon the basis of my summary of the arguments for republication in *TLNF*, the following claims, roughly in the order in which they are presented, seem to be of primary importance. In keeping with the divisions of the book, these claims can be classified into three categories: historical, biblical, and theological.

First, in the history of Reformed theology during the formative period of the sixteenth and seventeenth centuries, the idea that the Mosaic covenant in some sense republished the covenant of works was a commonplace, even the predominant view. Some form of the doctrine of republication was pervasive among the formative writers in the period of Reformed orthodoxy.

Second, though there were diverse formulations among Reformed theologians of the sense in which the Mosaic covenant republished the prelapsarian covenant of works, most of these formulations involved a "formal" or "hard" view of the republication of the covenant of works, not simply as a restatement of the requirements of the law of God but as a formal reinstitution of the covenant of works at some level.

Third, when the apostle Paul appeals to key OT texts that summarize essential features of the Mosaic covenant, especially Leviticus 18:5 and Deuteronomy 30:1–14, in passages like Romans 10:5–6 and Galatians 3, he interprets the Mosaic covenant as including the "works principle" that was an essential component of the prelapsarian covenant of works.

Fourth, when the apostle Paul treats the Mosaic covenant as an administration that republished the "works principle" of the covenant of works, he is not replying to a "legalistic" misuse of the Mosaic covenant or a feature of the Mosaic covenant that is being wrested (or abstracted) from its proper setting within the Mosaic covenant as an administration of the covenant of grace.

Fifth, the antithesis that the apostle Paul articulates in Galatians between the Abrahamic and Mosaic covenants is an antithesis between a covenant that is characteristically promissory and gracious and a covenant that is characteristically legal and condemning. In contrast to the unconditional and sovereignly gracious nature of the covenant of grace, the Mosaic covenant stipulates conditions that its recipients are unable to meet and that can only bring condemnation and death.

Sixth, the "works principle" that is an inherent feature of the Mosaic covenant functions typologically to teach Israel that its inheritance of and tenure as a corporate people in the Land of Promise was based upon her obedience to all the demands of the law.

Seventh, since the Mosaic administration included a republication of the natural law, which reveals a works principle that belongs to the essence of the original covenant of works, the Mosaic covenant necessarily republishes the covenant of works (VanDrunen).

And eighth, since believers in the new covenant are no longer under the law of Moses as a covenant of works, at least with respect to their conduct as members of Christ's spiritual kingdom, their conduct within the church is not governed by the law of Moses. Nor is the moral law as it was mediated through Moses the law that is written upon the hearts of believers in the new covenant (VanDrunen).

Postscript: Meredith Kline's View of the Mosaic Covenant

In the course of my summary of the arguments for the doctrine of republication, I have had occasion to refer to Meredith Kline's view of the Mosaic economy or covenant. Undoubtedly, Kline is one of the most influential advocates of the republication thesis among recent Reformed theologians.[17] Although many contemporary advocates of the republication view appeal to earlier writers in the period of Reformed orthodoxy to illustrate its presence throughout the history of Reformed theology,[18] the stimulus for the advocacy of this view among recent writers reflects the influence of the biblical-theological formulations of Kline. For this reason, before I turn directly to an assessment of the arguments that are integral to the case for the republication thesis, I wish to present a brief postscript on Kline's understanding of the unique role of the Mosaic economy in the course of redemptive history.

The starting point for Kline's formulation of the doctrine of the covenants is his emphasis upon a sharp distinction between the "inheritance principles" that govern the prelapsarian covenant of works and the postlapsarian covenant of grace. In Kline's understanding of the prelapsarian covenant of works, Adam's—and, in him, the human race's—inheritance of the fullness of life or eschatological glory was based upon a strict "works principle":

> A principle of works—do this and live—governed the attainment of the consummation-kingdom proffered in the blessing sanction of the creational covenant. Heaven must be earned. According to

17. The principal source for Kline's doctrine of republication is his *Kingdom Prologue*. For a recent book-length assessment of Kline's view, see Andrew M. Elam, Robert C. Van Kooten, and Randall A. Bergquist, *Merit and Moses: A Critique of the Klinean Doctrine of Republication* (Eugene, OR: Wipf & Stock, 2014).

18. Karlberg, *Covenant Theology*, 4, claims that this view was held by a "vast majority."

> the terms stipulated by the Creator it would be on the ground of man's faithful completion of the work of probation that he would be entitled to enter the Sabbath rest. If Adam obediently performed the assignment signified by the probation tree, he would receive, *as a matter of pure and simple justice*, the reward symbolized by the tree of life. That is, successful probation would be meritorious. With good reason then covenant theology has identified this probation arrangement as a covenant of works, thereby setting it in sharp contrast to the Covenant of Grace.[19]

As this statement of the works principle inheritance intimates, Kline insists upon the strictly "meritorious" nature of the works required of Adam in the covenant of works. To argue that there were elements of "grace" in the sense of unmerited favor undergirding the promise and administration of the prelapsarian covenant is theologically confused. In Kline's view, as soon as grace is introduced into the prelapsarian relationship between God as Creator and human beings as creatures, it is no longer possible to maintain the essential discontinuity and antithesis between the law and gospel. The legal obligations of the covenant of works enunciate a principle of inheritance that is rooted in God's essential justice: when the creature perfectly performs what the law demands, the inheritance of life is obtained in accordance with God's strict justice. In contrast to this principle of inheritance, the gospel enunciates an essentially different principle: the offending sinner who has demerited God's favor receives life as a free, unmerited grant or bestowal. Whereas the law requires perfect obedience in order for human beings to inherit the promise of life, the gospel promises life as a free gift. There is a stark contrast, accordingly, between the works-merit principle of the covenant of works and the grace-promise-faith principle of the covenant of grace.

According to Kline, any failure to recognize that the works principle promises life upon the basis of meritorious works will

19. Kline, *Kingdom Prologue*, 107 (emphasis added). The language of a "works principle" is characteristically Klinean, but is not found among writers of the orthodox period in Reformed theology so far as I have been able to determine.

have deadly consequences for a proper understanding of the work of Christ, the second Adam: "Indeed, the principle of works forms the foundation of the gospel of grace. If meritorious works could not be predicated of Jesus Christ as second Adam, then obviously there would be no meritorious achievement to be imputed to his people as the ground of their justification-approbation."[20] When Christ met all the obligations of the law, whether by means of his active conformity to the law's precepts (active obedience) or his passive endurance of the law's penalty (passive obedience), he genuinely merited the fullness of life for his people. The work of the second Adam, the Mediator of the covenant of grace, secured the inheritance of life for believers in a way that upholds God's strict justice by fully honoring the requirements of his holy law. Though the gift of life is a gift of sheer grace for believers, it was obtained by the meritorious work of Christ on their behalf. "In his probationary obedience the Redeemer gained the merit which is transferred to the account of the elect. Underlying Christ's mediatorship of a covenant of grace for the salvation of believers is his earthly fulfillment, through meritorious obedience, of his heavenly covenant of works with the Father."[21] Therefore, the covenant of grace and its freely bestowed benefit of eternal life are grounded upon Christ's obedience under the law. Through the obedience of Christ, which fulfilled all the legal requirements of the covenant of works, believers are granted the free gift of eternal life.

Kline also maintains that a failure to recognize the role of meritorious works within the covenant of works has similar negative consequences for a proper interpretation of the Mosaic economy in the covenant of grace. In the administration of the Mosaic covenant, it is evident that the inheritance principle of meritorious works plays a role at a certain level of the covenant's administration. Though Kline affirms the common Reformed view that the Mosaic economy was an administration of the covenant of grace, he believes it also illustrates the ongoing significance of the works principle of inheritance in the history of redemption. Although the Mosaic economy was "an

20. Ibid., 108.
21. Ibid., 109.

administration of grace on its fundamental level of concern with the eternal salvation of the individual," it was

> at the same time *on its temporary, typological kingdom level informed by the principle of works.* Thus, for example, the apostle Paul in Romans 10:14ff. and Galatians 3:10ff. (cf. Rom. 9:32) contrasts the old order of the law with the gospel order of grace and faith, identifying the old covenant as one of bondage, condemnation, and death (cf. 2 Cor. 3:6–9; Gal. 4:24–26). The old covenant was law, the opposite of grace-faith, and in the postlapsarian world that meant it would turn out to be an administration of condemnation as a consequence of sinful Israel's failure to maintain *the necessary meritorious obedience.* Had the old typological kingdom been secured by sovereign grace in Christ, Israel would not have lost her national election. A satisfactory explanation of Israel's fall demands works, not grace, as the controlling administrative principle.[22]

In this compact statement, Kline claims that the Mosaic economy functioned at one level—the typological—as an administration of the covenant of works. Like the first Adam, national Israel was placed under the administration of a works principle in respect to her inheritance of and tenure in the Land of Promise. Just as Adam was expelled from Eden for his failure to secure the promise of eternal life upon condition of meritorious obedience, so Israel was expelled from the land of Canaan for her failure to retain the Promised Land upon condition of obedience to the law of Moses. According to Kline, at the "typological" level of Israel's earthly inheritance of the land of Canaan, the Mosaic covenant republished and readministered the works principle of the covenant of works. The principle set forth in Leviticus 18:5, "do this [obey the requirements of the law of Moses] and you will live," confirms that the works-inheritance principle of the covenant of works functioned at the typological level of Israel's tenure in the land.

22. Ibid. (emphasis added).

In his characterization of the uniqueness of the Mosaic covenant, Kline maintains that it included two distinct levels of administration. At the typological level, the Mosaic covenant taught that Israel's tenure in the land was upon the "ground" of her covenant obedience to the law of Moses. However, at the fundamental level of the salvation of the elect, the Mosaic covenant taught that this was entirely based upon God's gracious and unmerited promise to Abraham.

> What we have found then is that once the typological kingdom was inaugurated under the Mosaic Covenant, Israel's retention of it was governed by a principle of works applied on a national scale. The standard of judgment in this national probation was one of typological legibility, that is, the message must remain reasonably readable that enjoyment of the felicity of God's holy kingdom goes hand in hand with righteousness. Without holiness we do not see God. But if the ground of Israel's tenure in Canaan was their covenant obedience, their election to receive the typological kingdom in the first place was emphatically not based on any merit of theirs (cf. Deut. 9:5, 6). Their original reception of this kingdom as well as their restoration to it after the loss of their national election in Babylonian exile, is repeatedly attributed to God's remembrance of his promissory commitments of grace to Abraham, Isaac, and Jacob (Exod. 2:24; 3:6ff.; 32:13; Deut. 9:27; 10:15; Lev. 26:42), pointing to the coming Messiah and the new covenant.[23]

While this summary of Kline's view of the Mosaic economy could be elaborated further, for our purposes the main lines of his doctrine of republication should be evident. According to Kline, the Mosaic economy is not an administration of the covenant of grace *simpliciter*. Rather, it contains elements of the covenant of works at the typological level of its administration, even though it remains fundamentally an administration of the covenant of grace. The law

23. Ibid., 323.

of Moses requires obedience upon the part of national Israel as a condition for Israel's inheritance of and continuation in the land of Canaan. In this sense, Israel is a kind of second Adam, whose land inheritance typifies the obligations of perfect obedience under the covenant of works that only Christ, the "last" and true Adam, fulfilled as the meritorious basis for the inheritance of eternal life on the part of believers. Israel's inability to secure her inheritance of the land by way of obedience to the law of Moses serves, within the framework of the administration of the covenant of grace throughout the history of redemption, to underscore the importance of Christ's active and passive obedience as the ground for the inheritance of life that believers receive through faith alone, apart from works. In Kline's biblical-theological appraisal of the uniqueness of the Mosaic economy, the history of Israel's inability to secure life through obedience to the requirements of the law confirms that the inheritance of life within the covenant of grace can only be obtained through the obedience of Jesus Christ, the Mediator of the new covenant.

3

The Covenant of Works and the Mosaic Economy (2):

Assessing the Case for "Republication"

In the previous chapter, I identified the most important arguments for the claim that the Mosaic economy included a republication in some sense of the covenant of works. The aim of this chapter will be to offer a critical assessment of the republication thesis. Just as my survey was necessarily selective, so my assessment will address some, but by no means all, of the arguments for the doctrine of republication. Since the various contributors to *TLNF* offer divergent views of the republication thesis, I will attempt as much as possible to identify the contributions to which my assessment is especially directed. Though it is a rather general criticism, it could be argued that the most problematic feature of the republication thesis is the vagueness of its principal claim. The repeated use of the phrase "in some sense" to modify the republication thesis begs the obvious question, "in what sense"? How precisely does the Mosaic administration republish the covenant of works? Some of the contributors to *TLNF* attempt to provide an answer to this question; others simply assume that the reader will understand the meaning of this language. Due to the ambiguity of the republication thesis, the challenge facing the critic of *TLNF* is similar to that facing someone who attempts to hit a moving target.

In keeping with the basic outline of *TLNF*, my evaluation will be organized in terms of the three parts of the volume. I will begin with a consideration of the broad historical argument that the doctrine of a republication of the covenant of works in the Mosaic administration was a commonplace among Reformed theologians in the formative period of the late sixteenth and seventeenth centuries. After a consideration of this historical claim, I will take up some of the biblical arguments of the second part of the volume. In the last section, I will identify and address briefly some of the theological dimensions and implications of the republication thesis.

An "Accommodated" Reading of the Sources

One of the difficulties confronting anyone who endeavors to interpret the history of the doctrine of the covenant in Reformed theology is the absence of any comprehensive account of this history. Though there are a number of secondary studies on particular Reformed theologians, the interpreter is confronted with a number of difficult choices in determining which doctrinal formulations belong to the consensus of Reformed covenant theology and which of them belong uniquely to a particular theologian. Historians of the orthodox period of Reformed theology are increasingly aware of the wide diversity of formulation that existed among the theologians of this period. The temptations that confront anyone who attempts to interpret the development of the doctrine of the covenant in this period include, among others, a selective reading of the sources or an anachronistic reading, which imposes categories of subsequent theologians upon those of an earlier period. The work of Richard Muller on the development of Reformed theology in the late sixteenth and seventeenth centuries, for example, illustrates the problem in terms of the debates regarding "Calvin and the Calvinists." Muller has persuasively argued that the interpretation of Calvin's theology was "accommodated" to a variety of twentieth-century theological concerns, particularly those of neoorthodoxy, and that in the process Calvin's theology was often not interpreted in its historical context.[1]

The question raised by the historical arguments of the contributors to *TLNF* can be put in similar terms: have the authors of

1. See Richard A. Muller, *The Unaccommodated Calvin: Studies in the Foundation of a Theological Tradition* (New York: Oxford University Press, 2000), esp. 3–18.

this volume "accommodated" their reading of the sources to demonstrate the claim that the republication thesis was a commonplace of Reformed theologians in this formative period? As I noted in my survey of *TLNF*, various authors throughout the book claim that the idea of republication was a commonplace of early Reformed theology, despite its absence in the formulations of many more recent Reformed theologians.

In order to test this historical claim, I propose to examine the positions of three Reformed theologians: John Calvin, Francis Turretin, and Herman Witsius. These theologians are arguably among the most important architects of traditional Reformed covenant theology.[2] Furthermore, both Turretin and Witsius are later figures who intentionally sought to articulate the "consensus" of Reformed theologians on disputed points. Rather than representing figures whose views were idiosyncratic or outside the mainstream of Reformed covenant theology, these figures articulated views that became fairly standard among Reformed theologians.[3] In addition to these important Reformed theologians, I will also evaluate the claims of the authors of *TLNF* by the standard of the WCF, which undeniably sets forth a codification in confessional form of the most basic, and common, features of traditional Reformed covenant theology.

2. For a treatment of a number of additional writers in the period of Reformed orthodoxy whose writings are relevant to the subject of republication, see Robert Letham, "'Not a Covenant of Works in Disguise' (Herman Bavinck): The Place of the Mosaic Covenant in Redemptive History," *MAJT* 24 (2013): 152–69. Letham's conclusion is similar to mine: though there were a few theologians who taught some version of a republication doctrine, they were in the "minority" and no version of this doctrine was adopted by any Reformed confession.

3. For a recent treatment of a Reformed theologian whose views on the Mosaic economy were outside of the mainstream, see Michael Brown, *Christ and the Condition: The Covenant Theology of Samuel Petto (1624–1711)* (Grand Rapids, MI: Reformation Heritage, 2012). Though Brown attempts to link Petto's view with more recent views that speak of a republication of the covenant of works in the Mosaic economy, Petto's view clearly does not serve this purpose well. For a critical review of Brown's study, see Ryan M. McGraw, "Review of Michael Brown, *Christ and the Condition*," *MAJT* 23 (2012): 152–55. Though my treatment of three leading theologians on the subject of the Mosaic economy is very selective, my principle of selection is simply the degree to which they represent mainstream and influential viewpoints that are largely codified in the Westminster Standards.

John Calvin

The danger of anachronism and overinterpretation is particularly pressing when it comes to an evaluation of Calvin's understanding of the distinctive nature of the Mosaic covenant within the history of redemption. It is commonly acknowledged that the doctrine of a prelapsarian covenant of works is not explicitly present in Calvin's theology, and even the claim that Calvin anticipated many components of the later bi-covenantalism of Reformed theology remains open to dispute.[4] To suggest that Calvin viewed the Mosaic administration as a republication of the covenant of works, therefore, is already liable to the obvious charge of an anachronistic reading of his formulations. However, Calvin does explicitly address the question of the special character of the Mosaic administration within the broader framework of the administration of the covenant of grace. In the course of addressing the peculiar nature of the Mosaic administration, Calvin makes statements about the law of Moses that prompt particularly Fesko and Ferry among the authors of *TLNF* to conclude that he conceived the Mosaic administration to be in some sense a covenant of works. In Fesko's interpretation, Calvin conceives of the Mosaic administration as both a covenant of grace and a covenant of works (31). And in Ferry's estimation, Calvin interprets the Mosaic administration as a "formal republication" of the covenant of works (95).

In order to evaluate Calvin's view of the distinctive nature of the Mosaic administration, we need to note two indisputable and fundamental features of his position, both of which are correctly acknowledged by Fesko in his contribution to *TLNF* (28–29). First,

4. For a defense of the thesis that Calvin anticipated many of the elements of the later Reformed doctrine of the covenant of works, see Peter A. Lillback, *The Binding of God: Calvin's Role in the Development of Covenant Theology* (Grand Rapids, MI: Baker Academic, 2001), 276–304; Andrew Woolsey, *Unity and Continuity in Covenantal Thought: A Study in the Reformed Tradition to the Westminster Assembly* (Grand Rapids, MI: Reformation Heritage, 2012) 253–343, esp. 336–43; and Cornelis P. Venema, "Calvin's Doctrine of the Imputation of Christ's Righteousness: Another Example of 'Calvin Against the Calvinists'?," *MAJT* 20 (2009): 37–44. For a recent case against this thesis, see Aaron Denlinger, "Calvin's Understanding of Adam's Relationship to His Posterity: Recent Assertions of the Reformer's 'Federalism' Evaluated," *CTJ* 44, 2 (2009): 226–50.

when Calvin uses the term "law," he does so in at least three distinct ways: (1) to refer comprehensively to the "whole religion of Moses" or to the Mosaic administration of the covenant of grace in its entirety;[5] (2) to refer to the moral law of God, which was set forth in the two tables of the Decalogue and in Jesus' summary of the law;[6] and (3) to refer to the specific statutes and requirements of the law, which can be distinguished into three parts, the civil, judicial, and ceremonial.[7] An assessment of the claim that Calvin viewed the Mosaic administration as a republication of the covenant of works must carefully attend to these distinct uses of the term "law." Failure to accurately identify Calvin's use of the terminology of "law" in his descriptions of the Mosaic administration will inevitably lead to a misinterpretation of his position.

The second feature of Calvin's view is his well-known insistence that the covenant of grace is *one in substance, though distinct in mode of administration*. At the outset of his consideration of the "similarity of the Old and New Testaments" in his *Institutes*, Calvin strongly asserts the unity of the covenant of grace throughout the entire course of the history of redemption: "Now we can clearly see from what has already been said that all men adopted by God into the company of his people since the beginning of the world were covenanted to him by the same law and by the bond of the same doctrine as obtains among us."[8] Shortly after this statement of the unity of the covenant, Calvin acknowledges the diversity of its forms of administration: "The covenant made with all the patriarchs is so much like ours in substance and reality that the two are actually one and the same. Yet they differ in the mode of dispensation."[9]

In the subsequent history of Reformed covenant theology, Calvin's insistence upon the unity of the covenant of grace through all

5. *Institutes*, 2.7.1 (*OS* 3.326).

6. Ibid., 2.8 (*OS* 3.343–98).

7. Ibid., 4.20.14–16 (*OS* 5.486–89). The distinction of the law into three types of statutes is traditional, and can be found in Thomas Aquinas's treatment of the law of God in his *Summa Theologiae*, rev. ed., 5 vols. (1920; repr., Allen TX: Christian Classics, 1981), 2.99.2–5.

8. *Institutes*, 2.10.1 (*OS* 3.403).

9. Ibid., 2.10.2 (*OS* 3:404).

its various administrations becomes a commonplace. Upon the basis of this far-reaching formulation, Calvin consistently maintains that all of the essential components that make the covenant of grace what it is belong to each of its administrations. Consequently, whatever may distinguish the Mosaic administration as a distinct administration of the covenant of grace belongs to the category of what Calvin terms "accidental" forms that are incidental to the covenant's nature. When Calvin and subsequent Reformed theologians employ the language of "substance" and "form" or "accidents" to refer to the distinct administrations of the one covenant of grace throughout history, they are employing a traditional category distinction from the philosophy of Aristotle. "Substance" refers to what makes something what it *is*, "accidents" refers to what belongs contingently to something. In the distinct administrations of the covenant of grace, including the Mosaic administration, there are elements that necessarily belong to each of these administrations as an administration of the covenant of grace. However, there are other features that belong only to a distinct administration of the covenant of grace at a particular moment in time.

Consistent with these features of his doctrine of the covenant of grace, Calvin first summarizes those features of the Old and New Testaments that belong to the substance of the covenant of grace in all of its administrations. According to Calvin, there were three features of the OT that belong to and are of one substance with the NT. First, the OT promise, however much it was framed in terms of earthly blessings and circumstances, was the same promise of "hope of immortality" in the fullness of God's spiritual kingdom as in the New. Second, "the covenant by which they [OT Israel] were bound to the Lord was supported, not by their own merits, but solely by the mercy of God who called them." And third, "they had and knew Christ as Mediator, through whom they were joined to God and were to share in his promises."[10] In all of these fundamental respects, the OT was substantially in harmony with the New. Believers in the OT trusted only in the Christ who was to come as the Mediator of

10. Ibid.

their salvation and blessing, just as believers in the NT trust in the Christ who has come for every blessing. If this were not so, it would be impossible to speak of Abraham as the father of all believers, and of his being justified by faith apart from works.

After devoting a chapter to a discussion of the essential features that belong to the covenant of grace and make it what it is in all of its administrations, Calvin turns to a series of differences between the covenants. These differences do not touch the substance of the covenant, but have to do with incidental features that distinguish its various forms or administrations. Five such features are distinguished: (1) in the OT, the spiritual blessings of the covenant were represented under temporal or earthly blessings, which reflected the infancy or immaturity of the OT church in comparison to the New; (2) the OT covenants set forth the substance and truth that belong to Christ in the form of "shadows" and "types" that prefigure the reality to come; (3) the OT's teaching is "literal," whereas the NT's teaching is "spiritual"; (4) the OT held the people of Israel in a kind of "bondage," but the NT grants freedom and assurance; and (5) in the OT the Lord focused upon setting apart one nation, but in the NT the gospel and its blessings are extended to all the nations of the earth.[11]

Regarding three of these differences (2, 3, 4), Calvin observes that they highlight the contrast between the "law," which he uses inclusively to include both the promises of the covenant and the publication of the law through Moses, and the "gospel," which he uses specifically to refer to the provision of salvation in Christ for all of the covenant people of the Lord.[12] None of these differences, however, touches the substance of the covenant or doctrine of salvation. In every administration of the covenant of grace, believers are saved through faith in Christ alone who is the one Mediator and Savior of his people. "Thus, God's constancy shines forth in the fact that he taught the same doctrine to all ages, and has continued to require the same worship of his name that he enjoined from the beginning. In the fact that he has changed the outward form and manner, he does

11. Ibid., 2.11 (*OS* 3.423–36).
12. Ibid., 2.11.10 (*OS* 3.432–33).

not show himself subject to change. Rather, he has accommodated himself to men's capacity, which is varied and changeable."[13]

To this point, there is nothing in Calvin's view of the covenant of grace that would suggest something like the idea of a republication of the covenant of works under the Mosaic administration. However, Fesko appeals to Calvin's language in describing the Mosaic covenant to support the idea that "with the dispensation of the Mosaic covenant there are two separate covenants, the *foedus legale* and *foedus evangelicum*, the ministries of Moses and Christ (2.11.4)" (30). Fesko further argues that these two covenants set forth antithetical principles, the "legal covenant" promising life through obedience, the "evangelical covenant" promising life through faith in Christ. In its administration, the Mosaic covenant was a legal covenant, but in its "substance" the Mosaic covenant was an evangelical covenant. While he acknowledges that Calvin denied the possibility of Israel obtaining life through obedience, he nonetheless concludes that Calvin viewed the Mosaic covenant as enunciating a "works principle" of inheritance that taught Israel to look to Christ alone for salvation (33).

There are two significant problems at this point with Fesko's interpretation of Calvin's view of the Mosaic administration. In the first place, Fesko misreads Calvin's language regarding a "legal" and an "evangelical" covenant. When Calvin uses this language, he is not referring to two covenants, which allegedly set forth different principles for obtaining life, but he is referring to two distinct administrations of the one (in substance) covenant of grace. In the section of the *Institutes* to which Fesko appeals for his conclusion that the Mosaic administration included two distinct covenants, Calvin clearly teaches that the "legal" and "evangelical" covenants are two administrations of one covenant, distinct only in their "accidents" but identical in their substance.

> Let us then set forth the covenant that he once established as eternal and never-perishing. Its fulfillment, by which it is finally

13. Ibid., 2.11.13 (*OS* 3.435–36).

> confirmed and ratified, is Christ. While such confirmation was awaited, the Lord appointed, through Moses, ceremonies that were, so to speak, solemn symbols of that confirmation. A controversy arose over whether or not the ceremonies that had been ordained in the law ought to give way to Christ. Now these were only the accidental properties of the covenant, or additions and appendages, and in common parlance, accessories of it. Yet because they were means of administering it, they bear the name "covenant," just as is customary in the case of other sacraments. To sum up, then, in this passage "Old Testament" means the solemn manner of confirming the covenant, comprised in ceremonies and sacrifices.[14]

In this passage, which follows shortly after Calvin's use of the language of a "legal" and an "evangelical" covenant, Calvin clearly affirms that the "legal" or Mosaic covenant was an administration of the covenant of grace. He does not mean to designate two covenants by this language, but, as is customary in his writings, he uses the terminology of "law" or a "legal covenant" in the comprehensive sense to refer to the Mosaic administration (or "the whole religion of Moses") of the one covenant of grace. When Fesko adduces this language to confirm that Calvin viewed the Mosaic covenant as "in some respect" a different covenant with a different principle of obtaining life and favor with God, he fails to attend with sufficient care to Calvin's explanation of this language in the immediate context.

In the second place, Fesko also misreads the contrast that Calvin subsequently draws in the *Institutes* between the "law" and "gospel." Fesko interprets Calvin's contrast to teach a real contrast between the Mosaic administration of the covenant of grace (at least at some level) and the gospel of Jesus Christ. According to Fesko, the contrast is that between the Mosaic covenant, which communicates a "works principle" for obtaining life, and the gospel, which communicates a promise of life by grace through faith in Christ alone. However, the passage that Fesko adduces for his understanding of this contrast

14. Ibid., 2.11.4 (*OS* 3.427).

shows that Calvin identifies the contrast as that between *a "legalistic" misappropriation of the law of Moses, abstracted from its setting within the broader administration of the Mosaic covenant and used as a means of justification before God, and the gospel.*

In the passage to which Fesko appeals, Calvin is explaining the contrast in Hebrews between the law and the gospel, and the reason the author appeals to the promise of Jeremiah 31:31–34. In his explanation, Calvin maintains that the contrast is between the law in the narrowest sense, namely, in terms of what it demands, promises, and threatens, and the gospel. However, this contrast is not between the Mosaic administration of the covenant of grace and the gospel, since the Mosaic administration also reveals God's promises of mercy and gracious correction of human depravity.

> For the apostle [author of Hebrews] speaks more opprobriously of the law than the prophet does—not simply in respect to the law itself, but, because of certain wretches who aped the law and, by their perverse zeal for ceremonies, obscured the clarity of the gospel. Their error and stupid predilection prompt Paul to discuss the nature of the law. It behooves us therefore to note that particular point in Paul. But both Jeremiah and Paul, because they are contrasting the Old and New Testaments, consider nothing in the law except what properly belongs to it. For example: the law contains here and there promises of mercy, but because they have been borrowed from elsewhere, they are not counted part of the law, when only the nature of the law is under discussion. They ascribe to it only this function: to enjoin what is right, to forbid what is wicked; to promise a reward to the keepers of righteousness, and threaten transgressors with punishment; but at the same time not to change or correct the depravity of heart that by nature inheres in all men.[15]

15. Ibid., 2.11.7 (*OS* 3.429–30). For a more complete summary of Calvin's distinction between Moses' general and peculiar offices, or between the whole religion of Moses and the "bare law" (*nuda lex*) wrested from its setting within the covenant of grace, see *ARC*, 232–36.

For Calvin, the law as such was never intended to play an independent role within the broader administration of the Mosaic covenant, which was an evangelical covenant that communicated the gospel of God's gracious promise of salvation through Christ. The contrast between the "law" and the "gospel," therefore, is not between the Mosaic administration and the gospel. In Calvin's view, when the apostle Paul and other NT writers oppose the "law" and the "gospel," they are speaking of the law in the narrowest sense, wrested from its evangelical setting and misappropriated by those who falsely boast of their justification before God through obedience to the law's demands. Though the law is holy and good, it can only demand perfect obedience and remind its recipients of the consequences of any failure to do what it requires. When the law is viewed in isolation from its evangelical setting, it can only condemn fallen sinners who are incapable of doing what it requires. Contrary to Fesko's reading of Calvin, there is no basis for interpreting Calvin to teach that the Mosaic administration included at some level a kind of "legal" covenant that republished the prelapsarian covenant of works.

Francis Turretin

The second Reformed theologian we consider is Francis Turretin (1623–87), a leading Reformed theologian of the orthodox period. Unlike Calvin, who was one of the principal architects of the earliest formulation of Reformed theology, Turretin deliberately sought to present the consensus of Reformed theology at the height of the period of Reformed orthodoxy. Turretin's principal theological work, *Institutes of Elenctic Theology*, was written, as its title intimates, in order to defend the consensus of Reformed theology against its theological opponents, whether within the Reformed community or within orthodox Lutheranism and Roman Catholicism.[16] For our purpose, which is to identify the way Reformed theologians viewed the Mosaic administration within the history of the covenant of grace, Turretin's handling of the question is of special value. Not only does Turretin offer his own conception of the unique place of the

16. *IET*. For a comprehensive treatment of Turretin's doctrine of the covenant, see *CCT*.

Mosaic administration within the broader history of the covenant of grace, but he also identifies the diversity of viewpoints among leading Reformed theologians of the period. Consequently, Turretin's exposition of the Mosaic covenant offers an especially significant piece of historical evidence for what may be described as a consensual or commonplace view among Reformed theologians on this feature of traditional Reformed theology.

Consistent with the scholastic form and method of his elenctic theology, Turretin offers a carefully nuanced and highly complex presentation of the doctrine of the covenant. In keeping with our limited purpose in this review, I will not attempt to trace out the complexities of Turretin's discussion, but focus upon the specific question of republication that is the concern of the authors of *TLNF*. However, before treating Turretin's handling of this specific question, I will begin with a brief summary of the main tenets of Turretin's doctrine of the covenant.

Unlike Calvin, who does not expressly distinguish between a prelapsarian covenant of works and a postlapsarian covenant of grace, Turretin maintains that life and fellowship with the triune God, whether as Creator or as Redeemer, is always communicated by way of covenant. In the prefall state, God covenanted with the human race, promising life upon condition of Adam's perfect and personal obedience and threatening death upon Adam's disobedience.[17] In the prefall covenant, which Turretin denominates a "covenant of nature," God gratuitously conferred upon Adam the right to eternal happiness upon condition of perfect obedience. Due to the infinite difference between God as Creator and man as creature, and due to the disproportion between the creature's obedience and the eternal life promised, Turretin clearly rejects the idea that Adam or the creature could "properly merit" life through obedience, though he acknowledges that, speaking improperly, we may affirm a kind of "covenanted merit" (*meritum ex pacto*) that derives "from the pact and liberal promise of God."[18] By virtue of Adam's disobedience and

17. *IET*, 1:574–75.
18. Ibid., 1:578.

fall, it is no longer possible for human beings to enjoy happiness in fellowship with God by means of this covenant of works. In distinction from the prelapsarian covenant of nature, Turretin affirms that God as Redeemer instituted the covenant of grace as the means to restore the elect in Christ to fellowship with himself and to obtain the blessing of eternal life. Turretin summarizes his commitment to the standard Reformed doctrine of bi-covenantalism in the following manner:

> [God] entered into a twofold covenant with men: first, a legal covenant (or one of works) with innocent man; another of faith and evangelical with fallen and sinful man. By the former, God promised eternal life to the man perfectly fulfilling the law and threatened the sinner with death according to the clauses, "do this and live" and "cursed is he who continueth not." By the latter, he promises to the believer safety in Christ and on account of Christ. The former was made with Adam before the fall and in him with all men. . . . The latter was entered into with the elect in Christ after the fall.[19]

In his extended treatment of the covenant of grace, Turretin addresses a series of questions such as the identity of the parties of the covenant, the promises and stipulations of the covenant, and the senses in which the covenant of grace is "conditional" or "unconditional." For our purpose, the most important questions that he addresses have to do with the unity of the covenant of grace in its diverse administrations throughout the history of redemption and the peculiar features of the Mosaic administration. In the course of his consideration of these questions, Turretin addresses explicitly the debates among Reformed theologians regarding whether the Mosaic administration was an administration of the covenant of grace, whether it was also an administration in some manner of the covenant of works, or whether it was a distinct covenant altogether, neither a covenant of works nor a covenant of grace. In his discussion of

19. Ibid., 2:174.

these topics, Turretin offers answers that are directly relevant to the republication thesis of the authors of *TLNF*.

On the topic of the unity of the covenant of grace, Turretin distinguishes the Reformed view from that of the Socinians, the Remonstrants (Arminians), and the Anabaptists. Contrary to these alternative views of the relation between the Old and New Testaments, the Reformed teach that the covenant of grace is "the same as to its substance and essential parts" in all of its diverse administrations. Whereas the substance of the covenant remains the same throughout redemptive history, the diverse administrations of the covenant differ only in respect to their "accidentals and the different modes and degrees of dispensation and manifestation."[20] In every administration of the covenant of grace, we find the same Mediator (Christ), the same obligation of faith in Christ, the same promise of spiritual blessings, and the same way of reconciliation and salvation. So far as the "intention" of God is concerned, therefore, the Mosaic administration, as an administration of the covenant of grace, rightly belongs to the covenant of grace and differs from the new covenant only in terms of its accidental features.

Within the framework of these fundamental themes of Reformed covenant theology, Turretin takes up specifically the subject of what is unique to the Mosaic administration of the covenant of grace. In doing so, he acknowledges that there is a lack of consensus, even among Reformed theologians, on this question.[21] Indeed, he admits that

> [t]he opinions of theologians vary on this subject. Some maintain that the Sinaitic covenant was a covenant of works; others that

20. Ibid., 2:194.

21. It is significant that, in his consideration of the Decalogue, Turretin observes a difference between the Reformed view and that of traditional Lutheranism. As he puts it, "[i]n assigning the difference between the Old and New Testaments the Lutherans differ also from our men and a question was agitated by them on this subject growing out of the sacramental controversy. They maintain that these two covenants are not only to be distinguished in substance, but also that the promise of grace is to be excluded from the old covenant" (*IET*, 2:234). For a summary of Turretin's assessment of the Lutheran view of the old covenant, see *CCT*, 265–69. It is interesting to observe that some of the representations

> it was a mixture of the covenant of works and the covenant of grace; others that it was properly neither a covenant of nature nor of grace, but a third covenant distinct from both in its whole species and was instituted to minister to the covenant of grace (and for this reason properly called "subservient"). Finally others (with whom we agree) say that it was a covenant of grace, but promulgated with the law and lying under it (which was sanctioned in the unusual manner of terror and servitude, in accordance with the state of the Israelite people and the age of the church at the time).[22]

As this statement of the differing views of the relation of the Mosaic administration to the covenants of work and of grace indicates, by the time of the writing of Turretin's *Institutes* considerable difference of opinion had emerged among Reformed theologians on the subject. Turretin's summary of these differences identifies at least four distinct opinions: (1) some viewed the Mosaic administration as a covenant of works; (2) some taught that the Mosaic administration was an admixture of the covenant of works and the covenant of grace; (3) a third opinion taught that the Mosaic administration was a distinct, subservient covenant, that was neither a covenant of works nor a covenant of grace; and (4) still others, with whom Turretin concurs, viewed the Mosaic administration as in substance a covenant of grace, though promulgating the law as a means to teach human inability and sinfulness and the need for the Mediator, Jesus Christ. In his consideration of these views, Turretin spends most of his time refuting the third opinion and arguing for the propriety of the fourth. With respect to the third or "subservient" covenant view, Turretin notes that it was primarily taught by John Cameron and Amyraut of the Amyraldian school. Though Turretin seems to permit some form of the other views within the boundaries of acceptable Reformed opinion, he expressly repudiates the idea that the Mosaic covenant "subserved" the covenant of grace

of the Mosaic covenant by authors of *TLNF*, especially in Gordon's chapter, resemble more the Lutheran view in this respect than the traditional Reformed view.

22. *IET*, 2:262.

by "inflaming" the children of Israel with a desire for the promise of the covenant of grace and restraining their sinful inclination toward disobedience.[23]

In defense of the fourth opinion, Turretin argues that the Mosaic administration was an administration of the covenant of grace. Since there are only two kinds of covenants, a covenant of works and a covenant of grace, he rejects outright the idea that the Mosaic administration was a third kind of covenant. For Turretin, the Mosaic administration was "as to substance and species . . . nothing else than a new economy of the covenant of grace."[24] The Mosaic covenant was no different in its substance than the covenant with Abraham, though by its promulgation of the law it was "clothed as to external dispensation with the form of a covenant of works."[25] The specific purpose of the Mosaic administration's promulgation of the law was not to reinstitute a covenant of works with Israel, but to remind Israel of her sinful inability to do what the law demands and thereby cultivate a more ardent thirst for the righteousness of Jesus Christ. The law served Israel as a pedagogue that led her by the hand to Christ and taught the people that there is no other basis for salvation than that which is found in him. In his elaboration of the place of the law, narrowly considered, within the Mosaic administration, Turretin offers an account that closely resembles the one we have already observed in Calvin.

> The Mosaic covenant may be viewed in two aspects: either according to the intention and design of God and in order to Christ; or separately and abstracted from him. In the latter way, it is really distinct from the covenant of grace because it coincides with the covenant of works and in this sense is called the letter that killeth and the ministration of condemnation, when its nature is spoken (2 Cor. 3:6, 7). But it is *unwarrantably abstracted here* because it must always be considered with the intention of God, which was, not that man might have life from the law or as a sinner might be

23. Ibid.
24. Ibid., 2:263.
25. Ibid.

> simply condemned, but that from a sense of his own misery and weakness he might fly for refuge to Christ.[26]

In this explanation, Turretin is making a point that we witnessed in Calvin's conception of the Mosaic administration. When NT writers (especially the apostle Paul) contrast the "law" of Moses and the covenant of grace in Christ, the contrast is not between the Mosaic covenant as such and the covenant of grace. The contrast is between the law, abstracted from its setting within the Mosaic administration and considered only in terms of what it demands and promises, and the covenant of grace. However, when the law, narrowly considered, is regarded as having been promulgated by God through Moses to teach Israel to find salvation through works of obedience, then the law has been turned to a design contrary to God's intention. Within the purposes of the God of the covenant, the Mosaic law was designed to serve the preaching of Christ and to point Israel to the only Mediator whose obedience could procure salvation. In a statement that both anticipates and opposes the appeal of the authors of *TLNF* to a passage like Galatians 3:12, Turretin observes that Paul speaks of the law "not as taken broadly and denoting the Mosaic economy, but strictly as taken for the moral law abstractly and apart from the promises of grace (as the legalists regarded it who sought life from it)."[27] In Galatians 3:12, accordingly, the apostle Paul is not equating the "law" with the Mosaic administration as such, and then sharply opposing the Mosaic administration to the covenant of grace. Rather, the apostle is contrasting what the law, wrested from its covenant setting, demands, and arguing against his legalistic opponents who pursued a righteousness that consisted in obedience to the law.[28]

26. Ibid., 2:267 (emphasis added).

27. Ibid., 2:267–68.

28. Turretin reiterates this point in the conclusion to his discussion of the question whether the Mosaic covenant was a covenant of works or a covenant of grace: "It is one thing to speak of the law in itself (which had the form of a covenant of works and was enacted not with the end of making alive, but to convict of transgression, extort the confession of debt and lead to Christ); another concerning the Sinaitic covenant itself, in which the law was enacted" (*IET*, 2:269). See *CCT*, 243–72, for an extensive discussion of Turretin's view of the "twofold economy" of the covenant of grace. Beach argues that Turretin

Though I will have occasion in what follows to consider further Turretin's view of the role of the law in the Mosaic economy, it does not appear from my summary thus far that Turretin understands it to function at some level as a covenant of works. To be sure, Turretin affirms that the law, narrowly considered, reminds Israel of the requirements and consequences of obedience, and thereby closes the door to justification and life by the works of the law. In this respect, the law reiterates the demands of the covenant of works and shows why the promise of life and blessing cannot be obtained through the law. However, in doing so the law serves the gospel of God's grace in Christ, demonstrating that the covenant of works has been wholly abrogated as an instrument for obtaining life. Part of God's purpose in giving the law within the broad framework of the Mosaic economy was to point Israel to Christ who alone fulfills all the obligations of the law on behalf of his people. To view the law as though it were given *covenantally* as a means for obtaining the blessing of life and justification would be to "abstract" the law from the promises of grace that are an integral part of the Mosaic economy. Indeed, such an abstraction of the law from its divinely intended place within the Mosaic economy is the error of the legalists whom the apostle Paul opposes in his letter to the Galatians. Though the Mosaic administration may include a *formal* republication of the law's obligations, together with the consequences that follow in the instance of obedience or disobedience to its requirements, it does not thereby reinstitute at some level the prefall covenant of works.

Herman Witsius

The third theologian of the Reformed tradition whom we consider is Herman Witsius. Witsius's views on the question of republication are important for two reasons. First, Witsius was a mediating

---

viewed the Mosaic economy as an administration of the covenant of grace, though the promulgation of the moral law, when distinguished from its setting within the evangelical promise, does have the "form" of the covenant of works, "showing humans what they owe God and the consequences of failing to live according to his will" (252). In Beach's estimation, however, Turretin subordinates this feature of the Mosaic economy to the level of a "form" or adjunct that does not materially alter the substance of the Mosaic covenant as a covenant of grace.

theologian who wrote toward the end of the formative period of Reformed theology and endeavored to resolve some of the ongoing disputes among Reformed theologians on this question and other features of covenant theology. And second, Witsius is also cited by authors of *TLNF* as a historical example who confirms the prevalence of the republication thesis in traditional Reformed covenant theology. In his summary of Witsius's view, Fesko, for example, argues that the republication thesis is more pronounced in Witsius than it was in Calvin. In addition to Calvin's view that the Mosaic law republished the works principle of the covenant of works, Fesko argues that Witsius also developed the typology of Israel's corporate subjection to the works principle. In his interpretation of Witsius's position, Fesko insists that the Mosaic administration was interpreted as a kind of second Adamic probation in which God "set forth a legal covenant before the nation of Israel, one by which they could earn their salvation through obedience" (37).[29]

In his well-known *The Economy of the Covenants between God and Man*, Witsius restates the classic bi-covenantalism of the Reformed tradition. Since Witsius's formulation of the covenant of works and the covenant of grace differs in no significant respect from that of Turretin, I will focus only upon his handling of the question of the distinctive character of the Mosaic administration in the economy of the covenants. Following the long-standing consensus of Reformed theologians, Witsius assumes throughout his discussion of the Mosaic administration that it was in substance an administration of the covenant of grace, however distinct it might be in its accidental or incidental features or forms. As Witsius explains it,

> The difference of the testaments consists in the different manner of dispensing and proposing the same saving grace, and in some

29. There is a confusing inconsistency in Fesko's account of the typology of Israel's subjection to the requirement of obedience to the law. Only a page after the quote cited, Fesko represents Witsius to teach that the Mosaic administration was neither an exclusive covenant of works nor an exclusive covenant of grace, but a "national covenant of 'sincere piety' that presupposes both covenants. This covenant of sincere piety in terms of the land inheritance did not require perfect obedience, but sincere obedience, which for the godly Israelite was the fruit of his faith" (38).

> different adjuncts and circumstances. Whatever was typical in that dispensation, and denoted imperfection, and an acknowledgment that the ransom was not yet paid, belongs to the OT. Whatever shews that the redemption is actually wrought out, is peculiar to the New Testament.[30]

On this cardinal assumption of Reformed covenant theology, Witsius is clear: the covenant of grace throughout history is one in substance, though distinct in form of administration. The question that arises, then, is what were the distinct features or "adjuncts" of the Mosaic administration as an administration of the covenant of grace?

Witsius introduces his discussion of whether the Mosaic administration with its promulgation of the law at Sinai was a covenant of works or of grace by offering four preliminary observations. First, it is undoubtedly true that the moral law promulgated through Moses is a "repetition of the doctrine concerning the law of the covenant of works."[31] The law, with its demands, rewards, and promises, repeats what was required of Adam before the fall and can only, when separated from the covenant of grace, condemn and curse its recipients who are fallen in Adam. Second, Witsius observes that the "tremendous signs of thunders and lightnings," which accompanied the giving of the law through Moses at Sinai, were a "repetition of the covenant of works."[32] Just as the covenant of works can only remind sinners of the condemnation and death that follow upon disobedience to the law of God, so these signs at Sinai reminded Israel of the threat of judgment and contrast in form with the "sweetness of the gospel." Third, though Witsius's language might suggest that the law republished and

30. Herman Witsius, *The Economy of the Covenants between God and Man: Comprehending a Complete Body of Divinity*, trans. William Crookshank, 2 vols. (1822; repr., Escondido, CA: Den Dulk Foundation, 1990), 1:308.

31. Ibid., 2:182. Witsius's observation that the Decalogue given through Moses repeats the moral requirements of the natural law of God before the fall into sin, corresponds to what Ferry in *TLNF* terms a "material republication" of the covenant of works. This is not to say that the law is given in the form of a "covenant" of works, but that the law of Moses, as to its essential content, repeats the content of the natural or moral law.

32. Witsius, *Economy*, 2:183.

placed Israel under a renewed covenant of works, he also observes that "[w]e are not, however, to imagine, that the doctrine of the covenant of works was repeated, in order to set up again such a covenant with the Israelites, in which they were to seek for righteousness and salvation."[33] The purpose of the giving of the law was not to renew the covenant of works, but "promote the covenant of grace" with its promises of life and blessing through God's mercy. And fourth, Witsius closes his preliminary observations on the Mosaic administration by noting that it included the "repetition of some things belonging to the covenant of grace."[34] When the Lord reveals his law through Moses, he does not do so without promises of friendship and blessing and of the provision of a Mediator and his "suretyship." If the Mosaic administration consisted only of the promulgation of the moral law through Moses, it could only fill its recipients with terror and exasperation. However, the Mosaic administration republishes the promises of the covenant of grace, even as it teaches Israel the impossibility of obtaining life through obedience to the demands of the law.

After these preliminary observations regarding the law of Moses, Witsius turns directly to the question whether it was a covenant of works or a covenant of grace. In his answer to the question, Witsius offers what can only be described as a perplexing answer. He begins with what appears to be a clear denial that the Mosaic law was a republication of the covenant of works. According to Witsius, the covenant made with Israel at Sinai "was not formally the covenant of works" for at least three reasons.[35] First, it is not possible that God would reinstitute the covenant of works with sinners, since they are not capable of the perfect obedience required in the covenant of works and of obtaining justification and life through such obedience. Second, the obedience required in the Mosaic covenant was a "sincere obedience, as an evidence of reverence and gratitude," and not a perfect obedience that was to be performed in order to obtain God's blessing. And third, the obligation of obedience in the Mosaic economy did not "conclude Israel under the curse, in the sense peculiar to

33. Ibid.
34. Ibid., 2:184.
35. Ibid.

the covenant of works, where all hope of pardon was cut off, if they sinned but in the least instance."[36]

Immediately after his denial that the Mosaic administration was in form a covenant of works, Witsius adds a point that we have seen previously in the formulations of Calvin and Turretin. In Witsius's interpretation of the apostle Paul's contrasting of the law and the gospel, the apostle is contending against "carnal Israelites," who did not regard the law in accordance with "God's purpose or intention" but who "mistook the true meaning of that covenant, embraced it as a covenant of works, and by it sought for righteousness."[37] Therefore, when Paul opposes the law of Moses and the gospel of justification through faith in Christ, he is not presuming that the law of Moses was "nothing but a covenant of works." Rather, Paul was teaching that "the gross Israelites misunderstood the mind of God, and basely abused his covenant; as all such do, who seek for righteousness by the law."[38]

Upon the basis of these considerations, which militate against the view that the law of Moses was formally a covenant of works, the reader would expect Witsius to argue that it was in fact only an administration of the covenant of grace. However, Witsius also rejects the teaching that the law of Moses was "formally a covenant of grace."[39] In order for the law of Moses to be a covenant of grace, it would have to include the promises of blessing and life, which can only be granted by God and received in the way of faith, and it would have to bestow the strength required in order for its obligations to be performed. Since the law of Moses includes neither the gracious promises of God's blessing nor the provision of the strength needed to perform what it requires, Witsius concludes that it is not a covenant of grace. If the law of Moses is neither formally a covenant of works nor formally

36. Ibid.

37. Ibid., 2:184–85.

38. Ibid., 2:185. Witsius appeals at this point to Calvin's interpretation of Romans 10:4, and to the apostle Paul's arguments in Romans 9:31–32 and Galatians 4 & 5.

39. Ibid. Perhaps part of the explanation for Witsius's hesitation to designate the law of Moses either a covenant of works or a covenant of grace, lies in the fact that he is speaking strictly of *the law* of Moses (the Decalogue), distinguished from the evangelical promise with which it is properly joined in the covenant of grace.

a covenant of grace, then what, Witsius asks, is it? In answer to this question, Witsius proposes that the law of Moses should be understood as a "national covenant between God and Israel, whereby Israel promised to God a sincere obedience to all his precepts, especially to the ten words; God, on the other hand, promised to Israel, that such an observance would be acceptable to him, nor want its reward, both in this life, and in that which is to come, both as to soul and body."[40] In this understanding of the law of Moses as a national covenant, we may say that it presupposes both the covenants of works and of grace, though it is not strictly one or the other. In some sense the law of Moses includes or is an admixture of the covenant of works, which teaches Israel that the Lord's blessing requires sincere obedience, and of the covenant of grace, which teaches Israel that the Lord's blessing is finally dependent upon his mercy and grace.

It is difficult to determine where Witsius's opinion of the peculiar nature of the Mosaic economy fits into the framework of his covenant theology as a whole, and how it lines up, for example, with the four views that Turretin discerns among Reformed covenant theologians. Witsius's view is not compatible with the "subservient" or "third" covenant view advocated by John Cameron and the Amyraldians. When Witsius describes the law of Moses as both a covenant of works and a covenant of grace, he seems to favor the second view that Turretin identifies, namely, that the Mosaic economy was an admixture of the covenants of works and of grace. However, much of Witsius's treatment of the question corresponds to the themes that we have seen previously in Calvin and Turretin, and cumulatively support the view that Witsius regarded the Mosaic covenant as substantively an administration of the covenant of grace. Among the writers we have considered, Witsius's position does seem to anticipate some of the emphases of authors of *TLNF*, particularly the idea that the Mosaic economy includes in some sense a formal republication of the covenant of works at the level of Israel's corporate or national life. But in this respect Witsius differs from the views of Calvin and Turretin, and in a way that is more confusing than it is clarifying.

40. Ibid., 2:186.

The Westminster Confession of Faith

The best source for determining the historic Reformed consensus on the doctrine of the covenant is undoubtedly the WCF. Among the classic symbols of the Reformed churches, the WCF clearly presents the consensus doctrine of the covenant in the period of Reformed orthodoxy. As is typically the case with confessional documents, the formulations of the WCF represent the common and accepted features of the doctrine, and leave aside those peculiar features that belong only to this or that theologian of the tradition. For example, even though it was fairly common by the time of the writing of the WCF to speak of an intra-Trinitarian "covenant of redemption" (*pactum salutis*), the WCF restricts its discussion of the covenant to the historical covenants before and after the fall into sin. Consequently, the WCF is an excellent standard to test the claims of the authors of *TLNF*. Is there any evidence that the WCF views the Mosaic administration as a kind of republication of the covenant of works?[41]

In chapter 7 of the WCF, which is titled "Of God's Covenant with Man," the Confession presents a classic statement of historic Reformed bi-covenantalism. The first article of chapter 7 underscores the importance of the doctrine of the covenant and offers a general definition of God's covenant with man. According to this article, all human beings were created in God's image and can only have "fruition of him as their blessedness and reward" by means of covenant (WCF 7.1). Even though human beings who bear God's image are obliged by nature to obey God, they would never be able to enjoy the perfection of eternal life without God's sovereign initiative or "voluntary condescension" to enter into covenant with them. For the Westminster divines, the covenant relationship between God and human beings as his image-bearers, whether before or after the fall, is always based upon God's free and unmerited condescension.

41. For a recent exchange on this question, see D. Patrick Ramsey, "In Defense of Moses: A Confessional Critique of Kline and Karlberg," *WTJ* 66, 2 (2004): 373–400; and Brenton C. Ferry, "Cross-Examining Moses's Defense: An Answer to Ramsey's Critique of Kline and Karlberg," *WTJ* 67, 1 (2005): 163–68. As their article titles indicate, Ramsey is arguing against the republication thesis, as it is represented in the works of Kline and Karlberg; and Ferry, one of the authors of *TLNF*, is arguing for it.

After making these fundamental points about the indispensability of the covenant to human blessedness and the nature of the covenant as a "voluntary condescension" on God's part, the Confession proceeds to distinguish and define the prelapsarian covenant of works and the postlapsarian covenant of grace. What distinguishes the covenant of works is that it promises Adam and all whom he represented life "upon condition of perfect and personal obedience" (WCF 7.2). By virtue of Adam's sin and disobedience, there is no possibility open to Adam or his posterity for life and blessedness upon the basis of the covenant of works. Consequently, God was "pleased to make a second, commonly called the *covenant of grace*; wherein he freely offereth unto sinners life and salvation by Jesus Christ; requiring of them faith in him, that they may be saved, and promising to give unto all those that are ordained unto eternal life his Holy Spirit, to make them willing, and able to believe" (WCF 7.3). The covenant of works and the covenant of grace are similar in respect to their source and promise. Both covenants originate with the triune God who voluntarily condescends to enter into covenant with his creatures. In the covenant of works, the parties are God, the triune Creator, and Adam and his posterity. In the covenant of grace, the parties are God, the triune Redeemer, and all who by faith are partakers of Christ and all his benefits. The life promised in the covenant relationship before and after the fall into sin is nothing less than the perfection of eternal life and blessedness in unbreakable communion with God. What distinguishes these two covenants as to their substance is that the first requires "personal and perfect obedience" as the condition for obtaining life, whereas the second requires faith in Christ, the Mediator.

The two concluding articles of Chapter 7 of the WCF are of special importance to the question of the unity of the covenant of grace throughout the history of redemption. In these articles, the Westminster divines embrace the formulation of Calvin and other Reformed theologians that the covenant of grace is one in substance throughout the course of history and in all its various dispensations.

> This covenant [of grace] was differently administered in the time of the law, and in the time of the gospel: under the law, it was

> administered by promises, prophecies, sacrifices, circumcision, the paschal lamb, and other types and ordinances delivered to the people of the Jews, all foresignifying Christ to come; which were, for that time, sufficient and efficacious, through the operation of the Spirit, to instruct and build up the elect in faith in the promised Messiah, by whom they had full remission of sins, and eternal salvation; and is called the old testament. (WCF 7.5)
>
> Under the gospel, when Christ, the substance, was exhibited, the ordinances in which this covenant is dispensed are the preaching of the Word, and the administration of the sacraments of Baptism and the Lord's Supper: which, though fewer in number, and administered with more simplicity, and less outward glory, yet, in them, it is held forth in more fulness, evidence and spiritual efficacy, to all nations, both Jews and Gentiles; and is called the new testament. There are not therefore two covenants of grace, differing in substance, but one and the same, under various dispensations (WCF 7.6).

Nothing in these confessional statements regarding the unity and diversity of the covenant of grace throughout the history of redemption differs in any significant way from what we have seen in the writings of Calvin, Turretin, and Witsius. The administration of the covenant of grace "under the law" refers broadly to the entire Mosaic economy. In the view of the Westminster divines, the Mosaic administration in its entirety foreshadowed the person and work of Christ as Mediator. Believers under the Mosaic economy were saved in the same way, and enjoyed the same spiritual blessings that are now enjoyed by believers after the coming of Christ.[42]

Though the authors of *TLNF* acknowledge these features of the WCF's conception of the Mosaic economy, they especially appeal to chapter 19 to argue for the view that the law of Moses "in some sense" republished the covenant of works (10–11, 43). In chapter 19, which

42. WCF 11.6 affirms, for this reason, that believers under the old covenant administrations of the covenant of grace enjoyed the blessing of free justification: "The justification

is titled "Of the Law of God," the WCF makes a number of important statements about the law within the context of the prelapsarian covenant of works and the postlapsarian covenant of grace. With respect to the covenant of works, the Confession notes that "God gave to Adam a law, *as a covenant of works*, by which he bound him and all his posterity to personal, entire, exact, and perpetual obedience" (WCF 19.1, emphasis added). Reiterating what was stated in chapter 7 regarding the covenant of works, the Confession affirms that the "promise of life" made to Adam would have been granted upon the basis of Adam's fulfillment of this condition.

In several subsequent articles of chapter 19, the Confession also affirms that the moral law of God continued after the fall to be "a perfect rule of righteousness" for all human beings created in God's image, and that it was communicated to Israel through Moses in the form of the Decalogue at Mount Sinai (WCF 19.2–5). In addition to the moral law, which was summarized for Israel in the Decalogue, God also gave Israel various ceremonial laws, which foreshadowed the coming of Christ and are abrogated under the new covenant (WCF 19.3). Of particular significance is the Confession's declaration regarding the moral law that God gave to believers under the Mosaic administration and that continues to "bind" believers to obedience under the new covenant in Christ.

> Although true believers be not under the law, as a covenant of works, to be thereby justified, or condemned; yet is it of great use to them, as well as to others; in that, as a rule of life informing them of the will of God, and their duty, it directs and binds them to walk accordingly. . . . The promises of it, in like manner, show them God's approbation of obedience, and what blessings they may expect upon the performance thereof; although not as due to them as a covenant of works. (19.6)

---

of believers under the old testament was, in all these respects, one and the same with the justification of believers under the new testament." Though the authors of *TLNF* do not deny this affirmation, it is noteworthy that it hardly receives much emphasis in their characterization of the Mosaic administration.

It is difficult to see what basis the authors of *TLNF* have for appealing to these articles in chapter 19 of the WCF to prove that the Mosaic economy in some sense republished the covenant of works. The Confession clearly affirms that the moral law, whether promulgated through Moses or by Christ himself, constitutes a "perfect rule of righteousness" that is abidingly normative for the conduct of God's people. Indeed, the moral law continues to obligate all creatures, "as well justified persons as others," to a pattern of conduct in respect to God and to others that is pleasing to God as their Creator or Redeemer. The moral obligations of obedience remain the same after the fall into sin as they were before, though the particular form or expression of these obligations may differ throughout the course of redemptive history. But this does not warrant the conclusion that the Mosaic economy was in some sense a republication of the covenant of works. As a matter of fact, the Confession expressly denies that the law was given through Moses "as a covenant of works." Unlike the covenant of works, which required "personal and perfect obedience" to the law as the condition for obtaining life and blessedness, the Mosaic economy requires faith in Christ alone for salvation. The obligations of the law under the Mosaic covenant as a covenant of grace are not set forth as a basis for the believer's justification, but to teach believers of their need for Christ and to encourage them in their life of grateful obedience.[43]

Summary

In my review of the covenant theology of three leading Reformed theologians, Calvin, Turretin, and Witsius, as well as my sketch of the covenant conception of the WCF, we have seen a consistent set of emphases. In every case, with the exception of Calvin who does not expressly articulate a doctrine of a prelapsarian covenant

43. Ernest F. Kevan, *The Grace of Law: A Study in Puritan Theology* (1964; repr., Grand Rapids, MI: Baker, 1976), 117, offers a helpful summary of the position set forth in the WCF, especially chaps. 7, 19: "The outcome of the debate [regarding the nature of the Mosaic economy among the divines] was that, on the whole, it was agreed that the Mosaic Covenant was a form of the Covenant of Grace; and this view was embodied in the *Confession of Faith*."

of works, a clear distinction is drawn between two substantially different covenants. The first covenant is the prelapsarian covenant of works, whose substance consists in God's promise of life to Adam and his posterity upon condition of perfect and personal obedience. The second covenant is the postlapsarian covenant of grace, whose substance consists in God's gracious promise of life to all who are united to Christ by faith and become thereby partakers of all his benefits. With respect to the postlapsarian covenant of grace, a clear consensus exists that this covenant, though diversely administered throughout the course of redemptive history, was one in substance. In all of its administrations, the covenant of grace promises life upon condition of faith in Jesus Christ. So far as the obligations of obedience under the covenant of grace are concerned, the moral law of God, which was known to Adam before the fall, serves as an abiding rule of conduct. However, the law of God, which was promulgated through Moses in the form of the Ten Commandments, does not function in any sense as a republication of the covenant of works. Though the law's moral demands remain the same, the law is not given through Moses or under any of the administrations of the covenant of grace as an instrument for obtaining the inheritance of life and blessing. Rather, the law functions in its first use to teach believers their need for Christ and his saving work, and in its third use to be a "rule of gratitude" for the sincere, though imperfect, obedience of God's redeemed people.

An Assessment of the Biblical Arguments

Though the historical argument for the republication thesis is a dominant feature of *TLNF*, the largest section of the volume consists of several articles that offer a biblical-theological case for the claim that the Mosaic administration republished the "works principle" of the prelapsarian covenant of works. The aim of the contributors to this section of the book is to confirm the biblical warrant for this view of the nature of the Mosaic administration. In keeping with the limitations of my review of *TLNF*, I will not engage all of the chapters in this section of the book, nor will I attempt to assess many of the details of the complex exegetical arguments of the authors. To do so would require nothing less than a biblical-theological monograph of considerable length. My assessment will focus only upon the articles that I summarized in my survey of the book and upon some of their most important arguments.

Furthermore, rather than attempt an independent exegesis of the key passages adduced by the authors for their respective versions of the republication thesis, I will simply contrast the handling of these passages in *TLNF* with the interpretation of several representative Reformed exegetes. My aim in drawing the contrast between the handling of these passages by contributors to *TLNF* and by other Reformed exegetes will not be to determine whose interpretation is finally to be preferred. Rather, it will be my aim to establish at least two points: first, that the biblical-theological arguments of the contributors do not clearly belong to the mainstream of historic Reformed biblical theology; and second, that the biblical-theological arguments of the authors rather reflect the far-reaching influence of a recent Reformed biblical theologian, Meredith Kline. If these two points can be established, then it seems to me that they undermine the larger claim of the authors of *TLNF*, namely, that their understanding of the republication thesis represents an integral part of the historic Reformed and biblical theology of the covenant.[44]

In order to organize my assessment of the biblical-theological argument for the republication thesis, I will address three topics: (1) the interpretation of the apostle Paul's use of Leviticus 18:5 in Romans and Galatians; (2) Galatians 3:6–14 and the Mosaic administration; and (3) the typology of the Mosaic economy in relation to its NT fulfillment. With respect to each of these topics, I will compare the positions of the authors of *TLNF* with alternative views

44. In this part of my assessment of *TLNF*, I do not in any way wish to impinge upon the legitimate "freedom of exegesis" that belongs to a proper confession of "Scripture alone" (*sola Scriptura*). Though Reformed exegetes are obligated to respect confessional boundaries in their exegetical labors, they are free to read the biblical data in a fresh and new way. The explorations and biblical-theological arguments of the contributors to *TLNF* legitimately invite further study and reflection. Nothing in my assessment is meant to undermine inappropriately the enterprise of biblical-theological study of the distinctiveness of the Mosaic economy.

that are more characteristic of biblical theologians in the Reformed tradition.

Paul's Use of Leviticus 18:5

Throughout *TLNF*, various contributors interpret the apostle Paul's use of Leviticus 18:5 in Romans 10 and in Galatians 3 to be clearly based upon the conviction that the Mosaic economy in some sense republished the covenant of works. In the biblical studies of Estelle and Gordon, this is a basic component in their arguments for republication.

In his chapter, Estelle argues that Paul views Leviticus 18:5 to communicate a covenant-inheritance principle that is antithetical to that of the covenant of grace, which promises life and blessing through the work of Christ and upon the basis of God's gracious initiative. In his description of the function of Leviticus 18:5, Estelle interprets the "works principle" it enunciates to serve two distinct purposes. On the one hand, Estelle maintains that this works principle was "republished" at Sinai to drive its recipients to acknowledge their sinful inability and to cause them to trust in "God's provision to accomplish the goal, that is, entitlement to the land of heaven" (131). On the other hand, Leviticus 18:5 served another function, namely, to teach Israel that obedience to the law "would be the meritorious grounds for Israel's continuance in the land, the typological kingdom" (136).[45] For his part, Gordon offers an interpretation of the use of Leviticus 18:5 that shows the radical contrast between the Mosaic administration as a covenant of works, which could only place its recipients under condemnation and death, and the Abrahamic administration as a covenant of grace, which promises justification and life to those who place their trust in Christ alone. In the view of Estelle and Gordon, Paul's use of Leviticus 18:5

45. Estelle's position on the nature and significance of the "works principle" in the Mosaic economy is difficult to interpret, since he seems to contradict himself. In the statement of the purpose of the "works principle," he sometimes speaks of it as though it required "meritorious" works that would be the basis for Israel's tenure in the land, as in this passage. But at other times, he describes the Mosaic economy's obligation of obedience as an obligation for "grateful" or "sincere obedience," an obedience that would serve as a witness to the nations (137).

demonstrates compellingly that the Mosaic covenant was in some sense a covenant of works that set forth a works principle antithetical to the grace principle of the gospel. Gordon's statement of the antithesis between the Mosaic covenant and the covenant of grace is less qualified than that of Estelle. However, both contributors insist that Paul appeals to Leviticus 18:5, not to oppose those who *misused* or *abused* the meaning of this passage within the broader framework of the Mosaic economy, but in accord with its proper meaning and significance.

Before I compare the way Estelle and Gordon interpret Paul's use of Leviticus 18:5 with that of other Reformed exegetes, it should be observed that they give little attention to the meaning of this text in its original, OT setting. While Estelle acknowledges the difference between Leviticus 18:5 in its "original setting" and in Paul's use of it (111), he does not offer an account of the difference. However, the reason Paul's appeal to Leviticus 18:5 raises a number of difficult exegetical questions derives precisely from this difference. In its original setting within the Mosaic economy, Leviticus 18:5 can scarcely be understood apart from other essential elements of the covenant of grace. For example, the obligations of obedience stipulated in Leviticus 18:5 assume the truth of Israel's redemption from bondage by God's outstretched arm, and are placed within this context in a manner that is similar to the promulgation of the law at Sinai. When the Lord calls his people to holiness, he does so as one who is holy, but also as one who graciously makes provision for the justification and sanctification of his people.

It is especially noteworthy that the statutes of the Mosaic covenant to which Leviticus 18:5 requires compliance include all the provisions in the Levitical legislation that concern the offering of sacrifices for the cleansing away of the guilt and pollution of sin. Indeed, all of the ceremonies of the law to which Israel is subject constitute a typological prefigurement of the person and work of Christ as Mediator and Savior. Furthermore, the Lord, who makes provision for the removal of the guilt and uncleanness of the people through the Levitical legislation, also promises the people that he will sanctify them (see, e.g., Lev. 22:32–33). In this context, Leviticus 18:5 can hardly be read to be a republication of the covenant of works, which obliges Israel to a perfect obedience as a basis for her blessing in the Land of Promise. This would not only wrest Leviticus 18:5 from its setting within the Mosaic economy and the Levitical legislation, but it would also suggest that this economy was no longer undergirded by the promises first made to Abraham, who was justified before God through faith alone and in no other wise than believers are justified in the NT economy. When Estelle and Gordon maintain that Leviticus 18:5 republished the covenant of works, they offer little or no explanation of how this comports with these fundamental features of the Mosaic covenant as an administration of the covenant of grace.

More important than their failure to explain how Leviticus 18:5 fits within the framework of a covenant administration that was substantively a covenant of grace, Estelle and (especially) Gordon dismiss a common Reformed interpretation of Paul's use of this text in Romans and Galatians. As we have seen in our consideration of the view of the Mosaic administration in Calvin, Turretin, and Witsius, these formative writers in the history of Reformed theology consistently interpret Paul to be addressing a "legalistic" abuse or misappropriation of the teaching of Leviticus 18:5. Remarkably, Gordon, in the course of his rather dismissive treatment of John Murray's view of the obligations of obedience under the Mosaic covenant, writes as though Paul's argument cannot possibly be read in any other way than the one he presents.[46] In offering his criticism of Murray, Gordon actually criticizes a rather standard view in the history of

46. Gordon's attack upon John Murray in his chapter seems to exceed the bounds of propriety for an academic essay in biblical theology. For example, he asserts that Murray not only could not have made any sense of Paul's argument in Galatians, but also that whatever he would have written would be "obfuscatory in the highest degree" (253). And, as if that were not enough, he adds, "I like to think that he [i.e., Murray] was aware that he was entirely flummoxed by Paul's reasoning, and that he therefore determined not to write anything about the matter until he could make some sense of it." In actual fact, Murray does address the matter directly in his commentary on the book of Romans, which includes an appendix on Paul's appeal to Leviticus 18:5, and which we will consider in what follows. Furthermore, Gordon neglects to note that Murray addresses the interpretation of Galatians 3 in his *Redemption Accomplished and Applied* (Grand Rapids, MI: Eerdmans, 1955), and that his lectures on Galatians at Westminster Theological Seminary are available to the public (see http://sites.google.com/site/themosaiccovenant/john-murray).

Reformed interpretation of Paul's argument in Galatians. Even were Gordon able to prove that Murray could have made "no sense" out of Paul's letter to the Galatians, as he alleges, he would still have to acknowledge that the interpretation of Paul's argument that he dismisses was fairly common, and probably predominant, among the principal exegetes of the tradition.

In the writings of Calvin, Turretin, and Witsius, Paul's appeal to Leviticus 18:5 in Romans 10 and Galatians 3 is interpreted quite differently than in the chapters by Estelle and Gordon. Each of these theologians interprets Paul's use of Leviticus 18:5 in terms of what might be called a "narrow" or "abstract" view of the law of Moses. Within the broader framework of the Mosaic administration of the covenant of grace, God's design and purpose in promulgating the law was twofold. On the one hand, the law was given to Israel after her redemption from bondage in Egypt as a comprehensive description of the kind of grateful and sincere obedience that the Lord properly expected from his covenant people. In Reformed theology, this is commonly termed the "third" and "principal" use of the law.[47] On the other hand, God's design in giving the law through Moses was also "pedagogical," since the law serves to expose human sinfulness and inability in order to drive its recipients to Christ, who is the "end" and "fulfillment" of the law. This use is typically termed the "first" or "pedagogical" use of the law. However, when the apostle Paul draws a contrast or speaks of an antithesis between the "law" and the "gospel," he is not teaching that the Mosaic administration in some sense republished the covenant of works and is, in this respect, contrary to the gospel. Rather, the apostle is opposing a kind of "legalism" that appeals to the "law" as an instrument for pursuing righteousness and justification before God upon the basis of works of the law.

In the interpretation of Calvin, Turretin, and Witsius, Paul's appeal to Leviticus 18:5 is understood within the context of his polemic with the legalism of his opponents. In their reading of Romans 10 and Galatians 3, Paul's appeal to Leviticus 18:5 aims to

47. Calvin regards the third use of the law as a rule of gratitude to be its "principal" use (*Institutes* 2.7.12 [*OS* 3:337]): "Tertius usus, qui et praecipuus est, et in proprium Legis finem propius spectat." On Calvin's view of the diverse uses of the law, see *ARC*, 229–47.

remind his legalistic opponents that the law, *narrowly and abstractly considered*, could never serve as an instrument of self-justification before God. In its narrow and abstract meaning, the law reveals only the demands and obligations of perfect obedience. These demands and obligations coincide with the moral law of God to which all image-bearers of God, including Adam before the fall, are subject. By means of the law, God reveals to his people what pleases him, namely, perfect conformity to his statutes. When the law with its demand for perfect obedience is separated from the promises and provisions of God's grace, it can only impress upon its recipients their sinful inability and the futility of obtaining acceptance with God on the basis of the works of the law.

Rather than cite again passages from each of these theologians to illustrate their interpretation of Paul's appeal to Leviticus 18:5, I will treat Calvin's comments on Romans 10:5 and Galatians 3 as illustrative of themes that are common to all of them.

In his commentary on Romans 10:5, Calvin explains Paul's appeal to Leviticus 18:5 by distinguishing between "the whole of the doctrine (*universam doctrinam*) taught by Moses" and "that part of it which belonged peculiarly to his ministry."[48] In his "universal office," Moses taught nothing that is contrary to the gospel. The Mosaic economy or administration of the covenant included the preaching of repentance and faith, and therefore it included "offering the promises, the free promises, of the divine mercy." In the discharge of his comprehensive office, Moses preached the gospel with its summons to faith and repentance. Within the context of the universal office of Moses, the law provided the people instruction in their duties and obligations of obedience. However, the apostle Paul appeals to Leviticus 18:5 as an example of Moses' peculiar office as a teacher of the demands and obligations of the law, which by God's design served as a means to instruct the people of Israel "in how many ways they were accursed and how far they were from being able to earn anything from God by their works. Being thus led to despair of attaining any righteousness of their own they were to flee to the haven of divine

48. Comm. Rom. 10:4–5, *CNTC* 8:222–23.

goodness—to Christ himself. This was the purpose of the ministry of Moses."[49] Though the ministry of Moses included a preaching of the gospel and its promises, Calvin observes that, in his particular office as a teacher of the law, Moses was called to teach the character of the righteousness of works and to remind the people of the rewards and punishments due to those who obey or disobey its precepts. When Paul contrasts the "law" of Moses and the gospel, the contrast is not between the universal office of Moses and the gospel, but between the peculiar office of Moses and the gospel. "Whenever the word *law* is used in this restricted sense, Moses is implicitly contrasted with Christ. We are then to see what the law contains in itself when separated from the Gospel. I must, therefore, refer to what I say here of the righteousness of the law not to the whole office of Moses, but to that part of it which was peculiarly entrusted to him."[50]

According to Calvin, in this passage Paul is opposing those who "put their trust for salvation" in their works performed in obedience to the law. When Paul speaks of those who are "of the works of the law," he is speaking of the Judaizers who sought to use the law as a means of self-justification before God.[51] Though the law of God is holy and good, by itself it can only "curse" all those who are unable to perform perfectly what it requires.

> [The apostle] concludes boldly that all are cursed because all have been commanded to keep the law perfectly, and this is because, in the present corruption of our nature, the ability is wanting. Hence we conclude that it is accidental that the law should curse, though at the same time perpetual and inseparable.[52]

In order to interpret Paul's appeal in this passage to Leviticus 18:5, it is necessary, according to Calvin, to bear in mind that his

49. Ibid., *CNTC* 8:223 (*CO* 49.97).

50. Ibid., *CNTC* 8:223 (*CO* 49.98).

51. Comm. Gal. 3:10–11, *CNTC* 11:53 (*CO* 50.208). Calvin's interpretation of the language, "of the works of the law," in Galatians 3:10 differs from that of Gordon who insists that Paul is not opposing those who misuse the law by "relying on" the works of the law as a means of self-justification (244–45).

52. Comm. Gal. 3:10–11, *CNTC* 11:53 (*CO* 50.208).

"language is adapted to these particular circumstances. The contradiction between the law and faith lies in the cause of justification."[53] While the law of God continues to serve believers as a rule of gratitude, the law of God serves, so far as justification before God is concerned, to show the impossibility of justification by works. When Paul adduces Leviticus 18:5 against his opponents, he is not offering a complete account of the law within the framework of the Mosaic covenant. Nor is he denying that, with respect to the believer's conduct, the law serves as a norm for the good works that faith necessarily produces. What the apostle wishes to deny is the claim that it is possible to do what the law requires and upon that basis obtain favor with God. In respect to the decisive question of justification, the law can only serve to remind sinners of their unworthiness and need for the work of Christ as Redeemer. As Calvin remarks, "[w]e admit that the doers of the law, if there were any, would be righteous. But since that is a conditional agreement, all are excluded from life because none offers the righteousness that he ought."[54]

Though there are a number of past and more recent interpreters of Paul's appeal to Leviticus 18:5 that follow in the trajectory of Calvin's view, I also wish to consider the way John Murray addresses this topic. Since Gordon singles Murray out for particular criticism and insists that he could not have offered a convincing interpretation of Paul's appeal to Leviticus 18:5, it is instructive that Murray does address the subject and follows closely the interpretation of Calvin.

In his commentary on the book of Romans, Murray devotes an appendix to the question of Paul's appeal to Leviticus 18:5 in Romans 10:5. Murray devotes special attention to this question since, as he acknowledges, Paul's use of Leviticus 18:5 seems to contradict the meaning of the passage in its OT context. In the OT economy of redemption, Leviticus 18:5 does not appear in a context "that deals with legal righteousness as opposed to that of faith."[55] Rather, Leviticus 18:5 seems to present the law in the same way as it is presented

53. Comm. Gal. 3:11–12, *CNTC* 11:54 (*CO* 50.209).

54. Comm. Gal. 3:12–14, *CNTC* 11:55 (*CO* 50.210).

55. John Murray, "Appendix B: Leviticus 18:5," in *The Epistle to the Romans*, 2 vols., NICNT (Grand Rapids, MI: Eerdmans, 1959, 1965), 2:249.

in Exodus 20, Deuteronomy 5, and in many other passages in the Pentateuch, namely, as a rule of gratitude that norms the conduct of a redeemed people in their life-fellowship with the Lord. According to Murray, Paul's use of Leviticus 18:5 cannot help but raise the question "could Paul properly have appealed to Lev. 18:5 as an illustration of works-righteousness in opposition to that of faith?"[56] In Murray's answer to this question, three "distinct relationships" are identified in which the principle enunciated in Leviticus 18:5, "the man that does shall live," has particular relevance.

First, in "a state of perfect integrity," Murray argues, the law of God reveals a "principle of equity in God's government."[57] Since the law discloses to human beings what accords with God's will, obedience to the law will invariably be pleasing to God and warrant his approbation and justifying verdict, whereas disobedience will always be displeasing to him and warrant his disapproval and condemnation. God always judges human conduct according to the truth, whether it be conduct that pleases or displeases him. In the state of Adam's integrity before the fall, it was possible for him to enjoy God's approval by doing what the law required. However, by virtue of Adam's fall and disobedience, the law of God as such can now only expose him and his posterity to condemnation and death, since all have sinned and fall short of God's glory. Since the fall of Adam, man's original relationship to the law is no longer operative. Now the law can only reveal the sinfulness of all human beings and their just liability to condemnation and death.

Second, "within the realm of sin" or the world subsequent to the fall of Adam, the principle, "the man that does shall live," must be regarded as "totally inoperative" as a means for obtaining favor and acceptance with God.[58] According to Murray, the absolute contrast that the apostle Paul wishes to set forth in Romans 10:5–6 between the righteousness of works and the righteousness of faith, is a contrast between *doing* what the law requires and *embracing* what God freely gives in Christ. When Paul adduces Leviticus 18:5

56. Ibid.

57. Ibid.

58. Ibid., 2:250.

to illustrate this contrast, he appeals properly to what the language of this text *by itself* expresses. Leviticus 18:5 expresses what "holds true when law-righteousness is operative unto justification and life and also express[es] the conception entertained by the person who espouses the same as the way of acceptance with God (cf. also Gal. 3:12)."[59] When the apostle Paul appeals to Leviticus 18:5 to prove the futility of obtaining a right standing with God on the basis of works, he properly demonstrates the futility of any such endeavor. No one is able to do all that the law requires, and therefore no one is able to obtain life through the works of the law.

And third, the purpose of Paul's quotation of Leviticus 18:5 is shaped by his polemic with those who would appeal to their works of obedience to the law as a basis for justification and life. In making his appeal to this passage, the apostle legitimately opposes any attempt to use the law as an instrument of self-justification. However, in Murray's judgment, the misappropriation of the law as a means to obtain life and justification before God by Paul's opponents, does not mitigate the proper use of the law as a norm for Christian obedience and sanctification. "But we must not suppose that doing the commandments as the way of life has ceased to have any validity or application. To suppose this would be as capital a mistake in its own locus as to propound works-righteousness as the way of justification. . . . In the realm of grace, therefore, obedience is the way of life. He that does the commandments of God lives in them."[60] When Paul adduces Leviticus 18:5 to expose the futility of any effort to obtain justification upon the basis of the works of the law, he does not thereby deny the legitimacy of an appeal to Leviticus 18:5 in support of a sincere and grateful obedience to the law of God. Nor does he deny the sense in which such sincere obedience is the way of life and blessing for the redeemed people of God.

From these comments of Murray's on Paul's use of Leviticus 18:5, it is apparent that he follows in all important respects the interpretive approach of theologians in the Reformed tradition whose

59. Ibid.

60. Ibid., 2:250–51.

views we have surveyed. Though several authors of *TLNF* challenge this interpretation, it represents a cogent and more common Reformed explanation of Paul's appeal to Leviticus 18:5 in Romans and Galatians.[61]

Galatians 3:6–14 and the Mosaic Administration

Perhaps the most provocative exposition of the republication thesis in *TLNF* is the chapter by Gordon that offers an interpretation of the contrast between the Abrahamic and Mosaic covenants in Galatians 3:6–14. Upon the basis of his reading of this passage, Gordon argues that these covenants are "characteristically" different. Whereas the Abrahamic covenant was unconditional and gracious, the Mosaic covenant was conditional and legal. Contrary to the Abrahamic covenant, which promised life and blessing through Christ, the Mosaic covenant enunciated a "works principle" that could only condemn and curse the people of God. In Gordon's interpretation, Paul's appeal to this contrast was not skewed by a legalistic misuse of the law of Moses by his opponents. Rather, Paul was appealing to the radical contrast between two principles of inheritance that characterized the Abrahamic and Mosaic covenants—the one a gracious, the other a works principle—in order to confirm the gospel of salvation by grace alone through faith alone.

In my assessment of Gordon's interpretation of Paul's argument in Galatians 3, I will follow the same procedure as in the previous section. I will begin with a summary of Calvin's interpretation of Paul's argument in Galatians 3, and then consider as well the interpretation of the argument by a more recent Reformed biblical theologian, Herman Ridderbos. My purpose in doing so will not be so much to refute Gordon's interpretation as such, but to establish the point that there are other, more common interpretations of Galatians 3 in the Reformed exegetical tradition, past and present.

I have already noted that Calvin interprets Paul's appeal to Leviticus 18:5 in Galatians 3:12 to illustrate the contrast between

61. For another example of this explanation by a Reformed exegete, see William Hendriksen, *Exposition of Galatians* (Grand Rapids, MI: Baker, 1968), 127–31.

the law and gospel on the issue of justification before God. Since no one is able to obey perfectly what the law requires, no one is able to be justified by the works of the law. With respect to the basis for the justification of believers before God, the law, narrowly considered, is opposed to the gospel. There is an antithesis between the righteousness of the works of the law and the righteousness of faith.

However, in the course of his exposition of Paul's contrast between the Abrahamic and Mosaic economies in Galatians 3, Calvin is at some pains to defend their full harmony and coherence. Calvin does not conclude from Paul's argument that the Abrahamic and Mosaic administrations are "characteristically" different, to use Gordon's language. In his interpretation of Paul's argument, especially the contrast the apostle draws between the promise given to Abraham and the law mediated through Moses, Calvin observes that the law of Moses was never intended to nullify or state a principle that opposes the promise. In order to sort out the complex argument of the apostle Paul, Calvin insists that we need to distinguish the different ways in which the apostle speaks of the law. Though there is a contrast between the law and the gospel on the question of justification, the law of Moses ultimately serves the ministry of the gospel promise. "I again repeat that if you do not understand that the promise is free, this statement will be quite empty, for the law and the Gospel are not at variance except that, in regard to justification, either the law justifies a man by the merit of works or the promise bestows righteousness freely."[62] The law was not given through Moses as a means or instrument of justification, for that, according to Calvin, would "make the promise of none effect."

According to Calvin, when Paul contrasts the law and the gospel in Galatians 3, he emphasizes only one of the uses of the law, namely, the pedagogical use whereby the law directs its recipients to Christ as the only Mediator. But Calvin hastens to warn against a possible misunderstanding of Paul's comments about the law. "Readers must be put on their guard on this matter; for I see many make the mistake of acknowledging no other use of the law than what is

62. Comm. Gal. 3:17, *CNTC* 11:59 (*CO* 50.213).

expressed here. But elsewhere Paul himself applies the precepts of the law to teaching and exhortation (2 Tim. 3.16). There this definition of the use of the law is not complete and those who acknowledge nothing else in the law are wrong."[63] In addition to the pedagogical use of the law as a teacher of sin and a schoolmaster that directs its recipients to Christ the Mediator, the law of Moses was given to Israel as a comprehensive rule of life. On the one hand, the law of Moses directs the people of Israel to look to Christ, who is the end or fulfillment of the law. Now that Christ has come, this peculiar function of the law is finished. In this way, the law of Moses was preparatory to the coming of Christ in the fullness of time. On the other hand, the law of Moses was given as a comprehensive rule of life, which reveals to the redeemed people of God the manner of life and grateful devotion that pleases the Lord. As a rule of conduct, the law of Moses is given within the context of God's gracious promise, not as an instrument for obtaining life and acceptance with God, but as an instrument for regulating Israel's sincere obedience to him.

> [Paul] affirms that under the reign of Christ there is no longer a childhood which needs to be ruled by a schoolmaster, and that consequently the law has finished its task. This is another application of the comparison. He had undertaken to prove two things: that the law is a preparation for Christ, and that it is temporary. But here again it may be asked whether the law is so abolished that it has nothing to do with us. I reply that the law, so far as it is a rule of life, is a bridle which keeps us in the fear of the Lord, a spur to correct the slackness of our flesh, in short, so far as it is profitable for teaching, correcting, reproving, that believers may be instructed in every good work, is as much in force as ever, and remains intact.[64]

For Calvin, Paul's argument does not warrant the conclusion that the Mosaic administration is opposed in any substantial way

63. Ibid., *CNTC* 11:61 (*CO* 50.215).
64. Ibid., *CNTC* 11:67 (*CO* 50.221).

to the gospel promise. Rather than being at odds with the gospel promise, the Mosaic economy has only "ended in so far as it differs in outward aspect from the covenant of grace."[65]

Though it would be instructive to review how other Reformed theologians in the orthodox period treat Paul's argument in Galatians 3, it is interesting to observe that a more recent Reformed biblical theologian, Herman Ridderbos, offers a strikingly similar interpretation to that of Calvin, in his magisterial work, *Paul: An Outline of His Theology*.[66] Ridderbos's interpretation of Paul's argument in Galatians 3 differs markedly from that of Gordon and follows closely Calvin's view of the Mosaic economy.

In his interpretation of the apostle Paul's view of the law of Moses, Ridderbos acknowledges that there is an apparent inconsistency between the way Paul treats the redemptive-historical function of the law in passages like Galatians 3 and 4, as well as Romans 10, and the "positive purpose" of the law in the OT economy.[67] In the OT economy, the law was given within the framework of redemption and served to regulate the conduct of the people of God in the Land of Promise. Within this framework, the law was not intended to serve as the basis for Israel's justification and life before God. The law was intended to set forth a positive rule of conduct for the people of God. However, in Paul's references to the law of Moses in Galatians 3 and 4, he speaks negatively of the law as a covenant "that brings forth children of slavery" and sharply contrasts the law with the righteousness of faith. According to Ridderbos, Paul's characterization of the law's function in these passages poses "an exceedingly complex problem" that can be put in the form of the question:

> [C]an the redemptive-historical significance Paul ascribes to the law be thought to be in harmony with the foundation on which the law was given in the OT (Exod. 20:2), and on which its

65. Ibid.

66. Herman Ridderbos, *Paul: An Outline of His Theology*, trans. John R. De Witt (Grand Rapids, MI: Eerdmans, 1975).

67. Ibid., 153.

> demand is intended to function, as appears from the whole OT revelation of God?[68]

Since the law was never given to Israel as an instrument for obtaining justification and life, Paul's contrast between the law and the promise in Galatians 3 seems inconsistent with the purpose and function of the law in the OT economy. In his treatment of this complex problem, Ridderbos offers several general observations that correspond at a number of points with emphases we have already witnessed in the writings of Reformed theologians, including Calvin, of the orthodox period.

First, Ridderbos notes that a resolution of the problem of Paul's negative appraisal of the law of Moses must be consistent with the apostle's teaching that the Mosaic administration also taught the righteousness of faith. "It should be maintained first that, for Paul the advent of Christ does not mean the great redemptive-historical incision in the sense that it was only with Christ that the possibility of faith had come, and that prior to it righteousness by the law was the only way of salvation assigned to Israel."[69] Ridderbos notes that the apostle Paul taught that "the way of faith . . . constituted the essence of the OT economy of redemption," and that Abraham was justified by faith and not by works (Rom. 4). Remarkably, the apostle Paul even appeals to pronouncements in the law of Moses to confirm the gospel of righteousness by faith (Rom. 10:6–13; Gal. 3:11; 4:21). Unless the apostle Paul contradicts himself, we must assume that his negative assessment of the law of Moses in Galatians 3 does not include a negative assessment of the Mosaic economy as a whole. For Ridderbos, it would be a mistake to conclude from Paul's argument in Galatians 3 that the apostle regarded the Mosaic economy to be at variance with the gospel promise previously revealed through the Abrahamic covenant. Such a conclusion would imply that the apostle Paul's view of the Mosaic economy was inconsistent and contradictory at key points.

Second, Ridderbos further argues that when Paul appeals to

68. Ibid.
69. Ibid., 154.

the law of Moses in a positive manner to confirm the gospel of salvation by grace through faith, he refers to the law in "the larger sense, and not the law 'consisting in commandments and ordinances.'"[70] In the course of his polemic against the Judaizers, Paul opposes not the Mosaic administration in its entirety, but the failure of his opponents to "see the law in the proper light." When the law is abstracted from its place within the broader framework of the OT economy, it can be viewed, as was true in the case of Paul's opponents, "as a means for setting up their own righteousness" before God. By isolating the law from its setting within the broader framework of the Mosaic administration, Paul's opponents were wresting the law to an inappropriate purpose, namely, as a means for obtaining righteousness and life before God.

Third, Ridderbos maintains that the apostle Paul engages his opponents by proceeding from their standpoint, namely, from the law "as it functioned in the synagogue's doctrine of redemption." The negative manner in which Paul describes the righteousness of the law can only be understood in terms of the position of his opponents, whose view of the law was opposed to the gospel of the righteousness of faith through Christ.

> Now, it is from this law, as it functioned in the synagogue's doctrine of redemption opposed by him, that Paul again and again proceeds, the law as he saw it before him in the life of the Jews, the law as he himself had also lived from it (Phil. 3:6), that is, the law before Christ and the law without Christ. That he is able to see the function of the law in another way as well, in the light of grace and of faith, as the rule for the new life, is apparent from the manner in which presently he will again connect the life that is from the Spirit with the law (Rom. 8:4, *et al.*). But in the antithesis with Judaism this function of the law does not arise, but the ultimate consequence is drawn from what takes place when the sequence of salvation and law is reversed, and the law itself is made a means of salvation. One can say, therefore, that

70. Ibid.

> in combating the Jewish doctrine of the law Paul starts from the Jewish standpoint and from thence makes plain what happens to the law and to man and what from God's side must happen when righteousness and life are anticipated from the law and not from the promise, from human volition and endeavor and not from the power of the Spirit.[71]

For Ridderbos, Paul's negative appraisal of the law represents a kind of *argumentum ad hominem*, an argument that proceeds from the mistaken standpoint of his opponents in order to prove the impossibility of any attempt to seize upon the law as an instrument of self-justification before God.

Fourth, after these preliminary observations about Paul's argument, Ridderbos identifies the most difficult question regarding Paul's negative evaluation of the law in a passage like Galatians 3. If Paul's argument proceeds from the false standpoint of his opponents, who sought to use the law as an instrument for self-justification, then the apostle "would in essence have taken his point of departure in a false position."[72] Moreover, if the apostle proceeds from the false standpoint of opponents, who seized upon the law as a means of self-justification before God, how can we explain Paul's appeal to Leviticus 18:5? To put the question in the sharpest terms, "[w]ould Paul . . . have cited Leviticus 18:5 in support of a false prophecy?"[73] On the surface, Paul's appeal to this passage seems to assume that the law not only requires obedience, but also that such obedience is in some sense the proper basis for obtaining life and salvation. Rather than opposing the standpoint of the Judaizers, this passage appears to argue that Moses taught the principle that life may be obtained on the basis of works.

In his response to this difficult question, Ridderbos identifies two possible explanations of what Paul is doing, each of which poses insuperable problems. The first explanation is that Paul does attribute the view of his opponents to Moses, and in doing so implies that Moses taught a view regarding the way of justification and life

71. Ibid., 154–55.
72. Ibid., 155.
73. Ibid.

before God that was based upon works. According to this explanation, Paul's appeal to Leviticus 18:5 means that he understood Moses to teach the propriety of pursuing a legal righteousness as a means of self-justification before God. In Ridderbos's judgment, this explanation cannot be correct, since Paul appeals elsewhere to Moses precisely to refute such a legalistic pursuit (e.g., Rom. 10:6).

The second explanation that Ridderbos identifies is especially significant, since it resembles closely the explanation offered by Gordon in *TLNF*. In this explanation, Moses is understood by Paul to have "posited two possibilities, of which the first (righteousness by the law) was intended by him as a way impossible for the sinner."[74] According to Ridderbos, there are two difficulties with this interpretation of Paul's argument and appeal to Leviticus 18:5. In the first place, Leviticus 18:5 in its original setting and in accordance with "the intention of Moses" communicates a "rule of the covenant," namely, that life and blessing within the covenant require obedience to God's statutes. The point of this text in its original setting is not to invite Israel to obtain life on the basis of her obedience, and to show thereby that such obedience is impossible. The point of the text, as is true of the giving of the law of Moses in general, is to summon Israel to grateful and sincere obedience. In his own understanding of the Christian life as a life of "faith working through love" (Gal. 5:6), the apostle Paul also affirms the positive place of obedience in the life of God's redeemed people. And in the second place, when Paul appeals to Leviticus 18:5 against those who seek to establish their own righteousness before God based upon obedience to the law, he properly reminds his opponents "that he who strives after the righteousness that is by the law is then bound to the word of Moses, that is, to do what the law demands." In Ridderbos's understanding of what Paul is doing, "[t]his is not an appeal to Moses in support of 'a false position,' but a binding of this position to its own point of departure: he who seeks righteousness in the law faces, as appears from the law itself, the requirement of doing (cf. Gal. 3:10, 12)."[75]

74. Ibid., 156.

75. Ibid. Moisés Silva offers a very similar interpretation of Paul's argument in Galatians 3. Silva notes that Paul's treatment of the law in Galatians, especially when he opposes

> What Paul means to say is this, that he who strives after the righteousness that is by the law is then bound to the word of Moses, that is, to do what the law demands. Likewise the wrong use of the law, to be zealous for the law without understanding, finds in the law itself the standard to which, if it is to have a chance of success, it must measure up. In that sense it can be said that Moses (or the law itself) "defines" the righteousness that is of the law.[76]

Ridderbos's explanation of Paul's argument conforms in all important respects with the one we have seen in Calvin and other Reformed covenant theologians. When Paul appeals to Leviticus 18:5, he is not offering a complete account of the nature of the Mosaic administration. Rather, Paul is showing to his opponents the futility of any attempt to make the law an instrument of justification before God. For, if the law is seized upon as an instrument of justification, then it places its recipients under the burden of doing all that the law requires.

Typology in the Mosaic Covenant

One feature of the biblical arguments for the doctrine of republication in *TLNF* that requires assessment is the typology of the

---

the law to the promise, is "colored" by the position of his opponents, who were seizing upon the law as a means of self-justification or as the "source" (not the "manner") of life before God. See Moisés Silva, *Interpreting Galatians: Explorations in Exegetical Method*, 2nd ed. (Grand Rapids, MI: Baker Academic, 2001), 187–95; Silva, "Abraham, Faith, and Works: Paul's Use of Scripture in Galatians 3:6–14," *WTJ* 63, 2 (2001): 251–67; and Silva, "Faith versus Works of Law in Galatians," in *JVN2*, 217–48. Interestingly, Silva rejects Meredith Kline's interpretation of Paul's view of the law in the argument of Galatians, noting its similarity with the views of historic Lutheranism and dispensationalism (*Interpreting Galatians*, 190). Silva also shares Ridderbos's (and Calvin's) view that, when Paul speaks in Galatians 3 of those who are "of the works of the law," he means to speak of those who "rely upon" or appeal to the law as an instrument of justification before God. See especially his "Faith versus Works," 222–26. This view is, as we have seen, strongly criticized by Gordon in his contribution to *TLNF*. See also Thomas R. Schreiner, *Romans* (Grand Rapids, MI: Baker, 1998), 551–62; and Schreiner, "Appendix: Mark Karlberg's View of the Mosaic Law," in *The Law and Its Fulfillment: A Pauline Theology of Law* (Grand Rapids, MI: Baker, 1993), 247–51. Schreiner follows in the trajectory of Ridderbos's and Silva's interpretation, and offers a critique of the kind of doctrine of the Mosaic administration that is represented in *TLNF*.

76. Ridderbos, *Paul*, 156.

Mosaic economy. When some of the authors speak of the typology of the Mosaic administration, they mean to refer in part to the way the Mosaic economy repeated the probation of Adam in the garden and pointed forward to the obedience of Christ, the "last" Adam (36–87, 97–98). Just as Adam was required to be obedient in order that he might obtain the promise of eschatological life, so Israel was required to be obedient in order that she might maintain tenure and enjoy blessings in the land of Canaan (118–19). At the administrative level, therefore, the Mosaic economy republished the works principle of the covenant of works in order to teach Israel to recognize her sinfulness and to point forward to Christ whose perfect obedience obtained the inheritance of eternal life for believers. With respect to Israel's corporate enjoyment and retention of her covenant inheritance, tenure, and blessing in the Land of Promise, the Mosaic covenant repeated the works-inheritance principle of the prelapsarian covenant of works. At the level of Israel's earthly inheritance, the Mosaic administration functioned typologically to reveal the need for the perfect obedience of Christ, who "merited" the inheritance of eternal life for the elect people of God. By means of the repetition of the works principle, Israel was taught the impossibility of obtaining her ultimate spiritual inheritance of eternal life in God's kingdom in any other way than through the obedience of Christ.

There are two observations that need to be made about this feature of the biblical argument of the authors of *TLNF*.

First, the stimulus and source for this understanding of the typology of the Mosaic covenant is undoubtedly the biblical-theological formulations of Meredith Kline. In the writings of Reformed theologians in what I have termed the "formative" period of the formulation of covenant theology, the language of a "works principle" in the Mosaic economy is not found. However, this language is frequently employed by Meredith Kline in his biblical theology of the covenants of works and of grace, and it is evident that Kline's formulations lie behind those of several of the authors of *TLNF*. The idea that the covenant of works was republished "in some sense" is a significant part of Kline's understanding of the distinctive nature of the Mosaic economy. In Kline's view of the

Mosaic economy, there are two levels or strata that reflect distinctive inheritance principles. At the basic and organic level of the Mosaic administration as an administration of the covenant of grace, the salvation of the individual member of the OT people of God was by grace through faith in Christ. However, at the level of the Mosaic economy as an administration that republished the covenant of works, Israel's national inheritance of and tenure in the Land of Promise was based upon a works principle. The following statement of Kline's view illustrates the basic similarity between his conception of the typological function of the works principle in the Mosaic economy and that of several of the authors of *TLNF*:

> [T]he old covenant order was composed of two strata and the works principle enunciated in Leviticus 18:5, and elsewhere in the law, applied only to one of these, a secondary stratum. There was a foundational stratum having to do with the personal attainment of the eternal kingdom of salvation and this underlying stratum, continuous with all preceding and succeeding administrations of the Lord's Covenant of Grace with the church, was informed by the principle of grace (cf., e.g., Rom 4:16). Because the Abrahamic covenant of promise found continuity in the Mosaic order at this underlying level, it was not abrogated by the latter. *The works principle in the Mosaic order was confined to the typological sphere of the provisional earthly kingdom which was superimposed as a secondary overlay on the foundational stratum.*[77]

A cursory reading of this rather complex statement of Kline's view demonstrates the significant parallels between his conception of the typology of the Mosaic economy and that of the authors of *TLNF*.

Second, the claim that the Mosaic economy republished the covenant of works in a typological manner with respect to Israel's inheritance and blessing in the land of Canaan begs some important

77. Meredith Kline, *Kingdom Prologue: Genesis Foundations for a Covenantal Worldview* (Overland Park, KS: Two Age Press, 2000), 321 (emphasis added). See also Meredith Kline, "Gospel until the Law: Rom 5:13–14 and the Old Covenant," *JETS* 34, 4 (1991): 434.

questions regarding the nature of biblical typology. Though this is a complicated topic in the history of theology, biblical types may be defined as those features, including events, persons, or institutions, of the OT that prefigure or foreshadow their NT realities.[78] Biblical typology focuses upon those features of the OT economy that typify, symbolize, and foreshadow features of the NT economy. As Geerhardus Vos observes, "[a] typical thing is prospective; it relates to what will become real or applicable in the future."[79] An obvious and important instance of biblical typology is the OT tabernacle and temple.

> The tabernacle affords a clear instance of the coexistence of the symbolical and the typical in one of the principal institutions of the Old Testament religion. It embodies the eminently religious idea of the dwelling of God with His people. This it expresses symbolically so far as the Old Testament state of religion is concerned, and typically as regards the final embodiment of salvation in the Christian state.[80]

For our purpose, it is important to observe that biblical typology assumes the essential similarity in meaning and symbolism between the OT type and the NT reality to which it points forward. To use the broad language of "promise" and "fulfillment," the types of the old covenant economy are promissory of their fulfillment in the new covenant economy.

From the vantage point of this understanding of the nature of biblical typology, it is difficult to make sense of the claim that the Mosaic administration functioned typologically as a kind of covenant of works, at least at the stratum of Israel's inheritance of temporal blessings. In order for this to be the case, a disjunction has

78. T. Norton Street, *How to Understand Your Bible*, rev. ed. (Downers Grove, IL: InterVarsity, 1974), 107, offers the following helpful definition of a biblical type: "A type can be defined as a divinely purposed, OT foreshadowing of a NT spiritual reality." For a more fulsome discussion of biblical typology, especially as it relates to the Mosaic economy with its types and ceremonies, see Geerhardus Vos, *Biblical Theology: Old and New Testaments* (Grand Rapids, MI: Eerdmans, 1948), 144–82.

79. Vos, *Biblical Theology*, 144.

80. Ibid., 148.

to be posited between Israel's inheritance of temporal blessings and her inheritance of spiritual blessings. In the usual view of Reformed covenant theology, however, the temporal blessings promised Israel are regarded typologically as a foreshadowing of the full spiritual blessing of fellowship with God in a renewed creation. The promise to Israel of blessing and life in the Land of Promise represented in the state of her immaturity a picture of the fullness of salvation in the life to come. Canaan was a type of the "city that has foundations, whose designer and builder is God" (Heb. 11:10). Moreover, in Kline's view of the typology of the Mosaic covenant, two radically opposed inheritance principles are posited, each of which is said to operate at a distinct level of Israel's life, the earthly and the spiritual. In the case of Israel's earthly inheritance, the operative principle is one of (meritorious) works; in the case of Israel's spiritual inheritance, the operative principle is that of grace alone. The problem with this conception is that the typology of the Mosaic economy does not foreshadow or prefigure, at least at the level of Israel's existence as a nation in the Land of Promise, the blessings that are granted freely and graciously to the new covenant people of God. The blessings are different in kind; and the principles for the inheritance of these blessings are radically different. To put the matter differently, because the Mosaic administration actually consists of two levels of covenant administration, one of works and the other of grace, it cannot function at both levels as a typological promise of the new covenant, which is essentially and exclusively a covenant of grace.

Since the problem with this understanding of the typology of the Mosaic covenant has been summarized by O. Palmer Robertson, I will conclude with his assessment of the way it conflicts with the general nature of biblical typology:

> Kline's view of the Mosaic economy as a "covenant of works" is fundamentally flawed at several points. He bases his case on the assumption that in God's redemptive covenants a distinction can be made between the basis of temporal benefits and salvific benefits. But in scripture these two aspects of redemption are both matters of grace. He must also assume that a difference

> in the basis for operation may be made between the typological experience of Israel and the redemptive experience. But Vos effectively makes the point that the typological can communicate in its essence nothing different than the symbolized reality it portrays (*Biblical Theology*, 145–46). Kline's definition of the Mosaic covenant as a covenant of meritorious works is also flawed by its effort to make a radical distinction between the basic nature of the Abrahamic and Davidic covenants in comparison with the Mosaic covenant. The same typological images present in the Abrahamic and Davidic covenants may be found in the Mosaic, and the same type of law condition in relation to promise is found in all three covenants. David admonishes his son/successor Solomon to "keep [God's] decrees and commands, his laws and requirements, as written in the law of Moses, so that . . . the Covenant Lord may keep his promise to me" (1 Kings 2:3–4 NIV). David obviously saw his covenant relation to the Lord as an extension of the Mosaic covenant and had no problem joining commandments to promises.[81]

Robertson's point is the same one that I wish to make. Consistent with the pattern of biblical typology, the promises and demands of the Mosaic economy are "typical" of the promises and demands of the new covenant economy. The redemption promised in the covenant of grace always requires the response of faith and sincere, albeit imperfect, obedience on the part of the people of the covenant. As it was in the covenant administration of Moses, so it is in the covenant administration of Christ.[82]

81. O. Palmer Robertson, *The Christ of the Prophets* (Phillipsburg, NJ: P&R Publishing, 2004), 364–65n6.

82. In this connection, it is instructive that Estelle finds Geerhardus Vos's treatment of the "Sinaitic covenant and legal merit" unclear, because Vos treats the obligations of obedience under the Mosaic covenant to be nonmeritorious and of one piece with the obligations of obedience under the new covenant economy. In my judgment, Vos's treatment of this topic is quite clear, even though it militates against the conception that Estelle and other authors of *TLNF* wish to defend. Vos, in his *Biblical Theology*, 127, states the matter nicely: "It is plain, then, that law-keeping did not figure at that juncture as the meritorious ground of life-inheritance. The latter is based on grace alone, no less emphatically than Paul himself places salvation on that ground. But, while this is so, it might still be objected that

Theological Ambiguities or Problems

Before concluding this critical review of *TLNF*, I wish to identify several theological ambiguities or problems that recur throughout the volume. Each of these ambiguities or problems warrants more elaboration than I will give them here. However, they are of sufficient importance to warrant notice and represent at best several important items of unfinished business in the elaboration and defense of the coherence of the republication thesis.

One in Substance, Diverse in Mode of Administration

The first of the theological ambiguities of *TLNF* is especially vexing. Though the authors of the volume profess their adherence to the historic Reformed theology of the covenants, they offer an account of the Mosaic economy that seems at odds with the classic Reformed position that there are only two covenants, a prelapsarian covenant of works and a postlapsarian covenant of grace, of which the Mosaic covenant is a particular administration. The traditional formula of Reformed covenant theology, that the covenant of grace is one in substance though diverse in administration, entails that the Mosaic covenant was *substantially* a covenant of grace and only *accidentally* distinct from other administrations of the covenant of grace. This means that the distinctive features of the covenant of grace, which distinguish it in substance from the covenant of works, characterize the Mosaic administration in its entirety. It also means that whatever features of the Mosaic administration distinguish it from

law-observance, if not the ground for receiving, is yet made the ground for the retention of the privileges inherited. Here it can not, of course, be denied that a real connection exists. But the Judaizers went wrong in inferring that the connection must be *meritorious*, that, if Israel keeps the cherished gifts of Jehovah through observance of His law, this must be so, because in strict justice they had earned them. The connection is of a totally different kind. It belongs not to the legal sphere of merit, but to the symbolico-typical sphere of *appropriateness of expression*." The point Vos is making can be stated more succinctly: OT believers were called to receive the redemptive promises of God by faith alone, but the faith of OT believers, like that of NT believers, was a faith "ever accompanied" by a sincere obedience to God's commandments. Believers are always saved by a faith that works through love in grateful devotion to God. To insist upon this does not raise the fearful specter of "merit" in the relation between believers and their covenant Lord, since the graces of free justification and progressive sanctification are freely granted by God himself to those whom he is pleased to save, namely, the elect.

other administrations of the covenant of grace belong to the category of adjuncts or accidents, which do not materially affect its nature or character.

The theological problem posed by the republication thesis can be stated rather simply. If what belongs to the substance of the covenant of works does not belong to the substance of the covenant of grace *in any of its administrations*, it is semantically and theologically problematic to denominate the Mosaic administration as *in any sense* a covenant of works. As I observed in my summary of the historic Reformed doctrine of the prelapsarian covenant of works, the substance of the covenant of works is the promise of God to grant life to Adam (and his posterity) upon condition of perfect and personal obedience. The way of life and blessing in the covenant of works is, as its name appropriately indicates, the way of obedience to all of the requirements of God's holy law. Adam's inheritance of life and blessedness in unbroken communion with his Creator was radically contingent upon his own obedience to the covenant's obligations. However, in the covenant of grace, the Lord promises graciously to grant to believers, upon the basis of the saving work of Christ as Mediator, the inheritance of life and blessing in fellowship with himself. Christ's mediatorial work includes not only his substitutionary endurance of the penalty of his people's disobedience to the law of God but also his substitutionary obedience to all of the law's requirements. Though the covenant of grace requires a believing reception of the promise of salvation upon the basis of the work of Christ, this reception, and all of the fruits of obedience that spring from true faith, are graciously bestowed upon the elect people of God. In all of its administrations, the covenant of grace promises life by grace alone through faith in Christ alone. Justification and life in fellowship with God is, in every administration of the covenant of grace, freely granted to believers for the sake of Christ's work as Savior. Because the Mosaic administration of the covenant includes everything that belongs to the substance of the covenant of grace, it communicated the same grace of Christ, albeit in the form of anticipatory types and shadows, as is communicated in the new covenant in Christ. The promises and obligations of the Mosaic economy are substantially the same as the promises and obligations of the new covenant economy.

When the fundamental and substantial differences between the covenant of works and the covenant of grace are acknowledged, it is difficult to see how the Mosaic administration could be in any sense a republication of the covenant of works. For this to be the case, as the authors of *TLNF* argue, the Mosaic administration would have to republish the requirement of personal and perfect obedience as the basis for Israel's inheritance of life and blessing in fellowship with God. The repetition of the "works principle" of the covenant of works in the Mosaic economy, to use the language of the authors of *TLNF*, would constitute at least one aspect of its administration of the covenant of grace. At some level of the covenant's administration, Israel's life and blessedness would be based upon meritorious works, or at least works that were the covenanted basis for some dimension of Israel's life in fellowship with God. The difficulty posed by this conception is that it ascribes to the Mosaic economy at some level a principle that is in substantial conflict with its essentially gracious character. To use the scholastic language of "substance" and "accidents," the authors of *TLNF* posit the presence within the Mosaic economy of a principle that belongs substantially to the economy of the covenant of works. In doing so, the Mosaic economy is viewed as though it included features at some level of administration that belong to the substance of a different covenant, namely, the prelapsarian covenant of works.

Another way of stating the theological problem posed by the republication thesis is to compare it to some of the views expressed during the history of Reformed reflection on the Mosaic economy. The viewpoint represented by the authors of *TLNF* seems closer to minority opinions that were represented in the history of Reformed theology, but that were never the consensus opinion. For example, in our summary of Turretin's view in the preceding, we noted that he identified at least four distinct views on the question of the peculiar character of the Mosaic administration. Two of these minority views, which Turretin and the majority of Reformed theologians repudiated, were the "mixed" covenant view, which regarded the Mosaic administration as a covenant of grace but also at some level as a covenant of works, and the "subservient" covenant view, which regarded the Mosaic administration as a characteristically legal covenant that was preparatory for the covenant of grace in Christ. Though it lies outside of the purview of this chapter to sort out the complexities of these various views of the Mosaic administration in the history of Reformed theology, there are considerable similarities between these alternative, albeit minority, viewpoints in the tradition and the view of the authors of *TLNF*. These similarities undermine the claim of the authors of *TLNF* to be representing the historic consensus of Reformed theology on the Mosaic administration.[83] They also confirm that the republication thesis does not cohere well with the general consensus that the Mosaic economy was substantially a covenant of grace with certain distinctive, accidental features.

The Covenant of Works, Voluntary Condescension, and the Covenant of Law

A second theological ambiguity in *TLNF* that requires brief comment arises in connection with the tendency of some authors to equate the moral law of God *as such* with the covenant of works. Though this tendency seems implicit in the general argument of the

83. For a description of these minority views, see *CCT*, 262–72, 301–16. Beach argues that Turretin represented the consensus view among Reformed theologians: "Turretin asserts that this covenant [the Mosaic] can be viewed in a bifurcated way: the first way, which is also the proper and principal way, is to view this covenant according to God's own intention and design, namely as leading to Christ; the second way is to view this covenant as separate from Christ and abstracted from him. . . . But this [second way] isn't how the Sinaitic covenant is properly considered, for the divine intention wasn't that 'man might have life from the law' or that humans as sinners 'might be simply condemned'; rather, the divine intention was that fallen persons, from a sense of their own misery and weakness, 'might fly for refuge to Christ'" (311). Another minority viewpoint in the Reformed tradition, Cocceius's doctrine of a gradual abrogation of the covenant of works through the successive administrations of the covenant of grace, also bears some similarities to the viewpoint represented by authors of *TLNF*. For a comprehensive study of Cocceius's covenant theology, see Willem J. van Asselt, *The Federal Theology of Johannes Cocceius (1603–1669)*, trans. Raymond A. Blacketer (Leiden: Brill, 2001). Interestingly, Cocceius denied that believers under the old covenant economy enjoyed a true "forgiveness of sins," but only a "passing over" of sins. Rather than being a traditional consensus viewpoint of Reformed covenant theology, the position on the Mosaic covenant espoused in *TLNF* has more similarities with these minority views.

book that the moral law as it was promulgated through Moses was in a sense a republication of the covenant of works, it becomes explicit in VanDrunen's argument in the theological section of the book. According to VanDrunen, the history of Reformed theology reflects an "ambiguity" regarding the prelapsarian covenant of works. While some theologians recognized that the natural or moral law of God was in itself a kind of covenant of works, promising life to those who perfectly obeyed its demands, threatening death to those who were disobedient, others viewed the covenant of works as distinct from the creation of man in God's image. In the view of theologians like Turretin and Herman Bavinck, for example, the covenant of works includes not only the natural obligation of human obedience to God's moral law, but also a positive revelation of God's will and promise of eschatological life. In the prelapsarian covenant of works, these theologians distinguish between the creation of Adam in God's image and the provisions of the covenant of works, which include God's initiative in revealing and granting to Adam the promise of eternal life upon the basis of his obedience and the threat of spiritual death in the event of his disobedience. According to VanDrunen, these theologians fail to recognize that the creation of man in God's image and the natural knowledge of the moral law of God are sufficient conditions for the covenant of works. For VanDrunen, the failure of these theologians to recognize the intrinsically covenantal nature of the natural law represents an ambiguity in traditional Reformed theology that has only recently been clarified in the biblical theology of Meredith Kline, who identifies *simpliciter* the creation of man in God's image with the prelapsarian covenant of works.[84]

VanDrunen's characterization of this "ambiguity" in historic Reformed theology is rather puzzling. There is little evidence that

84. See Kline, *Kingdom Prologue*, 92. For sympathetic elaborations of Kline's covenant theology, particularly his identification of creation and covenant, and his emphasis upon the idea of a "meritorious" works principle in the covenant of works, see Mark W. Karlberg, "The Original State of Adam: Tensions in Reformed Theology," *Evangelical Quarterly* 59, 4 (1987): 291–309; and Lee Irons, "Redefining Merit: An Examination of Medieval Presuppositions in Covenant Theology," in *Creator, Redeemer, Consummator: A Festschrift for Meredith G. Kline*, ed. Howard Griffith and John R. Muether (Greenville, SC: Reformed Academic Press, 2000), 253–69.

many covenant theologians in the orthodox period simply identified the covenant of works with man's creation in God's image and subjection to the moral law of God.[85] Rather than being an ambiguity in Reformed covenant theology, the distinction (without separation) between the creation of man in God's image and the institution of the prelapsarian covenant of works is nearly the unanimous opinion of the covenant theologians of the sixteenth and seventeenth centuries. VanDrunen's claim that there is an ambiguity in Reformed covenant theology on this point is belied by the express language of the WCF, when it describes the covenant as a "voluntary condescension" on God's part. Rather than being an ambiguity in the history of Reformed covenant theology, the consensus opinion expressed in the Confession views the covenant of works as a sovereign and voluntary initiative of God. In the traditional view of Reformed theologians, God not only reveals the covenant of works with Adam by means of what Geerhardus Vos terms a "preredemptive special revelation" but he also freely *grants* an entitlement to eschatological life upon the basis of Adam's personal and perfect obedience. Due to the radical disproportion between the infinite Creator and the finite creature, the obedience of Adam to the moral law of God could never obtain for him anything more than the title of an "unworthy servant" who had merely performed his duty. Obedience to the law of God is required of man as a creature, but God was under no obligation by nature to grant Adam the fullness of glorified life upon the basis of his personal and perfect obedience. When God voluntarily condescended to enter into a covenant with his image-bearer, Adam, he

85. See *CCT*, 57–61, 106–19, for a discussion of Turretin's and the consensus view of the majority of Reformed theologians. Beach's summary of Turretin's view on the relation of creation and covenant captures well the predominant opinion of Reformed covenant theology: "Turretin, however, in refusing to identify creation with covenant has not compromised the goodness of creation or somehow rendered it second-rate; rather, the Creator/creature relationship is incorporated into the covenant relationship and even presupposes it. What Turretin refuses to do, however, is to confuse these relationships, for creatures *as creature* are without rights before the creator. God does not owe humans eternal life as such. Moreover, God does not become the debtor of human beings by creating them, for creation is an act of freedom. This is why Turretin argues that unless God condescends to enter into a covenant relationship with humans, thereby choosing to become man's debtor through an act of goodness and love, they remain without rights before him."

conferred upon him and his posterity a covenanted right to eternal life that was an unmerited favor. Admittedly, it may be misleading to speak of "grace" in the prelapsarian covenant relationship, since the Scriptures ordinarily reserve the term for an unmerited favor that God grants to sinners who have demerited his favor and deserve only condemnation and death. However, the traditional and consensus view of Reformed theologians is that the covenant of works was a voluntary condescension on God's part that could never be "merited" in the proper and strict sense of the term.[86]

The point of my comments is not to settle the question whether Kline's treatment of the relation (or identity) between creation and covenant represents a clarification of a theological ambiguity in Reformed theology, as VanDrunen asserts. The point is that, on this as well as a number of other features of *TLNF*, the authors tend to accommodate their reading of the history of Reformed theology to contemporary theological concerns, especially the distinctive formulations of Meredith Kline.

The Abiding Validity of the Moral Law (Uses of the Law)

The third theological ambiguity in the arguments of the authors of *TLNF* concerns the abiding validity and function of the moral law of God as a rule of conduct for the covenant people of God. Though it may lie outside the purview of the particular focus of the authors, it is strange that little is said in *TLNF* about the positive role of the law of God, whether in the Mosaic or new covenant economies, as a norm for the sincere, albeit imperfect, obedience of God's covenant

86. For a treatment of the question whether Adam's obedience could "merit" the reward of life, see *IET*, 2:710–23; *RD*, 2:569–71; and *CCT*, 112–19, 196–202, 326–28. The following observation of Turretin is of particular significance to an understanding of the most common Reformed view: "Hence also it appears that there is no merit properly so called of man before God, in whatever state he is placed. Thus Adam himself, if he had persevered, would not have merited life in strict justice, although (through a certain condescension [*synchatabasin*]) God promised him by a covenant life under the condition of perfect obedience (which is called meritorious from that covenant in a broader sense . . .)." (*IET*, 2:712). In Turretin's understanding, we may only speak "improperly" of "merit" in the relation between Adam and his Creator. By virtue of the covenant that God condescends to make with Adam, there is a "connection" stipulated between Adam's obedience and the promised reward.

people. In the history of Reformed covenant theology, one of the important themes is the abiding validity of the Mosaic law as a rule of conduct not only for the people of Israel but for the new covenant believer in Christ. Calvin even denominates the use of the law as a rule of gratitude as its "principal" use, and at the same time denominates the law's first use, as a teacher of sin, as merely an "accidental" function owing to human sinfulness after the fall.[87] Even though it may be an argument from silence, it is remarkable to observe how seldom the authors of *TLNF* comment on the positive function of the law to norm the conduct of the covenant people of God. In one of the few instances where this function is addressed, Gordon takes strong exception to John Murray's claim that the covenant obligation of Israel to obey the law of Moses was substantially similar in nature to the obligations of obedience in the new covenant. And in the case of the argument of VanDrunen, it is not even clear whether the moral law, as it is summarized in the Decalogue of Moses, may be viewed as an abiding rule of conduct for the people of God within the spiritual kingdom of the church. In historic Reformed reflection upon the moral law of God, a far more vigorous and positive conception of the role of the law as a rule of gratitude is evident than that found in this volume.

In my estimation the failure of the authors of *TLNF* to affirm vigorously the positive function of the law as a rule of gratitude in the Mosaic economy is not accidental. Because the authors of *TLNF* view the moral law of God to express necessarily the "works principle" of the covenant of works, they do not have a stable theological basis for affirming the abiding validity of the moral law as a rule of gratitude. The argument of the authors seems to be something like the following: because the moral law of God, rooted as it is in God's holy and righteous character, always requires perfect obedience, and because God's moral government requires that obedience be rewarded and disobedience be punished—the moral law is essentially a covenant of works. For this reason, VanDrunen seems compelled to conclude that the moral law of God is no longer the rule of conduct for believers

87. Cf. n47 and n52, above.

in relationship to each other within the "spiritual kingdom" of the church of Jesus Christ. VanDrunen even goes so far as to suggest that the law that is "written upon the heart" of the new covenant people of God is not substantially the same moral law that was promulgated in the Decalogue through Moses. Even though the other authors of the volume do not explicitly make this claim, the implication of their arguments, which equate the law with its demands and consequences with the works principle of the covenant of works, seems to lead in the same direction. For the same reason, the authors assume that WCF 19 supports the republication thesis. However, when chapter 19 affirms the abiding validity of the moral law, it does so to emphasize the positive role of the law as a rule of conduct for the covenant people of God, and not to suggest something like the republication of the covenant of works through Moses.

Perhaps the theological problem at this point can be clarified further in terms of the traditional Reformed view of the various functions or "uses" of the law. In the Reformed tradition, the moral law of God is presumed to be an "abiding" and stable rule of righteousness for human conduct. The holy law of God that governed Adam's conduct as an image-bearer of God before the fall into sin is *identical* in its material content to the holy law of God that governs human conduct, and especially the conduct of God's covenant people, after the fall into sin. There is a great difference, however, between the function of the law within the framework of the covenant of works before the fall and the diverse uses of the law within the framework of the covenant of grace after the fall. Though the nature and demands of the holy law of God remain unchanged after the fall of Adam, the "uses" of the law within the covenant of grace diverge substantially from the "use" of the law before Adam sinned. In Reformed theology, the law has three distinct uses, each of which recurs throughout all of the administrations of the covenant of grace, including the Mosaic administration and the new covenant after the coming of Christ. In its first or "pedagogical" use, the law teaches believers to acknowledge their sin and inability to find favor and acceptance with God upon the basis of their obedience to the law. In this use, believers are taught to flee to Christ and to find in him the righteousness that alone answers to their need. In its second or "civil" use, the law serves to curtail human wickedness and rebellion, especially in the civil arena. Though the civil use of the law does not presume the inward regeneration of the heart, it does serve to restrain externally human sinfulness and disobedience. In its third and principal use, the law functions as a "rule of gratitude" that governs the conduct of believers in their life of grateful devotion to God. Even though believers are not perfectly sanctified in this life, their grateful obedience to the law of God is itself a fruit of the renewing work of the Holy Spirit and a benefit of the gospel of Jesus Christ. In the state of glorification, believers will be perfected in righteousness and be as holy in their personal conduct as they have already been declared through the grace of free justification in this life.

For the purpose of our assessment of the arguments of the authors of *TLNF*, it must be observed that, in none of these three uses of the law of God does the law function at any level as a kind of republished covenant of works. In all of its uses and promulgations after the fall into sin, the moral law serves the gracious purposes of the covenant of grace in Christ. Whether in its "first" or "third" uses, the law does not serve covenantally as a kind of repetition of the prelapsarian covenant of works. Rather, the law serves to communicate the gospel of Christ's person and work, not only in his obedience to all of its obligations on behalf of his people but also in his work of renewing his people in the way of increasing conformity to the law's obligations. In the striking words of Francis Turretin, in the history of redemption "the law is not administered without the gospel, nor the gospel without the law. So that it is as it were a legal-gospel and an evangelical-law; a gospel full of obedience and a law full of faith."[88]

Concluding Observations

Now that I have offered a critical assessment of the primary arguments of *TLNF*, I would like to conclude with several observations.

88. *IET*, 2:268.

These observations are intended to draw together some of the more important aspects of my assessment of the book.

First, though I have some serious reservations regarding the claims of the authors of *TLNF*, I recognize the difficulty of the topic addressed in this volume and, perhaps more importantly, the notable diversity of opinion regarding this topic in the history of Reformed theology. In the course of my review of *TLNF*, it should have been apparent that the question posed by the authors—does the Mosaic administration in some sense republish the prelapsarian covenant of works?—is not new or unknown in the history of Reformed reflection upon the biblical doctrine of the covenants. Already in the early period of Reformed theology, Calvin was aware of the similarities and differences between the diverse administrations of the covenant of grace in the history of redemption. In subsequent Reformed theology, a vigorous debate arose regarding the peculiar character of the Mosaic economy, especially in the light of the contrast between the law and the promise set forth by the apostle Paul in his argument in the letter to the Galatians. In the period of Reformed orthodoxy, the question of Paul's use of Leviticus 18:5 in Romans 10 and Galatians 3 was often discussed and disputed. Some theologians in the Reformed tradition were of the opinion that the Mosaic covenant reiterated the demands of the moral law, together with the consequences of obedience and disobedience, in a way that republished the stipulations and sanctions of the prelapsarian covenant of works. As we noted, especially in connection with Turretin's discussion of this question, several diverse answers were given as to how the Mosaic economy was related to the covenant of works. Viewed against the background of the history of Reformed covenant theology, the particular question of the distinctiveness of the Mosaic administration posed by the authors of *TLNF* is a legitimate one, and one with a long pedigree in the history of Reformed theology. That some contemporary Reformed theologians find the question itself to be puzzling or problematic does reflect, as the editors of *TLNF* observe, a loss of historical awareness and appreciation for the complex history of Reformed reflection on the covenant.

Second, underlying many of the arguments of the authors of

TLNF lies a proper desire to guard the biblical and Reformed doctrine of justification from corruption or distortion. In the historic Reformed view of justification, there is a radical contrast between the law and the gospel, when it comes to the question of the believer's justification and inheritance of life in communion with God. The law *as such* can only demand perfect conformity to God's holy will, and it can only communicate the consequences of obedience and disobedience. Under the conditions of human sinfulness since the fall and disobedience of Adam, there is no way whereby sinners can find favor and acceptance with God through the law. Indeed, the law can only lead to condemnation and death. Believers can only be justified upon the basis of the work of Christ, who fulfilled all the obligations (penal and preceptive) of the law of God on behalf of his people. In Reformed theology, the free justification of believers before God is solely based upon the granting and imputing to believers of the entire obedience and righteousness of Christ, consisting in his active conformity to the requirements of the law and his substitutionary endurance of its penalty. Though my review of *TLNF* offers a number of criticisms of the author's arguments, I fully concur with the authors' aim to uphold and teach the doctrine of justification by grace alone through faith alone upon the basis of the righteousness of Christ alone. As I put it in my description of *TLNF* on the book jacket, the "authors ably refute recent attacks upon the classic Reformed understanding of the grace of free justification on the basis of the entire obedience and sacrifice of Christ alone."

Third, while I recognize the manifest diversity of opinion on the question of the distinctive nature of the Mosaic economy in the history of Reformed theology, my primary objection to the arguments of the authors of *TLNF* is to what I have termed an "accommodated" reading of the sources. Though it is difficult to know finally "in what sense" the authors regard the Mosaic economy to republish the covenant of works, they all embrace some or another version of the republication thesis. Furthermore, they generally agree that the idea of republication was pervasive in the history of Reformed theology, even the predominant view of the tradition as a whole. I do not believe this interpretation of the history of the development of

Reformed covenant theology can stand up to careful historical scrutiny. The majority opinion of Reformed theologians of the orthodox period, and one that is codified in the WCF, is that there are two covenants, the covenant of works and the covenant of grace, that are *substantially* different. The substance of the covenant of works is the promise of life upon condition of Adam's personal and perfect obedience. The substance of the covenant of grace is the promise of life upon condition of faith in Christ, the Mediator. Since the Mosaic administration is an administration of the covenant of grace, which differs from other administrations only in its accidental or incidental features, it hardly seems appropriate to regard it as "in some sense" a republication of the covenant of works. Though it is difficult to determine the pedigree of the version of the republication thesis with which the authors of *TLNF* identify, it seems to be a view that finds its origins more in the recent writings of Meredith Kline than in the writings of theologians of the orthodox period.

Fourth, in my critical assessment of the republication thesis of *TLNF*, I have intimated that the historic Reformed distinction between the "three uses" of the law provides a better answer to the complex question that this thesis aims to resolve. Within the broad framework of the Mosaic administration as a covenant of grace, the first or pedagogical use of the law, which accords with God's own intention, serves to point the people of God to Christ as the only Mediator. In this "use" of the law, which Calvin terms an "accidental" use by virtue of the introduction of human sin through the fall of Adam, believers are taught to recognize their inability to obtain favor with God through the works of the law. In this way, the law serves the gospel and preaches Christ. This use of the law is not even unique to the Mosaic administration, since the law continues, even in the new covenant economy, to serve this purpose. But the law was never given to the people of God after the fall as a kind of covenant of works, that is, as an instrument that demands obedience as the basis at any level of the covenant for the obtaining of life and justification. Such a use of the law, which the apostle Paul opposes in Romans and Galatians, represents a legalistic misappropriation or abuse of the law of Moses. When the law is "wrested" from its evangelical setting and the gospel promise of the covenant of grace, it may be misappropriated as though it were a kind of covenant of works. But this misappropriation of the law does not accord with the divine intention undergirding the Mosaic economy and its promulgation of the law. Furthermore, the third and principal use of the law, in the Mosaic as well as in all other administrations of the covenant of grace, is as a perpetual and abiding rule of righteousness. Though we may speak, to use the language of Ferry, of a "material" identity of content between the moral law of God before and after the fall into sin, the law's function within the covenant of grace is entirely embraced within the framework of redemptive promise. The God of the covenant, who gave the Ten Commandments through Moses at Sinai, invites his redeemed people through the law to a life that pleases him.

And fifth, the tendency to identify the holy law of God with the covenant of works, or what the authors of *TLNF* term the "works principle" of covenant inheritance, creates an instability with respect to the Reformed view of the third use of the law. This instability becomes especially evident in VanDrunen's contribution to the volume. When VanDrunen argues for an identification of the moral law of God with the substance of the covenant of works, he finds it difficult, if not impossible, to affirm the moral law as an abiding rule of righteousness for the conduct of believers within the orbit of the spiritual kingdom of the church. In VanDrunen's view, since the law demands perfect obedience, and since the law necessarily promises eschatological life to its recipients upon condition of such obedience, the promulgation of the moral law of God necessarily republishes the substance of the covenant of works. The "logic" of this argument compels VanDrunen to argue that believers are not governed by the moral law in their relations with others within the spiritual kingdom. However, in historic Reformed covenant theology, the law of Moses, insofar as it republished the moral requirements of God's holy and unchangeable will, constitutes an abiding rule of conduct for the covenant people of God throughout the history of redemption. Though VanDrunen's theological argument for the identification of the covenant of works with the moral law may not be shared by other authors of *TLNF*, it does illustrate the need for further reflection on the subject of the role of the law of God within the framework of the covenants of works and of grace. The implication of the republication thesis, as it is stated by some of the authors, seems to undermine the positive function of the law within the administrations of the covenant of grace.

Part 2

Covenant and Election

4

Covenant and Election in the Theology of Herman Bavinck

In the historical development of Reformed theology, the doctrines of election and covenant are among the most important for the way Reformed theologians have sought to provide a synthetic account of Scripture's teaching. Interpreters of the Reformed tradition have often mistakenly viewed these doctrinal themes as "central dogmas," which provide a basis for a closed system of doctrinal truths, each deduced from a basic principle such as God's sovereignty or the realization of God's saving purpose in Christ through the covenant of grace in its various administrations.[1] Without a doubt, these two motifs have played a dominant role in the long history of Reformed reflection upon scriptural revelation. By emphasizing free and sovereign election, Reformed theology has stressed the monergism of divine grace in the salvation of sinners who bear God's image, but who have been "frightfully deformed" through the ravages of human sin and disobedience.[2] Nothing testifies more starkly

1. For critical assessments of and bibliography regarding the "central dogma" approach to the study of Calvin and the Reformed tradition, including a consideration of the "two traditions" thesis, which argues that the doctrine of the covenant was developed as a kind of theological counterweight to the doctrine of election, see Richard Muller, *After Calvin: Studies in the Development of a Theological Tradition* (New York: Oxford University Press, 2003), 63–80; *ARC*, 14–16; *HBP*, esp. 24–32; *CCT*, 22–60; Lyle D. Bierma, "Federal Theology in the Sixteenth Century: Two Traditions?," *WTJ* 45, 2 (1983): 304–21; and J. Wayne Baker, *Heinrich Bullinger and the Covenant: The Other Reformed Tradition* (Athens, OH: Ohio University Press, 1980).

2. This language is used by John Calvin to describe the consequences of the fall and human sinfulness. Cf. *Institutes*, 2.1–3.

to the truth that salvation is God's work from first to last than the theme of election. Reformed theology's attention to the unfolding of God's gracious purposes in Christ through various administrations of the covenant of grace also highlights its keen awareness of the historical texture of biblical revelation and the old covenant's fulfillment and realization in the work of Christ as Redeemer and Mediator of the covenant.

Despite the virtual unanimity of the Reformed theological tradition on the centrality of these themes of sovereign and merciful election and the historical administrations of the covenant throughout the history of redemption, the precise interplay between election and covenant has often occasioned considerable debate and controversy. Students of the history of Reformed theology in the Netherlands during the nineteenth and twentieth centuries are well aware of the protracted discussions in the Reformed churches during this time frame. Discussions often derived from diverse appraisals of the sacrament of baptism's significance as a sign and seal of the covenant promise. In some instances, divergent opinions regarding the nature of the covenant of grace, particularly its relation to election, generated not only theological controversy but also ecclesiastical divisions among the denominations. To represent these divergences in a somewhat schematic fashion, some theologians articulated the doctrine of the covenant from the standpoint of election; others approached the doctrine of the covenant from the viewpoint of the covenant's administration in history and sharply distinguished the covenant from particular election. The significance of these differences became especially evident in the way children of believing parents were viewed. Should such children be regarded as possessing the gospel grace the sacrament signifies or seals, unless they should fall away in unbelief and disobedience? Or should such children be viewed simply as recipients of an objective promise with an attached "condition" that may or not be fulfilled in them? Or should children of believers be regarded as possessing Christ's grace only upon their subsequent (to baptism) regeneration and conversion? These questions may seem subtle or insignificant, but they arose throughout the history of the Reformed churches in a way that invariably linked theological formulation with homiletical and ecclesiastical practice.[3]

An awareness of the relation between election and covenant in the Reformed tradition, and especially of the long history of controversy regarding this question among the Reformed churches of the Netherlands, provides the occasion for the subject in this and the next chapter of this volume. Herman Bavinck's handling of the doctrines of election and covenant is of special importance both for Reformed theology in general and for an understanding of the history of the period in which he played an influential role. Bavinck was a Reformed theologian of first rank at the end of the nineteenth and the beginning of the twentieth century, and the author of an influential four-volume *Reformed Dogmatics*. Among the topics Bavinck addresses, the doctrines of election and covenant have an especially important place. As with his handling of many theological topics, Bavinck's treatment of these themes displays an admirable grasp of biblical teaching, the history of theological reflection, the codification of the Reformed consensus in church confessions, and contemporary debates respecting these important themes. For these reasons, an exposition of Bavinck's treatment of these doctrines pays theological dividends for any careful student of Reformed theology.

Because Bavinck was also deeply involved in the ecclesiastical and theological debates of his period in the Netherlands, however, his treatment provides a window into the history and controversies within the Reformed churches at that time. On this topic, as with so many others, Bavinck played a mediating and pacifying role. By offering a balanced and moderate statement of the consensus of historic Reformed theology on this controversial subject, Bavinck also provides a model for handling these themes in a later ecclesiastical landscape when continued wrestling with these questions often fractures church community. Though I will note some of the

3. For a comprehensive treatment of this history, the debates regarding covenant and election, and the positions of various participants among the Reformed churches of the Netherlands, see E. Smilde, *Een Eeuw van Strijd over Verbond en Doop* (Kampen: J. H. Kok, 1946).

connections between Bavinck's formulations and the debates of his time, my primary aim is to summarize and analyze Bavinck's formulations of election and of the covenant. For this reason, I will largely limit my appeal to Bavinck's treatment of these doctrines in his four-volume *RD* and in several other theological works that contribute to an understanding of his position. Primary among these works are Bavinck's own one-volume abridgment of his dogmatics, *Magnalia Dei*,[4] and his extensive treatment of the debates regarding "calling and regeneration" in the Reformed churches of the Netherlands at the end of the nineteenth century.[5]

To provide an accurate account and assessment of Bavinck's position, I will begin with a distinct treatment of his handling of the doctrines of election and covenant. After that summary in this chapter, I will turn in the following chapter to his exposition of the interrelation between them, including his important contribution to the ecclesiastical controversies among the Reformed churches in the Netherlands in the late nineteenth and early twentieth centuries. These controversies were provisionally settled in 1905, when the synod of the Reformed Churches in the Netherlands adopted the so-called "Conclusions of Utrecht." Bavinck's role in the formulation of these "Conclusions" is crucial to understanding his view of the relation between election and covenant.

The Doctrine of Election

The nature of the link between God's purpose of election and the realization of his redemptive purpose in the historical unfolding

4. Translated into English as *Our Reasonable Faith* (*ORF*).

5. Herman Bavinck, *Roeping en Wedergeboorte* (Kampen: Ph. Zalsman, 1903). This volume has been published in English translation with the title *Saved by Grace: The Work of the Holy Spirit in Calling and Regeneration*, ed. J. Mark Beach, trans. Nelson D. Kloosterman (Grand Rapids, MI: Reformation Heritage, 2008). Throughout this chapter and the next, I will refer to the English translation of this work. However, references will also be given in parentheses to the Dutch original. For a treatment of the historical occasion for Bavinck's preparation of this volume, see J. Mark Beach, "Introductory Essay," in Bavinck, *Saved by Grace*, ix–lvi; Beach, "Abraham Kuyper, Herman Bavinck, and 'The Conclusions of Utrecht 1905,'" *MAJT* 19 (2008): 11–68; and Smilde, *Een Eeuw*, 152–210, 247–56.

of the covenant of grace remains my primary interest. Therefore, my summary of Bavinck's treatment of these topics in this chapter will be purposefully concise.[6]

The Dogmatic Location and Nature of the Divine Counsel

In the structure of his *Reformed Dogmatics*, Bavinck follows the traditional sequence of the doctrinal *loci*. After an introductory volume on theological *prolegomena*, which deals at considerable length with the formal questions of the nature of theology as a science and the doctrine of divine revelation, Bavinck turns in his second volume to the doctrines of God and man. Within the sequence of topics related to the doctrine of God, Bavinck considers God's eternal counsel only after a lengthy exposition of the knowability of God, the names of God, the incommunicable and communicable attributes of God, and the doctrine of the holy Trinity. This sequence reflects a pattern in the tradition of Western Christian theology that dates back to the medieval period and the great *Summa Theologiae* of Thomas Aquinas.[7] While there have been exceptions to this rule, Bavinck follows that pattern by locating his consideration of the

6. For older treatments of Bavinck's conception of election and covenant, see Smilde, *Een Eeuw*, 152–210; R. H. Bremmer, *Herman Bavinck als Dogmaticus* (Kampen: J. H. Kok, 1961), 198–208, 244–48, 355–62; and Anthony A. Hoekema, "Herman Bavinck's Doctrine of the Covenant" (Th.D. diss., Princeton Theological Seminary, 1953). In the abridged popular version of his dogmatics, *ORF*, Bavinck does not devote a separate chapter to the doctrine of election, but briefly treats the "counsel of God" as the basis and source for all of God's redemptive and re-creative work in history by means of the covenant of grace. Within the eternal counsel of God, there are three related components: God's gracious purpose of election; the achievement of the redemption of the elect through the eternal "counsel of redemption" in which the Son is appointed as head and representative of his people in the accomplishment of their redemption; and the divine appointment of the Holy Spirit as the One who will work out and apply the redemption of Christ to those whom God purposes to save. Cf. *ORF*, 266–68. In what follows, I will consider Bavinck's view of the "covenant of redemption" and its relation to the doctrines of election and covenant. For a recent treatment of Bavinck's formulation of the "counsel of redemption" or *pactum salutis*, see Laurence R. O'Donnell III, "Not Subtle Enough: An Assessment of Modern Scholarship on Herman Bavinck's Reformulation of the *Pactum Salutis* Contra 'Scholastic Subtlety,'" *MAJT* 22 (2011): 89–106. O'Donnell's article explores the relationship between Bavinck's formulation of the "counsel of redemption" and that of Reformed orthodoxy in the seventeenth century.

7. See Thomas Aquinas, *Summa Theologiae*, rev. ed., 5 vols. (1920; repr., Allen, TX: Christian Classics, 1981), 1.22–23.

doctrine of God's counsel, including the election of his people to salvation in Christ, within the framework of the doctrine of God.[8] Any true knowledge of the living and triune God, so far as it is derived from inscripturated divine revelation, must include a knowledge of the triune God's eternal plan or counsel.

At the outset of his treatment of the divine counsel, Bavinck affirms a traditional distinction in Christian theology between the knowledge of God's being and the knowledge of God's works. Even though all human knowledge of God must be derived from his comprehensive revelation of himself through his works and words, we must distinguish the knowledge of God as he necessarily and eternally exists with all of his attributes and the knowledge of God as he voluntarily chooses to act in respect to creation and history.[9] Human knowledge of God's names and attributes, as well as the "incommunicable attributes" of the persons of the holy Trinity, each distinguished from the others though comprising one, incomposite, and eternal Godhead, is knowledge of *who God is.* The knowledge of God's being is comprised of what can be known regarding God's "essential works" that are eternally and immutably true of who God is in the inexhaustible fullness of his triune life. This knowledge of who God is concerns the "works of God as he is in himself" (*opera Dei immanentia ad intra*). For example, to affirm God's "holiness" is to affirm that God is necessarily, immutably, and eternally holy, quite apart from his holy works in relation to the creation he chooses to call into existence and sovereignly rule. By contrast, the doctrine of God's eternal counsel and will belongs, broadly speaking, to the knowledge of *what God does in relation to the entire creation and history.* In

8. John Calvin, e.g., treats the topic of predestination toward the end of Book 3 of his *Institutes* (3.21–24), which describes the communication of God's grace in Christ to believers by the Holy Spirit through the Word of the gospel. In the theology of Karl Barth and the tradition of neoorthodoxy, it is usually argued that the traditional location of the doctrine betrays an approach to the knowledge of God that is "abstracted" from his revelation in Jesus Christ. See Karl Barth, *The Doctrine of God*, vol. 3.1 of *Church Dogmatics* (Edinburgh: T. & T. Clark, 1957), 76–93. For critical evaluations of this claim, see Richard A. Muller, "The Placement of Predestination in Reformed Theology: Issue or Non-Issue?," *CTJ* 40, 2 (2005): 184–210; and Paul Helm, "Calvin, the 'Two Issues,' and the Structure of the *Institutes*," *CTJ* 42, 2 (2007): 341–48.

9. *RD*, 2:342.

distinction from the "purely immanent works of God," we may speak of God's external works or his works as he "goes outside of his being," in order to reveal himself through his creation and providence.[10] Furthermore, these "external works of God" (*opera Dei externa*) are of two distinct kinds: "the works of God *ad intra* (inward) and the works of God *ad extra* (outward). The former are usually designated as 'decrees' and are all included in the one, eternal 'counsel of God.' These decrees establish a connection between the immanent works of the divine being and the external works of creation and re-creation."[11] In the strict sense, therefore, the doctrine of God's eternal counsel is based upon what the Scriptures teach regarding the works of God that have to do with his purpose or plan for creation and re-creation, but that remain inward or are to be distinguished from their realization in the course of the outworking of God's counsel.

According to Bavinck, the divine counsel and decrees of God possess three characteristics. First, all the ideas or components of the divine decrees are "derived from the fullness of knowledge that is eternally present in God."[12] God knows all things, whether "actual" or "possible." His knowledge is as inexhaustible and rich as his own being. What God knows about creation, providence, and re-creation, therefore, is his knowledge of what will become "actual" by virtue of his free decision, but this knowledge is not as exhaustive as his knowledge of himself and all that which is possible. Indeed, compared to the latter, God's knowledge of what belongs to his decrees, however rich and comprehensive it may seem to us, is but a "sketch, a summary, of the depths of both God's wisdom and knowledge."[13] Second, all of God's decrees are based upon "his absolute sovereignty" and freedom.[14] God is under no compulsion so far as his divine counsel

10. Ibid. The technical language Bavinck employs to distinguish these works or "operations" of the triune God is common to the tradition of Reformed theology. For definitions of the traditional understanding of these terms, see Richard A. Muller, *Dictionary of Latin and Greek Theological Terms: Drawn Principally from Protestant Scholastic Theology* (Grand Rapids, MI: Baker, 1985), 211–13.

11. *RD*, 2:342.

12. Ibid.

13. Ibid., 2:343.

14. Ibid.

is concerned. In his self-sufficiency, God does not need the world or find himself compelled to call the creation into existence in order to enrich himself. In this connection, we must sharply distinguish God's "knowledge of himself," which is necessary to who he is, and God's "knowledge of the world," which is based upon his freedom to determine how he will act in respect to the creation and history. And third, a distinction must be drawn between God's decrees and their realization in history. There is a difference between what God in his counsel determines, and what must necessarily follow in the course of the realization of his counsel in history. Even though God's decrees are free and sovereignly determined, when it comes to their realization in the course of history, we must affirm that "in due time they will be realized."[15]

The Doctrine of Predestination

Subsequent to his introductory comments on the dogmatic location and nature of God's counsel, Bavinck briefly summarizes scriptural teaching regarding God's decrees and the historical dispute between an Augustinian and Pelagian conception of God's counsel. In this summary, Bavinck observes that the NT provides a more clear and precise disclosure of the doctrine than the OT, though the entire teaching of Scripture is consistent regarding the sovereign purposes of God and their realization in the course of creation and re-creation. He also notes that the Augustinian doctrine of God's divine counsel has been the predominant and preferred view throughout the history of the church. Though this view was modified in a "semi-Pelagian" direction during the medieval period of scholastic theology, it was restored to greater purity by the Reformers, Luther and Calvin, during the sixteenth century, only to be abandoned or corrupted by later Lutheran and Arminian constructions.[16] One interesting and revealing feature of Bavinck is his careful reflection on the historic debate among Reformed theologians regarding the order of the decrees,

15. Ibid.

16. See ibid., 2:343–61, for Bavinck's survey of the scriptural teaching regarding the divine counsel, as well as the historical debates between Augustinian, Pelagian, and semi-Pelagian formulations of God's decrees.

whether "supra-" or "infralapsarian," although he does not directly address the contemporary debate within the Dutch Reformed churches on this question.[17] While Bavinck judges there are arguments, pro and con, that can be adduced for both positions, he views the complex components of God's counsel in their organic unity rather than in terms of their logical or temporal precedence.

The most significant part of Bavinck's treatment of the divine counsel is his definition of the nature of God's decree(s) in general, and his respective definitions of election and reprobation. Bavinck broadly defines the counsel of God as "his eternal plan for all that exists or will happen in time."[18] Despite important differences of understanding that have marked the history of theological reflection upon God's counsel, Bavinck notes how all Christian theology acknowledges to a greater or lesser degree that history unfolds in accordance with God's sovereign plan or will. Neither pantheism, which identifies what occurs in history with the being of God, nor deism, which views the world's history in relative independence from God's will, are satisfactory viewpoints from the standpoint of historic Christian theism. The counsel of God must be viewed to comprehend "all things that exist or will occur."[19] To exclude anything from the scope of God's eternal counsel would compromise God's independent existence and work as the Creator and Lord of all

17. "Supralapsarianism" is the view of the logical order of the elements of predestination that places the decree to elect and not elect "before" (therefore, *supra* or "above") the decree to permit the fall; "infralapsarianism" is the view that places the decree to elect and not elect "after" (therefore, *infra* or "under") the decree to permit the fall. The first appeals to the principle that "what is first in intention is last in execution" (*quod primum est in intentione, ultimum est in executione*). Bavinck's careful discussion of the differences between supralapsarianism and infralapsarianism, which includes a delineation of the relative merits and demerits of each view, likely reflects the debates of this period often associated with Abraham Kuyper, who favored the supralapsarian view, though not without some qualification. For a discussion of the historical setting of Bavinck's handling of this topic, including Kuyper's position on this question, see Beach, "Introductory Essay," xvi–xx; Beach, "'Conclusions of Utrecht,'" 17–21; and Smilde, *Een Eeuw*, 131–34. It is instructive to note that Bavinck shares Kuyper's criticism of the older views of the elements in God's decree of election; namely, that they did not give special place to God's purpose in creation but subordinated creation entirely to God's purpose to save the elect.

18. *RD*, 2:372.

19. Ibid., 2:373.

things. Whatever transpires in creation and in the whole subsequent course of providence and re-creation must be encompassed within the decree of God. Because the decree of God reflects the nature of its Author, we should think of this decree as "the eternally active will of God, the willing and deciding God himself, not something accidental in God, but one with his being, as his eternally active will."[20] The entire cosmos and its history represent the outworking of the divine counsel. Like the artist who can only "execute his vision in stages," so God executes his one, complex counsel in a series of temporal phases that reveal his nature and purpose.[21]

Within the broad framework of this general definition of God's counsel, Bavinck distinguishes between the decree as it pertains to all creatures and as it pertains to the destiny of humans and angels. In the traditional language of theology, the former and general counsel of God pertaining to all things was termed "providence," while the latter and more particular counsel of God pertaining to humans and angels was termed "predestination."

> While the name does not matter so much, what is important is that the decree of God encompasses all things, not just the determination of the eternal state of rational creatures (predestination), but the ordering and ranking of all things without exception. Predestination, accordingly, was not something considered in isolation, but was a part of God's decree for all things and only a particular application of it. . . . Predestination is providence insofar as it concerns the eternal destiny of humans and angels.[22]

The doctrine of predestination, therefore, sets forth the Scriptures' teaching regarding God's plan to save or not to save human beings who bear his image. Though Pelagianism has historically denied predestination as a component of God's all-comprehensive counsel, fearing it undermines the genuine freedom and responsibility of the creature, Bavinck maintains that Pelagianism is at odds with

20. Ibid.
21. Ibid., 2:374.
22. Ibid., 2:375.

scriptural teaching, the history of Christian theology, and human experience. However difficult the problem of the relation between God's counsel and creaturely responsibility, we must maintain that "by the infinitely majestic activity of his knowing and willing, [God] does not destroy but instead creates and maintains the freedom and independence of his creatures."[23] Pelagianism finally amounts to a denial of the Christian doctrine of creation, since it asserts that the creature may call into existence an act that is strictly unrelated to God and his will. Because the Pelagian doctrine of freedom posits an act unrelated to God's will and undetermined by any antecedent factor(s), it also undermines the foundation for God's "foreknowledge." Even God is incapable of knowing in advance an act that is absolutely indeterminate. In Pelagianism, "God's decree has become completely conditional and has lost its character as will and decree. It is nothing more than a wish whose fulfillment is totally uncertain. God looks on passively and adopts an attitude of waiting; humans decide. Caprice and chance sit on the throne."[24]

Since predestination refers to God's counsel pertaining to the salvation or non-salvation of humans and angels, Bavinck argues that it must be understood to include both reprobation and election. Because divine election constitutes the culmination of God's purposes in predestination, Bavinck treats reprobation first and then concludes with a consideration of election.

Bavinck emphasizes that reprobation is supported by the frequent testimony of Scripture about how God works out his will and purpose in all circumstances, including sin, unbelief, death, and eternal punishment. In all events, even the unbelief and condemnation of sinners who do not find salvation in Christ, God is actively accomplishing his inscrutable, wise, and just purposes. Despite the apparent attraction of a Pelagian denial of a decree of reprobation, Reformed theology must accept the teaching of God's Word that the will and hand of God are expressed in everything that happens. Without pretending to offer a solution to every problem, or a simple explanation

23. Ibid., 2:377.
24. Ibid., 2:382.

of what appears dreadful to human insight, Calvinism "invites us humans to rest in him [God] who dwells in unapproachable light, whose judgments are unsearchable, and whose paths are beyond tracing out."[25] Even the non-salvation of some must be regarded as an outworking of God's eternal counsel. However, Bavinck also observes that the decree of reprobation does not fit within the will and counsel of God in the same manner as the decree of election. The power and will of God in the decree of reprobation may not be affirmed at the expense of a proper view of God's justice. After all, we know from Scripture that, though sin is "not outside the will of God, it is definitely against it."[26] Though sin may not be the "efficient or impelling cause of the decree of reprobation"—if it were, all sinners would be reprobated—it is "the sufficient cause and definitely the meriting cause of eternal punishment."[27] The decree of reprobation undoubtedly has, as do all things, its ultimate cause within the will of God; but the act of reprobation never takes place apart from sin and culpability on the part of those who are not saved. There is not an exact parallel, therefore, between God's decree of reprobation and his decree of election.

Unlike the work of reprobation, the work of election is one in which God takes particular delight. In his purpose to grant salvation to some wholly and exclusively upon the basis of his grace, God acts in a manner that mirrors his perfections and achieves his culminating and consummate purpose. In reply to the Pelagian objection that particular election is unjust, Bavinck notes that all would be lost were salvation a matter of justice. "But now that election operates according to grace, there is hope even for the most wretched. If work and reward were the standard of admission into the kingdom of heaven, its gates would be opened for no one. . . . Pelagianism has no pity."[28] The sheer grace of divine election is the only basis for hope on the part of sinners who are incapable, because unwilling, of embracing Christ for salvation. Though it is often objected that election

25. Ibid., 2:395.
26. Ibid., 2:396.
27. Ibid.
28. Ibid., 2:402.

undermines the invitation of the gospel to respond to Christ in faith and repentance, Bavinck observes that no one has the right to conclude that they are outside the reach of God's electing grace. "No one has *a right* to believe that he or she is a reprobate, for everyone is sincerely and urgently called to believe in Christ with a view to salvation. No one *can* actually believe it, for one's own life and all that makes it enjoyable is proof that God takes no delight in his death. No one *really* believes it, for that would be hell on earth."[29] When it comes to the objects of God's decree of election, Bavinck observes that they are Christ and those who belong to his body, the church. Christ is appointed within the decree of election to be the Mediator and Redeemer of all those who are his members by faith. For this reason, the knowledge of election is always joined to faith in its embrace of the gospel promise in Christ. Moreover, it is not God's goal to elect simply an "aggregate of individuals" who are saved through the mediation of Christ. The goal and outcome of God's decree of election is nothing less than a renewed humanity in union with Christ. The elect represent in the purpose of God the realization of a new and glorified humanity in whom the entire organism of the human race is contemplated. In his decree of election, God loves not a loose collection of individuals but an organism that represents and consummates his love for the whole world.[30]

The Doctrine of the Covenant

In Bavinck's view of the divine counsel, it is evident that predestination and election have to do with God's eternal purpose to save his people in Christ, and that God's intention is no less than the redemption of a new humanity within his comprehensive work of re-creation. The doctrine of the covenant, in distinction from that of election, focuses upon the manner in which God accomplishes his purposes for human beings before and especially after the fall into sin. Bavinck discusses the doctrine of the covenant primarily in

29. Ibid.
30. Ibid., 2:404.

two places in his dogmatics. The first consideration of the covenant between the triune God and humans follows Bavinck's contemplation of the creation of man in God's image. The covenant is not to be regarded merely as a postfall means whereby God restores fallen sinners to fellowship with himself. Rather, the covenant is the divinely appointed instrument whereby from creation onward the triune God chooses to enjoy communion with his image-bearers in the historical unfolding of creation under human stewardship and dominion. The second occasion, a considerably more lengthy treatment of the doctrine of the covenant of grace, is Bavinck's introduction to the doctrine of the person and work of Christ. As was true of our summary of Bavinck's handling of the doctrine of election, our summary of his doctrine of the covenant will identify only the most important features of Bavinck's view. Once we have a clear sense of Bavinck's respective doctrines of election and covenant, we will take up the critical issue of their interrelation.

The Covenant with Adam ("Covenant of Works")

Bavinck introduces his discussion of the covenant between the triune God and all of humanity in Adam before the fall into sin by noting that, in the original state of integrity, Adam did not possess the image of God in isolation from the organic unity of the human race. Nor did Adam possess immediately the image of God in the fullest sense. In the scriptural conception of humanity, a clear distinction is evident between Adam and Christ, the second or last Adam. Even in the state of his original integrity, the first Adam did not yet possess the fullness of life that is secured only through Christ in the final state of glory. "As such, Adam, by comparison to Christ, stood on a lower level. Adam was the first; Christ the second and the last. Christ presupposes Adam and succeeds him. Adam is the lesser and inferior being; Christ the great and higher being. Hence, Adam pointed to Christ; already before the fall he was the type of Christ. In Adam's creation Christ was already in view."[31] This relationship between the first Adam and the last Adam is of

31. Ibid., 2:564.

special importance to a proper understanding of the original covenantal relationship between God and humanity. Only through the second Adam does the fullness of God's dwelling and communion with humanity (given partially in the original covenant relationship between God and man before the fall) find its eschatological realization and fulfillment.

In his introductory comments on the prefall covenant relationship, Bavinck observes that the doctrine of the prefall covenant is based upon several scriptural and theological themes that have deep roots in the history of Christian theology. In the scriptural representation of Adam's relationship with God before the fall, Adam's condition was "provisional and temporary and could not remain as it was. It either had to pass on to higher glory or to sin and death."[32] When God placed Adam under a probationary command of obedience, Adam was threatened with death in the event of his transgression and simultaneously promised a reward of life in the event of his obedience. The reward of eternal life set before Adam is consistently regarded throughout the Scriptures as the goal and outcome of the original covenant, as well as of the covenant of grace. Even though the express language of "covenant" is not used in the Genesis account of Adam's relationship with his triune Creator, Bavinck notes that it may be termed a covenant in Hosea 6:7, and it is certainly the case that the apostle Paul draws a clear "parallel" between Adam and Christ in Romans 5:12–21. Just as the disobedience of the first Adam brings condemnation and death to the whole human race, whom he represented as covenant head, so the obedience of Christ brings justification and life to those whom he represented as covenant head in the covenant of grace. In the history of Reformed theology, the formulation of the relationship between God and Adam in terms of the covenant was largely based upon theological reflection that sought to do justice to this parallel between Adam and Christ. Though Christian theology did not always recognize the implications of this parallel, it was implicit in the long-standing tradition since Augustine of distinguishing Adam's state before the

32. Ibid.

fall and the believer's state in Christ after the fall. The Augustinian distinction between Adam's ability not to sin (*posse non peccare*) and not to die (*posse non mori*) before the fall, and the inability to sin and die (*non posse peccare et mori*) that is bestowed upon the elect out of grace in Christ, requires the formulation of a pre- and postfall covenant.[33]

In the history of Reformed theology, the prefall covenant between God and humanity in Adam has been variously designated. Sometimes it is termed a "covenant of nature," since this covenant required obedience to the moral law of God that man knew by nature and was able to obey by virtue of the created gifts and integrity with which he was originally endowed. However, it is most commonly designated a "covenant of works," since the eternal life promised in the covenant was only able to be obtained "in the way of works, that is, in the way of keeping God's commandments."[34] Bavinck admits that the terminology of a prefall "covenant of works" is not employed in the Reformed confessions as it is in the Westminster Standards. The absence of this terminology does not alter the fact that all of the elements or components of the doctrine are present "materially" in BC 14 and 15, in HC 6–11, and in CD 3/4. These confessional articles provide clear testimony of the original state of humanity in Adam, the obligation of perfect obedience to the law of God, the promise of life upon condition of such obedience, and the consequence of Adam's sin and fall for the whole human race. Because Adam transgressed the covenant, he forfeited for himself and all his posterity any possibility of eternal life in unbroken and unbreakable communion with God. Now the only way to obtain such life is through faith in Christ, the last Adam, who alone is able to grant the fullness of glorified life to those who belong to him. In Bavinck's estimation, the fact that the Scriptures do not explicitly term the prefall state as a "covenant" relationship should not deter Reformed theologians from employing this term. In the Scriptures, it is common to speak of "covenant" as the "fixed form in which the relation

33. Ibid., 2:566–67.
34. Ibid., 2:567.

of God to his people is depicted and presented."[35] Therefore, however much the word may be in dispute, it ought to be acknowledged that the "matter is certain" (*de vocabulo dubitetur, re salva*).[36]

After his introductory comments on the propriety of viewing the original prefall relationship between God and man as a covenant, Bavinck offers several significant arguments for regarding all of the triune God's dealings with his image-bearers as covenantal in nature. The doctrine of a prefall covenant of works expresses a truth that is basic to the whole teaching of Scripture, namely, that "[a]mong rational and moral creatures all higher life takes the form of a covenant."[37] Whether in marriage, family, business, science, or art, human social relationships and interaction invariably take the form of covenants in which there is mutual obligation and intercommunion. This is no less true of the highest and all-embracing relationship between God as Creator and man as his creature. Indeed, there is no possible way human beings could enjoy

35. Ibid., 2:560.

36. In his defense of the doctrine of a prefall "covenant of works," Bavinck stands within the mainstream of historic Reformed theology on the continent of Europe as well as in the Presbyterian tradition. For examples of the consensus view of the tradition, as well as studies of the development and significance of the doctrine, see Zacharias Ursinus, *The Commentary of Dr. Zacharias Ursinus on the Heidelberg Catechism*, trans. G. W. Williard (1852; repr., Grand Rapids, MI: Eerdmans, 1954), 27–36, 97–101; Ursinus, "The Larger Catechism" in Lyle D. Bierma et al., *An Introduction to the Heidelberg Catechism: Sources, History, and Theology* (Grand Rapids, MI: Baker Academic, 2005), Q. & A. 10, 18, 36, 72, 135; Caspar Olevianus, *A Firm Foundation: An Aid to Interpreting the Heidelberg Catechism*, ed. and trans. Lyle D. Bierma (Grand Rapids, MI: Baker Academic, 1995), 9–10; Lyle D. Bierma, *The Covenant Theology of Casper Olevianus* (Grand Rapids, MI: Baker, 1996), 112–20; Bierma, "Covenant or Covenants in the Theology of Olevianus," *CTJ* 22, 2 (1987): 228–50; Peter A. Lillback, *The Binding of God: Calvin's Role in the Development of Covenant Theology* (Grand Rapids, MI: Baker Academic, 2001), 276–304; Paul Helm, "Calvin and the Covenant: Unity and Continuity," *Evangelical Quarterly* 55, 2 (1983): 65–81; Rowland S. Ward, *God & Adam: Reformed Theology and the Creation Covenant* (Wantirna, Australia: New Melbourne Press, 2003); Johannes Cocceius, *Summa Doctrinae de Foedere et Testamento Dei* (1648), par. 11 & 12.; Willem J. van Asselt, *The Federal Theology of Johannes Cocceius (1603–1669)*, trans. Raymond A. Blacketer (Leiden: Brill, 2001), 248–68; John Ball, *A Treatise on the Covenant of Grace* (London, 1645), 14–27; John Preston, *The New Covenant, or, the Saints Portion* (London, 1629), 313–40; *IET*, 1:569–83; 2:169–216; Herman Witsius, *The Economy of the Covenants between God and Man: Comprehending a Complete Body of Divinity*, trans. William Crookshank, 2 vols. (1822; repr., Escondido, CA: Den Dulk Foundation, 1990), 1:41–82.

37. *RD*, 2:568.

blessedness in fellowship with God other than through a covenant relationship. In the first place, the "infinite distance" between God as Creator and man as creature confirms that there is no possibility of communion with God without covenant. In order for God to commune with his image-bearer, not only as a "master" to "servant" but also as "father" to "son," he must "come down from his lofty position, condescend to his creatures, impart, reveal, and give himself away to human beings."[38] In the second place, the idea of covenant always implies a relationship of mutual obligation and commitment. As a mere creature, however, man does not possess of himself any "rights" before God. The creature may never place the Creator in his debt or under obligation, unless God first freely and graciously grants him rights within the context of a covenant relationship. "There is no such thing," Bavinck argues, "as merit in the existence of a creature before God, nor can there be since the relation between the Creator and the creature radically and once-for-all eliminates any notion of merit. This is true after the fall but no less before the fall."[39] In the prefall covenant as well as the covenant of grace after the fall, God grants, by virtue of his condescending goodness and unmerited favor, rights and privileges that would

38. Ibid., 2:569.

39. Ibid., 2:570. Bavinck rejects the idea of "merit" in the relationship between the creature and the Creator, particularly the traditional Roman Catholic distinction between two kinds of merit, "condign" and "congruent" (*meritum de condigno, meritum de congruo*). "Condign" merit is true or full merit and is based upon the good work of the Holy Spirit in the individual believer. "Congruent" merit is a half-merit or human work that does not truly merit God's grace, but receives its reward on the basis of God's generosity. See Muller, *Dictionary*, 190–92. Bavinck does not deny, however, that, whether we use the term "merit" in this context or not, the creature does have a right to the promised inheritance by virtue of the conferral of this right through the divinely initiated covenant relationship. Though Bavinck shies away from using the terminology of "merit" in the prefall covenant relationship, his position is consistent with earlier writers of the Reformed tradition who spoke qualifiedly of a kind of "covenanted merit" (*meritum ex pacto*). Bavinck does not hesitate to employ the language of "merit," however, to describe the obedience of Christ as the last Adam, who fulfills all of the obligations of the law on behalf of his people and thereby justly procures their covenant inheritance. For a summary of the traditional Reformed view that Bavinck affirms, see *IET*, 1:569–86, and esp. 2:712–24. Turretin allows that we may speak broadly and of "merit" in the relationship between Adam and God, if we mean only to say that, by virtue of the covenant relationship, Adam's obedience would justly secure his inheritance of eternal life.

otherwise be beyond man's reach. And in the third place, Bavinck argues that the idea of covenant corresponds to the nature of man as a moral and rational creation, with whom God interacts in a way that respects the unique capacity of his image-bearer to respond to God in free and heartfelt obedience.[40] In all his dealings with his image-bearers, God never treats human beings as he would an irrational or inanimate object. The beauty of the covenant is that it provides a framework within which a fully personal and responsible engagement may transpire between God and human beings, which is analogous to the marriage of a husband and wife, or the relationship between parent and child.

In the concluding section of his consideration of the prefall covenant, Bavinck argues that Reformed theology alone adequately captured the biblical understanding of this covenant. In historic Roman Catholic theology, the doctrine of man's state before the fall included the idea that God as Creator added to man's natural state the "free gift" (*donum superadditum*) of original righteousness and the promise of eternal life. Though this idea bears some formal resemblance to the Reformed understanding of the covenant of works and rightly acknowledges eternal life as an "unmerited gift of God's grace," it differs from the Reformed view by its radical distinction between nature and grace, particularly by its reintroduction of the concept of "condign merit" in the context of man's free cooperation with God.[41] In the Reformed conception of the prefall covenant, greater recognition is given to God's sovereign initiative in the "monopleuric" origin of the covenant relationship and in his gracious promise of eternal life. In the Reformed view, man as creature remains wholly dependent upon his Creator and finds a greater blessedness of glorious communion with God only in the way of obedience to the moral law of God. Moreover, unlike the traditional

40. *RD*, 2:570–71.

41. Ibid., 2:571–72. Though Bavinck closely links God's purpose of creation and the prefall covenant, he shares the majority opinion of the older writers that this covenant involves a distinct "voluntary condescension" on God's part and is not simply inherent in the Creator-creature relationship. See, e.g., *IET*, 1:574–78; and Witsius, *Economy*, 1:41–82. For a survey of this topic, including the identity of some Reformed theologians (e.g. Ursinus) who did not clearly distinguish creation and covenant, see *CCT*, 56–60.

view of Lutheran theology, namely, that Adam possessed in his original state of integrity the "highest possible blessing," the Reformed view never exaggerated the original state of Adam. In the Reformed conception, salvation in Christ brings more than the restoration, through the forgiveness of sins, of fallen man to his original state.[42] Rather, through the work of the last Adam, all who belong to him by faith and participate in the blessings of his saving work are granted the fullness of glory in the immutable and indefectible state that is eternal life. Only in the Reformed conception do we find a proper understanding of the parallel between the first Adam and Christ. In the Reformed doctrine,

> Christ does not [merely] restore his own to the state of Adam before the fall. He acquired and bestows much more, namely, that which Adam would have received had he not fallen. He positions us not at the beginning but at the end of the journey that Adam had to complete. He accomplished not only the passive but also the active obedience required; he not only delivers us from guilt and punishment, but out of grace immediately grants us the right to eternal life.[43]

Interestingly, Bavinck concludes his treatment of the doctrine of the prefall covenant with the same emphasis previously noted in his consideration of the doctrine of election. Just as God's purpose of election terminates not upon an aggregate of individuals but upon the whole organism of a new humanity in Christ, so God's intention in the covenant he establishes with humanity in Adam is to bring the whole of humanity to its appointed destiny in unbroken and glorious communion with himself. The image of God, which Adam possessed but in a less-than-perfect or consummate form, is only fully

42. *RD*, 2:572.

43. Ibid., 2:573. For a similar emphasis upon the significant difference between the Reformed and Lutheran views of the original state of man, see Geerhardus Vos, "The Doctrine of the Covenant in Reformed Theology," in *Redemptive History and Biblical Interpretation: The Shorter Writings of Geerhardus Vos*, ed. Richard B. Gaffin Jr. (Phillipsburg, NJ: Presbyterian and Reformed, 1980), 242–45.

expressed in the whole human race in its organic unity. Adam was not created as an isolated individual, but he was ordained by God as the covenant representative of the whole human race. God's journey with mankind begins with Adam, but this beginning is not to be confused with God's intended goal, which was that his image would be perfectly expressed only in his "finished image." "Only humanity in its entirety—as one complete organism, summed up under a single head, spread out over the whole earth, as prophet proclaiming the truth of God, as priest dedicating itself to God, as ruler controlling the earth and the whole of creation—only it is the fully finished image, the most telling and striking likeness of God."[44] The whole of humanity was by God's ordinance united both juridically and ethically in the first Adam. Therefore, by virtue of Adam's sin and fall, the entire human race has come under the judicial sentence of condemnation and death, and all of Adam's posterity have inherited a sinfully corrupted human nature. This also explains the unity of God's covenant with humanity, whether before the fall in the first Adam or after the fall in the last Adam. Christ, who is the one Mediator of the covenant of grace, is the "antitype" of the first Adam. By virtue of Christ's mediatorial work of perfect obedience to the Father and substitutionary endurance of the penalty of violating the law of God, all those who belong to Christ by faith constitute the new humanity in which God's original and abiding purpose is realized. In Christ believers are restored to union and communion with God, and upon the basis of his entire and perfect obedience are granted the title and inheritance of eternal life in consummate blessedness. Thus, Bavinck concludes that "[t]he covenant of works and the covenant of grace stand and fall together. The same law applies to both."[45] In the overarching purpose of God, Christ is the appointed Mediator who redresses all of the consequences of Adam's sin and transgression and procures for believers the fullness of their covenant inheritance, which is life in unbreakable and perfected communion with the living God.

44. *RD*, 2:577.
45. Ibid., 2:579.

The Covenant of Grace

Bavinck's conclusion of the prefall covenant between God and all humanity in Adam provides a natural link with his subsequent treatment of the covenant of grace in the context of an extended consideration of the Person and work of Christ as Mediator in the third volume of his *Reformed Dogmatics*. Rather than viewing the work of Christ merely as a remedy in the postfall situation for the consequences of Adam's sin, Bavinck views the work of Christ as the realization of God's original intention for covenant communion with his image-bearers. Through Christ, the last Adam and the only Mediator of the covenant of grace, fallen human beings are restored to covenant fellowship with God and obtain the consummate blessing of indefectible life in the community of Christ's body, the church. By means of the salvation of the elect in union with Christ, all of the great and encompassing purposes of God in creation and in redemption reach their fulfillment and goal. Before we turn to Bavinck's particular handling of the relation between God's purpose of election and the covenant he establishes with his people in Christ, therefore, we need to consider the principal elements of Bavinck's conception of the covenant of grace.

As the language of "covenant of *grace*" clearly indicates, the first principal feature of this covenant in its historical manifestation is that it reveals God's favor and disposition to enter into renewed communion with undeserving and fallen sinners. Through the disobedience of Adam under the prefall covenant of works, all of his posterity have been plunged into ruin and despair. There is no way back to communion with God by the covenant of works. However, God in his grace takes the initiative, immediately after the fall into sin, to restore his fallen image-bearers to communion with himself. This exhibits the uniqueness of the Christian religion over all forms of paganism. Rather than the fallen creature working to enter into communion with God, the great emphasis of biblical teaching rests upon the initiatives of God in coming to his fallen creatures to redeem them. "[I]n Scripture the grace of God comes out to meet us in all its riches and glory. Special revelation again makes God known to us as a Being who stands, free and omnipotent, above nature and has a character and will of his own."[46] Because Adam transgressed the law of God and forfeited for himself and his posterity any right under the original covenant to obtain the inheritance of life in communion with God, the grace of God after the fall always comes to expression in the form of a *new* and *gracious* covenant that "arises, not by a natural process, but by a historical act and hence gives rise to a rich history of grace."[47]

Following a long-standing tradition in Reformed theology, Bavinck appeals to the account of God's dealings with Adam after the fall in Genesis 3, especially verse 15, as the embryonic revelation of the covenant of grace in history. Although the terminology of covenant is not found in this passage, it contains in seed form a foreshadowing of the entire history of the covenant of grace and its ultimate realization in Christ, the true "seed of the woman," who would finally crush all opposition to and enmity against God. When God comes to Adam after the fall, he pronounces his curse, to be sure, but he does so in the context of a promise of blessing that triumphs over human sin. Through the fall into sin, Adam and Eve, in a manner of speaking, "covenanted" with Satan, the archenemy of God.[48] Through the "mother promise" of Genesis 3:15, however, God declares that he will break the bond of fellowship between Satan and the seed of the woman and join this people to himself in an irrevocable communion of life and blessing. In doing so, "God graciously annuls it [the covenant between Adam and the power of evil], puts enmity between the seed of the serpent and the woman's seed, brings the seed of the woman—humanity, that is—back to his side, hence declaring that from Eve will spring a human race and that that race, though it will have to suffer much in the conflict with that evil power, will

46. Ibid., 3:197.

47. Ibid.

48. In the history of the development of Reformed covenant theology, Caspar Olevianus was among the first to distinguish this "covenant with the Devil" from the "covenant of grace" that God first established with Adam after the fall. See Caspar Olevianus, *De Substantia foederis gratuiti inter Deum et electos* . . . (Geneva: Eustathius Vignon, 1585), 10, 253. See Bierma, *Caspar Olevianus*, 120–22, for a discussion of this theme in Olevianus. Characteristically, Bavinck's description here as elsewhere closely corresponds to traditional views.

eventually triumph."[49] In the promise made to Adam, God assures him of the continued propagation, development, and salvation of the human race. When Adam embraces this promise with childlike faith, God reckons his faith to him as righteousness. And so begins the course of redemptive history, which is the history of God's work of salvation in Christ and by means of the covenant of grace.[50]

It is significant that Bavinck, also following the tradition of earlier Reformed covenant theology, gives special attention to the meaning of the language of "covenant" in the Scriptures. Contrary to the trajectory of critical biblical scholarship in his day, which often argued that the theme of covenant emerges for the first time at a late point in the history of Israel, Bavinck maintains that the idea of the covenant emerges at the inception of God's work of redemption. Upon the basis of a careful analysis of the usage of the OT term for "covenant" (*berith*), Bavinck concludes that, when it refers to God's covenanting with his people, it contains three principal features: "an oath or promise that includes the stipulations agreed upon, a curse that invokes divine punishment upon the violator of the covenant, and a cultic ceremony that represents the curse symbolically."[51] When God enters into covenant with his people, he establishes a relationship of fellowship with himself that, by virtue of the accompanying oath of self-malediction, places his people "under the protection of God and so achieves a kind of indissolubility."[52] To the question whether the covenant relationship is a kind of mutual "agreement" between parties (bilateral) or a sovereign disposition or grant (unilateral), Bavinck answers that it depends upon how we view the nature of the covenant parties. Since the covenant of grace is initiated and sovereignly secured on God's part, it must be regarded as entirely unilateral in its origin and disposition. God graciously bestows his covenant blessing upon his people, imposes simultaneously the obligations of the covenant, and upholds the covenant in faithfulness in spite of the faltering and unfaithfulness of his people.

49. *RD*, 3:199.
50. Ibid., 3:200.
51. Ibid., 3:203.
52. Ibid.

> In this firmness and steadiness of the covenant of grace lies the glory of the religion we as Christians confess. . . . If religion is to be a true fellowship between God and humanity, fellowship in which not only God but also the human partner preserves his or her independence as a rational and moral being and along with his or her duties also receives rights, this can come into being by God's coming down to humans and entering into a covenant with them. In this action God obligates himself with an oath to grant the human partner eternal salvation despite his apostasy and unfaithfulness but by the same token, the human partner on his or her part is admonished and obligated to a new obedience, yet in such a way that "if we sometimes through weakness fall into sins we must not despair of God's mercy, nor continue in sin," since we have an everlasting covenant of grace with God.[53]

Because the covenant of grace is unilateral in origin and ultimately rendered effective unto salvation by virtue of God's abiding faithfulness, the most common form of the Hebrew term in the Septuagint is *diathēkē* ("disposition") and not *sunthēkē* ("agreement").[54] This linguistic convention confirms that the covenant is ultimately a sovereign bestowal of God whose faithfulness ensures the inviolability of the covenant relationship and guarantees that its promises will be realized in spite of the frequent infidelity of God's people. In this connection, Bavinck also observes that, though the language of the covenant is only infrequently rendered by the term, "testament," which suggests the guarantee of the reception of an inheritance upon the death of the testator, the biblical understanding of the covenant of grace includes the idea of a "testamentary disposition." In the sovereign working of God, Israel's unfaithfulness did not prevent the God of the covenant from gathering in the nation's place "the spiritual Israel, which according to God's election was gathered from all peoples, receives the goods of salvation from the Son as by a testamentary

53. Ibid., 3:204–5. The words in quotation marks are taken from the Form for Infant Baptism, used in the Reformed Churches of the Netherlands since the sixteenth century.

54. *RD*, 3:205.

disposition, stands in a child-Father relation to God, and expects salvation from heaven as an inheritance."[55]

After his general treatment of the central importance and nature of the covenant of grace to the biblical understanding of redemption, Bavinck devotes the remainder of his consideration of the doctrine of the covenant to six topics: (1) a survey of the history of the development of the doctrine of the covenant in Christian, and particularly Reformed, theology; (2) a relatively brief description of the doctrine of a "covenant of redemption" (*pactum salutis*); (3) the distinction between the covenant of grace in its broader and narrower sense; (4) the unity and differences between the various administrations of the covenant of grace throughout redemptive history, especially the difference between the "old" and "new" covenants; (5) the relation between the prefall covenant of works and the postfall covenant of grace; and (6) the relation between election and covenant. For the purpose of our summary of Bavinck's doctrine of the covenant, some of these topics are of greater importance than others. Since I will focus directly upon Bavinck's understanding of the relation between election and covenant in the next chapter, I will reserve comment on this topic until that point. Furthermore, since they are not of immediate importance to the subject of Bavinck's view of election and covenant, I will omit a consideration of Bavinck's interpretation of the history of covenant theology and the differences between the old and new covenants.

The "Covenant of Redemption" (Pactum Salutis)

Within the context of his evaluation of covenant theology's history, Bavinck considers what Reformed theologians termed the "covenant of redemption" or *pactum salutis*. Bavinck observes that Reformed theology, more than the Roman Catholic or Lutheran theological traditions, has distinguished itself historically by the way it fully developed the biblical conception of God's covenant. In the course of its reflection upon the way God initiated and administered the covenant of grace throughout history, Reformed

55. Ibid., 3:206.

theology pursued what way this covenant should be regarded to belong to God's eternal counsel. With characteristic interest in the all-comprehensiveness of God's eternal counsel, it is not enough for Reformed theology to view the covenant of grace merely in terms of its execution and administration throughout history. The question has to be raised regarding its background and foundation within the eternal counsel of the triune God, Father, Son, and Holy Spirit. The answer of historic Reformed theology was its distinctive formulation of the doctrine of an eternal, intra-Trinitarian covenant between the three Persons of the Trinity, which constitutes the basis for the realization of this covenant in time.[56]

Reflecting upon the doctrine of the "covenant of redemption," Bavinck affirms the essential components of the traditional formulation, though he conveys some misgivings regarding the "scholastic subtlety" of some of its expressions.[57] In spite of some questionable appeals to scriptural texts such as Zechariah 6:13 and the use of extrabiblical legal categories drawn from the realm of traditional jurisprudence, Bavinck affirms that the principal components of the traditional doctrine express a scriptural idea. Within the life and communion of the three Persons of the Trinity, we may posit the existence of a compact or agreement (a true *sunthēkē* or mutual concurrence of will and purpose) between the Father, who appoints the Son to be the Mediator of his people whom he chooses to give to him, and the Son, who willingly subjects himself to the Father's will, and the Spirit, who promises to furnish the Son with the power and gifts to accomplish his mediatorial task. In this "pact of salvation" between the three Persons, we witness, according to Bavinck, the

56. Among original and secondary sources on the development of the doctrine of an eternal intra-Trinitarian "covenant of redemption" in Reformed theology, see Bierma, *Casper Olevianus*, 107–39; Bierma, "Covenant or Covenants," 228–50; Johannes Cocceius, *Summa Theologiae ex Scripturis repetita* (1662), chaps. 31–43; Van Asselt, *Johannes Cocceius*, 218–44; *IET*, 2:177–78; Witsius, *Economy*, 1:281–83; Richard A. Muller, "Toward the *Pactum Salutis*: Locating the Origins of a Concept," *MAJT* 18 (2007): 11–66; J. Mark Beach, "The Doctrine of the *Pactum Salutis* in the Covenant Theology of Herman Witsius," *MAJT* 13 (2002): 101–42. For a treatment of the sources for Bavinck's formulation of the *pactum salutis*, see O'Donnell, "Not Subtle Enough," 89–106.

57. *RD*, 3:213.

"relationships and life of the three persons in the Divine Being as a covenantal life, a life of consummate self-consciousness and freedom. Here, within the Divine Being, the covenant flourishes to the full."[58] While the unity of the Trinity is particularly emphasized in the doctrine of the decrees of God, the doctrine of the "covenant of redemption" articulates the manner in which God realizes his redemptive purpose in fully Trinitarian categories. The work of salvation, accomplished through the instrument of the covenant of grace in its historical execution, is a work in which each of the three Persons of the Trinity performs a distinctive task, in accordance with the covenant between them. In the same way that the work of creation involved the respective and unified operations of the three Persons of the Trinity, so in the work of re-creation each Person fulfills a particular role upon the basis of the eternal covenant of redemption. Thus, we should not regard the historical administration of the covenant of grace as a kind of *ad hoc* remedy for the redemption of the elect, but rather as the realization in time of what the three Persons of the Trinity eternally resolved to accomplish.

> The pact of salvation . . . further forms the link between the eternal work of God toward salvation and what he does to that end in time. The covenant of grace revealed in time does not hang in the air but rests on an eternal, unchanging foundation. It is firmly grounded in the counsel and covenant of the triune God and is the application and execution of it that infallibly follows.[59]

As Bavinck's statement indicates, we should not think of this covenant and the covenant of grace as though they were *two* covenants.[60] Rather, we should regard the covenant of grace as the

58. Ibid., 3:214.

59. Ibid., 3:215.

60. The close link between the "covenant of redemption" and the "covenant of grace" is also underscored in Bavinck's *Saved by Grace*, 77 (108): "The covenant was established already in eternity with Christ as the Surety of His own. It did not come into existence for the first time within history. The covenant is rooted in eternity. Rather, the covenant existed at that point also in truth and in reality between the Father and the Son, and therefore immediately after the fall the covenant could be made known to man and be established

covenant of redemption coming to fruition in the course of the history of redemption. It is no historical accident that God the Father should send his Son in the fullness of time to fulfill the promises of the covenant of grace made prior to his incarnation. Nor is it an accident that the Son should choose to assume human flesh and undertake his work as Mediator. Nor is it accidental that the Spirit should furnish Christ with the necessary gifts required to fulfill his office as Mediator, or apply the benefits of Christ's mediation to the elect. All of the respective operations of the Father, Son, and Holy Spirit in the accomplishment of God's saving purpose stem from and express what was eternally covenanted between the Persons of the Trinity in the *pactum salutis*. Because the covenant of grace in its historical execution is founded upon this intra-Trinitarian compact, it can be understood in its unity and diversity. Furthermore, as an expression or execution of the eternal covenant of redemption, we can also affirm the inviolability and effectiveness of the covenant as the God-appointed instrument of redemption. The redemption that the covenant of grace effects for the covenant people of God, is a redemption that is of, from, and through God. Just as there is one God and Father of all who truly belong to the people of God, so there is one Son and Mediator, as well as one Spirit. Communion with the triune God, which is the goal to which the covenant of grace is ordained, is possible only upon the basis of the work of all three Persons in perfect unity and Trinitarian diversity.[61]

The Relation between the Pre- and Postfall Covenants

Following his discussion of the covenant of redemption, Bavinck briefly argues that the historical execution of the covenant of grace should not be viewed too narrowly, as though it terminated solely upon the salvation of the elect. In the scriptural representation of the covenant of grace, the first use of the term "covenant" occurs in connection with the "covenant of nature" that God established in

---

with man. Therefore, that covenant of grace, existing from eternity to eternity, functions within history as the instrumentality of all the redemption, the route along which God communicates all of His gracious benefits to man."

61. *RD*, 3:215–16.

the context of the worldwide flood in the days of Noah. The breadth of the promise that God makes in conjunction with the event of the great flood is a reminder, in Bavinck's judgment, that God's purposes of redemption are as wide in their compass as creation. The entire cosmos and all nations directly benefit from God's purpose to redeem his people from among the whole of the fallen human race. The creation is preserved, the nations are enabled to prosper, human culture advances, and the human sciences develop—all within the framework of God's overarching purpose of re-creation. With the redemption of his people in Christ, which is the principal goal of the covenant of grace in history, God also works in such a way as to renew and enlist the fruits of humanity's fulfillment of the cultural mandate in the accomplishment of his great purposes of redemption. In Bavinck's own words, "Nature and grace, creation and re-creation, must be related to each other in the way Scripture relates them. . . . Common grace and special grace still flow in a single channel."[62] God's purpose of redemption, accordingly, is, as we have previously noted, a purpose to redeem a new humanity and that purpose does not exclude, but includes, the re-creation of the cosmos. Re-creation, including the redemption of a covenant people, does not repudiate nature, but perfects it.

Of special importance to Bavinck's insistence that the covenant of grace is founded upon an eternal covenant of redemption and that it perfects rather than abandons God's work in creation, is his handling of the relation between the prefall covenant of works and the postfall covenant of grace. We should not view the covenant of grace as though it were at odds with the so-called covenant of works. The covenant of grace, rather, "was from the moment of its revelation and is still today surrounded and sustained on all sides by the covenant of nature God established with all creatures. Although special grace is essentially distinct from common grace, it is intimately bound up with it."[63] In order to appreciate the relation between these covenants, we need to clearly understand their differences and similarities.

62. Ibid., 3:216.
63. Ibid., 3:225.

The essential difference between the prefall and postfall covenants is that the latter is purely and only an expression of God's grace. All the blessings of the covenant of grace are to be understood in the strictest sense as "undeserved and *forfeited* blessings."[64] Though the covenant of works was indeed an expression of God's grace and favor toward humanity, which conferred covenant rights that man as creature did not deserve, it was nonetheless a covenant that required perfect obedience to the law of God as the way to eternal life. In the covenant of works, man is treated as a responsible creature, who is able to do what God's law requires and thereby obtain the covenant's blessings. The forfeiture of the blessings of this covenant occurs as the result of Adam's sin and disobedience, and fully accords with divine justice in the face of disobedience to God's holy and righteous law. In Adam the entire human race stands under the abiding obligation of perfect obedience and the sanction of condemnation and death on the basis of his failure to fulfill the righteous requirements of the law. "God stands by the rule that those who keep the law will receive eternal life. He posits this in his law, attests it in everyone's conscience, and validates the statement in Christ. But human beings broke the covenant of works; now they are no longer able to acquire life by keeping it. By the works of the law no human being can be justified."[65] Contrary to the "legalistic" character of this prefall covenant, we must understand the postfall covenant to be purely "evangelical." Everything that was forfeited under the terms of the prefall covenant is obtained and guaranteed in the postfall covenant by the provisions of God's grace in Christ.

> In distinction from and contrast to the covenant of works, God therefore established another, a better, covenant, not a legalistic but an evangelical covenant. But he made it, not with one who was solely a human but with the man Christ Jesus, who was his own only begotten, much-beloved Son. And in him, who shares the divine nature and attributes, this covenant has an

64. Ibid. (emphasis added).
65. Ibid.

> unwaveringly firm foundation. It can no longer be broken: it is an everlasting covenant. It rests not in any work of humans but solely in the good pleasure of God, in the work of the Mediator, in the Holy Spirit, who remains forever. It is not dependent on any human condition; it does not confer any benefit based on merit; it does not wait for any law keeping on the part of humans. It is of, through, and for grace. God himself is the sole and eternal being, the faithful and true being, in whom it rests and who establishes, maintains, executes, and completes it. The covenant of grace is the divine work par excellence—his work alone and his work totally. All boasting is excluded here for humans; all glory is due to the Father, Son, and Holy Spirit.[66]

The essential difference between the pre- and postfall covenants, therefore, is that in the covenant of grace every blessing that is bestowed through Christ, the Mediator of the covenant, is an undeserved and assured blessing that answers to what was lost and forfeited (demerited) under the covenant of works.[67] There is an important difference between a covenant that is based upon grace in the sense of unmerited favor and a covenant that is based upon and rendered effective by grace *in the sense of favor shown to undeserving sinners who have forfeited every covenantal claim upon that favor.* According to Bavinck, this difference between the covenants before and after the fall does not mitigate the fact that the law of God is fully upheld in both. Because God is unchangeably righteous, the demand of his holy law is maintained not only before the fall under the covenant of works but after the fall in the administration of the covenant of grace. No human being can find favor with God without doing what the law of God requires; this is as true in the covenant of grace as it was in the covenant of works. Therefore, in the covenant of grace, God does not act capriciously or arbitrarily. He always acts in a way that maintains and upholds the righteous requirements of his holy law. Indeed, after the fall into sin, the whole

66. Ibid., 3:225–26.
67. Ibid., 3:225.

human race comes to stand "under the law" in two respects: first, all remain obligated to do what the law requires in order to be pleasing to God; and second, all now come under the law in terms of its liability and penalty. After the fall into sin, the requirement of perfect obedience in order to obtain eternal life remains, but it has now been complicated by the additional requirement that payment be made for the debts disobedient sinners now owe God for their sins. "After the fall, therefore, God lays a double claim on humans: that of the payment of a penalty for the evil done and that of perfect obedience to his law (satisfaction and obedience)."[68]

Because the covenant of grace fulfills and meets the abiding obligations of obedience that were first stipulated in the covenant of works, it restores God's people to favor with God and secures their inheritance of eternal life in communion with him. Christ, as the Mediator of the covenant of grace, is the "anti-type" of Adam in the covenant of works. Adam, the original covenant head of

68. Ibid., 3:226. In this understanding of Christ's mediatorial work, Bavinck reflects the traditional Reformed view of Christ's "active" and "passive" obedience, which together constitute the imputed righteousness that is the basis for the justification of believers. The purpose of this distinction was not to divide Christ's obedience into two chronological stages (the first being his earthly ministry, the second being his sacrificial death upon the cross) or even into two parts, but to distinguish two facets of the one obedience of Christ. Christ's active obedience refers to his life of conformity to the precepts of the law; Christ's passive obedience refers to his life of suffering under the penalty of the law, especially in his crucifixion (Rom. 5:12–21; Phil. 2:5–8; Gal. 4:4). For traditional presentations of this distinction and its significance for justification, see *IET*, 2:646–59; *ST*, 379–82, 513–16; and James Buchanan, *The Doctrine of Justification* (1867; repr., Edinburgh: Banner of Truth, 1997), 314–38. For a perceptive comment on the link between the traditional Reformed view of Christ's "active obedience" and the original obligations of the prefall covenant of works, see Wilhelmus à Brakel, *The Christian's Reasonable Service*, ed. Joel R. Beeke, trans. Bertel Elshout, 4 vols. (Grand Rapids, MI: Reformation Heritage, 1992), 1:355: "Acquaintance with this covenant [i.e., the covenant of works] is of the greatest importance, for whoever errs here or denies the existence of the covenant of works, will not understand the covenant of grace, and will readily err concerning the mediatorship of the Lord Jesus. Such a person will very readily deny that Christ by His active obedience has merited a right to eternal life for the elect." On the theological significance of the covenant of works for the traditional Reformed view of the abiding obligations of God's law and the mediatorial work of Christ as the last Adam, see Richard A. Muller, "The Covenant of Works and the Stability of the Divine Law in Seventeenth-Century Reformed Orthodoxy: A Study in the Theology of Herman Witsius and Wilhelmus à Brakel," *CTJ* 29, 1 (1994): 75–100.

the human race, is "exchanged for and replaced by Christ," who is the covenant head of the new humanity.[69] Only within the history of Reformed theology has this correspondence and relationship between the covenant of works and the covenant of grace come to full development. Reformed theology recognized that Christ's work as Mediator of the covenant of grace obtained the righteousness and life for his people no longer able to be obtained through the covenant of works. Moreover, it also emphasized that the covenant of grace, so far as Christ's work is concerned, was for Christ a covenant of works. Christ's entire obedience and sacrifice constitute the basis for restoring his people to favor with God in a way that fully accords with the demands of God's righteousness. In the further explication of the doctrine of the covenant, Reformed theology also argued that the work of Christ in the covenant of grace was itself the fulfillment of the eternal "counsel of peace" (*pactum salutis*) in which Christ was appointed to and willingly assumed the office of Mediator. Some in the Reformed tradition went so far as to identify the covenant of redemption with the covenant of grace, and argued that, in the strictest sense, these two were essentially identical. By virtue of the foundation of the covenant of grace in the covenant of redemption, we may conclude that the covenant of grace is properly a covenant between God and Christ and "in him with all his own."[70]

In his evaluation of these developments in the history of Reformed theology, Bavinck hesitates to identify without qualification the covenant of redemption and the covenant of grace. Since Bavinck's commentary on the relation between the covenant of redemption and the covenant of grace is of particular significance to this question, it is worth quoting at length.

> Indeed, there is a difference between the pact of salvation and the covenant of grace. In the former, Christ is the guarantor and head; in the latter, he is the mediator. The first remains restricted

69. *RD*, 3:226–27.
70. Ibid., 3:227.

> to Christ and demands from him that he bear the punishment and fulfill the law in the place of the elect; the second is extended to and through Christ to humans and demands from them the faith and repentance that Christ has not, and could not, accomplish in their place. The first concerns the acquisition of salvation, is eternal, and knows no history; the second deals with the application of salvation, begins in time, and passes through several dispensations.[71]

I will consider further the implications of this important comment in my next chapter; however, it is clear that this comment is of direct significance for this question. In Bavinck's understanding, the covenant of redemption, which expresses the purpose of the triune God to save the elect and to do so by means of the different operations of the Father, Son, and Holy Spirit, expresses the divine counsel for the salvation of the elect. In the covenant of redemption, the "parties" are the triune God and all the elect in Christ; the non-elect are not directly contemplated in the covenant of redemption. In the covenant of redemption, Christ fulfills as guarantor all the "conditions" that must be met to accomplish the salvation of the elect. However, in the covenant of grace, which represents the historical execution in time of God's counsel of redemption, the situation is more complicated. Though Christ is the Mediator of the covenant of grace and secures all of its blessings for his own people, the parties of this covenant are the triune God and his covenant people (believers and their children, as well as all whom the Lord calls to himself) who are obliged in the covenant to respond to God's grace in the way of faith and obedience.[72]

Lest this distinction between the covenants of redemption and of grace be misunderstood, Bavinck adds that there remains a fundamental unity and connection between them. Just as Adam was the covenant representative and head of the human race before the fall, Christ is the covenant representative and head of the new humanity

71. Ibid.
72. Ibid., 3:227–28. Cf. *ORF*, 270–75.

after the fall. Unlike the first covenant, which could not secure the covenant inheritance of eternal life, the second covenant, because it is based upon the sure and perfect work of Christ guarantees and infallibly secures what it promises. "The covenant [of grace] is certain as a testament; it is a covenant of testaments and a covenantal testament. It involves no principle and is relatively immaterial whether one highlights the duality or the unity of the pact of salvation and the covenant of grace, provided it is clear that in the pact of salvation Christ can never even for a second be conceived apart from his own, and that in the covenant of grace believers can never even for one second be regarded outside Christ."[73]

Summary

This sketch of Bavinck's understanding of the covenant of redemption completes my survey of his exposition of the doctrines of election and covenant. Since the covenant of redemption is a pretemporal compact in which the triune God arranges the covenantal means to secure the salvation of the elect, there is an intimate and necessary connection between these doctrines. In broad terms, the covenant is the divinely-appointed instrument whereby the triune God achieves his saving purposes in time and history. If election is the doctrine that describes God's sovereign and gracious purpose to redeem his people in Christ, then covenant is the doctrine that describes God's chosen means to accomplish this purpose in time. Just as God displays his mercy and justice in his eternal decree to save the elect in Christ and to leave others

73. *RD*, 3:228. Due the the unity and distinction between the eternal "covenant of redemption" and the historical execution of this covenant in terms of the "covenant of grace," Bavinck vacillates in his use of the language of Christ as the "head and representative" of his people. In the "covenant of redemption," Christ is certainly the "head and representative" of the elect. The situation is more complicated in respect to the covenant of grace, however, since this covenant in its historical manifestation may be viewed in two ways: either in terms of its substance and reality (in which case, it is a covenant between the triune Redeemer and all the elect who truly belong to Christ by faith) or in terms of its administration (in which case, it is a covenant between the triune Redeemer and all believers together with their children, not all of whom are elect).

in their sins, so God displays his steadfast faithfulness and intra-Trinitarian communion in his covenantal administration of the history of redemption. In the following chapter, I will take up directly the way Bavinck describes this intimate interplay between election and covenant.

5

The Relation of Covenant and Election in the Theology of Herman Bavinck

In the previous chapter, I concluded my survey of Bavinck's understanding of the doctrines of covenant and election by summarizing his discussion of the relation between the covenant of redemption and the covenant of grace. According to Bavinck, the administration of the covenant of grace throughout redemption's history is founded upon and corresponds to the eternal covenant of redemption within the Godhead among the Father, the Son, and the Holy Spirit. God's way of redemption is thoroughly covenantal, whether in terms of the pretemporal and intra-Trinitarian covenant of redemption or the temporal covenant of grace, which is realized in time through the respective works of the three Persons of the Trinity in the economy of salvation.

My treatment in the last chapter of Bavinck's understanding of the covenant of redemption provides a natural bridge to the focus of this chapter. Whereas in the previous chapter I treated distinctly the doctrines of election and covenant in Bavinck's theology, in this chapter I want to take up the way Bavinck describes the relation between them. In the sequence of topics in Bavinck's *Reformed Dogmatics*, the relation between election and covenant immediately follows his discussion of the covenant of redemption. While Bavinck's treatment of the relation between election and covenant is rather brief and compact, he offers a carefully articulated statement of his conception of this relation. Because the covenant of redemption is a pretemporal compact within the Godhead and aims to accomplish God's eternal purpose of election in Christ, it constitutes a natural platform for Bavinck to address the relation between election and covenant.

In order to capture fully Bavinck's understanding of the relation between election and covenant, however, it is not enough to consider only his brief treatment in *Reformed Dogmatics*. During his ministry as a pastor and leading theologian in the Reformed churches of the Netherlands in the later nineteenth and early twentieth centuries, Bavinck played an important role in mediating a number of theological controversies in the Dutch Reformed churches directly concerning the doctrines of election and covenant. These controversies focused especially upon the doctrines of election, covenant, and the gospel promise signified and sealed to believers and their children in baptism. Consequently, my summary of Bavinck's view of the relation between election and covenant in this chapter will be divided into two parts. In the first part, I will treat Bavinck's discussion of this relation in the closing section of his exposition of the doctrine of the covenant in the third volume of his *Reformed Dogmatics*. And in the second part, I will consider Bavinck's discussion of the interrelation between the doctrines of covenant, election, and baptism, not only in the last volume of his *Reformed Dogmatics* but also in an important collection of essays on "calling and regeneration" published in 1903.

Covenant and Election in *Reformed Dogmatics*

Bavinck opens his discussion of the interrelation between covenant and election by observing that the doctrine of the covenant maintains "in a marvelous way . . . God's sovereignty in the entire work of salvation."[1] The covenant of grace surpasses the covenant of works "to the degree that Christ exceeds Adam."[2] Because all three Persons of the Trinity are intimately involved and at work in the accomplishment of the work of re-creation, the covenant of grace effectively accomplishes and secures the salvation of those whom

1. *RD*, 3:228.
2. Ibid.

God in his counsel is pleased to save. Nothing can frustrate the sovereign plan and purpose of God the Father, the representative and mediatorial work of God the Son, and the effectual application of that work by God the Holy Spirit to those who belong to Christ by faith. Throughout this great and majestic work of the triune God, it is God who works and graciously procures the salvation of his people. Viewed in this manner, the doctrine of the covenant, as much as the doctrine of election, underscores the monergism of divine grace and the glory of God's saving purpose and work. Covenant and election, each in its own manner, disclose the truth that salvation is God's work from beginning to completion.

However, after this opening note that covenant and election both underscore the truth of salvation by grace alone, Bavinck distinguishes them by the way God's grace engages human beings. In terms of the doctrine of election, we may say that God's image-bearers are utterly "passive" and purely the beneficiaries of God's gracious purpose. In terms of the doctrine of the covenant, however, this is not the case. At this point, Bavinck recalls his earlier discussion of the nature of the covenant as a suitable instrument for God's dealings with rational and moral creatures bearing the divine image. In the covenant of grace, God treats human beings as responsible partners who are placed in a relationship of fellowship with himself that is mutual and personal.

> Admittedly, the two are not so different that election is particular while the covenant of grace is universal, that the former denies free will and the latter teaches or assumes it, that the latter takes back what the former teaches. But the two do differ in that in election humans are strictly passive but in the covenant of grace they also play an active role. Election only and without qualification states who are elect and will infallibly obtain salvation; the covenant of grace describes the road by which these elect people will attain their destiny. The covenant of grace is the channel by which the stream of election flows toward eternity.[3]

3. Ibid., 3:229.

Though it is true that Christ acts as head and representative of his people in the covenant of grace, it is not true that Christ's work effaces the responsible partnership of those who belong to him by faith. Since Christ is not only the head of the covenant but also its Mediator, those embraced by the covenant of grace are obligated and placed under the demands of faith and repentance. Without the human response of faith to the covenant promise, together with its corresponding demand for repentance, it is not possible to speak of a covenant relationship between God and his people in Christ. According to Bavinck, this is the reason Reformed theologians have not hesitated to speak of the "conditions" of the covenant. Even though the language of "conditions" requires careful definition, it properly reflects the nature of the covenant of grace as it is administered in the history of redemption.[4]

Bavinck endeavors to articulate this difference between election and the covenant by distinguishing those senses in which the covenant is "unilateral," even "unconditional," and "bilateral" or "conditional." When viewed from the perspective of God's gracious initiative and bestowal of its saving blessings, the covenant is undoubtedly a work of God's grace.[5] God not only establishes the covenant and gathers his people to himself, but he also provides all that is needed for their salvation through the work of Christ, which is effectually applied and communicated to them by the Holy Spirit. In these respects, even the so-called "conditions" of the covenant, faith and repentance, are not to be viewed as anything other than the fruits or evidences of

4. Ibid., 3:230.

5. In *ORF*, 273, Bavinck offers a clear distinction between election, as one element of the eternal "counsel of redemption," and the manner in which God determines to accomplish and apply that redemption in terms of the *pactum salutis*, which undergirds the realization of redemption in time: "Election is not the whole counsel of redemption, but is a part, the first and principal part, of it. Included and established in that counsel is also the way in which the election is to be actualized—in short, the whole accomplishment and application of redemption. . . . In other words the counsel of redemption is itself a covenant—a covenant in which each of the three Persons, so to speak, receives His own work and achieves His own task. The covenant of grace which is raised up in time and is continued from generation to generation is nothing other than the working out and the impression or imprint of the covenant that is fixed in the Eternal Being. As in the counsel of God, so in history each of the Persons appears. The Father is the source, the Son is the Achiever, and the Holy Spirit is the one who applies our salvation."

the work of God's grace in his own. God graciously gives his people what he rightly demands of them through Christ and by the Spirit.[6] Nevertheless, in the "administration" of the covenant by Christ, those with whom God covenants are placed under the obligations of faith and obedience and the covenant "assumes this demanding conditional form."[7] The covenant of grace, which is indeed unilateral and proceeds from God and is rendered effective by him, "is destined to become bilateral, to be consciously and voluntarily accepted and kept by humans in the power of God."[8] In his description of the bilateral form of the covenant of grace, Bavinck argues that the covenant accentuates human responsibility, engages the whole person, and treats people, not as "inanimate objects" but as whole persons in the fullness of their created integrity. Thus, the covenant of grace, in a manner quite distinct from the doctrine of election, simultaneously accentuates divine sovereignty and human responsibility. In the covenant relationship, God's people come into their own and flourish in life and fellowship with God. In this way, "[t]he covenant of grace declares that God's honor and acclaim is [*sic*] not won at the expense but for the benefit of human persons and celebrates its triumphs in the re-creation of the whole person, in his or her enlightened consciousness and restored freedom."[9]

Another related difference between election and covenant, in Bavinck's estimation, is that election focuses primarily upon particular persons whom God knows by name, whereas the covenant focuses upon the person of Christ, the second Adam, in whom the entire organism of the human race is redeemed through the formation of

6. In a striking comment in *ORF*, 272, Bavinck observes that, if the covenant of grace is viewed in isolation from the doctrine of election, it will be understood finally as a kind of "covenant of works," that is, as a covenant that depends upon the human fulfillment of its conditions: "After all, when the covenant of grace is separated from election, it ceases to be a covenant of grace and becomes again a covenant of works. Election implies that God grants man freely and out of grace the salvation which man has forfeited and which he can never again achieve in his own strength. But if this salvation is not the sheer gift of grace but in some way depends upon the conduct of men, then the covenant of grace is converted into a covenant of works. Man must then satisfy some condition in order to inherit eternal life."

7. *RD*, 3:230.

8. Ibid.

9. Ibid.

a new humanity. "Election calls attention especially to individuals," whereas the covenant reminds us that the elect-in-Christ constitute the whole organism of a new humanity that is being gathered to God, not one individual at a time, but organically and in the historical line of the generations.[10] The doctrine of election has a narrower focus than the doctrine of the covenant. If we were to stay within the boundaries of God's purpose of election, we might conclude that God's purposes focus merely upon the salvation of a company of individuals. However, when we understand God's purpose within the setting of the historical administration of the covenant of grace, we must conclude that God's purposes focus upon nothing less than a new humanity, indeed the "whole of creation." "The covenant of grace is the organization of the new humanity under Christ as its head, as it links up with the creation order, and, reaching back to it, qualitatively and intensively incorporates the whole of creation into itself."[11] When we consider the rich and historically complex reality of the covenant in its various and distinct administrations, we observe that the divine work of redemption does not proceed contrary to the creation's structure and fabric, but takes the creation into itself and moves forward in a manner that respects the nature of human life and historical development.

The final, and perhaps most important, portion of Bavinck's consideration of the relation between covenant and election introduces a traditional distinction in the history of Reformed theology between the *historical administration* of the covenant of grace and the *saving communion* that this covenant effects for some, though not all, who fall under the covenant's administration in history. Though Bavinck's comments on this distinction are tantalizingly brief and suggest that he is not altogether satisfied with some historic formulations of it, it is of special importance that he nonetheless embraces a form of this distinction to explain the relation between covenant and election. According to Bavinck, not all those who come under the administration of the covenant of grace in redemption's

10. Ibid.
11. Ibid., 3:231.

history truly belong to Christ through faith. "It is self-evident," he observes, "that the covenant of grace will temporarily—in its earthly administration and dispensation—also include those who remain inwardly unbelieving and do not share in the covenant's benefits."[12] Historically, Reformed theologians have attempted to account for this reality by employing distinctions between an "internal" and an "external" covenant, between "covenant" and "covenant administration," or between an "absolute" and a "conditional" covenant.[13] The purpose of these distinctions was to explain the difference between those embraced within the covenant relationship in its historical administration (all believers and their children, all who belong to the "visible" church) and those who simultaneously and genuinely experience the salvation in Christ that the covenant communicates. Bavinck affirms this distinction, though he resists the tendency of some Reformed theologians to overstate it and "assume the existence of two covenants, one with the elect and the true believers, the other with external, not genuinely believing members of the church."[14] In Bavinck's conception, we should not view this distinction as though it warranted two separate covenants. Rather, this distinction allows us to express the undeniable truth that these two aspects of the one

12. Ibid.

13. This distinction is a common one in the history of Reformed theology, though it is variously articulated. Though it is sometimes alleged to imply two different covenants, Bavinck clearly opposes this implication and speaks rather of "two sides" of the one covenant. For examples of the use of this distinction, which is virtually equivalent to that between the "visible" and "invisible" church, see Zacharias Ursinus, *The Larger Catechism*, Q. & A. 118–40, in Lyle D. Bierma et al., *An Introduction to the Heidelberg Catechism: Sources, History, and Theology* (Grand Rapids, MI: Baker Academic, 2005); Lyle D. Bierma, *The Covenant Theology of Caspar Olevianus* (Grand Rapids, MI: Baker, 1996), 66–67, 74–75, 105, 112; *IET*, 2:205–16; Herman Witsius, *The Economy of the Covenants between God and Man: Comprehending a Complete Body of Divinity*, trans. William Crookshank, 2 vols. (1822; repr., Escondido, CA: Den Dulk Foundation, 1990), 1:281–91; and *ST*, 284–90. Anthony Hoekema, "Herman Bavinck's Doctrine of the Covenant" (Th.D. diss., Princeton Theological Seminary, 1953), 129–34, 228–38, argues that Bavinck does not develop this distinction in as clear and thorough a manner as Geerhardus Vos. Though this criticism is warranted, all of the elements articulated in Vos's treatment of the distinction are present throughout Bavinck's writings. For Vos's handling of this distinction under what he terms the "dual aspect" of the covenant, see G. Vos, *Dogmatiek*, vol. 1, part 1 (Grand Rapids, MI: mimeographed, 1910), 102–38.

14. *RD*, 3:231.

covenant of grace never wholly overlap or "coincide" in this world. Not all who belong to the covenant in its broad and administrative sense are, strictly speaking, among the elect who are joined to Christ and beneficiaries of his saving work in faith. Nevertheless, we should not view this distinction in a way that "splits apart" or places these aspects "side by side" each other. Only God knows infallibly who are his, and he alone will definitively separate the genuine from the ingenuine members of the covenant in the day of judgment. In the meantime, though it is true that some are only "in" the covenant (*in foedere*) while others are also "of" the covenant (*de foedere*), we should proceed according to "the judgment of love" and regard those who are embraced within the covenant as "allies" so long as they "walk in the way of the covenant."[15]

The importance of this distinction between the covenant in its administration and the covenant in its saving outcome will become more apparent in our next section, which treats Bavinck's handling of the relation between election, covenant, and the sacrament of baptism. Here it is sufficient to note that it addresses the heart of the difficult question of the relation between election and covenant. In Bavinck's view, the circle of election and the circle of covenant, at least in its historical administration, do not coincide, though they do overlap significantly. Since God is pleased to realize his purpose of election through the instrumentality or "channel" of the covenant of grace, there is the closest and most intimate relation between them. However, since not all who are embraced within the historical administration of the covenant receive its saving blessings in the way of faith, we are compelled to acknowledge that the circle of the covenant is wider than the circle of election.[16] Furthermore, the ultimate

15. Ibid., 3:232.

16. Cf. Herman Bavinck, *Saved by Grace: The Holy Spirit's Work in Calling and Regeneration*, ed. J. Mark Beach, trans. Nelson D. Kloosterman (Grand Rapids, MI: Reformation Heritage, 2008), 149 (215–16), where Bavinck speaks of the "external and internal sides of the covenant of grace": "According to the saying of Augustine, there are sheep outside and wolves inside the sheepfold of the church of Christ upon earth. The external and internal sides of the covenant of grace do not correspond fully to each other. There are many who according to our estimate belong within the dispensation of the covenant of grace and nevertheless do not share in the essence and the spiritual benefits of that covenant. In

explanation for this perplexing circumstance, namely, that not all of those who fall under the covenant administration receive its saving blessings, must be found in God's purpose of election, in accordance with which God grants faith to some but not all.

Election, Covenant, and Infant Baptism

Thus far our treatment of Bavinck's view of election and covenant has been largely based upon what he teaches explicitly regarding these subjects in his principal theological writings, the four-volume *RD* and his popular summary of his dogmatics in *ORF.* However, further light is shed upon Bavinck's conception of the relation between the doctrines of election and covenant in his reflection on the implications of this relation for the administration of the sacrament of baptism, especially to the children of believing parents. Bavinck labored in the context of an ecclesiastical environment that had witnessed during the nineteenth and early twentieth centuries a protracted series of controversial debates regarding these implications. Though it is not my purpose to provide an account of this history, or even of Bavinck's role in these debates, it is instructive to witness the way Bavinck handles this subject, not only in his formal work on Reformed dogmatics, but in his 1903 book on "calling and regeneration" (Eng. trans.: *Saved by Grace*). In this volume, which was based upon a lengthy series of articles in the church periodical, *De Bazuin* (*The Trumpet*), Bavinck aimed to contribute to a resolution of some of the primary differences that had emerged within the Reformed community of which he was a member.

At the risk of oversimplifying these debates, it should be observed that they were especially directed to the role the doctrines of election and covenant play in understanding the significance of the baptism of children. The recurring question that emerged in the debates of Bavinck's time was how should we regard the children of believing parents who receive the sign and seal of the covenant promise in

---

connection with the means of grace, the sign and the thing signified are not always united with other."

Christ through the sacrament of baptism? Among Bavinck's contemporaries, two broad answers represented very different emphases so far as the doctrines of election and covenant are concerned.

Some theologians, proceeding from the standpoint of election, maintained that such children should be assumed to possess the fullness of God's grace in Christ, which the sacrament visibly signifies and seals. Since God's promise is addressed in the strictest sense only to the elect, those who receive this promise in baptism should be assumed to possess all the benefits of salvation in Christ that flow from divine election—regeneration, conversion, union with Christ and its accompanying benefits of justification, sanctification, and perseverance. In its most rigorous form, theologians who virtually identified covenant with election sometimes expressed themselves in such a way as to suggest that the ground or reason for the baptism of such children is their assumed election and regeneration. Moreover, since the promise of grace that baptism visibly confirms actually belongs only to the elect, these theologians included some who drew the conclusion that the baptism of nonelect children was an "unreal" or only an "apparent" baptism. This tendency to proceed from the standpoint of election in the understanding of the administration of the covenant (identifying covenant with election) was associated with the theological views and formulations of Abraham Kuyper, Bavinck's contemporary and predecessor as professor of dogmatics at the Free University in Amsterdam, and those who were influenced by him.[17]

17. For sketches of this approach and its proponents, see E. Smilde, *Een Eeuw van Strijd over Verbond en Doop* (Kampen: J. H. Kok, 1946), 118–51, 211–22, and 303–19; and J. Mark Beach, "Introductory Essay," xxvii–xxxvi, in Bavinck, *Saved by Grace*; Beach, "Abraham Kuyper, Herman Bavinck, and 'The Conclusions of Utrecht 1905,'" *MAJT* 19 (2008): 41–52, 63–67. Though proponents of this approach, especially Kuyper, were often interpreted to teach either a doctrine of "baptismal regeneration" or the baptism of the children of believers upon the basis of their "assumed regeneration" (in the Dutch: *veronderstelde wedergeboorte*), this is not necessarily the case. What this approach encouraged is a strong confidence that the grace of Christ, which is signified and sealed to the children of the covenant in baptism, properly belongs to such children unless they should grow up to show themselves to be unbelieving. It also emphasized the "unconditionality," in the strict sense, of the covenant promise, since this promise properly belongs only to the elect. In North American Reformed church history, this approach with its tendency to view the covenant strictly in terms of the doctrine of election, is represented by the Protestant Reformed Churches. For a theological defense of this approach, see Herman Hoeksema, *Reformed*

Other theologians, proceeding from the standpoint of the covenant in its administration and preferring to keep the doctrine of election out of view, maintained that we should view the baptism of the children of believers only in terms of the objective administration of the covenant. All baptized children ought to be regarded in the same way and upon the basis of the promise of the covenant that was communicated to them sacramentally in their baptism. This does not warrant the assumption that all such children are elect, since the promise that baptism attests is "conditional" in the sense that it requires faith on the part of its recipient. Nor does it warrant the idea that the baptism of the children of believing parents is grounded upon the assumption of the (election and) regeneration of such children. When the church baptizes the children of believing parents, it does not proceed upon the basis of any assumption (or "presumption") regarding their regeneration, but upon the basis of the scriptural teaching regarding the administration of the covenant. In this approach, all baptized children should be regarded in the same manner, namely, as those who have received the visible sign and seal of the covenant promise in Christ, which obliges them to respond in the way of faith. Viewed from the standpoint of the covenant's administration, such children either prove to be faithful to the covenant in the way of faith and obedience, thus receiving the salvation that is promised them in Christ, or prove to be unfaithful in the way of unbelief and disobedience, thus coming under the curse of the covenant. If we regard such children simply from the standpoint of the covenant promise and its obligations, we will avoid the temptation to speculate regarding the election and regeneration of such children. On this approach, it is possible not only to emphasize the "conditional" nature of the covenant relationship but also speak appropriately of those who become "covenant breakers" through their failure to live by the terms of the covenant relationship. Among advocates of this approach to the question, some emphasized the reality of the objective promise that the sacrament

---

Dogmatics (Grand Rapids, MI: Reformed Free Publishing, 1966), 283–336, 682–700; and Hoeksema, *Believers and Their Seed* (Grand Rapids, MI: Reformed Free Publishing, 1970).

of baptism attests, others emphasized the obligation of such baptized children to undergo a conversion experience subsequent to their baptism.[18]

Admittedly, this is only a very schematic representation of the viewpoints expressed among Bavinck's contemporaries. Within the broad framework of these two tendencies—one viewing the covenant from the standpoint of election, the other viewing the covenant strictly in terms of its historical administration—there were many variations and permutations on these two divergent views. Rather than trace out the diversity of opinions expressed in these debates, I will summarize Bavinck's most important comments on these questions in his 1903 volume and in related sections of the fourth volume of his *Reformed Dogmatics*, which in its second and final edition was published some years later. In his 1903 work, *Saved by Grace*, Bavinck comments on the debates of the period, particularly on some of Abraham Kuyper's views regarding the question whether regeneration or the new birth by the Holy Spirit is effected with or without the use of the means of grace (Word and sacraments). In the course of his lengthy and, at times, highly complex and theologically careful handling of this question, Bavinck makes several points that are directly related to his conception of the relation between election and covenant. These comments include especially his understanding of the following subjects: (1) the priority of the covenant relationship in the salvation of God's people, which requires that we understand "calling" to precede "regeneration" in the ordinary sequence of the "order of salvation" (*ordo salutis*); (2) the special circumstance of the election and salvation of children of believing parents who die as infants, which requires that we recognize that regeneration may sometimes occur without the ordinary use of the "means of grace"; (3) the relation between the baptism of covenant children and their regeneration; and (4) the propriety of preaching to covenant members in a way that summons them to conversion and self-examination.

18. For sketches of this approach and its proponents, see Smilde, *Een Eeuw*, 7–64, 223–45, 286–302. Smilde's account of the history of the Reformed churches of the

Calling Ordinarily Precedes Regeneration

The first occasion for Bavinck to comment on covenant and election in *Saved by Grace* arises in connection with his consideration of the historic Reformed view of the covenant of grace and the church. Reformed theologians have traditionally placed "calling" before "regeneration" in the "order of salvation" (*ordo salutis*) because this best conforms to the nature of the covenant and its obligations. In the Reformed understanding of the covenant, children of believing parents receive the means of grace, the Word and sacrament, upon the basis of their gracious inclusion within the church. Though the sacrament of baptism is not the basis for membership in the covenant community, it is an important attestation of such membership. Consequently, while the baptism of the children of believers visibly signifies and seals their incorporation into the covenant of grace, Reformed theologians never viewed the sacrament to be "absolutely necessary to salvation." The grace of the Holy Spirit can and may be communicated to such children, even when they may not have received the sacrament of baptism. However, in order to confirm that God is pleased to embrace the children of believers within the covenant, they receive the sign and seal of this covenant in baptism and are placed thereby under the obligation to respond with faith and obedience to the covenant promise. In Bavinck's words,

> God is so good that in His electing and in the dispensing of His grace, He follows the line of generations and receives into His

---

"Secession" tradition (1834) illustrates that already in the early years of these churches a number of controversies on the subject of election, covenant, and infant baptism were occasioned by proponents of this approach. Among the older sources that represent this view and that are cited by Smilde, see K. J. Pieters and J. R. Kreulen, *De Kinderdoop volgens de Beginselen der Gereformeerde Kerk, in haar Gronden, Toedieningen en Praktijk* (Franeker, Neth.: T. Telenga, 1861). In the history of North American Reformed churches, this approach and its tendency to view the covenant strictly in terms of its historical administration is best represented by the Canadian Reformed Churches. For historical and theological presentations of this approach, see J. Faber, "American Secession Theologians on Covenant and Baptism," in Klaas Schilder, *Extra-Scriptural Binding: A New Danger* (Neerlandia, AB: Inheritance, 1996), 38–41; J. Kamphuis, *An Everlasting Covenant* (Australia: Free Reformed Churches, 1985); and J. Van Genderen, *Covenant and Election*, trans. C. Pronk (Neerlandia, AB: Inheritance, 1995).

> covenant both parents and their seed together. So the children of believers are to be viewed as holy, not by nature but through the benefit of the covenant of grace, in which they together with their parents are included according to God's arrangement.[19]

Therefore, in the ordinary communication of God's grace in Christ, the covenant of grace with its appointed means of Word and sacraments is the instrument through which God is pleased to save his people. Because the covenant obliges believers and their children to respond in faith to the means of grace, including the sacrament of baptism, Reformed theologians have historically insisted that the calling of the gospel normally precedes regeneration. All members of the covenant community are summoned through the Word and sacraments to believe the gospel promise and to walk in obedience before God.

While Bavinck argues that calling ordinarily precedes regeneration in the order of salvation, he also observes that regeneration, which in its narrow sense is a work of the Holy Spirit alone, is absolutely necessary in order to enable members of the covenant community to respond appropriately in faith and repentance. No member of the covenant community could respond to the gospel summons in faith, unless God graciously grants what the Word and sacrament require. This indisputable truth is of particular significance to the question of the relation between election and covenant. According to Bavinck, we must recognize that God's purpose of election is realized by means of the administration of the covenant, and that this purpose is inseparably joined to the covenantal means that God has appointed. Though not all who are placed under the administration of the covenant of grace are ultimately saved, God does grant his grace in the way of the covenant.

> Faith is not a condition *unto* the covenant, but a condition *within* the covenant: the route to be followed in order to become partaker and to enjoy all the commodities of that covenant. Yet faith

19. *Saved by Grace*, 68 (95).

> itself is already a fruit, a benefit of the covenant, a gift of God's grace and thus a proof that God has received us in His covenant. For God bestows all the gifts of His grace in and along the pathway of the covenant.[20]

In this statement, which is illustrative of Bavinck's view of the close, yet distinct, nature of election and covenant, Bavinck affirms the way God realizes his saving purpose through the administration of the covenant of grace. In the administration of the covenant, a relationship is established between God and believers together with their children. Only through the covenant, which requires faith and obedience, does God grant salvation in Christ to his people. However, the doctrine of election must always be invoked in order to give a scriptural account of the way salvation in the covenant is entirely God's work of grace from beginning to completion.

The Election and Salvation of Covenant Infants

The second occasion for broaching the subject of election and covenant in *Saved by Grace* is of particular significance. In the history of Reformed theology, special attention has been devoted to the difficult pastoral and theological question of the election and salvation of the children of believing parents whom God calls out of this life in their infancy. The CD devote a specific article to this question (1.17), which declares that the "godly parents ought not to doubt the election and salvation" of such children.[21] In his comments on this subject, Bavinck observes that the "uniform confession" of the Reformed churches affirms the salvation and election of the children of believing parents who die in their infancy. However, he also adds that there were two opinions regarding the significance of this confession. Some theologians, noting that not all the children who come under the administration of the covenant are elect children, stopped short of expressly declaring "with full certainty that all

20. Ibid., 76–77 (108). For a similar argument, see *ORF*, 272–73.

21. In the following two chapters of this volume, I offer an extended study of Article 1.17 of the CD in its historical context.

covenant children dying in infancy belonged without exception to the elect."[22] Others adopted what Bavinck terms a "broader position." In this position, such a child should be viewed strictly in terms of the promise of the covenant and on this basis as having been received by God in grace and having "become a partaker of salvation at death." Because these children were incapable of violating the covenant or rejecting its promise, they should be regarded as elect children who are objects of God's saving purpose in Christ. His comments on this second approach make it apparent that it is the one Bavinck prefers. However, Bavinck adds that this confession in the CD is presented in a "subjective" or pastoral manner, encouraging parents not to doubt the election and salvation of their children. Furthermore, the confession does not speak abstractly, but aims to encourage "godly parents" who may be tempted to doubt God's grace toward their children in a circumstance of special distress. In these comments on the Reformed confession, Bavinck clearly distinguishes between election and covenant, observing that some who are embraced within the covenant may not be elect in the strict sense, since they forfeit the covenant's blessings through unbelief and impenitence. At the same time, Bavinck underscores the intimate link between election and covenant, when he embraces the historic Reformed view regarding the election of the children of godly parents who die in their infancy. Though Bavinck distinguishes between election and covenant, he also seeks to bind them in the most intimate unity.

Baptism and Regeneration

The relevant comments on election and covenant that I have considered thus far are of direct importance to one of the principal issues Bavinck addresses in *Saved by Grace*, namely, the relation between the baptism of children of believing parents and their regeneration. I have already observed that Bavinck appeals in this work to the doctrine of the covenant in order to support the traditional order between calling and regeneration in salvation. Since the covenant is

22. *Saved by Grace*, 83 (117).

the ordinary instrument whereby God achieves his saving purpose, the means of grace consist of the Word and sacraments, each of which obliges its recipients to respond in faith and repentance. Though no one is able to believe or repent without the grace of regeneration, ordinarily the call of the covenant comes before the work of regeneration. Furthermore, in his reflection on the election and salvation of the infant children of godly parents who die before they are capable of responding to the gospel's call, Bavinck defends the traditional view that such children are regenerated without the use of the ordinary means of grace. Though the regeneration of those who are saved ordinarily takes place within the covenant through the use of the Word and sacraments, the unusual circumstance of such children reminds us that regeneration is ultimately a work of the Holy Spirit and there is a place for speaking of an "immediate" regeneration. In Bavinck's handling of these subjects, he clearly affirms that regeneration may occur prior to and, at least in the case of elect infants, apart from the ordinary use of the means of grace. The distinction between "immediate" and "mediate" regeneration, accordingly, is a necessary one, and has been commonly employed by Reformed theologians. Though this distinction may be abused in a way that inappropriately separates regeneration from the Spirit's use of the means of grace, it is necessary to preserve the exclusive role of the Spirit in authoring the new birth.

Although Bavinck recognizes the need to speak of "immediate" regeneration in the case of the elect infants of believing parents and in order to preserve the Spirit's exclusive role in authoring the new birth,[23] he is very circumspect in his analysis of the relation between regeneration and the baptism of the children of believers. In the history of Reformed theology, many theologians regarded regeneration to occur before or even at the time of the baptism of such children. They did so upon the basis of their understanding of the covenant promise that baptism confirms and the close link between the covenant and God's purpose of election. When God promises to grant salvation in Christ to those with whom he covenants (believers and

23. Bavinck also notes that "immediate" regeneration obtains in the case of all persons who are "incapable of receiving the external calling through the ministry of the Word, such as deaf mutes and the like" (*Saved by Grace*, 69 [96]).

their children), we may be confident that the children of believers possess the grace that the sacrament signifies and seals. In the older tradition of Reformed theology, accordingly, it was common for Reformed theologians to draw this inference from the baptism of the children of the covenant.[24]

In his consideration of this question, Bavinck offers a number of observations regarding how we should view the relation between the baptism of covenant children and the question of their regeneration. First, Bavinck concurs with the historic consensus of Reformed theology that baptism, though a sacrament that attests the need for and reality of regeneration by the Spirit of Christ, does not effect regeneration. The doctrine of baptismal regeneration fails to distinguish between the work of the Spirit in regeneration and the use of the sacraments as a visible confirmation of the gospel promise. It also ascribes to the sacrament an intrinsic power that it does not possess and that is contradicted by the fact that some baptized persons do not (at or subsequent to their baptism) embrace the covenant promise in the way of faith and repentance. Second, Bavinck argues against the tendency of some of his contemporaries, including Kuyper, to suggest that the ground for the baptism of such children is their "presumed regeneration." According to Bavinck, we do not baptize the children of believing parents on any other ground than the command of God, who stipulates that such children are members of the covenant and therefore ought to be baptized.[25] And third, Bavinck mildly criticizes

24. *RD*, 4:511; *Saved by Grace*, 85 (120).

25. See *RD*, 4:531: "[the] basis for baptism is not the assumption that someone is regenerate, nor even that [there is] regeneration itself, but only the covenant of God." Bavinck adds that we should not base the baptism of such children upon "subjective opinion" but "in accordance with the revealed will of God and the rule of his Word." Despite Bavinck's criticism of Kuyper at this point, he does affirm the long-standing Reformed view that, in accordance with the "judgment of charity," we ought to regard the baptized children of believing parents to possess the grace promised them unless there is evidence forthcoming to the contrary (*RD*, 4:511). It is instructive that Bavinck also took a different view of the language in the traditional baptism formulary, that the children of believers are "sanctified in Christ" and ought to be baptized. Whereas Kuyper took this language to refer to "internal renewal by the Holy Spirit," Bavinck took it to refer to an inclusion within the administration of the covenant. See Bavinck, *RD*, 4:511; Abraham Kuyper, *E Voto Dordraceno: Toelichting op den Heidelbergschen Catechismus*, 4 vols. (Amsterdam: J. A. Wormser, 1892–95), 2:541ff; Beach, "Introductory Essay," xxxii–xxxvi; and Beach,

Abraham Kuyper's emphasis upon the "assumed regeneration" of such children. Not only is such an assumption an uncertain basis for baptism, but it also may encourage speculation that desires "to know more than God has revealed in His Word."[26] Since we do not know whether the regeneration of such children precedes, accompanies, or follows their baptism,[27] we should exercise caution in the assumptions we make respecting them. What we do know regarding these children is that they are included within the covenant of grace, that they should accordingly receive the sign and seal of their inclusion in baptism, that they are called to respond to God's gracious promise in the way of faith and obedience, and that God graciously works by the Spirit of regeneration to enable them to respond appropriately. Though we have good reason to be confident that God will grant regeneration to such baptized children, and though we may not unduly separate baptism and regeneration for this reason, we should avoid the temptation to speculate on this subject or say more than we are warranted to say on the basis of scriptural teaching.[28]

The Propriety of the Call to Conversion and Self-Examination

In his reflection on the relation between baptism and regeneration in *Saved by Grace*, Bavinck critically evaluates two problematic views expressed by his contemporaries. In Bavinck's assessment, each of these views was one-sided and tended to encourage a lack of balance in the way the preaching of the gospel was carried on within the

---

"'Conclusions of Utrecht 1905,'" 45–51, 66–67.

26. *Saved by Grace*, 91 (130).

27. Ibid., 89 (127): "even as God merely according to His pleasure has chosen certain people unto salvation, He is also entirely free to regenerate them at whatever time pleases Him."

28. Cf. *RD*, 4:511, where Bavinck notes that there was a historical occasion for the hesitation among Reformed theologians of the eighteenth and nineteenth centuries to link closely baptism and regeneration. With the "neglect of discipline" in this period (cf. "nominal" Christianity), it became more problematic to affirm very confidently the "unity of election and covenant" or the link between regeneration and baptism. This perceptive observation on Bavinck's part illustrates the close interplay between historical context and theological formulation.

context of the administration of the covenant of grace.[29] On the one hand, some theologians so emphasized the assumed regeneration of all baptized members of the covenant community that they undermined the legitimate call to conversion and self-examination that is issued through the preaching of the gospel. In this view, the preaching of the call to conversion, if it is urgently pressed upon the children of believing parents, may tend to suggest that the regeneration and salvation of such children are in doubt until and unless they respond properly to the gospel call.[30] On the other hand, some theologians so separated the administration of the covenant and the sacrament of baptism from the reality of the work of the Spirit in regeneration that they undermined the legitimate confidence that believers may have in the promises of the covenant to them and their children. Rather than presume the salvation and regeneration of the children of believing parents, this view tends to presume the non-salvation and non-regeneration of such children until evidence of the work of God's grace in their lives is forthcoming. At the risk of considerable simplification, the first of these views proceeds in preaching from the standpoint of the "presumed regeneration" of all baptized members of the covenant; the second of these views proceeds from the standpoint of the "presumed non-regeneration" of such members.[31] In the first view, the circle of the covenant is virtually identified with the circle of election. In the second view, the circle of election tends to be viewed as a relatively small one within the much broader circle of

29. Bavinck identifies a kind of "Methodistic" or pietistic preaching that does not proceed upon the basis of the covenant in addressing the covenant community (including children), and a kind of overly presumptive preaching that proceeds from the assumed regeneration of the covenant community and its members. See *Saved by Grace*, 119–28 (172–87).

30. Ibid., 90–94 (129–35).

31. The language of "presumed" or "assumed" or even "presupposed" regeneration translates the Dutch expression *veronderstelde wedergeboorte*. When this language is used to reflect the position of A. Kuyper and others, it suffers from two misleading implications: that advocates of this language teach a doctrine of "baptismal regeneration" and are being unduly "presumptuous" in the way they view baptized children. Neither of these implications, however, adequately captures the point that Kuyper and others were making when they used this language. For a further comment on this terminology in Kuyper's writings, see Beach, "Introductory Essay," xxvii–xxxii, esp. n55; Beach, "'Conclusions of Utrecht,'" 41–45, esp. n131, 51–52.

the covenant in terms of its historical manifestation. According to Bavinck's argument in *Saved by Grace*, neither of these two views does justice to the relation between election and covenant.

In evaluating the first of these views, Bavinck maintains that it fails to distinguish adequately the sacrament of baptism, which by God's command is to be administered to all the children of believers, with the work of the Holy Spirit in regeneration, which we know from Scripture and experience is not granted to all such children.[32] This first approach also fails to reckon seriously with the fact that some baptized members of the covenant community do not respond in faith and obedience to the covenant's promises and obligations. Due to the important distinction between the covenant and election, we may not assume that all members of the covenant in its historical administration are elect and regenerated by the Holy Spirit. Corresponding to the nature of the covenant in distinction from divine election, there remains a place in the preaching of the gospel, even when it addresses those who are members of the covenant, to emphasize the urgent need for true conversion. Furthermore, since it is possible for baptized members of the covenant community to fail to respond in the way of faith and repentance to gospel overtures, the preaching of the Word should include a call to "self-examination" on the part of those who are embraced within the covenant.[33] Because the circles of election and of the gathered community of the church do not perfectly coincide, it is always legitimate, even within the context of the covenant people of God, to call all members of the covenant to true conversion in the way of genuine faith and repentance. Likewise, it remains legitimate, even pastorally obligatory, to warn the members of the covenant community, professing adults and baptized children alike, to examine themselves to see whether they are truly in the faith and possess the grace promised in the gospel.[34] The proper administration of the covenant of grace leaves no room for any kind of complacency or easy presumption that all members of the covenant community are regenerated and truly saved.

32. *Saved by Grace*, 117–18 (169–70).
33. Ibid., 126–27 (184–86).
34. Ibid., 127–28 (185–87).

While for these reasons Bavinck demurs from an exaggerated emphasis upon the close connection, even identity, between election and covenant (presumed regeneration), he also cautions against the kind of pietism that approaches all baptized children of believers as though they were unregenerate unless evidencing true conversion. Undoubtedly it is permissible, even necessary, to summon earnestly all members of the covenant community to faith and repentance. However, Bavinck cautions against the "pietistic" tendency to separate baptism and regeneration in such a way that the non-regeneration of baptized children is virtually assumed until evidence to the contrary is forthcoming. Since there is an intimate connection between God's purpose of election and his bestowal of Christ's grace through the instrumentality of the covenant, we ought to regard baptized children to be regenerate as a kind of "judgment of charity."[35] Although it is undeniable that the visible community of the church, which includes all professing believers and their children, includes some who are not genuinely saved, we should nonetheless address the people of God from the standpoint of the covenant promise and regard them to consist of "God's beloved, God's elect, called to be saints, believers."[36]

In his consideration of the complex debates of his time, therefore, Bavinck steers a steady and moderate course between the more extreme views of some of his contemporaries on the relation between election and covenant.

Concluding Observations

Having considered Bavinck's treatment of the doctrines of election and covenant, not only in his principal theological writings but in his 1903 treatise on "calling and regeneration," we may now draw some conclusions regarding his position. These conclusions are based upon the exposition of Bavinck's theology that I provided in the foregoing, and will accordingly be stated in a relatively concise manner.

35. *RD*, 4:511.
36. *Saved by Grace*, 117 (169).

Each of them aims to capture the principal themes and characteristic formulations of Bavinck's theological position.

First, throughout his exposition of the doctrines of election and covenant, Bavinck exhibits a consistent pattern of theological reflection and method. Upon the basis of a deep and rich acquaintance with scriptural data, the Reformed confessions, and the history of Reformed theology, Bavinck articulates in a fresh and creative way the broad consensus of historic Reformed theology on these topics. The characteristic features of Bavinck's theological work are clearly evident in his treatment of these principal themes of Reformed theology. Though it would be unfair to say that Bavinck offers only a repristination of the traditional consensus, it is certainly true that, at every point, Bavinck remains within the broad center of what might be termed "catholic" Reformed theology. At points in Bavinck's treatment of election and covenant, he offers a correction or modification of some feature of Reformed theology. For example, he eschews the alternatives of "supra-" and "infralapsarianism" in his doctrine of predestination, and he shares Kuyper's critical observation that, in the traditional understanding of God's decrees, insufficient emphasis was given to God's positive purpose for creation in its original state and consummate glory. However, throughout his exposition of these doctrines, especially within the context of debates among his contemporaries, Bavinck proves again and again to be a "mediating" figure who resists the one-sidedness and lack of synthetic unity in theological formulation that often marked their divergent positions. Scriptural fidelity, confessional sympathy, historical consciousness, antipathy to simplistic solutions—these qualities mark Bavinck's theological labor and constitute, as much as the distinct positions he espouses, an important aspect of his legacy as a Reformed theologian.

Second, whereas some interpreters of the Reformed tradition have maintained that the doctrines of election and covenant represent two divergent modes of Reformed theology, Bavinck's handling of these doctrines exhibits a keen awareness of their comprehensive unity and interrelation. Though election and covenant are distinguished, they both express, broadly, one of the principal motifs of Reformed theology, namely, that the redemption of a new humanity through the work of Christ, the Mediator, is a work of sheer and sovereign grace. The triune God's work of re-creation is rooted in eternity and finds its source in the living, eternal, and active will of God to redeem a new humanity in Christ, the last Adam. The eternal counsel of God embraces all things, not only the redemption of fallen sinners through the work of Christ, but also the re-creation and glorification of the entire cosmos. Predestination is the dimension of the triune God's eternal counsel that pertains especially to the redemption of the elect. Though distinct from election, the doctrine of the covenant pertains to the divinely appointed manner whereby this elective and redemptive purpose will be achieved. In Bavinck's conception of the interrelation between election and covenant, it is important to observe that the covenant of grace in its historical execution in time is itself rooted in the intra-Trinitarian "covenant of redemption." Each of the three persons of the Godhead—the Father, the Son, and the Holy Spirit—compacted together (or mutually concurred in will, purpose, and appointment) from all eternity to secure the redemption of the elect through the mutual "operations" of each. The covenant of grace in its historical administration is no "accident" of history. Nor is it an "afterthought" in the eternal counsel of the triune God. From the beginning of the history of the covenant, even before the fall into sin, until its consummation, the Father purposed to commune with his people through the Son of his good pleasure; the Son purposed to humble himself in his incarnation and the fulfillment of his office as Mediator; and the Holy Spirit purposed to communicate the manifold benefits of Christ's mediation to his people. The covenant of grace in its historical expression is tethered to its basis and foundation in God's eternal counsel of peace (*pactum salutis*). Thus, in Bavinck's theology, it is unthinkable that election and covenant could be played off against each other, or that the doctrine of the covenant could provide an alternative, more historical, mode of expressing the monergism of Reformed soteriology.

Third, in his formulation of the doctrine of the covenant, Bavinck embraces and defends the historic Reformed doctrine of a prelapsarian "covenant of works" and a postlapsarian "covenant of grace." He also affirms a distinction between the covenant of grace in its historical realization and the foundation of this covenant in the intra-Trinitarian "covenant of redemption" or *pactum salutis*. In his reflection upon these distinct features of a biblical and Reformed theology of the covenant, Bavinck exhibits a sophisticated grasp of the Reformed tradition and resists tendencies among some Reformed theologians to overemphasize the differences between these distinct phases of the covenant on the one hand or to overstate the uniformity between them on the other.

In Bavinck's estimation, the doctrine of the covenant expresses a central theme of biblical religion, namely, that the triune God created human beings in his image and for the purpose of being placed in a life-relationship of communion with him. Only the doctrine of the covenant does justice to the nature of man as a rational and moral creature, capable of enjoying union and communion with the living God in service to him and in dominion over creation. The doctrine of the covenant also underscores the goodness and grace of God, who initiates the covenant, stipulates its requirement of perfect obedience, maintains it in justice and truth, and grants the creature covenantal "rights" before him. Bavinck simultaneously affirms the prelapsarian covenant was graciously initiated and bestowed by the triune God, and required perfect obedience in order for humanity in Adam to attain fullness of life in consummate and unbreakable communion with God.

An especially significant feature of Bavinck's formulation of the doctrine of the covenant is the way he carefully articulates the relation between the prelapsarian "covenant of works" and the postlapsarian "covenant of grace." Whereas in the prefall covenant, Adam was the head and representative of the organism of humanity, in the postfall covenant Christ is the head and representative of the organism of the new or re-created humanity. Within the unfathomable depths of God's eternal purposes for creation and re-creation, the first Adam was a "type" of the last Adam, and the original aim of God was to be realized only through Christ. There are significant features of unity and interrelationship, therefore, between the pre- and the postfall covenants. Both are rooted in God's unmerited favor and goodness. Both promise the consummate blessing of eternal life in communion with the triune God. Both require human beings to find favor with God only in the way of perfect obedience and fidelity. But there are also significant and undeniable differences between them. The "last Adam," Christ, is greater than the first and secures infallibly for his own the covenant blessing of eternal life. The grace shown before the fall to undeserving human beings is surpassed in the grace of Christ, which is shown after the fall to undeserving sinners who have willfully forfeited in Adam any and every claim upon God's favor. Furthermore, the obligations of obedience that must be met in order for sinful human beings to find favor with God now include not only perfect obedience to the abiding stipulations of God's moral law ("active obedience") but also a perfect satisfaction of the penalty for disobedience ("passive obedience"). The glory of the covenant of grace in its historical unfolding is that it perfectly and infallibly achieves God's covenant purposes for his people in union with Christ, the last Adam. Christ's mediatorial work includes the meeting of these obligations on behalf of his people. In Bavinck's conception of the covenant, we must distinguish between the pre- and postfall covenants, but not in such a way as to separate them. Even the "covenant of works" is taken up into and made to subserve God's gracious purpose for the redemption of humanity in Christ, which entails the realization of the eschatological goal of the covenant, the inheritance of eternal life.

In the same way that Bavinck distinguishes without separating between the pre- and postfall covenants, he also insists upon the distinct, yet inseparable, relation between the "covenant of redemption" and the "covenant of grace." On several occasions, Bavinck notes that these should not be construed as *two* covenants, but as the same covenant viewed from the perspectives of God's eternal counsel and the realization of that counsel in time. The importance of recognizing the unity between the covenant of redemption and the covenant of grace lies, in Bavinck's judgment, in the way the latter ultimately depends upon God's grace and faithfulness for its effectiveness. Unless the triune God undertakes to accomplish all that is required in the covenant of grace for the redemption of the elect, the covenant of grace can easily be transfigured into a new kind of "covenant of works." Since the covenant of grace in its historical administration takes an explicitly *conditional form*, obliging believers and their children to walk before God in the way of faith and obedience, it might be inferred that the salvation of those with whom God covenants finally depends upon their faithfulness in fulfilling these conditions. Contrary to this inference, Bavinck insists that the "conditions" of the covenant of grace are ultimately met upon the basis of God's eternal counsel of redemption. In the covenant of grace, God gives to believers and their children the blessings obtained for them by Christ and conferred upon them through the Holy Spirit. The covenant of grace is, therefore, *unconditional*, when viewed from the standpoint of God's eternal purpose and gracious disposition in the "covenant of redemption." However, the covenant of grace is also "conditional," when viewed from the standpoint of the covenant people's obligations to respond in faith and live out of the blessings of the covenant in Christ. Viewed from the standpoint of the certain realization of God's purpose to grant his people eternal life in fellowship with Christ by the Spirit, the covenant of grace has a "testamentary" character. It is a divine gift or disposition whose fruition and blessing ultimately depend upon God's gracious initiative and faithfulness to his promise. When viewed from the standpoint of its administration in the history of redemption, the covenant of grace has the character of a *mutual* fellowship or friendship between two parties, the triune Redeemer and his covenant people (believers and their children).

Fourth, Bavinck affirms with some qualification a long-standing distinction between the covenant in its *historical administration* and the covenant in *its reality and substance* as saving fellowship with the triune God. In the history of theological reflection on the doctrines of election and covenant, this distinction, though variously expressed, was employed to account for the fact that not all members of the covenant community enter into the blessings of the covenant that result from Christ's work as Mediator and head of his people. The circle of election and the circle of the covenant, at least in terms of its manifestation in history, do not coincide, even though they significantly overlap. Some members of the covenant community in the broad sense of the "visible church" prove to be unbelieving and impenitent. Other members of the covenant community enter into the fullness of the blessings of the covenant in the way of faith, which is ordinarily produced in them by the Holy Spirit through the use of the Word and sacraments of the covenant. At this juncture, Bavinck resists the temptation to go in one of two directions in understanding the relation between election and covenant. On the one hand, he does not equate election and covenant, and thereby exclude from the covenant those who are not "children of the promise" in the strict sense (Rom. 9:6–8). It is possible for those who are embraced by the covenant to fail to respond properly to its obligations of faith and obedience. In this way, some members of the covenant community "break" the covenant relationship and thereby come under the greater judgment of God for sinfully forfeiting the privileges that were theirs under the covenant. On the other hand, Bavinck also rejects any approach that would isolate the covenant in its administration from the doctrine of election. In Bavinck's judgment, when the covenant is separated from election in this manner, it quickly devolves into a relationship whose effectiveness and blessings ultimately depend upon the human party's faithfulness. Contrary to these apparent solutions to difficult theological and pastoral questions, Bavinck maintains the close interconnection between election and covenant. The doctrine of election preserves the doctrine of the covenant from falling into a form of synergism. The doctrine of the covenant preserves the doctrine of election from devolving into a form of "fatalism" that leaves no room for human responsibility. Though it is somewhat simplistic to formulate Bavinck's position in these terms, it might be argued that Bavinck views the doctrine of election to underscore God's sovereignty in salvation and the doctrine of the covenant to underscore human responsibility in the conferral of salvation.

And fifth, within the framework of his comprehensive understanding of the doctrines of election and covenant, Bavinck charts a careful course between the opposing views of his contemporaries on the significance of the baptism of children of believing parents. Unlike some who suggested that the children of believers should be baptized on the assumption of their election and regeneration,

Bavinck clearly insists that the only basis for the baptism of such children is the scriptural teaching that they are proper recipients of the covenant promise. Since God is pleased to include the children of believers in the covenant relationship, thereby honoring the created order and the significance of the line of generations, the church properly administers the sacrament of baptism to them. Such children are included within the covenant of grace and therefore ought to receive the sign and seal of its promise in the sacrament of baptism. Moreover, because Bavinck conceives of the covenant as the pathway whereby God's eternal counsel of redemption is executed, he also affirms the long-standing view of Reformed theologians that there is a close link between the sacrament and the grace that the sacrament confirms. Though Bavinck opposes as "speculative" any attempt to determine whether regeneration occurs before, during, or subsequent to baptism, he does emphasize that the children of believers ought to be regarded as genuine beneficiaries of the covenant of grace unless they should prove obstinate in unbelief and disobedience. The confidence we may have in the election and salvation of such children is based upon the promise of the covenant and the faithfulness of God to that promise.

However, since we also know from Scripture and by experience that not all those who come under the administration of the covenant enter through faith into the enjoyment of its saving benefits in Christ, we are also obliged, in Bavinck's view, to urge with all seriousness that covenant children (indeed, all members of the covenant community) respond to the gospel call in the way of genuine faith. Because the circle of election and the circle of the covenant do not wholly coincide, there is always room within the administration of the covenant for a serious summons to conversion and self-examination, lest the covenant relationship become the occasion for undue complacency or presumption. Upon the basis of his comprehensive understanding of election and covenant, Bavinck characteristically seeks to avoid the errors of those who identify election with covenant and those who exclude election from their formulation of the covenant. Thus, in his contribution to the debates among his contemporaries on the subject of election, covenant, and infant baptism, Bavinck makes careful use of his comprehensive theology of election and covenant.

Though there are many lines of intersection between Bavinck's reflection on election and covenant and ongoing debates in the Reformed community in North America, I will resist the temptation to trace them out here. My aim in this and the previous chapter remains to offer an analysis of Bavinck's handling of these doctrines in his principal theological writings and in the context of the debates of his time. This purpose is not incompatible, however, with the further task of addressing these important themes of Reformed theology in the contemporary context. My observations regarding Bavinck's contribution to a Reformed understanding of these themes in his day suggest that an acquaintance with his theology may be, among others, a good place to become acquainted with the rich tradition of Reformed reflection on them. Such acquaintance is a necessary prelude to further discussion of these topics in the context of contemporary debates.

6

The Election and Salvation of the Children of Believers Who Die in Infancy:

A Study of Article 1.17 of the Canons of Dort (1)

A common prejudice against the biblical teaching concerning election claims that it undermines the assurance of salvation. If the salvation of believers depends ultimately upon God's sovereign choice to save some and not others, fatalism is introduced into the order of salvation. After all, who can withstand the will of God (cf. Rom. 9:19)? It is alleged that the specter of uncertainty overshadows God's grace toward us in Jesus Christ. Since no creature is privy to the "secret things" of God, including the specifics of his sovereign election, believers cannot be confident of God's good will toward them in Christ. Consequently, the teaching of election undermines assurance of salvation. According to this prejudice, the reality of God's foreordination of the salvation of some and the non-salvation of others reduces his choice to arbitrariness.[1]

Despite this common misrepresentation, a cursory reading of the CD (the most definitive and universal statement of the Reformed

1. For an extended treatment of the charge of "arbitrariness" against the doctrine of election, see G. C. Berkouwer, *Divine Election*, trans. Hugo Bekker (Grand Rapids, MI: Eerdmans, 1960), 53–101. Though Berkouwer rejects the charge of arbitrariness, he seems to do so by affirming divine election in Christ while denying any parallel nonelection of others (ibid., 172–217, esp. 180).

view) indicates that the key notes throughout this confession are praise toward the triune God for his amazing, undeserved grace in Christ and a remarkable confidence in his invincible favor. A fair-minded reader of the Canons could scour every article of the five heads of doctrine and discover no evidence for fatalism or uncertainty. Because salvation does not hang upon the thin thread of their own initiative and perseverance, but upon the solid chain of God's electing purpose in Christ, believers may be assured of their salvation. Sovereign and merciful election allows believers to thank God on one hand, and rest confidently in his gracious favor in Christ on the other.[2] For the authors of the Canons, the teaching of election serves "the honor of God's name . . . and the comfort of anxious souls."[3]

The note of assurance that pervades the Canons comes to remarkable expression in an article in the First Head of Doctrine, dealing with the subject of "Divine Election and Reprobation." After a series of articles that set forth the biblical teaching regarding God's election of his people in Christ and his reprobation of others, Article 1.17 addresses the question of the election and salvation of the children of believers "whom God calls out of this life in infancy."

> Since we must make judgments about God's will from his Word, which testifies that the children of believers are holy, not by nature but by virtue of the gracious covenant in which they together with their parents are included, godly parents ought not to doubt the election and salvation of their children whom God calls out of this life in infancy.[4]

2. H. Kaajan, *De Groote Synode van Dordrecht in 1618–1619* (Amsterdam: De Standaard, n.d.), 175, points out that this pastoral character of the Canons was by design.

3. This language is used in the "Rejection of False Accusations" with which the Canons conclude. The original Dutch and Latin texts of the Canons are published in J. N. Bakhuizen van den Brink, *De Nederlandse Belijdenisgeschriften*, 2nd ed. (Amsterdam: Bolland, 1976), 230–78.

4. "Quandoquidem de voluntate Dei ex Verbo ipsius nobis est iudicandum, quod testator liberos fidelium esse sanctos, non quidem natura, sed beneficio foederis gratuiti, in quo illi cum parentibus comprehenduntur, pii parentes de Electione et salute suorum liberorum, quos Deus in infantia ex hac vita evocat, dubitare non debent" (Bakhuizen van den Brink, *Belijdenisgeschriften*, 236). In the Dutch, the language "ought not to doubt" is "moeten . . . niet twijffelen."

In this Article, which seems to intrude rather unexpectedly into the sequence of the preceding articles, the authors of the Canons deal with a question regarding election that had arisen in debates in the Reformed churches prior to the convening of the Synod of Dort in 1618–19: What may we believe regarding the election of the children of godly parents whom God calls out of this life in infancy? The remarkable feature of Article 17 is that it expresses a good confidence regarding God's favor toward such children. In this teaching of the Canons, sovereign and merciful election, far from casting a shadow over the question of assurance, seems rather to undergird and fuel a robust confidence in God's favor toward the children of believers.

My purpose in this chapter and the next will be to examine CD 1.17 to ascertain what it reveals about the relation between the teaching of election and the theme of the assurance of salvation. This Article deserves special attention not only because it witnesses so directly to the prominent theme of assurance in the Canons, but also because it has been relatively neglected in the study of the Canons. Though this question may not be as pressing for many Reformed believers today as it was at the time of the framing of the Canons, it remains a crucial question and provides an important window into Reformed teaching. It also illustrates the intimate interplay between the doctrines of election and covenant, since the assurance this Article affirms is based upon the disclosure of God's grace through the promise of the covenant.

In our consideration of this Article, I will start with a treatment of the background and occasion for its inclusion in the Canons. A proper interpretation of the meaning of this Article requires careful attention to the circumstances that prompted the authors of the Canons to include it in the final draft of their confession. I will then consider the deliberations of the Synod of Dort, which led the delegates to adopt the final language of Article 1.17. These deliberations are an important key to a proper interpretation of this Article's meaning. Though it has not been the subject of much direct debate in the history of the Reformed churches,[5] my analysis in the next

5. An exception to this neglect is the recent article by N. H. Gootjes, "Can Parents Be

chapter will also take up the question of how this Article has been interpreted by Reformed theologians. Before concluding with several observations regarding this Article's teaching, I will also comment on the similarities and dissimilarities between what it affirms and what is taught in the WCF, which addresses in its own way the salvation of "elect infants." My thesis will be that Article 1.17 offers an important affirmation of the confidence believers may have in the election and salvation of their children whom God calls to himself in infancy.

The Background and Occasion for Article 1.17

I noted that Article 1.17 appears to intrude into the sequence of articles under the Canons' First Head of Doctrine on election and reprobation. Though the Article properly belongs to the Canons' teaching regarding election, it introduces a particular question into the more general statement of Scripture's teaching summarized in the First Head of Doctrine. The impression of a break in the articles of the First Head of Doctrine is not surprising, since Article 17 was not included in the first draft of the Canons and was only added at the encouragement of some delegates in order to answer a common Arminian objection to the teaching of sovereign election. A proper understanding of this Article requires, therefore, that we begin our consideration of it by noting the background and occasion for its ultimate inclusion in the final form of the Canons.

The reason for the inclusion of this Article is mentioned in the important "Rejection of False Accusations" that concludes the CD. There the authors of the Canons refer to those who, contrary to "truth, equity, and charity," claim that the Reformed teaching of election implies that

> many infant children of believers are snatched in their innocence from their mothers' breasts and cruelly cast into hell so that

Sure? Background and Meaning of Canons of Dort, I, 17," *Lux Mundi* 15, 4 (1996), 2–6. Though a popular consideration of Article 1.17, Gootjes's article provides a helpful statement of the historical discussion of its teaching.

> neither the blood of Christ nor their baptism nor the prayers of the church at their baptism can be of any use to them.[6]

In this description of the Arminian complaint against the Reformed teaching of election, the authors of the Canons did not engage in an ecclesiastical form of "shadow boxing," but identified a common Arminian accusation. By alleging that the doctrine of election entailed that many children of believers were reprobate, and that their parents could have no assurance of their salvation, the Arminian party sought to stir up opposition to the Reformed view. To appreciate the background to this allegation, we need to recall briefly the circumstances that led to the convening of the Synod.[7]

When the great Synod of Dort was convened by the States General of the Netherlands in 1618, the aim of the Synod was to settle a dispute within the Reformed churches of the Netherlands regarding the doctrine of election. The instigator of the dispute over BC 16 was Arminius, professor of theology at the University of Leiden. Early in the seventeenth century, Arminius began to raise objections to the doctrine's traditional formulation. A number of theologians

6. "Multos fidelium infantes ab uberibus matrum innoxios abripi et tyrannice in gehennam praecipitari, adeo ut iis nec Baptismus, nec Ecclesiae in eorum Baptismo preces, prodese queant" (Bakhuizen van den Brink, *Belijdenisgeschriften*, 278). B. B. Warfield, "The Development of the Doctrine of Infant Salvation," in *Studies in Theology* (1932; repr., Grand Rapids, MI: Baker, 1981), 435n78, suggests that the likely source for the language used by the Arminians in describing the Reformed view is Calvin's reply to Castellio. In Calvin's reply to Castellio, however, the reference is not to the children of believers, but to the general truth that God reprobates some children who die in infancy. Upon the basis of this language, the Arminians charged all Reformed churches with the teaching that God reprobates the deceased infant children of believers and unbelievers alike. See also Gootjes, "Parents," 3.

7. For the background to the convening of the Synod of Dort, see L. H. Wagenaar, *Van Strijd en Overwinning: De Groote Synode van 1618 op '19 en Wat aan Haar Voorafging* (Utrecht: G. J. A. Ruys, 1909), 1–256; W. Robert Godfrey, "Tensions within International Calvinism: The Debate on the Atonement at the Synod of Dort, 1618–1619" (Ph.D. diss., Stanford University, 1974), 10–69; Louis Praamsma, "The Background of the Arminian Controversy (1586–1618)," in *Crisis in the Reformed Churches*, ed. Peter Y. De Jong (Grand Rapids, MI: Reformed Fellowship, 1968), 22–38; Donald Sinnema, "The Issue of Reprobation at the Synod of Dort (1618–19) in Light of the History of This Doctrine" (Ph.D. diss., University of St. Michael's College, 1985), 136–213; and Keith D. Stanglin, "'Arminius *avant la lettre*': Peter Baro, Jacob Arminius, and the Bond of Predestinarian Polemic," *WTJ* 67, 1 (2005): 51–74.

and pastors sympathetic to Arminius's views met in January of 1610 in Gouda. At this meeting, the Arminian party prepared a petition to be presented to the civil authorities. In this "Remonstrance," the Arminians expressed their views on the doctrine of election in five articles. These opinions of the Remonstrants form the background to the Five Heads of Doctrine in the CD, each of which offers a Reformed response to the Arminian article on the point in dispute. The Synod delegates, who represented not only the Dutch churches but also the Reformed congregations throughout Europe, met to formulate a consensus on the Reformed teaching and to reject the Arminian errors in the Dutch church.

The objection addressed in Article 1.17 of the Canons was first formally stated at the 1610 meeting of the Remonstrants in Gouda. In the written statements stemming from this meeting, the Arminians expressly rejected any teaching

> that God . . . has decided to deliver some from this fall and corruption to declare his mercy, and to leave in damnation others, young as well as old, and even some children of covenant people, who are baptized in the name of Christ, when they die in infancy, to declare his righteousness.[8]

Though this statement does not identify any particular source for or instance of the teaching it rejects, it clearly implies that the Reformed doctrine of election taught the reprobation of at least some of the covenant children of believing parents who die in infancy. Therefore, the Arminian party specifically raised the uncertainty regarding the election of the children of believing parents. This protest, as the Canons' concluding "Rejection of False Accusations" confirms, was frequently included among the litany of Arminian objections against Reformed teaching.

To appreciate the force of this particular objection of the Arminians, we must consider the historical context of its powerful,

8. As quoted and translated by Gootjes, "Parents," 3. The original text is found in J. Trigland, *Kerckelycke Geschiedenissen* (Leiden: Adriaen Wyngaerden, 1650), 525.

emotional appeal. In the early seventeenth century, the infant mortality rate was much higher than is often the case today. The death of an infant child touched nearly every family. Many Reformed believers were likely to have witnessed the deaths of several of their children.[9] The complaint of the Arminians, therefore, was a particularly poignant one, since it robbed parents of any assurance regarding the salvation of their deceased children. According to the Arminian claim, parents of such children have no basis to be certain of their election and salvation. Because the Reformed churches teach that God sovereignly elects some and reprobates others, the Arminians believed such parents could derive no comfort from the covenant promise to their children, signified and sealed to them in baptism. Since God's choice of election discriminates even between those with whom he covenants, the covenant can provide no sure basis for certainty regarding the election of such children. For many, if not most, Reformed parents, this charge was not an abstract point of theology, but a painful addition to their grief over the loss of their children. Not only did they sorrow over the death of their children, but they also faced an even greater sorrow, the fear of the eternal loss and condemnation of their children under the wrath of God.

The background and occasion for the inclusion of Article 1.17, therefore, can be found in this common Arminian complaint against the Reformed understanding of election. By including this article in the final draft of the Canons, the delegates to the Synod of Dort sought to refute a false accusation of the implications of their convictions about God's election of his people in Christ.

The Synod of Dort and Article 1.17

In order to appreciate the inclusion of Article 1.17 in the First Head of Doctrine of the Canons, some features of the work of the Synod of Dort need to be noted. After the Remonstrants appearing

9. Gootjes, "Parents," 3: "The average recorded mortality rate in France around this time was between fifteen and thirty percent for babies born alive. Between the ages of one

at the Synod were dismissed early in the proceedings, the Synod adopted a particular procedure to address the Arminian controversy.[10] All of the distinct delegations from various branches of the Reformed churches throughout Europe were invited to present their respective "judgments" (*iudicia*) on the five disputed Arminian opinions. Several of the professors of the Dutch churches were invited to present their judgments as well. Only after receiving and compiling these initial judgments did the Synod appoint a committee to write the Canons. After this committee completed its work, the delegations were again offered the opportunity to respond with comments on the draft document. Upon the basis of the delegation's responses to their draft of the Canons, the draft committee then revised and supplemented its initial document for deliberation and eventual adoption by the Synod as a whole.

The actions of the Synod that led to the adoption of Article 1.17 have to be viewed in light of this procedure. Among the materials from the Synod that are relevant to our interpretation of this Article, we need to note the following: (1) the initial judgments (*iudicia*) of the delegates, including the Dutch theologians, that address the question of the election of the children of believers whom God calls out of this life in their infancy; (2) the subsequent request that the draft committee include an article on this subject, since it was not included in the original draft document; (3) the initial proposal of the draft committee for Article 1.17; and (4) the revised and final form of Article 1.17. If we are to achieve clarity regarding the significance and meaning of this Article, each of these items requires careful attention.

---

and five, about eighteen percent of the children died." Gootjes cites the following sources for this data: L. Stone, *The Family, Sex and Marriage in England 1500–1800*, rev. ed. (Mammondsworth, U.K.: Penguin, 1985), 54–58; and L. Clarkson, *Death, Disease and Famine in Pre-industrial England* (Dublin: Gil and MacMillan, 1975), 5.

10. For a treatment of the procedure of the Synod in handling the Remonstrant delegates, see Sinnema, "Reprobation," 214–74, 286–92; and Godfrey, "Tensions," 132–64. My description of the Synod's procedure only highlights its most important features. Prior to the Synod's appointment of a committee to draft the Canons, Johannes Bogerman, president of the Synod, had prepared his own draft document. This document became an important reference point for the committee appointed to draft the Canons.

The Initial Statements of the Delegates

A number of the initial statements or "judgments" of the various delegations and theologians at the Synod of Dort addressed indirectly or directly the Arminian charge regarding the reprobation of the infant children of believing parents. These judgments not only confirm the importance of this Arminian charge against sovereign election, but they also provide a helpful window into the thinking of the various delegations present at the Synod. Though the final, adopted version of the Canons expresses the consensus judgment of the Reformed churches on this question, an awareness of the historical circumstances helps set a context for interpreting the language of Article 1.17. These judgments are rather extensive, but we will consider each of them in turn since they provide important testimony to the range of opinion among the synodical delegates. An awareness of these judgments helps to establish a matrix within which to interpret the final opinion of the Synod and is also important since some critics of Article 1.17 draw heavily upon them.

Among the judgments presented initially to the Synod on the election or reprobation of the children of believing parents, the following are of particular significance.[11]

The English Theologians. The initial judgment presented to the Synod by the English delegation contains an extensive statement on the election of young children. In the section of their judgment that addresses unscriptural propositions concerning election, the English theologians consider the specific proposition that "there is no election of little (*kleine*) children who die before reaching the use

11. These judgments are printed in *Acta of Handelingen der Nationale Synode*, ed. J. H. Donner and S. A. van den Hoorn (Leiden: J. H. Donner, n.d.). In the following, I am making use of the English translations of these judgments that are provided by Homer Hoeksema in his *The Voice of Our Fathers: An Exposition of the Canons of Dordrecht* (Grand Rapids, MI: Reformed Free Publishing, 1980), 269–76. On a number of occasions, however, I have slightly modified Hoeksema's translations to reflect more accurately the original. Hoeksema, for example, often translates the Dutch "jonge" with the English "little," when it would better be translated "young" or "infant." Unfortunately, Hoeksema does not cite the sources of his quotations from the synodical *Acta*. Sinnema, "Reprobation," 341–71, also cites and translates some relevant portions of these judgments, though his interest is in the broader question of the doctrine of reprobation.

of reason." The most pertinent section of the English delegation's opinion states that "Scripture presupposes that the names of some little ones are written in the book of life, and that they shall appear before the throne of God, Revelation 20:1; and shall be admitted into the new Jerusalem, Revelation 21:27. . . . Similarly Luke 18:16, 'For to such is the kingdom of heaven'. . . . Hence they were chosen unto this in Christ."[12] The interesting feature of the English delegation's judgment is that it does not directly address the issue of the election and salvation of the children of believing parents who die in infancy. The judgment of the English theologians argues simply that the unconditional election of God includes the election of children, contrary to the denial of this proposition by the Remonstrants. As such it does not directly answer the particular accusation of the Arminians that the believing parents of children who die in infancy can have no assurance regarding the election of such children.

The Swiss delegates. In the initial judgment prepared by the Swiss delegates, the following proposition was offered on the subject of the election of children of believers who die in infancy:

> That there is an election and reprobation of children, as well as of adults, we cannot deny before God, who mercifully loves and irreprehensibly hates those who are not yet born. But as concerns the children of believers, since God by virtue of the covenant of grace is their God, and since Paul calls them holy who are born of a believing father and mother, and since the Lord of heaven declares them heirs of the heavenly kingdom, if they die in their infancy, before the years of discretion, we hope the best of them (*wij hopen van hen het beste*). And we doubt not (*wij twijfelen niet*) that the angels of such children, who are ministering and very loving spirits [to them] from their tender youth, who always behold the face of God, are especially sent out for their sake, and faithfully serve in their office.[13]

12. *Acta*, 348.
13. Paragraph 8, On Predestination, *Acta*, 376.

Unlike the judgment of the English delegates, the judgment of the Swiss delegates addresses directly the point of the Arminian objection. Contrary to the Arminians' charge, this judgment maintains that believers hope the best for such children, and also states that they do not doubt that the angels of such children will be sent out for their sake.[14]

The Nassau and Wettaravian delegates. The third judgment that addressed the accusation of the Arminians in the preparatory phase of the Synod of Dort's handling of the First Head of Doctrine is that of the Nassau and Wettaravian delegates. Summarizing the true teaching of the Reformed churches, these delegates presented a brief proposition on the election and salvation of the children of believing parents: "Although it is true that God may condemn children because of original sin, nevertheless, Christian parents must in no wise doubt (*moeten . . . geenszins twijfelen*) concerning the salvation of their children; for the promise is to them and their children, Gen. 7:7 [*sic*]; Mark 10:16; Acts 2:39."[15] Like the judgment of the Swiss delegates, this judgment uses language that calls believing parents not to doubt the salvation of their children, appealing to the covenant promise that is extended to them. It speaks generally of the salvation of children of believing parents, however, without specifically addressing the issue of those children who die in infancy.

The Bremen delegates. Of all the judgments of the synodical delegates that address the Arminian accusation, none is more forthright than that of the Bremen delegates. Among its propositions was the following:

> Concerning only the children of believers who die before they are able to understand the teaching, we judge that God loves them, out of that same good pleasure for Christ's sake, through Christ,

14. Though we will have occasion to return to Homer Hoeksema's interpretation of these judgments in a subsequent section of this chapter, it is noteworthy that he declares that the Swiss delegates "do not dare to say anything positive and objective about the children of believers who die in infancy" (*Voice*, 271). This comment does not seem to do justice to the rather "objective" claim of the Swiss judgment that God sends his angels to secure their welfare (salvation) on the occasion of their death.

15. *Acta*, 380.

> and in Christ, out of which he loves the adults; therefore, they also, with a view to the covenant, are holy. In order to confirm this, they are initiated by holy baptism and put on Christ.[16]

This proposition clearly identifies the particular question that the Arminian accusation raises, namely, the election and salvation of the children of believers who die in infancy. It also affirms without reservation that such children are to be regarded as loved by God in Christ. The basis for this confidence is to be found in the covenant of grace, which is signified and sealed to such children in baptism.

Three Dutch professors. The judgment presented to the Synod by three Dutch professors, Polyander, Thysius, and Walaeus, expressly addresses the Arminian proposition that there is no election or reprobation of young children. In the opening portion of their judgment, the three Dutch professors maintain that "[t]here is a vast difference in the condition of those little children who are born of non-covenant parents, since Scripture declares the latter to be unclean, alienated from Christ and from the covenant of grace."[17] After noting that the children of non-covenant parents are alienated from Christ, the judgment goes on to cite several Scripture passages that speak to the different and privileged status of the children of covenant parents (1 Cor. 7:14; Gal. 2:15; Eph. 2:12; Gen. 17:7; Matt. 19:14; Acts 2:39). Upon the basis of the teaching of these passages, the opinion of the three Dutch professors draws a conclusion regarding the election and salvation of such children who die in infancy.

> From these passages we conclude that the children of believers who die in their infancy must be reckoned among the elect (*onder de uitverkorenen moeten gerekend worden*), since they are graciously delivered from this life by God before they have broken the conditions of his covenant. But concerning the children of unbelievers, who are outside of the church of God, we deem

16. Ibid., 397. Cf. Hoeksema, *Voice*, 272, who maintains that "even this opinion does not make a flat, objective statement concerning all children of believers who die in infancy."

17. *Acta*, 606.

> that men ought to leave them committed to God's judgment. For those who are without, God shall judge, 1 Cor. 5:13.[18]

In this conclusion, the Dutch professors address the specific accusation of the Arminians and claim that believers ought to regard their children who die in infancy to be elect. In support of this claim, they adduce an argument from the consideration that such children have not broken the conditions of the covenant and would not, accordingly, be subject to God's judgment on that account. This argument adds to the scriptural case that is present in the other judgments we have considered. It also testifies to the special focus of their response to the Arminian accusation. Though believers ought to leave the question of the salvation of the children of unbelievers to God's judgment, they have reason to be confident of the salvation of their own children when they die in infancy without breaking covenant with God.

Sybrandus Lubbertus. In a separate judgment, the Dutch theologian Lubbertus indicated his agreement with the opinion of the

18. Ibid. Hoeksema, *Voice*, 272, terms the statement about not having broken the conditions of the covenant "unsubstantiated." However, it was common among Reformed theologians prior to the Synod of Dort to distinguish between infant children, who were not capable of breaking the covenant and being excluded from its promises, and those who had reached an age of discretion, who were able to break the covenant and forfeit its blessings. For this reason Zwingli and Bullinger, the leading theologians of the Reformed churches of the Rhineland and architects of the Reformed doctrine of the covenant, expressed confidence regarding the salvation of those children of believers who died in infancy. Warfield, *Studies in Theology*, 429–31, appeals to evidence that this was Zwingli's view, but states that he is unaware of any evidence in Bullinger's writings to confirm Philip Schaff's contention that he taught a similar view. I believe the evidence for Bullinger's view is found in his great treatise on the covenant, which carefully distinguishes those who are included in the covenant by virtue of their not having or being able to violate its conditions, and those who prove themselves to be "carnal" when they reach "the age of reason" and "neglect the conditions of the covenant." See Heinrich Bullinger, "A Brief Exposition of the One and Eternal Testament or Covenant of God," in J. Wayne Baker, *Heinrich Bullinger and the Covenant: The Other Reformed Tradition* (Athens, OH: Ohio University Press, 1980), 106–7, 130–31. On the subject of the infant children of believers who die before they break the covenant, Bullinger writes: "Wherefore we conclude that infants who are born of faithful parents and who die either before they have begun to live or before they could be inscribed among the people of God with the sacred sign of the covenant cannot be damned with the support of this text [Gen. 17:14]. For God is speaking of despisers of the covenant who are adults. . . . We believe, moreover, such infants to be saved by the grace and mercy of God" (131).

three Dutch professors. Lubbertus also added his own opinion, which was subscribed to as well by the three professors. Contrary to the Arminian denial of an election or reprobation of children, Lubbertus stated,

> Scripture proves this point, Romans 9:7. 'Neither because they are Abraham's seed are they all children'; and verse 6, 'For they are not all Israel, who are out of father Israel.' Besides, the promise belongs to the little children of the Church, Acts 2:39. 'For to you is the promise and to your children.' To the others, who are outside of the Church, there is no promise given.[19]

Lubbertus's opinion makes the general point that there is an election and reprobation of children and that this election and reprobation may even distinguish between children of covenant parents. But it does not speak as directly or affirmatively of the specific question regarding how believing parents should view their children who die in infancy. The reader is left to infer from Lubbertus's reference to Acts 2:39 at the end of his opinion that parents should view these children from the standpoint of the promise of the covenant.

Franciscus Gomarus. In addition to these judgments by several Dutch professors, the Synod also received a judgment from the eminent theologian and opponent of Arminius, Franciscus Gomarus. Against the unscriptural teaching of Grevinchovius, an Arminian theologian, that there is no election of little children since that they have no "foreseen faith," Gomarus observed that

> [t]he young (*jonge*) children of those who are in the covenant of God through Christ, and of those who are true believers, we piously believe to be also elect (*gelooven wij Godvruchtelijk, dat mede verkoren zijn*), in case they die before reaching the age of understanding, according to the indication of the formula of the covenant, "I am your God, and the God of your seed," Gen. 17 and Acts 2:39. But, in case they arrive at the age of understanding,

19. *Acta*, 615.

> then we acknowledge that only those who believe in Christ are elect, for these alone are saved according to the gospel.[20]

Gomarus's judgment, like that of the three Dutch professors, Polyander, Thysius, and Walaeus, speaks specifically to the question in dispute. In the particular circumstance of "true believers" whose young children die in infancy, we may piously believe that such children are elect. With the same care for precision in his judgment, Gomarus also makes the point that played a role in the thinking of the other Dutch professors, namely, that these children belong to a special category of persons with whom God covenants, those who in the nature of the case have not responsibly (having reached the age of understanding) broken the covenant relationship. The preciseness with which Gomarus defines those children whom believers may regard as elect, allows him at the same time to acknowledge that not all of those with whom God covenants in the covenant of grace are elect.

The delegates from the Particular Synod of South Holland. The judgment presented to the Synod by the Particular Synod of South Holland includes an interesting opinion on the subject. Though this opinion encourages believing parents not to doubt the election and salvation of their young children, it also adds a general comment about the possibility of the reprobation of some children of believers. This addition is somewhat unique among all the preliminary judgments on the question that were presented to the Synod.

> That all young children, by reason of original sin, are subject to everlasting condemnation, and that reprobation may take place even in the case of little children who live and grow up (*bij hun leven en opwassen plaats hebbe*), they [the delegates] hold that holy Scripture and experience testify clearly enough. But whether reprobation may also take place in the case of young children of believers who die in their early childhood before the age of speech, without actual sins (*stervende in hunne jong sprakelooze*

20. Ibid., 619–20.

> *kindsheid zonder werkelijke zonden*), concerning this they are of the opinion that men should not curiously inquire (*niet nieuwsgieriglijk hebbe te onderzoeken*); but seeing that there are testimonies of Holy Scripture which cut off for believing parents all reason for doubting (*alle oorzaak afsnijden van te twijfelen van de verkiezing*) concerning the election and salvation of their young children, therefore, they hold that men should be at peace and satisfied with this; Gen. 17:7; Matt. 19:14; Acts 2:39; 1 Cor. 7:14, and similar passages.[21]

Even though this opinion allows for the possibility of the reprobation of some children of believers who "live and grow up," it pointedly warns against any speculative conclusion that young children of believers who die in infancy may be among those whom God reprobates. In the special case of such children, parents have no basis whatsoever to doubt their salvation by virtue of their standing as children embraced by the promises of the covenant of grace.

The Utrecht delegates. The judgment of the Utrecht delegates speaks at some length on the scriptural teaching that God elects and reprobates young children, a teaching that the Arminians had expressly denied. In their judgment, however, the Utrecht delegates do not address as directly the particulars of the Arminian objection regarding the reprobation of the young children of believers who die in infancy. No distinction, for example, is drawn between children who die in infancy and others who may reach an age of maturity. Nor is there any direct affirmation regarding how believing parents should regard the election and salvation of their children who die in infancy. However, the judgment of the Utrecht delegates does include the argument that the promise of the covenant to the young children "comes from nowhere else than from election unto salvation."

> If there is no election of young children, then there is also no promise of salvation, nor salvation for them. For salvation, and the promise of salvation, comes from nowhere else than from

21. Ibid., 634.

> election unto salvation (*Want de zaligheid, en de belofte er van, is nergens anders uit, dan uit de verkiezing ter zaligheid*). Now the promise belongs to young children, "I am your God and the God of your seed." "To you and to your children is the promise"; "your children are holy." And salvation belongs also to them, "Let them come unto me, for such is the kingdom of heaven."[22]

In the opinion of the Utrecht delegates, the assurance of the election of young children derives from the promise of the covenant that is extended to them together with their parents.

The Drenthe delegates. The last judgment that we consider is the judgment of the Drenthe delegates. In their judgment, the Drenthe delegates distinguished carefully between the young children of unbelievers who die in infancy and the young children of believers who die in infancy. Regarding the deceased children of unbelievers, their opinion states that they may be judged to be reprobate; regarding the deceased children of believers, however, their opinion states that the parents of such children can have a "sure hope" of their election.

> Here we may say something concerning young children (among whom we also include adults who have been insane from the beginning of their life), namely, concerning those young children who die in their infancy. 1. The little children of unbelievers who die in their infancy we judge to be reprobate; 1 Cor. 7; Rom. 11. Hence the contrary doctrine falls away: 1. the heathen shall be saved if they use the good light of their reason; 2. no one is condemned on account of original sin. But matters stand differently with respect to the young children of believers who die in infancy; concerning these we say the following. 1. Little children of believers, even though they die in infancy, can nevertheless be rejected by God, and left in their misery, if God should will to use his right. . . . 2. Meanwhile believing parents can nevertheless have a sure hope concerning the salvation of such little children

22. Ibid., 655.

> (*van de zaligheid van hunne zoodanige jonge kinderen, eene zekere hoop hebben*). For we never read in Scripture that such children were ever reprobated. But on the contrary the same Scripture testifies of the good inclination of God towards such children; Gen. 17:7; Matt. 19:14; Acts 2:39.[23]

One noteworthy feature of this judgment is the argument from the absence of any scriptural testimony that the children of believers who die in infancy may be reprobate.

These judgments confirm a keen interest and desire among the delegations to respond to the untrue accusation of the Arminian party regarding the election of the children of believers who die in infancy. They illustrate that the delegates wanted the Synod's Canons to include a statement regarding the propriety of a positive judgment respecting the election of such children. Though some express their opinion in more unqualified terms than others, most of them ask for a forthright statement that would encourage parents not to doubt the election and salvation of their children in such circumstances.

The Request for Article 1.17

Surprisingly, the first draft of the Canons did not include any reference to the election of the young children of believers who die in infancy. Even though many of the initial judgments that were presented before the Synod of Dort included comments on this subject, the committee authorized to prepare a draft of the Canons chose not to include an article on it in the first draft. In this respect, the draft Canons followed the precedent of an earlier set of Canons that had been written by the president of the Synod, Bogerman, and that were among the materials available to the committee as it prepared its first draft for consideration by the Synod.[24] For example, in their comments on Bogerman's earlier draft statement, the Overijssel delegates had argued that it would be appropriate for the Synod to address the subject of the election of infant children of the covenant, not only to

23. Ibid., 689–90.
24. Sinnema, "Reprobation," 412.

answer the Arminian complaint but also to lend comfort to believing parents.[25]

The absence of any comment on the Arminian complaint regarding the Reformed view of election, especially in terms of its implications for the election and salvation of infant children of believers, was bound to provoke some reaction from the various delegations at the Synod. Indeed, in the discussion of the initial judgments of the various delegations to the Synod, a number of delegates had expressed their desire that a statement be included that would address the Arminian complaint. It is not surprising, therefore, that some of the delegates strongly advised that such a statement be included in a revised version of the committee's draft Canons. The advice of the Swiss delegates captures well the sentiment of these delegates.

> We are surprised that nothing at all is decided or defined about the election and reprobation of infants. It certainly seems right to us that regard must be paid to the vileness by which the Remonstrants are accustomed to make the orthodox doctrine of predestination hateful for pregnant women. And clearly there is scarcely anything—experience is witness—which can cause women (especially the feminine sex in childbirth) more hurt than to hear something debated concerning the salvation or damnation of their young. Hence those [apparently other delegations] do not badly—perhaps with good cause—give advice who would grant some moderate and sound (*moderatum et solidum*) canon not only to assuage the doubt of believing parents about their infants but also to counter the vileness of opponents.[26]

It is evident that this advice of the Swiss delegates enjoyed the support of many of the delegates, since it became the occasion for the draft committee's subsequent submission of a draft Article 1.17 for the consideration of the synod.

25. Ibid., 412. For a copy of the Swiss request, see Klaas Dijk, *De Strijd over Infra- en Supralapsarisme in de Gereformeerde Kerken van Nederland* (Kampen: J. H. Kok, 1912).

26. Sinnema, "Reprobation," 412–13. The translation is Sinnema's and is taken from an original source (Zurich, Manuscript B235, fol. 242r.).

The Committee Draft of 1.17

At this point in the story of the formulation of Article 1.17, the matter becomes a bit more complicated. In his dissertation on the subject of reprobation at the Synod of Dort, Donald Sinnema calls attention to perhaps the earliest draft of the Article, which was written in the hand of Polyander, a member of the draft committee. In this draft, there is evidence that an early proposal for the Article differed somewhat from the draft that was eventually presented to the Synod. This difference is apparent from the written statement of Polyander, which Sinnema reproduces as follows:

> Although, properly speaking, God knows those who are his, 2 Tim. 2:19, and we are not to investigate his hidden judgment, nevertheless the Scripture says 1 Cor. 7:14 [at the end stands an alternative to the preceding words: Since we must make judgments about God's will from his Word, of which Gen. 17:7, Act. 2:39, 1 Cor. 7:14 testify] that the children of believers are holy, not according to nature, but by virtue of a gracious covenant in which they together with their parents are comprehended, pious parents ought not to doubt the election and salvation of their children whom God in their infancy ==== calls from this life but to believe concerning them from ==== the promises of the covenant that the kingdom of heaven belongs to them. It is so far from being the case that they ought to suppose ==== some of them even from their mother's breast ==== torn and ==== into the eternal damnation of hell.[27]

27. Sinnema, "Reprobation," 413 (quoting from Hague Manuscript I.5.18 [second document]). The translation is mine, and is based upon the following reproduction of Polyander's handwritten note by Sinnema: "Etsi Deus proprie novit qui sint sui, 2 Tim. 2:19, et de occulte ipsius judicio nobis non sit serutandum, tamen cum Scriptura dicat 1 Cor. 7:14 [at the end stands an alternative to the preceding words: Quandoquidem de voluntate Dei ex verbo ipsius nobis est judicandum, quod testator Gen. 17:7, Act. 2:39, 1 Cor. 7:14] liberos fidelium esse sanctos, non quidem natura, sed beneficio foederis gratuiti in quo illi cum parentibus comprehenduntur, pii parentes de electione et salute suorum librorum quos Deus in infantia ==== ex hac vita evocat dubitare non debent, sed credere ad eos ex ==== vi promissionis foderalis pertinere regnum caelorum. Tantum abest ut opinari debeant ==== nonnullos ex iis aliquos ab uberibus matrum ==== abripi et ==== in gehennae damnationem aeternam." Sinnema notes that the conclusion of this draft of

The interesting feature of this handwritten draft of Polyander is that it originally began with a concessive clause ("Although, properly speaking, God knows those who are his. . . .") that might open the door to some uncertainty regarding God's electing purpose with respect to the infant children of believers. According to the opening language of Polyander's draft, we must acknowledge that the "hidden judgment" of God remains unknown to us. This "hidden judgment" concerns God's perfect knowledge of the elect and nonelect, a knowledge to which we do not have access. By calling attention to the "hidden judgment" of God, the language of Polyander's first draft allowed the possibility of the reprobation of the deceased children of believers within the secret will of God, even though it also encouraged parents not to doubt the election of such children.

Polyander's handwritten draft of Article 1.17, however, reveals that this element of uncertainty regarding God's secret will, which was present in an early draft of the Article, would soon be removed by the draft committee. In the draft committee's eventual recommendation to the Synod, the proposed Article was identical to the present form of Article 1.17.[28] In this draft proposal to the Synod, the opening phrase of the Article emphasizes that believers make judgments about God's will upon the basis of his revealed Word. No reference is made to the hidden judgment of God. Rather, believing parents are strongly encouraged to be assured of the election and salvation of their children when they die as infants. By emphasizing the positive confidence believing parents may have regarding the election of their infant children, the proposed Article eliminates a possible occasion for uncertainty on the subject. Remarkably, after this draft proposal was presented to the Synod, the draft committee considered altering its language once more at the request of the delegates from the Palatinate. When the draft committee invited responses to their

Polyander was to reappear in the final form of the Canons, in the closing "Rejection of False Accusations." The adopted form of the Canons omits any reference to Matt. 19:14, and places the references to 1 Cor. 7:14, Gen. 17:7, and Acts 2:39 in the margin (though the language of the Article clearly means to allude to these passages).

28. In the draft presented to the synod, however, this Article was numbered Article 1.18.

proposed Article, the Palatine delegates stated that "[w]e prefer that the entire formula presented by us before be retained, because concerning God's will it is well-known from his Word that 'not all who are from Israel are of Israel' (Rom. 9:6). There [in the committee's proposal], however, nothing is defined about the first cause, but it remains in the order of secondary causes."[29] Despite this request for a change in the Article, which would add a reference to God's "hidden judgment" that had earlier been removed, the Synod ultimately decided to retain the Article in the form in which it was first proposed by the draft committee.

The Final Form of 1.17

Though it might appear unnecessary to rehearse the details of the complicated prehistory of Article 1.17, an acquaintance with this history is directly relevant to a proper understanding of the Article as it was finally adopted. Despite the diversity of opinions in the judgments of the various delegations, the consensus of the Synod of Dort is expressed in the Article as it has been received by the Reformed churches to this day. In its final form, Article 1.17 speaks to the Arminian accusation in clear terms: believing parents, who are to make judgments about God's will upon the basis of his revealed Word, ought not to doubt the election and salvation of their infant children whom God calls to himself. Therefore, the Arminian accusation that the Reformed churches teach the reprobation of (some of) these children and deprive believers of any assurance regarding their election and salvation is false and does not accord with truth or charity. The doctrine of election, particularly in respect to the question raised by the Arminians' accusation, supports a robust assurance of God's favor toward his people, including their deceased infant children. This assurance rests solidly upon what is revealed respecting

29. Sinnema, "Reprobation," 414 (quoting from Hague Manuscript I.5.15). Sinnema notes that nothing is said to this effect in the original "judgment" (*iudicium*) of the Palatine delegation, though the opinion expressed was held by the Heidelberg theologian David Pareus in his annotation of Bellarmine's *De Amissione Dei*. . . . Sinnema appeals to this request of the Palatines to argue that Article 1.17 does not exclude the possibility that some such children of believers might be reprobate at the level of God's "hidden will."

these children in the Word of God, namely, that they are embraced by the covenant promise in Christ and set apart as holy.

Based on our study of the occasion for the writing and adoption of Article 1.17, the next chapter will explore how this Article should be interpreted. While Article 1.17 expresses a consensus opinion among the Reformed churches, we will see that it has been liable to different interpretations within these churches.

7

The Election and Salvation of the Children of Believers Who Die in Infancy:

A Study of Article 1.17 of the Canons of Dort (2)

One of the remarkable features of CD 1.17 is that it does not seem to have provoked any substantial debate throughout the history of the Reformed churches. I am unaware of any specific cases in which office-bearers were charged with deviating from the teaching of this Article. The conclusions that seem to follow from the apparent absence of such cases is that the Reformed churches have consistently embraced the teaching of Article 1.17 and that there is really no basis for significant disagreement among those who subscribe to it.

Before we draw such sanguine conclusions, however, we need to consider whether Article 1.17 has been uniformly interpreted by Reformed theologians. Despite the relative absence of controversy regarding this Article among the Reformed churches, there is evidence of some differences of opinion regarding its teaching. At the risk of oversimplification, these differences can be categorized as two distinct interpretations. The first, which might be termed the "definite" or "objective" one, insists that Article 1.17 forthrightly affirms the election of the children of believing parents who die in infancy. The second, which might be termed the "pastoral" or "subjective" one, argues that Article 1.17 speaks only of the hope that believing parents should have with respect to their infant children.[1]

A Definite Declaration of Election

The first interpretation of Article 1.17 claims that its encouragement to believing parents is rooted in a confident judgment that their children who die in infancy are elect and saved. On this reading of Article 1.17, doubt is excluded. Though advocates of this view acknowledge that Article 1.17 is expressed in a pastoral form, encouraging parents "not to doubt" the election and salvation of such children, they emphasize that the confidence expressed in the Article could not be sustained if this were only a "subjective" hope. Several arguments have been set forth to defend this interpretation.

First, this interpretation has the sanction of a long-standing tradition of interpretation and is represented in commentaries on the CD. As we noted in our summary of the various judgments of the delegations at the Synod of Dort, several of them are formulated in a manner that forthrightly affirms the election and salvation of the deceased children of believing parents. This is true in the judgments of the Swiss, the Bremen, the Utrecht, and the Drenthe delegations and is the position defended by the five Dutch professors at the Synod. These judgments provide evidence that a significant,

1. N. H. Gootjes, "Can Parents Be Sure? Background and Meaning of Canons of Dort, I, 17," *Lux Mundi* 15, 4 (1996), 2, characterizes these two views nicely, when he notes that the first takes the Article to "determine the salvation of these infants," and the second takes it to "determine [only] the attitude of the parents." While the language may be misleading, one could speak of the first as the "objective" and the second as the "subjective" reading of Article 17. Opinions differ as to the historical consensus of Reformed theologians on the election of the deceased infant children of believers. Cf. B. B. Warfield, "The Development of the Doctrine of Infant Salvation," in *Studies in Theology* (1932; repr., Grand Rapids, MI: Baker, 1981), 429–38, who argues that this is the prevalent Reformed view; and *RD*, 4:725, which claims that "[t]he Reformed were inclined to believe that all children who were born in the covenant of grace and died before reaching the age of discretion attained to blessedness in heaven, though in this connection as well many of them made a distinction between elect and reprobate children and did not dare to attribute salvation with certainty to each of these children individually." No doubt there remains a diversity of opinion among Reformed theologians. The first or objective reading of Article 1.17, however, insists that the CD gave confessional expression to the prevalent view.

if not prevalent, portion of the delegations at the Synod of Dort favored a strong testimony to the election of such children. Moreover, in their comments on this Article, many Reformed theologians have taken it to be a straightforward affirmation of the election and salvation of the children of believing parents who die in infancy. For example, in 1818 Thomas Scott wrote that "[t]he salvation of the offspring of believers, dying in infancy, is here scripturally stated, and not limited to such as are baptized."[2] In his commentary on the Canons, which was written early in the twentieth century, M. Meijering summarizes his discussion of Article 1.17 with the following statement: "When God-fearing parents cry over their precious gifts they could only briefly enjoy having, they may look up together and remind one another: Our children were fruits early ripe for heaven. And with this they can comfort one another."[3] Among these commentators, it is observed that the language, "ought not to doubt," is a *litotes*. Though this language expresses the matter negatively, it intends to express a positive sentiment. Accordingly, one commentator observes,

> We have to take the words "ought not to doubt" as a *litotes*. That is a figure of speech seemingly diminishing the meaning but in fact used to strengthen it. "He is not a fool" means in fact: "He is very smart." We must therefore take "ought not to doubt" as "must be firmly assured." Believing parents must be firmly assured over the election and salvation of their children who died in infancy.[4]

These comments attest the presence of a commentary tradition that understands Article 1.17 to express, albeit negatively and

2. Thomas Scott, *The Articles of the Synod of Dort, Translated from the Latin, with Notes* (1818; repr., Harrisburg, PA: Sprinkle Publications, 1993), 270.

3. M. Meijering, *De Dordtsche Leerregels* (Groningen: Jan Haan, 1924), 82.

4. Joh. Francke, "Zijn de Kinderen der Gelovigen, die God in hun Kindsheid uit dit Leven Wegneemt, Wedergeboren?," *De Reformatie* 44, 42 (1969), 330. See also T. Bos, *De Dordtsche Leerregelen* (Kampen: J. H. Kok, 1915), 66–76; Abraham Kuyper, *E Voto Dordraceno: Toelichting op den Heidelbergschen Catechismus*, vol. 3 (Kampen: J. H. Kok, n.d.), 6–12; C. den Boer, *Om 't Eeuwig Welbehagen* (Utrecht: De Banier, 1974), 79–82.

pastorally, a strong certainty regarding the election and salvation of the deceased children of believing parents.[5]

Second, the definite interpretation of Article 1.17 also appeals to the particular occasion for its formulation.[6] This was the Arminian accusation that the Reformed view taught the reprobation of some (but not necessarily all) children of believing parents who die in infancy. The formulation's purpose is to offer a rebuttal that would prove the Arminian accusation to be false and baseless. If sufficient weight is given to the occasion for the formulation of Article 1.17, it hardly seems adequate to say that its authors only intended to speak to the attitude of believing parents in such circumstances. If the Article merely encouraged a subjective hope that such children were elect, though all the while granting the real possibility that some among them were reprobate, it would not provide an adequate answer to the Arminian accusation. Indeed, a reading of Article 1.17 that would allow for the possibility of the reprobation of such children within the secret will of God would lend support to, perhaps even confirm, the validity of the Arminian accusation. The less definite reading of the Article does not seem consistent with the emphatic way the conclusion of the Canons rejects the Arminian misrepresentation of Reformed teaching on this subject. The only answer that would prove the falsity of the Arminian accusation would be one that positively affirmed the election and salvation of such covenant children.

Third, we have already observed that the various delegations to the Synod of Dort presented their judgments on the Arminian accusation. Though these judgments reflect a spectrum of opinion on this accusation, most of them called for a positive statement that would

5. For another interpretation of Article 1.17 that takes this view, see J. G. Vos, *The Covenant of Grace* (Pittsburgh, PA: Crown and Covenant Publications, n.d.), 21–24.

6. Gootjes, "Parents," 2–6, lists five "reasons" that Article 1.17 should be read as an expression of certainty regarding the election of these infants: (1) only a statement of certainty would answer the Arminian accusation; (2) the insistence of the various delegations that the Synod include a positive, forthright statement on the matter; (3) an evasive answer would not have satisfied the request of the delegations for a positive statement; (4) the draft presented by the committee to the Synod initially included Matt. 19:14 as a proof text; and (5) the wording of the text of Article 1.17. Though there is some overlapping between Gootjes's "reasons" and the arguments I identify, my summary follows a different sequence than Gootjes's and combines his second and third reasons for the sake of clarity.

affirm the election and salvation of the children of believers who die in infancy. The strong desire for such an affirmative statement is evident from the fact that Article 1.17 was unanimously approved by the Synod for inclusion in the final form of the Canons. In the form that was approved, no uncertainty is cast upon the affirmation of the election of such children, even though the Palatine delegation asked for the inclusion of a sentence that referred to the secret will of God and left room from that standpoint for the inference that some deceased infant children of believers might be reprobate. The sentiments expressed in the judgments of some of the delegations, however, called for a much more definite and less evasive answer to the Arminian accusation. The final form of Article 1.17 provides that kind of definite answer. In the light of these considerations, it does not seem likely that the Synod would be satisfied with an answer that would allow the possible inference that some of these children were ultimately reprobate within the secret will of God.[7] The latter inference seems inconsistent with Article 1.17's insistence that we are to make judgments about the matter upon the basis of the Word of God and the promise of the covenant of grace.

Fourth, the "Rejection of False Accusations" at the conclusion of the Canons declares emphatically that the Arminian accusation is false. To appreciate the significance of this claim, it needs to be remembered that this accusation characterizes the Reformed churches as teaching that "many infant children of believers are snatched in their innocence from their mothers' breasts and cruelly cast into hell so that neither the blood of Christ nor their baptism can be of any use to them." Since Article 1.17 purports to answer to this

7. Though I do not cite it as a separate ground for this view, it should be remembered that some of these judgments especially emphasized the fact that these children were not in a position to break the covenant. Though some with whom God covenants may break the covenant and come under its sanctions, this circumstance does not apply in the case of children of believers who die in infancy. Vos, *Covenant of Grace*, 23, stresses this point in his consideration of the question: "It is true that some of the children of believing parents are not of the elect, and turn out to be covenant-breakers. But an infant that dies before reaching years of discretion cannot be a covenant-breaker; it cannot despise and violate the obligation of the Covenant of Grace. Therefore we have the best of reasons for believing that all children of believing parents dying in infancy are not only within the Covenant of Grace, but also of the number of the elect and shall certainly be saved."

accusation, it should not be interpreted to permit the view that some of these infant children may in fact be reprobate. The point of the closing "Rejection of False Accusations" is that the Arminian accusation was a false and uncharitable misstatement of the Reformed view. However, if Article 1.17 were stating something less than a definite affirmation of the election of these children, the Arminian accusation could not be declared false or untrue. If any room were left for believing parents to be unsure of the election of their children who die in infancy, the Arminian accusation would seem to retain something of its persuasiveness.

And fifth, the pastoral form of Article 1.17 does not mean that it falls short of a positive affirmation of the election and salvation of the children of believing parents who die in infancy. Though it is alleged that the language "ought not to doubt" speaks only to the subjective attitude such parents may have in the circumstance of the death of their infant children, this language is used because it answers precisely to the form of the Arminian accusation. The accusation of the Arminians was not simply that these children may be reprobate. Rather, the accusation was that believing parents could have no assurance of the salvation of their infant children because they might be reprobate within the secret will of God. Because this was the nature of the Arminian accusation, it was appropriate for the Synod of Dort to adopt a statement that spoke directly to the confidence parents may have in this circumstance. A simple statement of the truth, namely, that such children are elect, would not suffice to answer the pointed complaint of the Arminians. N. H. Gootjes summarizes this argument well, when he observes that

> Canons of Dort I, 17 does not fall short of certainty, rather, it moves beyond a statement of fact by directly addressing the situation of the parents. It begins by pointing out the certainty that their children are holy in virtue of the covenant of grace. Then it turns to the parents to comfort them on this basis that they ought not to doubt. Rather, they should trust the words of God: 1 Cor. 7:14, Gen. 17:7 and Acts 2:39. It is radically against the intention of this confession to use the practical direction of this

> statement to undermine the certainty of the doctrine. The parents are comforted on that [*sic*] basis that God himself promised salvation. Before the certainty of God's promises the doubt of parents melts away.[8]

For these reasons, rather than leave uncertain the election and salvation of such children, the first interpretation of the pastoral word of Article 1.17 insists that nothing less than a certain affirmation of their election could press upon believing parents the duty to be confident in this circumstance.

A Pastoral Encouragement of Good Hope

Despite the arguments that Article 1.17 expresses a strong certainty regarding the election of the deceased children of believing parents, some interpreters take a less definite view. In their opinion, Article 1.17 stops short of expressing a positive certainty regarding the election and salvation of such children. According to this reading of Article 1.17, believing parents are encouraged to have a good hope that their infant children are elect, but this is not tantamount to an affirmation of their election within God's secret will and purpose. Article 1.17 speaks to the *attitude* that believing parents should cultivate upon the death of their infant children. But it does not purport to speak objectively of the election and salvation of such children.

Though this interpretation of Article 1.17 seems to have fewer advocates than the stronger interpretation that we have already considered, it does have some able and clear defenders. Among those, the Protestant Reformed writers Herman Hoeksema and Homer Hoeksema have presented a fairly vigorous argument for a more subjective understanding. In this reading, Article 1.17 encourages believing parents to have hope respecting the salvation of their children who die in infancy, but this is a "subjective" attitude that leaves open the status of such children within the hidden judgment of God.

Herman Hoeksema's comments on this Article are surprisingly

8. Gootjes, "Parents," 5.

critical. After acknowledging the important pastoral and historical occasion for the inclusion of the Article in the final form of the Canons, Hoeksema nonetheless observes that "[t]he article leaves much to be desired as far as clarity and sharpness of definition are concerned; and it cannot be denied that in the form in which the matter is here cast it really cannot be considered an item for a confession."[9] The reason Hoeksema judges the Article to be inappropriate for a confessional statement is that it does not express "a definite view concerning the salvation of children who die in infancy."[10] If the Article had expressed such a definite view, it would not have spoken of how believing parents "ought not to doubt the election and salvation" of their children, but would have positively affirmed "that the children of believers whom God takes away in their infancy are saved according to their election."[11] While he acknowledges that many interpreters take this definite view, Hoeksema is convinced that the Article speaks only to the attitude of parents in this circumstance and "does not express an objective item of faith."[12] Hoeksema also notes that the Article provides no help to parents who may be unsure if their children belong to the category of infants or whether they may have reached the age of discretion. As he describes the teaching of this Article, the definition of such infants remains "rather elastic" and undetermined.[13]

In addition to the subjectivity and uncertainty that characterize the language of the Article, Hoeksema adds another argument against taking it as a definite statement. Since we know from the Scriptures (Rom. 9) that not all those who fall within the "sphere" of the covenant are elect, we cannot infer from the apparent covenant

9. Herman Hoeksema, *Believers and Their Seed*, trans. Homer Hoeksema (Grand Rapids, MI: Reformed Free Publishing, 1971), 149.

10. Ibid.

11. Ibid.

12. Ibid., 150.

13. Ibid. Hoeksema cites the example of children as young as seven or eight years of age who can give a credible expression of faith in Jesus Christ. This argument from the uncertainty as to who is an "infant" according to the language of 1.17 seems to me an abstraction from the concrete circumstance that is being addressed. The language of "infants" in this Article is clarified in the closing "Rejection of False Accusations," which speaks of the "infant children" of believers who are "snatched in their innocence from their mothers' breasts."

status of such children that they are elect and saved according to the sovereign will of God. "From their being in God's covenant by reason of birth from believing parents the salvation of infants does not simply follow as a necessary conclusion."[14] Upon these considerations, and his rejection of the legitimacy of appeals to scriptural texts that are often cited to support Article 1.17, Hoeksema concludes that "such a general proposition cannot be expressed."[15] The most the church could say on the question addressed in Article 1.17 is that "the Lord saves *His seed* out of our seed."[16]

Homer Hoeksema's discussion of Article 1.17 in *The Voice of Our Fathers* is very similar to that of Herman Hoeksema. He also argues that the "negative and subjective viewpoint" of the Article confirms that it speaks only to the attitude of believing parents in the circumstance of the death of their infant children.[17] Since the Article does not express a definite conviction regarding what the church "believes concerning the truth of God's Word according to the Scriptures," Homer Hoeksema concludes that it is "of little doctrinal or confessional value."[18] Unlike Herman Hoeksema, who bases his discussion almost entirely upon the text of Article 1.17, Homer Hoeksema appeals to the judgments of the various delegations at the Synod of Dort. According to him, these judgments confirm that it was not the intention of the delegates to the Synod to express a definite conviction

14. Hoeksema, *Believers*, 153.

15. In addition to the texts cited by the delegates to the Synod of Dort (Gen. 17:7; Matt. 19:14; Mark 10:13–16; Acts 2:39; 1 Cor. 7:14), Hoeksema notes that some proponents of the election of such children appeal (inappropriately, in his view) to passages like 2 Sam. 12:15–23 and 1 Kings 14:12–13.

16. Hoeksema, *Believers*, 158. In view of the force with which Hoeksema writes against Article 1.17, it is interesting to observe that his unhappiness with this Article never became a significant issue in the Protestant Reformed Churches. It should also be observed that Hoeksema's opinion has no official standing in the Protestant Reformed Churches. For example, in a "Response" to a letter to the editor in the *Standard Bearer*, February 15, 1991, 223–24, David Engelsma expressed his disagreement with the view of Hoeksema. According to Engelsma, a professor at the seminary of the Protestant Reformed Churches, the point of Article 1.17 "is not that godly parents have no reason to doubt of the election and salvation of their children who die in infancy, but it is understandable and permissible that they doubt anyway. They *may not* doubt. They are *obliged* not to doubt."

17. Homer Hoeksema, *The Voice of Our Fathers: An Exposition of the Canons of Dordrecht* (Grand Rapids, MI: Free Reformed Publishing, 1980), 276.

18. Ibid., 277.

regarding the election and salvation of the children of believers who die in infancy. Some of these judgments speak in explicitly subjective terms, affirming the "good hope" that parents may have in this circumstance. Others acknowledge the scriptural teaching that "the lines of election and reprobation are carried through also in regard to infants," and thereby acknowledge that some children of believers may be reprobate according to God's hidden judgment.[19] In summarizing his view, Homer Hoeksema identifies four considerations that support a subjective interpretation of Article 1.17: (1) the primary point of doctrine that is affirmed against the Arminian view is the scriptural teaching of the election and reprobation of infants, not the "narrow question of the salvation of children of believers who die in infancy";[20] (2) not one of the judgments of the various delegations expresses "a purely objective and scripturally established statement in regard to the salvation of infants of believers who die at an early age";[21] (3) the Scripture passages appealed to in the judgments of the delegates to the Synod (Gen. 17:7; Matt. 19:14; Mark 10:13–16; Acts 2:39; 1 Cor. 7:14) do not teach that all the children of believing parents who die in infancy are elect; and (4) the judgments of the delegations to the Synod of Dort prove that "the Synod by no means intended to express as a hard and fast ecclesiastical statement of doctrine that all children of believing parents who die in infancy are elect and are saved on the basis of the testimony of Scripture, but that the Synod exactly avoided such a statement."[22]

19. Ibid., 270.

20. Ibid., 276.

21. Ibid. In our discussion of these statements above, we had occasion to point out that this description by Homer Hoeksema is not an adequate representation of their teaching.

22. Ibid., 277. Though I have cited several passages from the writings of two prominent Protestant Reformed theologians on Article 1.17, it should be noted that their view is similar to the view that seems to be prevalent within the tradition of the Netherlands Reformed Churches. For a defense of this view by a Heritage Netherlands Reformed theologian, see J. R. Beeke, "Children Dying in Infancy: Young People Ask (9)," *Banner of Truth* 54, 1 (1988): 22–23. Beeke appeals to the judgments of some of the delegations at Dort to argue that "they did not believe that each particular child dying in infancy of believing parents would enter into glory." According to Beeke, Article 1.17 affirms merely that God "normally" works salvation along covenantal lines, though there may be "Esaus" among the deceased infant children of believers. In this connection, it is interesting to observe that Wilhelmus à Brakel, in *The Christian's Reasonable Service*, ed. Joel R. Beeke, trans. Bartel

Though I believe the first interpretation, which maintains that the Article forthrightly affirms the election of the deceased infant children of believers, is more likely, the position and arguments of Herman and Homer Hoeksema testify to the continued presence among the Reformed churches of this second, "subjective" interpretation of Article 1.17.

Article 1.17 and the Westminster Confession of Faith: A Comparison

Before I conclude this chapter with several observations about the interpretation of Article 1.17, it would be well to consider a question seldom broached in older discussions of the Article: what difference, if any, is there between the affirmation of CD 1.17 and the affirmation of WCF 10.3? In chapter 10.3 of the WCF, the Westminster divines affirmed that "[e]lect infants, dying in infancy, are regenerated, and saved by Christ, through the Spirit, who worketh when, and where, and how he pleaseth: so also are all other elect persons who are uncapable of being outwardly called by the ministry of the Word." Upon an initial reading of the language of chapter 10.3, it appears that it might be addressing the same question addressed in Article 1.17 of the Canons. Since both confessions make affirmations about the election of infants who die in their infancy, there seems an obvious overlap. Because both these confessional statements express the common faith of the Reformed churches, some comment is in order regarding the relation and compatibility between them.

Though we could explore this subject at some length, we will restrict our discussion to the dissimilarities and similarities of these two confessional statements.

Elshout, 4 vols. (Grand Rapids, MI: Reformation Heritage, 1992), 2:506, offers a fairly strong opinion regarding the salvation of the children of believers who die in infancy: "[A]ll children of members of the covenant (irrespective of whether these members are converted or unconverted) who die in infancy—be it prior to or after the administration of baptism—must be considered as saved by virtue of God's covenant in which they were born and in consequence of which they are children of the covenant." While à Brakel clearly denies that all children of believers are elect and partakers of salvation (2:506), he does not hesitate to affirm the assurance that Article 1.17 affords to believers whose children die in infancy.

Dissimilarities

The most obvious dissimilarity between these two confessional statements is that they address quite different questions. In our analysis of Article 1.17 of the Canons, I emphasized that it was written to answer a false accusation of the Arminians. According to this Arminian objection to the doctrine of election, the Reformed view undermined any possible basis for believing parents to be assured of the election and salvation of their children who die in infancy. Article 1.17 answers this objection by stressing that the basis for assurance in these circumstances is the revealed will of God in Scripture. The statement in the WCF, though it speaks about the election of infants, addresses a very different question. Chapter 10 of the WCF deals with the subject of "effectual calling." In the first article of chapter 10, the WCF affirms that effectual calling occurs in the lives of those whom God has predestined to life, and that it ordinarily takes place through the means of Christ's Word and Spirit. Within this setting, the interest of WCF 10.3 is to explain how "elect infants," who are unable to make use of the "ordinary means" for effectual calling, are nonetheless able to be saved according to God's purpose and will. The answer of WCF 10.3 is that all are saved by virtue of God's electing purpose, though in the case of elect infants who die in infancy, their salvation is effected by the Spirit of regeneration in an extraordinary manner.

In addition to this fundamental dissimilarity between the two confessional statements, there is another that is of lesser significance. Article 1.17 of the Canons treats only the issue of the election of covenant children who die in infancy. It does not speak to, or even warrant inferences regarding, the possible election of infant children of nonbelieving, non-covenantal parents. The only persons in view in this Article are the children of believing or godly parents. By contrast, the statement in WCF 10.3 describes a more general category of persons, namely, all elect infants who die in infancy, whether as the children of believing or of unbelieving parents. Though there is room to debate whether WCF 10.3 makes any positive affirmation regarding the election and salvation of the deceased, infant children of nonbelieving parents, it approaches the subject of children who die in infancy in a broad and general manner.[23] However, there is no room for debate whether Article 1.17 of the Canons makes any positive affirmation regarding the election and salvation of all children who die as infants. It clearly does not. Among the judgments of the various delegations to the synod, some speak of the reprobation of the children of unbelievers while others speak with more reserve. However, nothing in the final form of Article 1.17 speaks directly to this subject. By comparison, WCF 10.3 opens the door to the inference that, if any of the children of nonbelieving parents who die in infancy are elect, they will undoubtedly be saved, though without the use of the ordinary means of grace.

Similarities

If sufficient attention is paid to the different questions addressed by Article 1.17 of the Canons and chapter 10.3 of the WCF, there does not appear to be any basis for claiming they are contradictory. Each confession addresses the election of deceased infants from a different perspective, but neither makes any affirmation inconsistent with the other. This is evident from the similarities between them.

The most significant similarity is their common teaching about God's sovereign election of his people. The basic assumption of both confessional statements is that salvation or non-salvation depends ultimately upon God's sovereign and merciful election of some persons and not others. That children who die in their infancy are saved can only be ascribed to God's electing grace and purpose toward them in Christ. Neither confession permits the idea that such children are saved because of their innocence or because of anything

23. Consequently, some Presbyterian theologians who hold to WCF 10.3 have argued that it permits (though without positively asserting) the position that all deceased infants, whether born of believing or nonbelieving parents, are elect and therefore saved. See Warfield, *Studies in Theology*, 429–44. CD 1.17 does not speak directly to the question of the possible election of some or all children of nonbelieving parents. As Warfield himself acknowledges, the Canons, though they positively teach the certain election of all deceased infant children of believers, are "agnostic" on the question of the election or nonelection of the deceased infant children of nonbelievers (*Studies in Theology*, 435). Vos, *Covenant of Grace*, 24, argues correctly that by its silence on the question WCF 10.3 does not support the assertion that there is a class of "nonelect infants dying in infancy."

that is in them or that they have done. Salvation for all persons, whether they die as children in their infancy or they live to a ripe old age, wholly depends upon God's sovereign choice. On this fundamental, biblical, and Reformed teaching, these confessional statements fully concur.

Though a more subtle similarity, it should also be observed that both confessional statements concur that the deceased children of believing parents are not excluded from salvation by virtue of their inability to make use of the ordinary means of salvation. In the case of WCF 10.3, this point is explicitly addressed and affirmed. In the case of Article 1.17 of the Canons, this point may be inferred. If believing parents may be confident of the election and salvation of their children whom God calls out of this life in their infancy, they may also be confident that such children are able to enter the kingdom by virtue of their new birth through the Spirit of regeneration. God's electing purpose is invincible and will be effected upon the basis of Christ's mediatorial work and the Spirit's application of that work to all the elect. Both of these confessional statements are built upon fundamental biblical and Reformed tenets more fulsomely stated in other sections of their respective confessions.

The implication of the dissimilarities and similarities between these two respective confessional statements seems clear. Because these two statements do not contradict each other, a Reformed believer can in good conscience affirm both without fear of inconsistency. However, because these two statements address quite distinct questions from different points of view, it is also possible that a Reformed believer who subscribes to WCF 10.3 might not be prepared to subscribe to Article 1.17. What may be expressly affirmed in Article 1.17 is not expressly affirmed or necessarily implied in WCF 10.3. All Reformed believers, however, whether they hold to the CD or the WCF, must agree with the affirmation of WCF 10.3 that "elect infants, dying in infancy" are regenerated without the ordinary use of the means of grace. Or, to express the matter differently, WCF 10 expresses a truth that is common to the confessions of the Reformed churches, namely, that salvation for any person depends entirely upon God's sovereign and electing grace. Article 1.17, by comparison, may express a truth that is particular to the CD and constitutes one of its unique contributions to the Reformed confession of sovereign election.

Concluding Observations

I observed in the introduction to my treatment of CD 1.17 that it represents a striking illustration of the character of the Reformed teaching about election. Though this Article has been relatively neglected in historical treatments of the Canons and the Reformed view of God's electing purpose in Christ, it provides an important example of the Reformed churches' emphasis upon the twin themes of God's glory as the sovereign Savior of his people and the believer's comfort in his gracious favor. The doctrine of election accents the sheer graciousness of salvation through Christ and constitutes a sure basis for comfort in the gospel promise. Any interpretation of CD 1.17 must recognize how this Article in its own way testifies to both of these themes. Considering the synodical proceedings that led to the adoption of Article 1.17 and the two primary interpretations of the Article that I have discussed in this chapter, four general conclusions seem warranted.

First, any interpretation of Article 1.17 requires careful attention to the precise question that it answers. Unless this question is properly defined, we will not be in a position to determine accurately what is affirmed in this Article. The question is not merely the general question whether God unconditionally elects and reprobates infants, which was denied by the Arminians and affirmed by the Reformed delegates to the Synod of Dort. Neither is Article 1.17 addressed to the general question whether there may be elect as well as nonelect persons with whom God covenants in the historical administration of the covenant of grace. The judgments of the various delegations to the Synod of Dort indicate there was a general consensus that not all children of believing parents are elect. The opinions of these delegations include, for example, references to Romans 9, which teaches that some children of believing parents, like Esau, may be reprobate within the will and purpose of God.

But these general points of biblical and Reformed teaching were not the specific focus of Article 1.17.[24] Rather than speaking broadly to these kinds of questions, Article 1.17 answers specifically a question regarding the election and salvation of the children of believing parents whom God calls out of this life in their infancy. As some of the judgments of the delegates are careful to observe, God did not will that these children should live and grow to an age of discretion. They are children who, in the nature of the case, were not in a position to break the gracious covenant that God had established with them and their parents. The persons whose election and salvation are addressed in Article 1.17 are a special class of persons within the framework of the covenant of grace. The Arminian accusation was that the parents of such children could not be sure of their salvation, since they might well be reprobate within the secret will of God. The specific question to which Article 1.17 speaks, then, is whether believing parents may be confident of the election and salvation of these children.

Second, if we bear in mind the specific question to which Article 1.17 provides an answer, a good case can be made for what I have termed the "definite" interpretation of this Article. The arguments set forth in support of what I have termed the "stronger" reading of Article 1.17 all concur at this point. A definite affirmation of the election and salvation of the children of godly parents who die in infancy seems well suited to answer satisfactorily the Arminian objection summarized in the Canons' closing "Rejection of False Accusations." If Article 1.17 only encouraged a "strong presumption" or "hope" that such children are elect within the purpose of God, it could leave the door slightly open to the Arminian objection. Even a strong, hopeful attitude that such children are elect might open the way to continued doubt concerning their election and salvation.

24. For a treatment of the general Reformed consensus on the relation between sovereign election and the covenant of grace, including an acknowledgment that God's purpose of election does not embrace all believers and their children with whom God covenants in the covenant of grace, see Geerhardus Vos, "The Doctrine of the Covenant in Reformed Theology," in *Redemptive History and Biblical Interpretation: The Shorter Writings of Geerhardus Vos*, ed. Richard B. Gaffin Jr. (Phillipsburg, NJ: Presbyterian and Reformed, 1980), 234–67, esp. 258–67. See also chap. 8 of this volume, which addresses in a general way the topic of covenant theology and baptism.

The less definite interpretation of the Article does not provide a clear rebuttal of the Arminian complaint, namely, that the Reformed view provides believing parents insufficient warrant to be confident of the election of such children.

Another difficulty with the subjective or pastoral-encouragement view of Article 1.17 is that it may not preclude a speculative appeal to the secret will and judgment of God in a manner that undermines assurance. The argument for the subjective view emphasizes that God's electing will ultimately distinguishes between some children of believers who are genuinely recipients of the covenant promise (election) and others who are not (reprobation). It also observes that some children of believing parents grow up and fall away in unbelief, and that this accords with the sovereign purposes of God. When proponents of the second view apply these general truths taught in Scripture to the particular persons who are envisioned in Article 1.17, they conclude that Article 1.17 could not provide a definite affirmation of the election and salvation of all such children. However, a possible weakness in this line of reasoning is that it may undermine a basis for assurance, not only in the case of the deceased infant children of believers, but also in the case of any believer.[25] A speculative approach to the problem of assurance (one that appeals to God's secret, unrevealed will) is discouraged by the opening phrase of 1.17, when it states that we "must make judgments about God's will from his Word." The way of assurance for believing parents set forth in Article 1.17 is the same way of assurance that all believers must follow, lest the assurance of election

25. The Reformed confessions consistently teach that believers may have an assurance of their election, which is based principally upon the revealed promise of the gospel. See e.g., HC 20–23; CD 5.10; and WCF 18. The WCF even speaks of an "infallible assurance," which can only be based upon "the divine truth of the promises of salvation." Any introduction of a speculative consideration regarding the secret judgment of God could only undermine such assurance, not only in the case of the infant children of believing parents who die in infancy, but also in the case of any believer. Cf. Cornelis P. Venema, "The Doctrine of the Sacraments and Baptism according to the Reformed Confessions," *MAJT* 11, 1 (2000): 64n51: "The argument of the Canons is that, if our knowledge of God's grace toward us in Christ is based upon the Word and sacraments, and not upon some impossible insight into the particulars of the divine decree, then we have an adequate basis for confidence regarding the salvation of the children of believing parents."

and salvation never be more than a hopeful attitude regarding what may only possibly be the case. When Article 1.17 says that we must make judgments about the election and salvation of such children upon the basis of God's revealed Word, it reflects a long-standing Reformed conviction that the revealed Word of God in the gospel is the "mirror of election" and the principal basis for the assurance believers may have of God's favor.[26]

Third, despite these arguments for the stronger or more definite interpretation of Article 1.17, it must be acknowledged that the second interpretation has some arguments in its favor as well. As I noted in the introduction to this chapter, there is no evidence in the history of the Reformed churches that the more subjective reading of Article 1.17 has been treated as a failure to honor its teaching. Defenders of the less definitive viewpoint argue that the Article aims primarily to speak a pastoral word of comfort to godly parents of covenant children who die in their infancy. Such godly parents are encouraged not to doubt that these children will be saved, basing their assurance upon the promise of the covenant of grace that also embraces their children. The Article also warns against the temptation to "make judgments" that inappropriately inquire into the secret things of God's eternal counsel. So long as the Article is interpreted and pastorally applied in a manner that encourages, rather than discourages, parents in this circumstance, it can scarcely be argued that its pastoral intention is being denied. When Reformed believers decline to interpret the argument as a definite statement regarding the salvation and election of all such children, they need not thereby deny the comfort and encouragement that it provides them. Since the Reformed churches have never judged between the two broad interpretations of Article 1.17 that I have identified, and advocates of each interpretation have been free

26. For this reason, Reformed theologians often use the language of Christ as the "mirror" of the believer's election. See *Institutes*, 3.24.5: "But if we have been chosen in him, we shall not find assurance of our election in ourselves; and not even in God the Father, if we conceive him as severed from his Son. Christ, then, is the mirror wherein we must, and without self-deception may, contemplate our own election." For a similar emphasis in Heinrich Bullinger, see *The Decades of Heinrich Bullinger* (1849–52; lithographic reprint of 4 volumes in 2, Grand Rapids, MI: Reformation Heritage, 2004), 3:187–88.

to advance arguments for their views, the freedom to hold one or the other of these views has always been maintained in the history of the churches that subscribe to the CD.[27]

And fourth, my treatment of Article 1.17 confirms one of the characteristic features of the doctrine of election in the CD and the Reformed tradition. In the specific case of the deceased children of believing parents, the authors of the Canons desired a clear statement that would comfort such parents and belie the false accusation of the Arminian party. Despite the Arminian charge that the doctrine of election can only undermine the assurance of salvation, the affirmation of Article 1.17 declares that, in the death of infant children of believers, God's sovereign and merciful election is a solid basis for assurance regarding their salvation. For such children to be saved, God must love them in and for the sake of Christ. Indeed, no one is saved whom God does not graciously choose to save in Christ. This holds true for children as much as for adults. As members of the fallen race in Adam, the children of believers whom God calls out of this life in infancy are saved solely by virtue of God's gracious favor. Far from intimating any uncertainty or doubt respecting the assurance of their election, this Article declares an assurance that is securely founded upon the biblical and Reformed teaching regarding election and its revelation through the Word of the gospel. In doing so, it illustrates what we noted at the outset of this essay: the biblical and Reformed teaching regarding election serves to safeguard the singular honor of God, who sovereignly and graciously saves his people in Christ, and to undergird the believer's confidence in his gracious and invincible favor.

27. The permission to hold to one or the other of the two interpretations of Article 1.17 that I have identified is an illustration of what is technically called the *animus imponentis* ("the intention of the imposing body"). The evidence from the divergent views of the divines at the Synod of Dort, and the historical treatment of this Article by the assemblies of the Reformed churches, confirms that the churches have always permitted a degree of liberty in the interpretation and application of it.

8

Covenant Theology and the Baptism of the Children of Believers[1]

> "The argument in a nutshell is simply this: God established His church in the days of Abraham and put children into it. They must remain there until He puts them out. He has nowhere put them out. They are still then members of His Church and as such entitled to its ordinances."[2]

Benjamin Breckinridge Warfield, the great Presbyterian theologian in the tradition of the old Princeton Theological Seminary, was not known for his terse writing style. In his polemics with the Reformed Baptist theologian Augustus Hopkins Strong on the subject of infant baptism, however, he was uncharacteristically brief. According to Warfield, the whole issue concerning the proper recipients of the sacrament of baptism comes down to the question, who belongs to the church? Baptism, as a sign and seal of God's covenant promise, must be administered to all those with whom God covenants. Since God covenants with believers and their

1. This chapter is a revised version of Cornelis P. Venema, "Covenant Theology and Baptism," in *The Case for Covenantal Infant Baptism*, ed. Gregg Strawbridge (Phillipsburg, NJ: P&R Publishing, 2003), 201–29. It is included here because it addresses in a particular way the relation between covenant and election.

2. B. B. Warfield, "The Polemics of Infant Baptism," in *Studies in Theology* (1932; repr., Grand Rapids, MI: Baker, 1981), 408.

children, they are entitled to the divinely appointed ordinances that administer the covenant. The baptism of the children of believing parents, therefore, is an act performed in obedience to the divine institution of the sacrament as a sign and seal of the covenant of grace. Because God covenants with believers *and their children*, the church baptizes them on the ground of their membership in the church and covenant people of God.

Warfield's uncharacteristically blunt conclusion aptly identified the central matter in the long-standing debate between paedobaptists and Baptists.[3] This debate can be reduced to one principal question: does the covenant of grace in its NT administration embrace the children of believing parents in the same way as in its OT administration? However complex and diverse may be the arguments, pro and con, over the subject of infant baptism, this remains the overriding issue.

Precisely because the debate between paedobaptists and Baptists centers upon the doctrine of the covenant of grace, particularly the similarity and dissimilarity of the covenant in its OT and NT administrations, it can hardly be resolved merely by appealing to specific biblical texts. Typically, in the polemics regarding paedobaptism, Reformed authors appeal to texts that *imply* a continuation of the OT practice of including children within the covenant community. Baptist authors counter by pointing out that *no single text* in the NT expressly teaches that children ought to be baptized. Both sides in the debate, ironically, employ a kind of argument from silence to make their case. Paedobaptists argue that the silence of the NT confirms the continuation of OT practice. After all, if the children of believing parents had been excluded in the new covenant, this surely would have become a bone of contention in the early church, which in its beginnings was comprised largely of Jewish Christians. Baptists respond by pointing out the connection often made between faith and baptism, arguing that in the NT faith ordinarily is required prior to the administration of the sacrament of baptism.

3. Throughout this chapter I will use "Baptists" as a term to designate those who reject the baptism of children of believing parents and insist upon the practice of believer's baptism.

Rather than enter into the history of polemics regarding paedobaptism or the exegesis of the most pertinent biblical passages in dispute, my purpose in this chapter is to set forth the main lines of the covenant theology that undergirds the paedobaptist position. The Reformed practice of baptizing believers and their children, as Warfield rightly maintained, is largely based upon an understanding of the biblical doctrine of the covenant of grace. In the principal writings of the Reformers of the sixteenth century,[4] and in the great confessional symbols of the Reformed tradition,[5] the one argument for paedobaptism that repeatedly stands out is the covenant argument. Children, like adult believers, are to be baptized because they belong to the covenant community in Christ.

To summarize the covenant theology that supports the paedobaptist position, we will proceed in a series of steps, moving from the more general and basic elements of covenant theology to its specific implications regarding the proper recipients of Christian baptism. We will begin with an extended treatment of the doctrine of the covenant of grace. What do we mean by the covenant of grace, and do the various administrations of this covenant represent *one* unitary covenant or *several* disparate covenants? After treating the doctrine of the covenant of grace, we will take up more briefly the particular issue of the role and use of sacraments in the covenant's administration. Who appoints the sacraments at various stages in its administration and for what purpose? Within the more immediate context of the doctrine of the sacraments, we will then turn to the sacrament of baptism, its relation to the rite of circumcision in the OT, and its peculiar new covenant significance. Only after having

4. See, for example, *Institutes*, 4.16.

5. For a summary of the Reformed confessions' teaching, see Cornelis P. Venema, "The Doctrine of the Sacraments and Baptism according to the Reformed Confessions," *MAJT* 11 (2000): 21–86, esp. 80–82. HC 74 well represents the consensus of these confessions, when it answers the question, "Are infants also to be baptized?" as follows: "Yes; for since they, as well as adults, are included in the covenant and Church of God, and since both redemption from sin and the Holy Spirit, the Author of faith, are through the blood of Christ promised to them no less than to adults, they must also by baptism, as a sign of the covenant, be ingrafted into the Christian Church, and distinguished from the children of unbelievers, as was done in the old covenant or testament by circumcision, instead of which baptism was instituted in the new covenant."

laid a foundation in the doctrine of the covenant and its sacraments will we be in a position to address the particular question in dispute: who ought to be baptized? Anticipating possible Baptist objections to the argument, the chapter will conclude with a brief consideration of two common Baptist criticisms of Reformed covenant theology.

The Covenant of Grace

To summarize the biblical and Reformed doctrine of the covenant of grace is a daunting task. The history of Reformed theology since the sixteenth-century Reformation is, in some respects, a history of the development and articulation of covenant theology. Just as the Reformed tradition is known for its emphasis upon sovereign and gracious election, so it is known for its emphasis upon the communication of God's grace in Christ to his people by means of covenant.

One of the best points of reference for a summary of the theology of the covenant is the classic statement in the WCF. Though the other Reformed symbols assume the doctrine of the covenant, only the WCF gives it formal and thorough expression. In chapter 7, "Of God's Covenant with Man," the Confession offers the following key summary affirmations:

1. The distance between God and the creature is so great, that although reasonable creatures do owe obedience unto him as their Creator, yet they could never have any fruition of him as their blessedness and reward, but by some voluntary condescension on God's part, which he hath been pleased to express by way of covenant.
2. The first covenant made with man was a *covenant of works*, wherein life was promised to Adam; and in him to his posterity, upon condition of perfect and personal obedience.
3. Man, by his fall, having made himself incapable of life by that covenant, the Lord was pleased to make a second, commonly called the *covenant of grace*; wherein he freely offereth unto sinners life and salvation by Jesus Christ; requiring of them faith in him, that they may be saved, and promising

to give unto all those that are ordained unto eternal life his Holy Spirit, to make them willing, and able to believe.

4. This covenant was differently administered in the time of the law, and in the time of the gospel: under the law, it was administered by promises, prophecies, sacrifices, circumcision, the paschal lamb, and other types and ordinances delivered to the people of the Jews, all foresignifying Christ to come; which were, for that time, sufficient and efficacious, through the operation of the Spirit, to instruct and build up the elect in faith in the promised Messiah, by whom they had full remission of sins, and eternal salvation; and is called the old testament.
5. Under the gospel, when Christ, the substance, was exhibited, the ordinances in which this covenant is dispensed are the preaching of the Word, and the administration of the sacraments of Baptism and the Lord's Supper: which, though fewer in number, and administered with more simplicity, and less outward glory, yet, in them, it is held forth in more fullness, evidence and spiritual efficacy, to all nations, both Jews and Gentiles; and is called the new testament. There are not therefore two covenants of grace, differing in substance, but one and the same, under various dispensations.

According to this summary statement of the biblical doctrine of the covenant, in order to enjoy a life-relationship or fellowship with man, his image-bearer, the triune God voluntarily condescends to enter into covenant with him. This was already true prior to the fall into sin, when God as Creator covenanted to grant Adam life and eternal blessedness upon the condition of his perfect obedience.[6] However, after the fall into sin, which ruptured the communion between the triune Creator and his image-bearing creature, the covenant of grace was established by the triune Redeemer to restore fallen man to saving fellowship with himself. The God of the Scriptures

6. For a treatment of the prelapsarian "covenant of works," see Charles Hodge, *Systematic Theology*, vol. 2 (1871; repr., Grand Rapids, MI: Eerdmans, 1952), 115–22; *RD*, 2:563–88; *ST*, 211–18; and chap. 1 of this volume.

is a covenant God, and the creature who bears his image is a covenant creature. The union and communion with God that comprise man's peculiar life and blessedness are covenantal in nature. Covenant expresses the manner in which the triune God enters into and maintains fellowship with his people.

The covenant of grace is, accordingly, the means instituted by God's mercy to restore fallen sinners to communion with himself. Having forfeited through sinful rebellion any claim upon God's favor, sinners lie under the curse of death and separation from God. Only in virtue of God's gracious initiatives in coming to his people and restoring them to communion with himself do fallen sinners find salvation and life. These initiatives, according to scriptural revelation, are always covenantal in nature.

The Nature of the Covenant Relationship

In the history of Reformed theology, there has been considerable debate and even divergence of opinion regarding the precise nature of the covenant relationship. In the older writings, the tendency was to treat the covenant as a kind of agreement between two parties.[7] Francis Turretin, for example, in his *Institutes of Elenctic Theology*, defines the covenant of grace as "a gratuitous pact entered into in Christ between God offended and man the offender. In it God promises remission of sins and salvation to man freely on account of Christ; man, however, relying on the same grace promises faith and obedience."[8] However, in more recent discussions of the covenant of grace, the sovereign and unilateral initiative of God has received greater prominence. Though it was clearly recognized by the older writers that God alone effectively brings the covenant relationship to bear fruit through the mediation of Christ and the working of the Holy Spirit, recent writers have especially accented this feature of the covenant relationship.[9] The covenant relationship is, in its origin and

7. See John Murray, *The Covenant of Grace: A Biblico-Theological Study* (1954; repr., Phillipsburg, NJ: Presbyterian and Reformed, 1988), 5–7.

8. *IET*, 2:175.

9. See, e.g., Murray, *Covenant of Grace*; O. Palmer Robertson, *The Christ of the Covenants* (Phillipsburg, NJ: Presbyterian and Reformed, 1980); and Meredith G. Kline,

administration, an initiative and work of God's undeserved grace and mercy.

The covenant relationship is marked by communion between God and his people. This relationship involves mutual promises and obligations. God makes promises and stipulates obligations, and so binds himself to his people as a husband to his wife, or as a father to his children.[10] For their part, the covenant people of God are invited to embrace the covenant promises by faith and to acknowledge their corresponding obligations. This mutuality and fellowship, which mark the union and communion of the covenant relationship, however, do not reflect a *parity* between God and his people in the covenant. God takes the initiative in establishing the covenant. He graciously administers and sustains the covenant. And he ensures the fruitfulness of the covenant. The triune God begins, maintains, and finally realizes his covenant purpose of saving communion with his people.

The Covenant Promise

Because the covenant of grace is a sovereign initiative of God's undeserved grace, the basis of the covenant's blessings is found in the covenant promise. In Genesis 3:15, often called the *protevangelium* or "first gospel" promise, the Lord comes to Adam and Eve after the fall and pledges to provide a seed of the woman who will "bruise the head" of the serpent. Though little is told about the covenant of grace in this passage, it does reveal God's gracious purpose to redeem a people for communion with himself and to provide a Savior, born of the woman, who would destroy the tempter and his work. This passage anticipates the subsequent events of God's covenant with Noah and his family (Gen. 9:9), and of the formal establishment of the covenant of grace in Genesis 12 and 15, and especially Genesis 17.

In the accounts of the formal establishment of the covenant of

---

By Oath Consigned: A Reinterpretation of the Covenant Signs of Circumcision and Baptism (Grand Rapids, MI: Eerdmans, 1968). Robertson's biblical-theological study is an outstanding survey of the biblical history and diverse administration of the covenant of grace.

10. These are some of the dominant metaphors utilized in the Scriptures to describe God's relationship with his people. See e.g., Ps. 103:13–14; Mal. 3:17; Jer. 3:6–10; 31:20–22; Hos. 1:14–2:3; Luke 3:38; Eph. 5:21–33.

grace in Genesis, the Lord comes to Abram and promises to make of him a great nation and to bless all the families of the earth through him (Gen. 12:2–3). The Lord also promises to grant to Abram a son and through him descendants more numerous than the stars of the heavens (Gen. 15:4–5). When Abram believes this promise, God reckons this to him as righteousness (15:6; cf. Rom. 4; Gal. 3:8) and, by means of a self-maledictory oath ceremony, confirms his pledge to do as he has promised. Then, in the great account of the establishment of the covenant of grace in Genesis 17, the Lord God comes once more to Abram and reaffirms his promise: "Behold, my covenant is with you, and you shall be the father of a multitude of nations. . . . And I will establish my covenant between me and you and your offspring after you throughout their generations for an everlasting covenant, to be God to you and to your offspring after you" (vv. 4, 7).

Any tracing of the way in which God graciously deals with his covenant people throughout the course of the history of redemption, beginning with Abraham, Isaac, and Jacob and finally fulfilled in the person and work of Jesus Christ, will quickly reveal that it is a story of God's covenant faithfulness through and through. What sustains this history is not the faithfulness of God's people, but rather the extraordinary and undeserved faithfulness and perseverance of God. However many promises the Lord God makes to Israel, these all find their "yes and amen" in Christ (2 Cor. 1:20). The prophecies of the OT find their fulfillment in the coming and work of Christ (Luke 24:44). The covenant of grace is, therefore, a covenant ultimately rooted in God's gracious promise to provide salvation for his people through Jesus Christ.

Though the covenant of grace, throughout its diverse administrations from Noah to Abraham to Moses to Christ, includes a great number of promises, some specific and typical to Israel, others more basic and enduring, the one great promise is the promise of salvation in communion with God through Christ.[11] This promise includes such blessings as the forgiveness of sins and acceptance with God (free justification), the renewal of life in obedience by the working of

11. For a summary of the biblical evidence for this claim, see *ST*, 277.

the Spirit, and the final glorification of life in unbroken fellowship with God. These promises are sure and certain of fulfillment, for they are as immutable as God who extends them and secures their realization by the work of Christ through his Spirit. As the WCF puts it, in the covenant of grace God "freely offereth unto sinners life and salvation by Jesus Christ . . . promising to give unto all those that are ordained unto eternal life his Holy Spirit, to make them willing, and able to believe" (WCF 7.3).

The Covenant Obligation

Though the covenant of grace is initiated and maintained by God's undeserved favor toward his people, it nonetheless obligates believers to embrace God's promises by faith. Because the covenant involves mutual promises and commitments, those with whom God covenants are obligated to respond to him in faith and obedience. For this reason, WCF 7.3 speaks of God's "requiring of them [sinners] faith in him [Christ], that they may be saved." Just as God graciously commits himself in covenant to his people, so his people are called to live before him in love and devotion. God's covenant faithfulness summons his people to a corresponding faithfulness, even as a husband who loves his wife invites her to love and be subject to him. In this way, there is mutuality in the covenant relationship. Those whom God loves must in turn love God and others with him (Ex. 20; Deut. 6:5; Mark 12:30–31).

Just as the Bible records God's promises in particular dispensations of the covenant, so it records his people's corresponding obligations. When God first entered into a covenant relationship with Abraham, he demanded among other things that Abraham walk before him and be blameless (Gen. 17:1). When God subsequently covenanted with the children of Israel under Moses at Sinai, he gave Israel the Ten Commandments (Exodus 20) together with an elaborate system of ceremonial and civil law. Likewise, with the coming of Christ and the preaching of the gospel of God's grace under the new covenant, God's people are called to faith in Christ and obedience to his law ("the law of Christ," Gal. 6:2). The promised blessings of covenant life and fellowship with God require faith and repentance.

One of the more difficult questions in the formulation of covenant theology is whether the covenant is *conditional* or *unconditional.* On the one hand, it would seem that the covenant of grace is unconditional. God sovereignly and unilaterally establishes the covenant. He maintains and fulfills immutably his promises to his people. As we shall see more fully when we consider Christ as the Mediator of the covenant of grace, God the Father secures the covenant's blessings for his people by sending his Son to accomplish their redemption through his atoning sacrifice and the outpouring of his Spirit. *Everything that God demands of his people in the covenant of grace, he graciously grants them in Christ.* Not only are the covenant's obligations preceded by God's gracious promise, but these obligations are fulfilled for and in believers by the triune God, Father, Son and Holy Spirit, in their respective operations. God's demands are born of grace and fulfilled in us by grace. In these respects, the covenant of grace is unconditional, excluding every possible form of "merit" whereby the faith and obedience of God's people would be the basis for their obtaining life and salvation.

However, when the covenant is viewed from the work of Christ and the manner of its administration, it is conditional. Covenant blessings are contingent, for example, upon the work of Christ in fulfilling the conditions of obedience first set down in the prefall covenant of works (Rom. 5:12–21). The curse due to the covenant breaker who violates in one particular what the law requires, was borne by Christ upon the cross (Gal. 3:13). In these and other respects, Christ's work procures the blessings God promises to those with whom he covenants (Eph. 1:3). Furthermore, the obligations of faith and obedience, though not meritorious conditions, are necessary responses to the covenant's promises and are instrumental to the enjoyment of the covenant's blessings. Faith and obedience, of course, are themselves the fruits of God's grace toward his people in Christ. They are God's gifts, for salvation is of grace alone, not of works lest anyone should boast (Eph. 2:5–10).[12] Yet, they are also

12. For a classic Reformed treatment of the way salvation, including both the benefits of free justification and sanctification, is graciously granted to us by the triune God, Father, Son, and Holy Spirit, see *Institutes*, 3.1–11. The covenant's obligations are fulfilled in us,

the response of God's people to his grace, and indispensable to the receiving and enjoying of what the covenant communicates. Without faith and repentance, the sinner may have no expectation of God's favor or blessing.

The Covenant Parties

The question as to whether the covenant of grace is conditional or unconditional, raises another, closely related question regarding the covenant that is equally difficult: with whom does God covenant? The elect only? Or believers and their children, not all of whom are elect? Throughout the history of theological reflection upon the covenant of grace, Reformed theologians have answered this question with one of these two answers. Some have also addressed this question by speaking of the "dual aspect" of the covenant.

The first of these answers—that God covenants with the elect only in the covenant of grace—is suggested by WCF 7.3, when it says that God promises in this covenant "to give unto *all those that are ordained unto eternal life* his Holy Spirit, to make them willing, and able to believe" (emphasis added). WLC 31 more clearly suggests this when it states that "[t]he covenant of grace was made with Christ as the second Adam, and in him with all the elect as his seed."[13] In the strictest sense of the covenant as a saving communion with God, the parties of the covenant of grace are the triune God and his elect people.

The grounds often given for this answer, which is the opinion of many if not the "great majority" of Reformed theologians, are several.[14] First, when the covenant of grace is viewed from the vantage

according to Calvin, by the Spirit who grants faith to the believer and simultaneously renews him in holiness. For a comprehensive study of Calvin's view, see *ARC*, esp. 132–92.

13. The Westminster Standards, however, clearly teach that the covenant of grace, in its concrete administration, also includes in a more general way some who are not elect. This is evident from the distinction drawn between the "visible" and "invisible" church in WCF 25, and the way the recipients of baptism are described in chap. 28.

14. *ST*, 273, claims that the "great majority" of Reformed theologians take this view. However, he also acknowledges that, among these theologians, most also admit that there is another and broader sense in which God covenants with some who are not elect in the particular sense of God's "purpose of election" (cf. Rom. 9:6–13).

point of God's sovereign counsel and purpose, it is seen in terms of God's electing intention to provide his Son as the representative head of his people whose salvation he accomplishes and guarantees. Because the covenant of grace is the historical means to effect the triune God's saving purposes for his elect people, the covenant is, strictly speaking, designed for and effectual in securing the salvation of all those whom the Father elects, for whom the Son atones, and in whom the Spirit effectively works faith and repentance.[15] Second, the covenant of grace is made with those who are "in Christ," that is, with those for whom Christ's mediation is the sure basis of their salvation. Not all those who are Abraham's seed are in Christ in this sense (compare Gen. 21:12; Rom. 9:8; Gal. 3:16, 29; 4:28), and therefore a distinction has to be made between those who are "children of the promise" in the strict sense and those who are not. The promise of salvation is effectual and fruitful in those called according to God's purpose of election, but some, like Esau, are not full heirs of the promise. Third, because the salvation of those with whom God covenants is the fruit of God's sovereign design and working, it cannot depend upon the uncertain faithfulness of sinners. If salvation were finally to rest upon the basis of covenant obedience, it would no longer be by grace, nor would it bring any assurance of the covenant's blessing. Salvation or non-salvation in the covenant of grace may not be explained merely from the fact that one covenant member is faithful and the other is not. This would be a form of Arminianism, which makes election contingent upon covenant faithfulness. And fourth, if the covenant is viewed not merely as a "means to an end" but as an "end in itself," then what it promises must be a reality in the

15. For this reason, Reformed theologians historically have spoken of a "covenant of redemption" or *pactum salutis*. This "covenant of redemption" represents the pretemporal counsel between the Father, Son, and Holy Spirit to provide redemption for the elect by means of their respective works in the covenant of grace. The Father, accordingly, purposes to send his Son to make atonement for the elect, and, together with the Son, purposes to bestow the Spirit to apply the benefits of Christ's atonement to the elect. For representative treatments of this covenant of redemption, see Hodge, *Systematic Theology*, 2:357–62; Geerhardus Vos, "The Doctrine of the Covenant in Reformed Theology," in *Redemptive History and Biblical Interpretation: The Shorter Writings of Geerhardus Vos*, ed. Richard B. Gaffin Jr. (Phillipsburg, NJ: Presbyterian and Reformed, 1980), 245–52; and *ST*, 265–72.

experience of those with whom God covenants. Since the covenant relationship expresses the fullness of friendship and fellowship with God, it is not possible that the nonelect could be members of it.

Despite these substantial reasons for affirming that the covenant of grace is made with the elect only, many Reformed theologians have nonetheless maintained that the covenant embraces all believers and their children, not all of whom are elect in the strict sense. These theologians, while acknowledging that the life and salvation promised in the covenant of grace are inherited only by the elect, argue that the covenant promise, together with its accompanying obligation, is extended to Abraham and his seed. In the administration of the covenant of grace throughout the course of redemptive history, there are many among the covenant community *who break covenant with God and become liable to his covenant wrath*. In the OT and NT, members of the covenant community are warned against the danger of unbelief and impenitence. Such disobedience carries the fearful prospect of God's judgment. The blessings promised in the covenant belong to those who believe and obey. However, the curses of the covenant will undoubtedly fall upon those who despise their covenant birthright and refuse the gracious promise extended to them (Hebrews; 1 Peter 4:17). The only way to avoid the false presumption that all those with whom God covenants are guaranteed salvation (because they are presumably elect) is to recognize that there may be covenant breakers who ought to be cut off from God's people. Such covenant breaking and its consequence, though it may contradict the saving purpose for which the covenant of grace was instituted by God, reminds us that the circle of the covenant is wider than the circle of election.

In order to resolve this question, therefore, Reformed theologians have sought to distinguish in a variety of ways between all those with whom God covenants (believers and their children) *in the wider sense of the covenant's administration* and those in whom the covenant comes to fruition (the elect) *in the narrower sense of the covenant's communion of life*.[16] Sometimes referred to as the

16. For a discussion of this so-called "dual aspect" of the covenant, see Vos, "Doctrine

"dual aspect" of the covenant, this distinction aims to acknowledge that the covenant embraces all believers and their children as recipients of the gospel promise and obligation, on the one hand, while simultaneously acknowledging that some fall away in unbelief and disobedience, on the other hand. Though the unbelief and disobedience of some with whom God covenants is an *anomaly*—it prevents the covenant breaker from entering into covenant life and salvation—it is nonetheless real and undeniable. There are nonelect persons in the covenant who do not respond to the promise in faith and obedience. The presence of such persons "under" the covenant, however, should not be viewed as an evidence of failure on God's part in communicating his grace to his own. For it is in the way of the covenant that God grants life and salvation to those whom he has elected to save.

The Covenant Mediator

All the blessings promised by God to believers and their children in the covenant of grace find their basis and surety in Christ. This was as true of the old covenant believer as it is of the new. The central figure in the story of redemption related in the Scriptures is Jesus Christ, the son of Abraham, the son of David (Matt. 1:1). Not only is he the focus and content of all the promises of God in Scripture, from the "mother promise" of Genesis 3:15 to the promise of the consummation of the covenant in Revelation 21–22. But he also obtains for his people the life and salvation offered through the covenant of grace (Matt. 1:21). He is the promised "seed" through whom the blessings of the covenant are extended to all the families of the earth (Gal. 3:16). He is the one who crushes the head of the Serpent and brings salvation for his people in fulfillment of the covenant first made with Abraham (Luke 1:72). All the ceremonies and prophecies of the OT find their goal and fruition in Christ, of whom they spoke and toward whose coming they looked (Luke 24:44; 2 Cor. 1:20; Heb. 1:1–2; 2 Peter 1:19).

---

of the Covenant," 258–67; John Murray, *Christian Baptism* (1952; repr., Phillipsburg, NJ: Presbyterian and Reformed, 1980), 51–53; and *ST*, 284–89.

The Unity of the Covenant

A critical theme in covenant theology, as articulated historically in the Reformed tradition, is the insistence on *one* covenant of grace throughout redemption history. To use John Calvin's well-known language, the covenant of grace is one in substance, diverse in mode of administration.[17] However diverse and particular the dispensations of the covenant of grace—so that we may even speak of "covenants" in the plural (Rom. 9:4)—they do not differ as to substance.

There are a number of biblical arguments supporting this claim.

First, the covenant promise of life and salvation is described in the same way throughout the Scriptures. When God first entered into an everlasting covenant with Abraham, he promised, "[I will] be God to you and to your offspring after you" (Gen. 17:7). This language is used of the covenant made at Sinai under Moses (Ex. 19:5; 20:2), of the covenant made on the Plains of Moab (Deut. 29:13), of the covenant with David (2 Sam. 7:14), and of the new covenant in Christ (Jer. 31:33; Heb. 8:10). When John depicts the consummate state (Rev. 21:1–8), he records Christ using this language to describe the unbroken communion God will enjoy with his people in the new heavens and earth. All the OT and NT blessings of life and fellowship with the triune God are summed up in the covenantal promise of union and communion with God.

Second, the Mediator of the covenant is the same in every administration of the covenant of grace. Jesus Christ, according to the writer of Hebrews, is "the same yesterday and today and forever" (13:8). When Abraham, the father of all believers, trusted God, he placed his trust in Jesus Christ (Gal. 3:16; cf. John 8:56). All those who are heirs with Abraham of the covenant promises are heirs through faith in Jesus Christ (Gal. 3:16–29). Christ's sole mediatorship is reflected in Revelation, which speaks of those whose names have been "written before the foundation of the world in the book of life of the Lamb that was slain" (Rev. 13:8). It is also reflected in Hebrews, which speaks of "the blood of the eternal covenant" (Heb.

17. *Institutes*, 2.10.1: "The covenant made with all the patriarchs is so much like ours in substance and reality that the two are actually one and the same. Yet they differ in the mode of administration."

13:20). Christ is the one through whom all believers receive every spiritual blessing in the heavenly places (Eph. 1:3). He is the one mediator between God and men (1 Tim. 2:5), and his is the only name given among men whereby they can be saved (Acts 4:12).

Third, the gospel preached in the old covenant is the same gospel preached in the new covenant. The apostle Paul states in Galatians 3:8, "And the Scripture, foreseeing that God would justify the Gentiles by faith, preached the gospel beforehand to Abraham, saying, 'In you shall all the nations be blessed.'" This gospel was declared at the beginning of redemption's history to Adam (Gen. 3:15), was reaffirmed in God's covenant with Abraham, and finds its fulfillment in the birth and ministry of Jesus Christ in the fullness of time.

Fourth, the obligation of the covenant of grace is essentially the same throughout the course of its successive administrations. Abraham believed God and it was reckoned to him for righteousness. In so doing, he set an example of faith for all believers who receive the promise, not by works performed in obedience to the law, but by faith in Christ. Jews and Gentiles alike obtain salvation by faith alone, not by works (Rom. 4:9–25; Gal. 3:7–9, 17–18). The gracious promise of the covenant precedes the giving of the law, thereby teaching us that salvation is by grace alone through faith alone, and not on account of the righteousness of works.

For these reasons, the covenant of grace, throughout its diverse administrations, is essentially one and the same covenant. Though OT believers embraced Christ by faith under the veil of the law's shadows and ceremonies, they embraced the same Mediator by the work of the same Spirit and thereby enjoyed the same fundamental blessings of salvation—favor with God and renewal of life in consecration to his will.

The Sacraments of the Covenant

In the administration of the covenant of grace, the Scriptures reveal that God has appointed the sacraments as a means of confirming to his people the covenant promise and its corresponding obligation. These sacraments are visible signs and seals of the covenant, which God ordains as a means of attesting to his people the life and salvation promised in the gospel.

To guide us in our summary of the nature and function of the covenant's sacraments, we will once again use the WCF as a standard statement of the Reformed view. The following articles from chapters 27, "Of the Sacraments," and 28, "Of Baptism," are especially important to our purpose:

1. Sacraments are holy signs and seals of the covenant of grace, immediately instituted by God, to represent Christ and his benefits; and to confirm our interest in him: as also, to put a visible difference between those that belong unto the church, and the rest of the world; and solemnly to engage them to the service of God in Christ, according to his Word.
2. The grace which is exhibited in or by the sacraments rightly used, is not conferred by any power in them; neither doth the efficacy of a sacrament depend upon the piety or intention of him that doth administer it: but upon the work of the Spirit, and the word of institution, which contains, together with a precept authorizing the use thereof, a promise of benefit to worthy receivers. (chap. 27)
3. Baptism is a sacrament of the new testament, ordained by Jesus Christ, not only for the solemn admission of the party baptized into the visible church; but also to be unto him a sign and seal of the covenant of grace, of his ingrafting into Christ, of regeneration, of remission of sins, and of his giving up unto God, through Jesus Christ, to walk in newness of life. Which sacrament is, by Christ's own appointment, to be continued in his church until the end of the world.
4. Not only those that do actually profess faith in and obedience unto Christ, but also the infants of one, or both, believing parents, are to be baptized.
5. The efficacy of Baptism is not tied to that moment of time wherein it is administered; yet, notwithstanding, by the right use of this ordinance, the grace promised is not only offered, but really exhibited, and conferred, by the Holy Ghost, to

> such (whether of age or infants) as that grace belongeth unto, according to the counsel of God's own will, in his appointed time. (chap. 28)

The Nature and Function of Sacraments

The starting point for an appreciation of the nature and function of the sacraments is their divine authorship. God appoints sacraments, in addition to the communication of the gospel of salvation in Christ through the preaching and teaching of the Word, as a means of grace. The sacraments are not human inventions, which primarily serve to declare the faith of those who are members of the covenant community. They are not "badges" of a Christian profession, but "tokens" of God's grace toward his people. They are God-ordained instruments to communicate the grace of the covenant to its members. In the OT and NT, the sacraments were instituted by the covenant Lord as an integral part of his administration of the covenant of grace.

What distinguishes the sacraments from the preaching and teaching of the Word is their use of visible signs and seals. In the sacraments, God consecrates the sacramental elements to a holy use, employing them as visible confirmations of the invisible grace of the covenant. The sacraments visibly *represent* the gospel promise of life and salvation in Christ. There is a correspondence in the sacrament between the visible sign and the grace to which it points. The water of baptism, for example, signifies the washing away of sin through the blood of Christ and the regenerating Spirit. The bread of the Lord's Supper vividly portrays the body of Christ given for the remission of sins. The sacraments are also seals that authenticate and assure believers of the truth of the covenant's promise. The sacraments display and confirm the veracity of God's Word.

The WCF emphasizes that the efficacy of the sacraments depends upon the Spirit's working in and through them to confirm the gospel promise. Just as the Spirit uses gospel preaching to create and nourish faith, so the Spirit uses the visible word of the sacrament to nourish and confirm the faith of believers. However, this working of the Spirit through the sacraments is not owing to any intrinsic power in the sacrament itself. The sacraments wholly depend upon the Spirit's power and remain instrumental to the communication of the grace of God in Christ. They require the same response as does the Word, namely, faith in Christ and a consecration to God. The sacraments do not *by themselves* work regeneration and faith in their recipients. Nor are they administered on the basis of the presumed regeneration of their recipients, as if the sacrament attested to the state of grace of its recipient.

Circumcision and Baptism

In the dispute between paedobaptists and Baptists regarding the proper recipients of the sacrament of baptism, one of the more crucial questions concerns the similarity and dissimilarity of the sacraments of circumcision and baptism. Baptist authors typically argue that these sacraments of the OT and NT, respectively, are radically different in their meaning and significance. Because circumcision and baptism vary so widely in meaning, no conclusions may be drawn from the OT practice of circumcising the male children of covenant members to the NT practice of baptism. Reformed authors counter this argument by noting that these sacraments have considerably more in common than what distinguishes them. Just as the sacrament of circumcision in the OT signified and sealed incorporation into the covenant community, so the rite of baptism in the NT is an initiation into the community of Christ and his people. The similarities between the two sacraments are, so far as their essential meaning is concerned, far more weighty than their dissimilarities.[18]

Though Baptists often argue, for instance, that circumcision was only a sign of outward membership in the nation of Israel and not a sign of a spiritual blessing, this is clearly contradicted by the biblical accounts of its significance. In the passage that records the appointment of circumcision, the sacrament is virtually identified with the covenant relationship itself, which is a relationship of communion and fellowship between the Lord and his people (Gen.

18. For a discussion of the relation of circumcision and baptism, see Pierre Ch. Marcel, *The Biblical Doctrine of Infant Baptism*, trans. Philip E. Hughes (London: James Clarke, 1953), 82–95.

17:11). Circumcision is a sacrament that, like the covenant which it signifies and seals to believers and their children, in its deepest meaning stands for fellowship with God. As a visible sign and token of an invisible grace, circumcision specifically reminded the children of Israel of their need to remove the defilement of sin (cf. Deut. 10:16; 30:6; Jer. 4:4). The sacrament of circumcision was a bloody sign of the need to remove the sin whose guilt and corruption constitute an insuperable obstacle to fellowship with a holy God. Moreover, in the argument of the apostle Paul in Romans, we are taught that circumcision was for Abraham a sign and seal of "the righteousness that he had by faith" (4:11). Abraham's circumcision was not merely a sign that he would be the father of the Jewish nation, but it was also a seal of his justification through faith alone, apart from works. In this Abraham became, says the apostle, "the father of *all* who believe without being circumcised." Circumcision, therefore, was a sign and seal of the most basic and glorious spiritual blessings: covenant communion and fellowship with God, the need for removal of sin's defilement as an obstacle to favor with a holy God, and the righteousness of faith whereby believers become acceptable to God.

Because these spiritual blessings belong to the covenant circumcision signified and sealed to OT believers, it is not surprising to find the apostle Paul treating baptism as the new covenant counterpart to circumcision (Col. 2:11–13). In the new covenant, circumcision no longer functions as a sign and seal of fellowship with God (Gal. 2:3). The Lord appointed baptism as a sign and seal of fellowship with the triune God and incorporation into Christ's church (Matt. 28:16–20). Baptism now portrays the spiritual circumcision "made without hands, by putting off the body of the flesh" (Col. 2:11). The spiritual blessings represented by circumcision in the old covenant are, in the context of the new covenant realities of Christ's coming, death, and resurrection, now represented by baptism. Believers receive a sign and seal of their communion with Christ and of their having put off their former sin-dominated nature. This spiritual circumcision occurs through union with Christ, which is signified and sealed by the sacrament of baptism. What was formerly confirmed through circumcision is presently confirmed through baptism: the forgiveness of sins (Mark 1:4; Acts 2:38; Heb. 10:22), the washing away of sin through fellowship with Christ (Rom. 6:2–10; 1 Cor. 6:11; Eph. 5:26; Col. 2:12), regeneration, and fellowship with Christ and his body (Acts 2:40–41; 1 Cor. 12:13).

"The Promise Is . . . to Your Children"

Now that we have considered several of the key elements of covenant theology, including the nature and function of the sacraments as God-appointed media to signify and seal the covenant promise in Christ, we are in a position to draw the conclusion to which this theology inevitably compels us.

We know from the biblical history of the covenant of grace that, in the OT administration, God promised communion and fellowship with himself to Abraham and his seed. Believers and their children were embraced within the covenant promise and favor of God. In this way, the faithfulness of Israel's covenant-keeping God was extended from generation to generation, as an everlasting covenant whose blessings would ultimately expand to all the families of the earth. These covenanted blessings, however, placed believers and their children under corresponding obligations of faith and obedience. God promised his covenant love unto a thousand generations of those who loved him and kept his commandments. To confirm this covenant relationship, God gave his people the sacrament of circumcision. This sacrament was a sign and seal of God's promise, a sacrament of inclusion or initiation into the covenant relationship with all of its promises and obligations.

But what of the new covenant in Christ? According to the biblical revelation, this covenant *fulfills* the promises of the old: Christ is the One in whom all the promises of God have their yes and amen. The seed promised under the old covenant, the One through whom the blessings of the covenant would extend to all the peoples, is none other than Christ himself (Matt. 1:1–17; Gal. 3:16). Those who believe in Christ are heirs of the covenant, children of Abraham who are reckoned righteous by faith, even as he was. In this new covenant administration, the covenant promise of communion and fellowship with the living God is fulfilled by the work of Christ, the Mediator, and the ministry of the Spirit whom he poured out at Pentecost. The covenant promise of life and salvation is now offered to sinners who are called by means of the gospel to faith and repentance. However much greater and richer the new covenant administration in Christ, it does not displace the old covenant. Rather, the new covenant in Christ's blood is the fulfillment of all the old covenant foreshadowed. In this new covenant administration, God has appointed a sacrament to signify and seal to his people the promises and obligations of the gospel. Through baptism, believers are initiated into the fellowship of the triune God and his people, separated from the world of unbelief and sin, and incorporated into the body of Christ. By means of this sign and seal of spiritual circumcision, God represents and attests the life and salvation that come through the work of Christ.

The one great question that arises in the debate between paedobaptist and Baptist at this point, then, is, how does the new covenant administration differ from the old, so far as its subjects or recipients are concerned? The promise and obligation remain the same. The Mediator is the same. The same gospel is preached. However, the sacramental rite of inclusion among the people of God differs. Whereas formerly believers and their children were circumcised, now baptism has come in its place as a sacramental means of signifying and sealing the covenant promise and its obligation. But is there a further difference in the covenant's administration? Must we conclude that, whereas children were formerly recipients of the promise, they are no longer? Is the new covenant administration, so far as its proper recipients are concerned, *more restricted, less encompassing in its reach*, than had been the case previously?

The answer to this question appears in the apostle Peter's sermon at Pentecost. Baptists often quote Peter's admonition to repent and be baptized as illustrating the necessity for faith and repentance as prerequisites to baptism, but they tend to gloss over his words immediately following—"For the promise is for you *and for your children, and for all who are far off, everyone whom the Lord our God calls to himself*" (Acts 2:39). At this critical turning point in the history of redemption, on the day of the Spirit's outpouring at Pentecost, Peter reaffirms the OT covenant promise. The first sermon preached in the epoch of the founding of the church after Pentecost embraces the old covenant promise, which includes children of believing parents and all families of the earth to whom the promise of salvation in Christ will be extended.

Far from any hint of restriction upon the covenant's reach—children now being excluded whereas previously they were included—the apostle Peter clearly announces the richer extension of God's promise. Not only is the promise for believers, but it is also for their children. And it is also for all believers among the peoples of the earth.

Though this may not be the "proof text" that Baptists are looking for—it does not say that the children of believing parents are to be baptized, nor does it provide an unambiguous account of the Christian baptism of such children—it is strong evidence nonetheless. The language of this text has no apparent significance apart from what it assumes, namely, that God's grace was always extended to believers and their children, from generation to generation, incorporating them into his household and numbering them among his beloved children. Wrested from its natural home within the context of the biblical theology of the covenant of grace, this passage would stand out as an inexplicable "bolt out of the blue." However, when read against the background of the old covenant administration, it makes perfectly good sense. The Lord is now fulfilling his promise to Abraham and his descendants after him—the promise of salvation in Christ comes to believers, their children, and all the families of the earth. A more compelling testimony than this is hard to imagine, that the new covenant in Christ continues to embrace believers *and their children*. Only now the promise is more clearly revealed to embrace all whom the Lord God is calling into fellowship with himself through Christ.

Answering Two Common Objections

In the history of the debate between paedobaptists and Baptists, many different arguments have been employed. Advocates of one or the other position have adduced a variety of exegetical, historical, and theological considerations to support their position. Two common Baptist objections to the paedobaptist position are particularly related to the subject of this chapter—covenant theology and the baptism of children of believers. To conclude our summary of covenant theology and baptism, therefore, we will briefly note these objections and the covenantal or paedobaptist response to them.

Encourages Nominalism

One of the most frequent objections to paedobaptism is the claim that it encourages complacency on the part of those who are baptized. Infants are incapable of the faith and repentance required for receiving the gospel promise and its corresponding obligation. Their incorporation into Christ and the fellowship of his body, therefore, occurs without their believing reception of the gospel promise or consent to its obligations. As a practical matter, this means that unbelieving and impenitent persons are admitted into the church, the body of Christ, without having experienced the regenerating work of the Holy Spirit evidenced in conversion. Churches that practice infant baptism, for this reason, cannot avoid including a whole class of persons in the church who are Christians only in "name" and not in truth. The historical problem of what is sometimes called a "halfway covenant" is an illustration of the undesirable consequences of this practice. Nominal members of the church, who have given no visible confirmation of the regenerating work of the Holy Spirit, are permitted to present their children for baptism. And even though Reformed churches expressly repudiate the idea of sacramental regeneration, as though the sacrament worked salvation *ex opere operato* ("by virtue of the work performed"), the practice of paedobaptism inevitably encourages the notion that the children are automatically saved. When the rite of Christian baptism is administered to children, nominalism and complacency are never far behind.

There are several points that need to be made in reply to this objection.

First, there is a difference between baptism's proper use and improper use. Unless it can be demonstrated that nominalism is an inherent feature of the paedobaptist view, this objection addresses only an improper practice that fails to emphasize baptism's obligations. Nothing, however, that we have seen in the covenant theology undergirding the practice of paedobaptism encourages nominalism. The sacramental sign and seal of incorporation into the fellowship of Christ always demands from believers and their children a response of faith and repentance. The privileges of covenant membership do not diminish, but rather accentuate the responsibilities of the covenant. The sacrament of baptism, whether administered to adult believers or the children of believers, places all recipients under the same gracious promise and corresponding obligations. Admittedly, the language of "infant baptism" may inappropriately suggest that baptism, when administered to the children of believing parents, has a different meaning than when administered to adult believers. "Infant baptism" is one kind of baptism; "adult baptism" is another. It cannot be too strongly emphasized, however, that baptism signifies and seals the same promises to, and places the same demands upon, children as it does upon adult believers.

Second, the argument that the inclusion of children through baptism in the covenant of grace encourages nominalism, could equally well be used against the OT practice of circumcision. If baptizing the children of believing parents in the new covenant necessarily encourages a complacent view of covenant membership, then circumcising children of believing parents in the old covenant would likewise encourage complacency. However, as we have seen in our consideration of the respective significance of circumcision and baptism, these sacraments equally emphasize the privileges and responsibilities of the covenant relationship.

And third, the practice of "believer's baptism" no more ensures against nominalism than does baptism of the children of believing parents. Insisting that faith and repentance, as subjective attestations of the regenerating work of the Holy Spirit, are prerequisite to baptism does not protect the church from baptizing those whose faith and repentance are counterfeit. All the true marks of regeneration, including faith and repentance, can be counterfeited, and no church or believer has the capacity, which alone belongs to God, to discriminate infallibly between the true and the untrue. There is nothing, therefore, in the Baptist position that provides a hedge against the sacrament of baptism being administered to non-regenerate persons. Nor, as the history of the churches, paedobaptist and Baptist alike, attests, is there any lack of evidence of the toleration by Baptist churches of nominalism on the part of baptized church members. Baptist churches are no more protected from nominalism by their doctrine of believer's baptism than Reformed churches are encouraged to nominalism by their doctrine of paedobaptism.

Implies Baptismal Regeneration

One of the great difficulties in the dispute between paedobaptist and Baptist is the difficulty of mutual understanding. The paedobaptist position is, as we have argued, the fruit of a broadly covenantal understanding of the Scriptures. It is framed by a coherent set of convictions regarding the substantial unity of the covenant of grace throughout the course of redemption's history and the nature of the sacraments as God-appointed signs and seals of the covenant promise. The Baptist position, by contrast, is the fruit of a quite different set of convictions about the covenant of grace in its diverse administrations. Within the framework of the Baptist position, the old and new covenants substantially diverge in their promises and demands as well as in their sacraments. The Baptist view of the sacraments insists that they are primarily means to attest the faith and repentance of their recipients. They are a means of declaring the subjective spiritual state of believers. By means of the sacraments, believers *address God and others.* This is quite far removed from the paedobaptist conviction that, in the sacraments, *God addresses his people, believers and their children and as many as he calls to himself.*

It is essential to bear this in mind, when considering another common Baptist objection to paedobaptism, namely, that it implies a doctrine of baptismal regeneration. According to this objection, the chief reason the paedobaptist position encourages nominalism is that it *presumes the regeneration of the children of believing parents*, apart from their conscious response to the gospel's call. Despite the paedobaptist insistence that the sacraments do not work *ex opere operato*, and despite the Reformed churches' insistence that all baptized children must respond to their baptism in faith and repentance, the Baptist suspects the paedobaptist of harboring a doctrine of baptismal regeneration. The Reformed practice of infant baptism betrays a continuing commitment to the kind of sacramentalism taught by Roman Catholic and Lutheran churches. However many disclaimers the paedobaptist might make to this objection, the Baptist regards the paedobaptist position as a veiled form of baptismal regeneration.

The problem with this objection is that it reflects a fundamentally different view of the sacraments of the covenant of grace than that taught within the framework of covenant theology. Because the Baptist views the sacrament of baptism as an attestation of conversion, he regards the baptism of children as evidence that the paedobaptist presumes these children's regeneration. Because baptism is principally a profession of the spiritual state of its recipient, all who receive the sacrament are presumed to be in that state. This represents, however, a fundamental misapprehension of the covenantal view. The doctrine of the covenant, so far as it undergirds the practice of infant baptism, teaches that *the only ground for administering the sacrament is that of covenant membership*. Adult believers and their children are baptized for the *same reason*—the Lord is pleased to signify and seal to them that they belong to him and his people and are recipients of his gracious promise in Christ and under the obligations of love and fidelity toward him. When the question of the sacrament's recipients arises, it arises in a specific way. The question is not, is this person truly regenerate? (which only God can answer in any case) but rather, is this person one to whom God wishes to address the promise and demand of the covenant?

Warfield, therefore, put it correctly as well as succinctly, when he summarized the covenant argument for paedobaptism: "God established His church in the days of Abraham and put children into it. They must remain there until He puts them out. He has nowhere put them out. They are still then members of His Church and as such entitled to its ordinances."[19]

19. Warfield, *Studies in Theology*, 408.

Part 3

Covenant Theology in Recent Discussion

9

Covenant, Justification, and the "Federal Vision" (1): An Introduction[1]

In the recent history of the Presbyterian and Reformed churches in North America, a number of authors have advanced what has become popularly known as the "Federal Vision" (hereafter FV). Though some advocates of positions associated with the FV do not believe it is appropriate to refer to it as a well-defined movement, there is no doubt that such a movement exists. Whatever differences may exist among its proponents, the FV represents a number of common teachings that have particular significance for an understanding of the covenant of grace and the gospel benefit of justification by faith alone. Proponents of the FV have vigorously promoted their views through their public writings, theological conferences, and a variety of internet media. One of the predominant claims of the FV, as the name "Federal" Vision itself confirms, is that the biblical doctrine of the covenant has not been adequately understood in many Reformed churches, and that the implications of the covenant for

1. This chapter and the following two chapters are a revision of a draft report that I wrote on behalf of a study committee appointed by Synod 2007 of the United Reformed Churches in North America. Since the original report was written for the URCNA, these chapters appeal frequently to the "Three Forms of Unity," namely, the HC, the BC, and the CD—the subordinate standards of the URCNA. For a copy of the report as it was received by Synod 2010 of the URCNA, see *Acts of Synod London 2010: Seventh Synod of the United Reformed Churches in North America, July 26–30, 2010* (London, ON: Cornerstone United Reformed Church, 2010), 727–801.

the church's life and ministry have also not been fully appreciated.[2] The controversial nature of the FV stems from the way a number of FV writers have reformulated, revised, or even rejected aspects of the understanding of the covenant in the Reformed tradition, whether in its confessional or theological expressions.

Although the FV is not a monolithic movement, certain themes recur in the writings of many leading proponents. Before I assess the FV in two subsequent chapters, I will begin in this chapter with a brief sketch of the emergence of the FV, as well as a general description of the principal claims of FV authors. These claims involve a revision of some aspects of the historic Reformed doctrine of the covenant of grace and of the principal benefit of the covenant, justification by grace alone through faith. Once the distinctive claims of the FV movement are identified, we will be in a position to evaluate them in the chapters to follow.

A Brief Sketch of the Emergence of the Federal Vision[3]

It is important to observe that the language of "Federal Vision" did not originate with those who have criticized some of its themes and emphases. In January 2002, Steven Wilkins, pastor at the time of the Auburn Avenue Presbyterian Church (PCA) in Monroe, Louisiana, invited a number of speakers to the church's annual pastor's conference to articulate and defend their advocacy of the "Federal Vision." These speakers included Wilkins himself; Steve Schlissel, pastor of Messiah's congregation in New York City; Norman Shepherd, a retired CRC pastor and former professor of systematic theology at Westminster Theological Seminary; and Douglas Wilson, pastor of Christ Church in Moscow, Idaho. Since

2. The term "federal" in "Federal Vision" stems from the Latin term for covenant, *foedus*. Thus, one way to interpret the FV is to regard it as an attempt to articulate a comprehensive understanding of the covenant of grace that will resolve a number of long-standing questions in the Reformed tradition.

3. For treatments of the history and emergence of the FV, see *Justification: A Report from the Orthodox Presbyterian Church* (Willow Grove, PA: Committee on Christian Education of the OPC, 2007), 11–18; and Guy Prentiss Waters, *The Federal Vision and Covenant Theology: A Comparative Analysis* (Phillipsburg, NJ: P&R Publishing, 2006), 1–29.

Shepherd was unable to attend this meeting, John Barach, at the time a pastor of the Grande Prairie URC, was invited to speak in his place.[4] Though it is sometimes suggested that the FV is only an intramural debate among North American Presbyterians, the roster of speakers at this conference illustrates that the FV has had significant representation in a broad spectrum of Presbyterian and Reformed denominations in North America.

The 2002 Auburn Avenue Conference can be regarded as the point at which a growing debate about the FV commenced within several Presbyterian and Reformed church communions. Shortly after the 2002 Conference, the Reformed Presbyterian Church in the United States (RPCUS) strongly condemned the FV as being out of accord with the Westminster Standards on the doctrines of the covenant and justification.[5] Among the objections raised against the FV, the following were most important: the denial of a prefall "covenant of works"; the blurring of the distinction between the law and the gospel; the rejection of the teaching of the imputation of the "active obedience" of Christ as a ground for the believer's justification before God; the tendency to include the "works" faith produces as part of faith in its instrumentality for justification; a kind of sacramentalism that ascribes efficacy to the sacraments apart from the response of faith on the part of their recipients; and a tendency to identify covenant membership with election to salvation in Christ. Despite some diversity of expression and viewpoint among proponents of the FV, these issues have continued at the center of the debate regarding the compatibility of the FV with the Reformed standards or confessions.

In response to serious criticisms that were brought against some aspects of the FV, Wilkins invited Barach, Schlissel, and Wilson to join him in a discussion with critics of the FV at Monroe, Louisiana,

4. Recordings of the lectures that were delivered at this conference are available at www.auburnavenue.org.

5. The decisions of the General Assembly of this denomination are available at www.rpcus.com. A minister of this denomination, John Otis, has written a book-length critique of the FV. See John M. Otis, *Danger in the Camp: An Analysis and Refutation of the Heresies of the Federal Vision* (Corpus Christi, TX: Triumphant Publications, 2005).

in January 2003. Participants in this discussion also included Joseph Pipa, president of Greenville Presbyterian Theological Seminary; Carl Robbins, pastor of the Woodruff Road Presbyterian Church (PCA) in Greenville, South Carolina; Morton Smith, professor at several Presbyterian seminaries and former stated clerk of the PCA; and R. C. Sproul Jr., editor of *Tabletalk* and director of the Highlands Study Center. When this discussion did not achieve a resolution of the controversy over the FV, another conference was held in Florida in August 2003 under the auspices of Knox Theological Seminary. Participants in this private discussion included not only those who had met earlier in January in Monroe, Louisiana, but also several others who were sympathetic to or critical of FV teachings.[6] Though this discussion did not take place before an ecclesiastical audience, the various presentations, including several critical evaluations of the FV, were later published in book form.[7]

Since the time of these early discussions between proponents and critics of the FV, debate regarding its emphases has continued in a variety of Reformed and Presbyterian churches. Proponents of a number of FV teachings have held conferences and published books that defend the FV positions against their critics.[8] Several Presbyterian and Reformed denominations have mandated studies of the FV, including the Orthodox Presbyterian Church, the Reformed Church in the United States, the Presbyterian Church in America, and the Orthodox Christian Reformed Churches. All of the study committee reports of these denominations have reached conclusions sharply critical of a number of FV emphases.[9] Both

6. Participants at this conference who were sympathetic to the FV included Peter Leithart, pastor of Trinity Reformed Church in Moscow, Idaho, and Rich Lusk, assistant pastor at the time of AAPC. Participants who were critical of the FV included Christopher A. Hutchinson, associate pastor of Trinity Presbyterian Church (PCA) in Statesboro, Georgia; George Knight III, adjunct professor of New Testament at GPTS; and Richard Phillips, pastor of First Presbyterian Church (PCA) in Coral Springs/Margate, Florida.

7. *TAAT.*

8. Among these books, the following are of special importance: P. Andrew Sandlin, ed., *Backbone of the Bible: Covenant in Contemporary Perspective* (Nacogdoches, TX: Covenant Media Press, 2004); and *TFV.*

9. As noted earlier, the OPC study committee report is available in book form. The reports of the PCA (www.byfaithonline.com), the RCUS (www.rcus.org), and the OCRC

Westminster Seminary in California and Mid-America Reformed Seminary have offered public testimonies that judge elements of the FV movement to be contrary to the Word of God and the Reformed confessions.[10] The faculty of Westminster Seminary in California and Mid-America Reformed Seminary have also published books and articles, and conducted public conferences, that criticize a number of FV teachings, particularly its denial or uncertainty regarding the imputation of Christ's active obedience in the justification of believers.[11] The advocacy of children at the Lord's Table, which is one of the most common practical fruits of the FV understanding of the covenant of grace, has also been addressed by the broader assemblies of several Reformed and Presbyterian denominations.

While this brief rehearsal of the emergence of the FV movement does not tell the whole story, it is enough to demonstrate the need to achieve clarity regarding the FV and its characteristic themes. These themes all revolve around a revised version of the doctrine of the covenant and related doctrinal issues. In the opinion of FV authors, a more consistent covenant theology offers to resolve a series of doctrinal issues that have played an important role in the history of Reformed theology. These doctrinal issues include such prominent topics as election, assurance, ecclesiology, the sacraments, the relation of law and gospel, and the nature of faith as the sole instrument of justification.

The Doctrine of the Covenant

The FV movement, as its name indicates, primarily focuses upon the doctrine of the covenant. In this respect, it is a movement that must be of special interest to the Reformed churches, which

(http://www.cambridgeocrc.org/ocrcresources.htm) are available online or in the respective Acts of their synods or general assemblies.

10. The statement of the Westminster Seminary in California is available at www.wscal.edu. The statement of the Board and Faculty of Mid-America Reformed Seminary is available in booklet form: *Doctrinal Testimony regarding Recent Errors* (Dyer, IN: Mid-America Reformed Seminary, 2007).

11. See, e.g., R. Scott Clark, ed., *Covenant, Justification, and Pastoral Ministry: Essays by the Faculty of Westminster Seminary California* (Phillipsburg, NJ: P&R Publishing, 2007); and *GFA*, 232–56.

have always viewed the relationship between the triune God and his people, whether before or after the fall into sin, as a covenantal relationship. It could even be said that the original "covenant vision" is not the FV movement, but the Reformed faith in its understanding of God's gracious initiative in establishing his covenant with his people in Christ. That the FV movement emphasizes the covenantal character of God's dealings with his image-bearers is, for this reason, unexceptional and even to be commended. However, there are some features of the FV understanding of the covenant relationship between God and his people that are distinctive. These distinctive features of the FV viewpoint on the covenant are the reason that this movement has generated so much controversy in the churches.

Covenant and Salvation

In the writings of proponents of the FV, the saving significance of the covenant that God establishes with his people is strongly emphasized. The covenant relationship, especially the covenant of grace that God initiates between himself and believers and their children is not simply a means whereby God accomplishes the salvation of fallen sinners. The covenant relationship itself is a saving relationship, which unites believers and their children in true communion with God through Jesus Christ, the Mediator of the covenant of grace. The covenant relationship is salvation, and all who are members of the covenant people of God—believers together with their children and all whom God calls into membership in the church of Jesus Christ—enjoy all the benefits of saving union with Christ. Rich Lusk, a proponent of the FV, offers a clear statement of this emphasis:

> On the one hand, some so totally identify covenant and election that to be in covenant and to be elect are one and the same. . . . At the other extreme are those who identify the covenant with the visible church, but make covenant membership a matter of mere externals. . . . Against both of these distortions, we must insist that *the covenant is nothing less than union with the triune God, nothing less than salvation*. . . . So when someone is united

> to the church by baptism, that person is incorporated into Christ and into his body; that person becomes bone of Christ's bone and flesh of his flesh.[12]

In this statement, Lusk distinguishes between election and covenant but still insists that all who are included in the covenant are, in the proper sense, truly and savingly joined to Christ. All who are members of the covenant community are genuinely united to Christ and participants in all the benefits of his saving work.

Another proponent of the FV, John Barach, makes similarly strong and remarkable claims regarding what it means to be a member of the covenant people of God. According to Barach, "[t]he covenant is not just a bare legal relationship. The covenant is not just a means to an end, the goal of salvation. The covenant in history is the early form of that final goal. It is a bond of love with the triune God of Scripture. God chose you to have the bond with Him in Christ."[13] In this understanding of the administration of the covenant of grace in the course of the history of redemption, all those with whom God covenants genuinely enjoy salvation in union with the triune God. While Barach does acknowledge that not all who begin to enjoy covenant salvation will persevere, since God has only chosen them to salvation "for a time," he insists that all who are embraced within the covenant are thereby truly saved, at least for a period.[14] In Lusk's and Barach's view of the covenant of grace, membership in the covenant community, which includes believers and their children, must be understood in the strongest sense to include full participation in the saving blessings of Christ's work as Mediator. Consistent with this identification of covenant membership and true, saving communion with Christ, proponents of the FV reject any distinction, however it is expressed, between those members of the "visible" church who may truly be members of Christ by faith and those who are only "externally" members of the covenant people

12. Rich Lusk, "Covenant and Election FAQs," http://www.hornes.org/theologia/rich-lusk/covenant-election-faqs (emphasis added).

13. John Barach, "Covenant and Election," in *TAAT*, 154.

14. Ibid.

of God. Distinctions between the covenant in its historical administration and the covenant as a saving communion of life, between the "visible" and "invisible" church, between "external" membership in the covenant and "internal" or saving membership, are frequently rejected by FV proponents, who insist that all members of the covenant community are savingly united to Christ.[15]

Covenant and Election

Closely allied to the FV emphasis upon the identity of covenant and salvation is its emphasis upon the "objectivity" of the covenant and its significance for our knowledge of God's election of his people in Christ. Though FV proponents do acknowledge that not all members of the covenant community are "elect" in the strict and confessional sense of this language,[16] they often employ the language of "election" in a way that suggests the election of all members of the covenant community. Consistent with their undifferentiated view of all who are covenant members, some proponents of the FV speak at times as though covenant membership and election coincide. In doing so they leave the distinct impression that not all those who are "saved" in the covenant for a time, or who are "elect" by virtue of their inclusion within the covenant, are necessarily saved or elected to perseverance in the way of salvation.

John Barach, for example, has emphasized the FV's teaching that election and covenant are virtually coincident.

> But then who is in Christ? Those who have been incorporated into Christ, brought into Christ, those who have been baptized into Christ. . . . Covenantal election and individual election aren't actually all that far apart. We can distinguish them perhaps, but we cannot and may not divide them completely. What is the connection? The connection has to do with God's promise, God's speech to us. God has promised every covenant member that he or she is elect in Christ. . . . When God speaks to his people and

15. See, e.g., ibid.; Steve Wilkins, "Covenant, Baptism, and Salvation," in *TAAT*, 262–67; and Lusk, "FAQs."

16. See "A Joint Federal Vision Statement," http://www.federal-vision.com/.

> calls them elect, he is not simply predicting that this will happen, he is making a pledge to them. . . . His promise is that he administers his salvation to us by speaking to us. . . . And God in the gospel and through baptism, promises us that he unites us to Christ. . . . What's missing in Jesus? In him you have redemption, righteousness, justification, sanctification, the Holy Spirit, glorification, and election. The whole package of salvation . . . is found in Christ.[17]

This remarkable statement is typical of the way some FV writers equivocate in their use of the language of "election." On the one hand, Barach's statements could be interpreted to mean that there is a kind of "corporate election" which encompasses the entire number of those who belong to the covenant community, though not all of these members are "savingly elect" in the sense of the Reformed confessions' use of the language of election. On the other hand, Barach fails to draw a clear distinction between covenantal election and individual election. Without emphasizing the necessary response of faith to the covenant promise, a faith that savingly unites the believer to Christ and his benefits, Barach wants to affirm that all covenant members are individually elect and true beneficiaries of Christ's saving work with all of its benefits. Since membership in the covenant is salvation, and since election is unto salvation, what Barach calls a "connection" between covenant and election becomes more than a connection. For this reason, he rejects the idea that we should regard covenant members to be elect in the sense of a "charitable judgment" about them.[18] Covenant and election are identified and, as we shall see in the following, serious problems are created when it is further acknowledged that not all saved and elect members of the covenant persevere in the way of faith.

17. John Barach, "Covenant and Election," lecture, Auburn Avenue Pastor's Conference, 2002, 87–90.

18. John Barach, "Covenant and History," lecture, Auburn Avenue Pastor's Conference, 2002. Cf. E. Calvin Beisner, "Concluding Comments on the Federal Vision," in *TAAT*, 311.

The Prefall Covenant

Another common theme in the writings of FV proponents is that the historic Reformed view of the prefall covenant between the triune God and the human race in Adam needs to be significantly revised. The problem with the Reformed understanding of the prefall covenant, which is commonly termed a "covenant of works," is that it introduces the unbiblical idea of "merit" into the relationship between God and man. Furthermore, the Reformed understanding fails to acknowledge the underlying unity of the covenant between God and his people, whether that covenant is administered before or after the fall into sin.

In the Reformed view of the prefall covenant of works, the triune Creator "voluntarily condescended" to establish a covenant relationship between himself and the human race in Adam.[19] The aim of this covenant was to grant to Adam and his posterity the blessing of eternal life and glorification in unbreakable communion with God "upon condition of perfect and personal obedience." The promise of this original covenant relationship was an implicit promise of eternal life, which was sacramentally signified and sealed by means of the "tree of life" in the garden of Eden (Gen. 3:24). The sanction of this original covenant relationship was the explicit threat of death, both physical and spiritual, in the event of human disobedience and transgression. When God stipulated the command that Adam should not eat of the "tree of the knowledge of good and evil" (Gen. 2:16–17), he subjected Adam, as covenant representative and head of the human race, to a "probationary testing," which concentrated the absolute demand of obedience to God's law in the form of a particular prohibition. As a result of Adam's sin and disobedience, the entire human race has come under condemnation that brings death. Though all human beings are subject to this original covenant

19. WCF 7.1–2: "The distance between God and the creature is so great, that although reasonable creatures do owe obedience unto him as their Creator, yet they could never have any fruition of him as their blessedness and reward, but by some voluntary condescension on God's part, which he hath been pleased to express by way of covenant. The first covenant made with man was a *covenant of works*, wherein life was promised to Adam; and in him to his posterity, upon condition of perfect and personal obedience."

relationship as fallen sinners in Adam and are incapable of obtaining life by obedience to the law, Christ, the "last Adam," has fulfilled all of the obligations of the law on behalf of his people and thereby obtained for them justification and life in restored fellowship with God (Rom. 5:12–21). The significance of the Reformed formulation of the "covenant of works" is that it provides the biblical framework that is indispensable to any proper appreciation of Christ's mediatorial work in the covenant of grace. Whereas Adam was obliged to perfect obedience in order to obtain the promised reward of eternal life in fellowship with God, believers are obliged to receive the superabounding grace of God in Christ by means of the empty hand of faith alone, which rests in Christ's perfect and sufficient obedience that secures their covenant inheritance. In the historic Reformed view, the "condition" that must be met in the covenant of grace is not the believer's personal and perfect obedience to the law, but a heartfelt trust in Christ whose righteousness is wholly sufficient to restore his people to full and indefectible communion with God.[20]

According to a number of proponents of the FV, the Reformed view fails to account for the structural similarities between the prefall and postfall covenants. In both covenants, union and communion with God are based entirely upon God's grace or undeserved favor toward those with whom he covenants. When we distinguish between a prefall covenant of "works" and a postfall covenant of "grace," our language fails to do justice to the grace upon which the original (and every) covenant relationship depends. Furthermore, in all covenant relationships, union and communion with God require that those with whom God covenants live in obedience to his law,

20. WCF 7.3: "Man, by his fall, having made himself incapable of life by that covenant [of works], the Lord was pleased to make a second, commonly called the *covenant of grace*; wherein he freely offereth unto sinners life and salvation by Jesus Christ; requiring of them faith in him, that they may be saved, and promising to give unto all those that are ordained unto eternal life his Holy Spirit, to make them willing, and able to believe"; BC 22: "We believe that, to attain the true knowledge of this great mystery, the Holy Spirit kindles in our hearts an upright faith, which embraces Jesus Christ with all His merits, appropriates Him, and seeks nothing more besides Him. For it must needs follow, either that all things which are requisite to our salvation are not in Jesus Christ, or if all things are in Him, that then those who possess Jesus Christ through faith have complete salvation in Him."

an obedience that springs from gratitude and filial devotion. When Adam was obliged to obey God perfectly, he was obligated to render the obedience of faith, namely, to serve God from a "heart of faith alone, in a spirit of loving trust."[21] Similarly, when believers in Christ are graciously restored to covenant fellowship with Christ, they are placed under the renewed obligation of the obedience of faith. Without the obedience of faith, which is the condition of the covenant of grace even as it was the condition of the "covenant of life" before the fall, believers cannot be justified or assured of their covenant inheritance or eternal life. Due to these common features of the prefall and postfall covenants, we may speak of the way of blessedness in all covenants as "by grace through [the obedience of] faith."[22]

In their reformulation of the doctrine of the covenant, especially the distinction between the prefall and postfall covenants, FV writers often criticize the Reformed view for continuing to uphold the idea of "merit" in the relationship between the creature and the Creator. In the older view, according to FV authors, the relationship between Adam and the triune Creator is construed on analogy like that between an employee and an employer or a servant and a master. Adam's obedience is the required payment or "wages" that he owes God, the basis upon which he would receive what was "due" him as an obedient servant. Furthermore, in the older doctrine, the work of Christ is also viewed in terms of the idea of "merit." By his complete obedience under the law, Christ "merited" justification and life for all those who by faith receive his righteousness as a free gift. The problem with this entire conception of the covenant relationship, and even of Christ's work in redemption, is that it fundamentally misconceives the nature of the covenant fellowship between God and his people. Not only does it deny what is true of the covenant before and after the fall into sin, namely, that it is based upon God's grace

21. "Joint Federal Vision Statement."

22. Norman Shepherd, "Law and Gospel in Covenantal Perspective," pamphlet published by Norman Shepherd (2004), 9. Shepherd expresses clearly the FV tendency to diminish the differences between the prefall and postfall covenant relationship when he says "[w]hat is promised [in the Adamic, Noachic, and Abrahamic covenants] is a gift of grace and it is received by a living, active, and obedient faith."

or undeserved favor, but it also undermines the obedience of faith in the covenant of grace as a necessary (pre-) condition for the believer's inheritance of eternal life. On the one hand, the older view diminishes the grace of God in the prefall covenant. And on the other hand, the older view undermines the legitimate obligations of obedience in the postfall covenant of grace.

Law and Gospel in the Covenant

To appreciate the significance of the FV criticism of the formulation of the prefall and postfall covenants, it is important to note the way FV authors treat the distinction between the "law" and the "gospel." In the Reformed tradition, a sharp distinction is drawn between the law of God, which requires that human beings created in God's image obey perfectly all of its commandments, and the gospel of Jesus Christ, which promises believers free justification and acceptance with God on the basis of the righteousness of Christ alone. In the Reformed view of the gospel benefit of justification, only the perfect obedience of Christ under the law, whether to its precepts (active obedience) or its penalties (passive obedience), is a sufficient basis for satisfying the requirements of God's justice and enabling the believing sinner to be right with God. When the believer is clothed with the fullness of Christ's righteousness under the law, he is able to be justified or placed in the status of innocence and holiness before God. Though the Reformed confessions affirm the continued use of God's law as a "rule of gratitude," they clearly distinguish between the law and the gospel when it comes to the great question of the believer's justification. No "works of the law" of any kind constitute even a part of the believer's righteousness before God or the basis upon which he is justified.[23]

In the judgment of a number of FV writers, this contrast between the law and the gospel depends upon an unbiblical understanding of the prefall "covenant of works." In the FV view, because the Reformed view teaches that Adam's obedience would "merit" his inheritance of eternal life under the covenant of works, it also teaches

23. HC 3–23, 59–64; and BC 22–23.

that the work of Christ, the last Adam, graciously fulfills the requirements of this covenant and thereby "merits" for believers their acceptance before God. Furthermore, since it is alleged that the Reformed view regards any works performed in obedience to the law within the framework of a "works-merit paradigm," FV writers believe it is unable to do justice to the obligations of obedience to the law within the covenant of grace. However, when we view the prefall covenant as a gracious covenant, which required Adam to live before God in grateful obedience, FV writers claim that there is no basis for regarding Adam's works as meritorious. Similarly, when we recognize that the covenant of grace also requires that God's people respond to his grace with an obedient faith (or the obedience of faith) in order to be justified and secure their inheritance, they believe we have no reason to fear that this introduces any "merit" into the covenant relationship. The "works of the law" that the Scriptures condemn, when they speak of justification by faith and apart from works, are not the works that belong to faith but works that are performed in order to merit acceptance with God.[24] Just as the prefall covenant promised blessing to Adam in the way of an obedient faith, so the postfall covenant of grace promises blessing to those who respond to it in the way of an obedient faith. Rather than drawing a sharp contrast between the law and the gospel, we need to recognize, according to FV authors, that grace (or gospel) and law are like two sides of one coin.[25]

The Doctrine of the Church and Sacraments

Based on the FV's reformulation of several features of Reformed teaching regarding the covenant, the FV also argues for a particular understanding of the doctrine of the church and the sacraments. If we properly understand the nature of the relationship between God

24. Shepherd, "Covenantal Perspective"; and Shepherd, "Thirty-four Theses on Justification in Relation to Faith, Repentance, and Good Works," Thesis 24, www.hornes.org/theologia/norman-shepherd/the-34-theses.

25. See Lusk, "A Response to 'The Biblical Plan of Salvation,'" in *TAAT*, 128: "The law did not require perfect obedience. It was designed for sinners, not unfallen creatures. Thus the basic requirement of the law was covenant loyalty and trust, not sinless perfection."

and his people, particularly in the administration of the covenant of grace, we must revise some features of the historic Reformed understanding of the church as a covenant community. In the writings of FV authors, this becomes apparent in three areas: (1) the Reformed distinction between the "visible" and "invisible" church; (2) the efficacy of the sacraments; and (3) the admission of covenant children to the Lord's Supper.

The Distinction between the "Visible" and "Invisible" Church

In the history of the Reformed churches, a distinction is commonly drawn between the so-called "visible" and "invisible" church. Though this distinction is variously defined, its most basic function is to acknowledge that not all professing believers and their children, who belong to the concrete, visible expression of Christ's church in the world, are truly saved and members of Christ by faith. Since the visible church includes some who are not genuinely "of" the church, or who are not "elect" in the strict sense, this language serves to distinguish between the church as a community of professing believers and their children, not all of whom savingly belong to Christ by faith, and the church as God alone knows it as the "whole number of the elect."[26]

Several proponents of the FV have rejected this Reformed distinction because it is incompatible with the FV's claim that covenant membership and saving union with the triune God coincide. They also believe it suggests too sharp a distinction between the circle of the covenant and of election. For example, John Barach has argued that, because "the doctrine of election goes hand in hand with the doctrine of the church," we may affirm, upon the basis of their baptism, that believers and their children "are among the elect *now*."[27] Though it is unclear how literally he wants to use this language, Barach also adds that this affirmation is no mere "wish or boast," but

26. WCF 25.1–2. Cf. BC 29, which in treating the marks of the true church notes that "we speak not here of hypocrites, who are mixed in the Church with the good, yet are not of the Church, though externally in it."

27. Barach, "Covenant and Election," in *TAAT*, 155.

ought to be the confident conviction of all who are baptized.[28] Douglas Wilson, another advocate of the FV, has expressed similar reservations regarding the original Reformed distinction, since it allegedly undermines the importance of membership in the visible church.[29] Wilson proposes that we should distinguish between the "historical" (as it visibly exists now) and "eschatological" (as it will perfectly exist in the future consummation) church. According to FV writers, the distinction between the "visible" and "invisible" church or a similar distinction between an "internal" or "external" membership in the covenant of grace, creates insoluble pastoral problems of assurance (Am I truly a member of Christ? Am I elect?). Contrary to the implications of the distinction between the visible and invisible church, FV authors argue that we should affirm that all members of the covenant community are truly in Christ. As I noted previously, while FV writers acknowledge that some members of the covenant people of God may not persevere in the way of salvation, they want to insist that all members of the covenant are nonetheless in true and saving union with Christ.[30] In the FV view, the "objective" character of membership in the covenant and church of Jesus Christ is undermined, when we distinguish between the church as it visibly exists and as it known only to God.

The Efficacy of the Sacraments (Baptism)

While there are differences of opinion among advocates of the FV on the doctrine of the sacraments, one of the primary themes of the FV is that the Reformed churches need a renewed appreciation for the efficacy of the sacraments in the communication of God's grace in Christ. Corresponding to their emphasis upon the close connection between covenant and salvation, or between covenant and election, FV writers frequently maintain that the sacraments are

28. Ibid. Cf. Beisner, "Concluding Comments," in *TAAT*, 308–9.

29. See Douglas Wilson, *"Reformed" Is Not Enough: Recovering the Objectivity of the Covenant* (Moscow, ID: Canon Press, 2002), 59: "a Christian is one who would be identified as such by a Muslim. Membership in the Christian faith is objective—it can be photographed and fingerprinted."

30. Barach, "Covenant and Election," lecture. Cf. Beisner, "Concluding Comments," in *TAAT*, 308–9.

effectual means of grace, which genuinely communicate the grace of Christ and participation in his saving work to all their recipients. In the view of many FV writers, the Reformed churches have not adequately developed a strong view of the effectiveness of the sacraments in the salvation of those who belong to the covenant community.

This FV emphasis upon the efficacy of the sacraments comes to prominent expression in the understanding of the sacrament of baptism, especially the baptism of children of believers. For example, in his defense of paedobaptism, Rich Lusk insists that the sacrament of baptism does something that even the Word preached does not accomplish. In his interpretation of Acts 2, especially verse 37, Lusk argues that

> [p]reaching alone is insufficient to make them [believers and their children] participants in Christ's work of redemption. . . . Baptism, not preaching per se, is linked with forgiveness and the reception of the Spirit. Clearly, Peter believes God will give them something in baptism that they have not received through preaching alone. Baptism will consummate the process of regeneration begun by the Word preached.[31]

In this statement, the sacrament of baptism is understood to be *constitutive* of its recipients' membership in the covenant of grace. Whereas Reformed sacramental theology would speak of the Spirit producing faith through the Word and *confirming* it through the use of the sacraments, Lusk's view ascribes to the sacraments the power to effect communion with Christ in the fullest sense of the term. By virtue of their baptism, believers and their children are constituted members of Christ and participate in the fullness of his redemptive work on their behalf. All of the benefits of Christ's saving mediation are imparted to all those who are incorporated into the covenant community by means of baptism.

31. Lusk, "Some Thoughts on the Means of Grace: A Few Proposals," http://www.hornes.org/theologia/rich-lusk/some-thoughts-on-the-means-of-grace.

Another example of this emphasis upon baptism as an effectual means of incorporating believers and their children into Christ is provided by Steve Wilkins. As I previously noted, in his understanding of the relation between covenant, baptism, and salvation, Wilkins also proceeds from the conviction that covenant membership involves full, saving communion with the triune God. All persons who are incorporated into the covenant of grace enjoy "a real relationship, consisting of real communion with the triune God through union with Christ. The covenant is not some *thing* that exists apart from Christ or in addition to Him (another *means* of grace)—rather, the covenant *is* union with Christ. Thus, being in covenant gives all the blessings of being united to Christ."[32] According to Wilkins, the sacrament of baptism is the instrumental means whereby this covenant union with Christ is effected. All who are baptized, accordingly, enjoy the fullness of participation in Christ and are the recipients of all the blessings of such participation, including regeneration, justification, and sanctification.[33] Though it is possible for such persons who through baptism are united to Christ to fall away in unbelief and impenitence, thereby losing the real benefits of salvation that were once their possession, Wilkins maintains that baptism is the means of incorporation into Christ and places its beneficiaries in possession of all the benefits of his saving work.[34]

These kinds of unqualified affirmations of the saving efficacy of the sacraments in FV writings are not incidental. They follow naturally from the kind of undifferentiated view of covenant and church membership that characterizes FV teaching generally. If membership

32. Steve Wilkins, "Covenant, Baptism, and Salvation," in *TAAT*, 262.

33. Ibid., 262–64.

34. Similar unqualified statements of the efficacy of the sacraments, especially the sacrament of baptism, can be found sprinkled throughout the writings of FV authors. See, e.g., Douglas Wilson, "Sacramental Efficacy in the Westminster Standards," in *TAAT*, 236: "Worthy receivers of the sacrament of baptism and the Lord's Supper are effectually saved by these sacramental means through the working of the Holy Spirit and the blessing of Christ." Waters, *Federal Vision*, 198–257, offers extensive evidence of FV statements relating to the efficacy of the sacraments. For a critical evaluation of the FV exaggeration of the efficacy of the sacraments, see William B. Evans, "'Really Exhibited and Conferred . . . in His Appointed Time': Baptism and the New Reformed Sacramentalism," *Presbyterion* 31, 2 (2005): 72–88.

in the covenant community entails salvation and warrants a confident affirmation of the election of its members, the sacraments, which signify and seal to all their recipients the promises of the gospel, should be viewed as saving ordinances, which effectively unite believers and their children with Christ and his church. Since membership in the covenant community is tantamount to saving union with Christ, and since baptism is the means to effect such membership, it seems to follow that baptism saves by uniting covenant members to Christ so that they are flesh of his flesh, bone of his bone.

Children at the Lord's Table

A particularly instructive example of the implications of these FV teachings is the question whether the children of believing parents should be admitted to the sacrament of the Lord's Supper. Since "ideas have legs," it is not surprising that one of the most obvious and practical implications of FV teaching is that all baptized children should be admitted to the Lord's Table.

I have had occasion at several points to observe the claim of FV authors that *all* covenant members without exception—believers and their children who are recipients of the covenant promise and the accompanying sacrament of covenant incorporation, baptism—enjoy a full and saving union with Christ. Though Reformed theologians have historically distinguished between those who are "under the administration" of the covenant of grace and those who truly enjoy the saving "communion of life" that the covenant communicates, we have seen how FV proponents often reject as inappropriate any such distinction between covenant members. Within the framework of this unqualified definition of what it means for all believers and their children to be members of the covenant of grace, we have also seen that FV writers strongly emphasize the efficacy of baptism as a sacrament of incorporation into Christ. The FV emphasis upon the significance and efficacy of baptism is of particular relevance to the question whether children of believing parents should be admitted to the Table of the Lord. Since the baptism of the children of believers effectively unites them to Christ and grants them full participation in his saving work, baptism by itself is thought to provide a sufficient warrant for admitting such children to the Table of the Lord without requiring a preceding profession of faith.[35]

The common advocacy of paedocommunion on the part of most FV writers, therefore, is no accident, but follows from the most basic FV features. Advocacy of paedocommunion is a necessary consequence of the FV doctrine of the covenant of grace and its sacraments. Within the framework of the FV understanding of what is true of all covenant members, and of baptism's effectiveness as constitutive of their incorporation into Christ, the warrant for admission of believers' children to the Table of the Lord should be apparent. It is a simple matter of theological and covenantal consistency to move from the reality of covenant membership and saving union with Christ, which are the possession of all believers and their children under the covenant of grace, to the reception of children at the Lord's Table. In the view of many FV writers, to exclude children from the Table of the Lord denies their privileges as members of Christ. The children of believing parents, who already possess Christ in his fullness, may scarcely be denied a participation in Christ by means of the sacrament that Christ appointed to strengthen communion with himself and to nourish faith. At stake in the debate regarding the admission of children to the Lord's Table is nothing other than a consistent covenantal hermeneutic or way of interpreting Scripture. Consequently, those who advocate the admission of children to the Lord's Table upon the basis of their covenant membership regard the historic practice of the Reformed churches on this question to be baptistic and inconsistent.[36]

35. Perhaps recognizing the danger of this kind of understanding of paedobaptism as an effectual instrument of salvation, Lusk has posited the notion of a kind of "paedofaith" that embraces the promise that baptism communicates. See Rich Lusk, *Paedofaith: A Primer on the Mystery of Infant Salvation and a Handbook for Covenant Parents* (Monroe, LA: Athanasius, 2005); and Lusk, "Baptismal Efficacy and Baptismal Latency: A Sacramental Dialogue," *Presbyterion* 32, 1 (2006): 36.

36. For a brief summary of this argument, see Gregg Strawbridge, "The Polemics of Infant Communion," in *The Case for Covenant Communion*, ed. Gregg Strawbridge (Monroe, LA: Athanasius, 2006), 147–65. For a recent critical evaluation of this argument, see Cornelis P. Venema, *Children at the Lord's Table? Assessing the Case for Paedocommunion* (Grand Rapids, MI: Reformation Heritage, 2009).

Assurance, Perseverance, and Apostasy

One of the primary motivations that underlies the FV is the desire to resolve certain pastoral problems that have surfaced in the history of the Reformed churches. A frequent charge of FV writers is that many Presbyterian and Reformed churches have aggravated the problem of the assurance of salvation by failing to articulate a biblical view of the covenant of grace. Furthermore, because many Reformed believers have viewed the covenant of grace from the perspective of the doctrine of election, they have also failed to do justice to the biblical warnings against apostasy and covenant breaking on the part of those who belong to the covenant people of God.

Assurance of Salvation

The FV solution to the problem of the believer's assurance of salvation should be readily apparent from what I have already noted in respect to the FV's doctrine of the covenant and the sacraments. According to FV authors, the Reformed churches historically have been plagued by the question as to how believers ought to be assured of their own salvation. Rather than basing such assurance upon the "objective" promises God makes in the covenant of grace, or upon the efficacy of the sacramental communication of the grace of Christ in baptism, believers have been encouraged to look within themselves for concrete signs of their regeneration. Several FV authors maintain that this accounts for the tendency to engage in a kind of "morbid introspection," a looking inward to ascertain evidences of the work of God's grace in the individual believer's life, as the pathway to obtaining assurance of salvation.[37] Because of the uncertainty and unreliability of Christian experience, however, this introspective or subjective approach to the assurance of salvation is unable to grant the believer any secure confidence before God.

The solution to the problem of assurance proposed by FV authors is to base the assurance of salvation on the status of believers

37. See, e.g., Barach, "Covenant and Election," lecture; Barach, "Covenant and Election," in *TFV*, 38; Steve Wilkins, "Apostasy and the Covenant II," lecture, Auburn Avenue Presbyterian Church Pastor's Conference, 2002; and Waters, *Federal Vision*, 125–56.

as members of the covenant community and to appeal to the efficacy of the sacraments as a reliable basis for confidence. A common theme among writers of the FV is that their view of the covenant and its sacraments resolves a problem that many Reformed churches have only aggravated. John Barach offers an especially clear statement of this solution:

> [H]ow do you know that promise [of the covenant] is really for you and not just for other people in the church, people who've advanced further in their sanctification or who've had some special experience that convinced them of God's love? The answer is that you've had a special experience. You've been baptized. All God's salvation—from election to glorification—is found in Christ. And when you were baptized, God promised to unite you to Jesus Christ. That's what it means to be baptized into Christ. You're united to Jesus and all His salvation is for you. At baptism, God promises that you're really one of His elect: I will be your God and you will be my child. And God never hands out counterfeit promises.[38]

In his comments on the problem of assurance in the Reformed churches, Steve Wilkins makes a similar claim. Rather than look to a subjective experience of conversion as the basis for assurance, believers and their children should be directed to their membership in the covenant and their reception of the sacrament of baptism. When believers look to their "objective" membership in the covenant community, they have a sure basis for the assurance of salvation. Moreover, this assurance is more than a "judgment of charity." It is an assurance that is based upon what we know to be true in the strongest possible sense.[39] As another FV writer concisely expresses it,

38. John Barach, "Baptism and Election," lecture, Auburn Avenue Presbyterian Church Pastor's Conference, 2002, in response to a question posed to Steve Schlissel, as cited by Waters, *Federal Vision*, 134–35. Also see Barach, "Covenant and Election," in *TFV*, 38.

39. See, e.g., Barach, "Covenant and History," lecture; and Wilkins, "Covenant, Baptism, and Salvation," in *TAAT*, 259–65.

"The gospel is preached, the water was applied, the Table is now set. Do you believe? The question is a simple one."[40]

Perseverance and Apostasy

Even though the FV emphasis upon the assurance of salvation, based upon objective covenant membership and efficacy of the sacraments, might appear "presumptuous," it is interesting to observe that there is another emphasis also present in the teaching of the FV. Since the covenant is always "conditional," requiring the obedience of faith on the part of those with whom God covenants, FV writers stress the need for an obedient faith that perseveres to the end and does not fall away into apostasy. Because all members of the covenant community are obliged to new obedience, failure to continue in the way of faithfulness to the covenant will ultimately prove spiritually fatal. One of the themes of FV writers, accordingly, is the theme of perseverance in the way of covenant faithfulness, lest covenant members lose their salvation through their disobedience.

I have already noted the way some FV writers speak of the salvation of those who belong to the covenant community as one that may be experienced only "for a time." Since "covenant election" does not coincide with "election" in the proper sense of God's eternal purpose, it is possible for covenant members to fall away from a salvation that they once possessed. In September 2002, the session of the Auburn Avenue Presbyterian Church adopted a "Summary Statement of AAPC's Position on the Covenant, Baptism, and Salvation." In this statement, the possibility of covenantal apostasy on the part of persons who have genuinely experienced saving union with Christ is affirmed.

> God mysteriously has chosen to draw many into the covenant community who are not elect in the ultimate sense and who are not destined to receive final salvation. These nonelect covenant members are truly brought to Christ, united to Him in the Church by baptism and receive various operations of the

40. Wilson, *"Reformed" Is Not Enough*, 130.

> Holy Spirit. Corporately, they are part of the chosen, redeemed, Spirit-indwelt people. Sooner or later, however, in the wise counsel of God, these fail to bear fruit and fall away. In some sense, they were really joined to the elect people, really sanctified by Christ's blood, really recipients of new life given by the Holy Spirit. God, however, withholds from them the gift of perseverance, and all is lost. They break the gracious new covenant they entered into at baptism.[41]

Among FV writers, it is frequently argued that Christ's words in John 15:1–8, which speak of some who do not abide in the vine and bear its corresponding fruit, describe the reality of some who enjoy a true communion with Christ but subsequently fall away through apostasy and lose what was once theirs.[42] Because the covenant is always conditioned upon a persevering and obedient faith, those who fall away through unbelief and disobedience lose their salvation in Christ and all its accompanying blessings.

Though it would not be difficult to multiply examples of this kind of emphasis within the writings of FV proponents, the FV understanding of perseverance and apostasy should be fairly transparent. Because all those who belong to the covenant people of God by baptism are genuinely incorporated into Christ and thereby participate in the saving benefits of his work of Mediator, failure on their part to meet the conditions of the covenant may entail the loss of saving blessings that were once their possession. Since FV authors resist any distinctions between some within the covenant community who are only "externally" or "apparently" in union with Christ and others who are truly and savingly in union with Christ, they are compelled to regard covenant apostasy as tantamount to a kind of

41. "Summary Statement of AAPC's Position on the Covenant, Baptism, and Salvation," www.auburnavenue.org. For a survey of similar statements by FV authors, see Waters, *Federal Vision*, 146–67.

42. See, e.g., Wilkins, "Covenant, Baptism, and Salvation," in *TFV*, 63–64; Norman Shepherd, "The Covenant Context for Evangelism," in *The New Testament Student and Theology*, vol. 3 of *The New Testament Student*, ed. John H. Skilton (Nutley, NJ: Presbyterian and Reformed, 1976), 51–75; and Douglas Wilson, "The Objectivity of the Covenant," *Credenda/Agenda* 15, 1 (2012): 4–5.

"falling from grace" or the loss of a temporary election and salvation. Even though the FV emphasizes the close connection between covenant, election, and salvation, the FV also stresses the necessity of meeting covenant obligations to ensure the blessings of salvation in Christ. This means that covenant members must be faithful in the way of an obedient and persevering faith, lest they risk the loss of what was once theirs when they were first incorporated into Christ through baptism.

10

Covenant, Justification, and the "Federal Vision" (2): *Covenant and Election*

In light of my previous chapter's overview of the FV movement, we now face the challenge of assessing the distinctive emphases of the FV. In doing so, it is important to recognize that there has always been room for a diversity of opinion and formulation within the boundaries of the Reformed confessions. The history of the Reformed and Presbyterian churches reflects a fairly wide spectrum of opinion regarding the doctrine of the covenant and related issues pertaining to the doctrine of the church and sacraments. On the topic of the assurance of salvation, for example, some Reformed churches have emphasized the "objective" grounds for assurance in the gospel promise: the sacraments and the witness of the Holy Spirit by these means. Others have been inclined, for fear of complacency or presumptuousness, to emphasize the "subjective" experience of God's grace through the working of the Holy Spirit. For this reason, my assessment of the FV will endeavor to acknowledge points where diversity of opinion is permissible. However, it will also be necessary to identify emphases in the FV that are problematic and at odds with the historic consensus of Reformed theology, particularly in respect to the important doctrine of justification.

Due to the complexity of the issues involved, my assessment of the FV is divided into two parts. In this chapter, I will begin with a critical evaluation of the manner in which FV authors have described the relation between covenant and election. And in the following chapter, I will focus especially upon the implications of the FV for an understanding of the doctrine of justification by faith alone.

Covenant, Election, and Salvation

As I noted in my survey of the claims of the FV movement, several FV proponents argue for the closest possible relationship between covenant, election, and salvation. When God covenants with his people (believers and their children), he graciously elects them to a true and saving communion with himself. All who are members of the covenant people of God may legitimately proceed from the conviction that they are "elect in Christ" and possess accordingly all the saving benefits of Christ's work as Mediator. With respect to the doctrine of justification, this means that all covenant members enjoy all gospel benefits, including justification, by virtue of their membership in Christ and his church.

From the standpoint of the confessions, this FV identification of covenant, election, and salvation is at best overstated and at worst seriously unbiblical. By equating covenant, election, and salvation, FV proponents are unable to maintain clearly that those whom God elects in Christ will unfailingly be granted the fullness of salvation in unbreakable communion with God. Since not all those with whom God covenants in history are "elect" in the proper sense of the term, especially as election is defined in BC 16 and the CD, we may not assert in an unqualified manner that they are all elected unto salvation and participate in the saving benefits of Christ's mediatorial work. Within the framework of this identification of election and covenant, some FV authors speak of covenant members who, though elect and saved in Christ, do not persevere in the covenant and subsequently lose their salvation. However, in the Reformed confessions, God's gracious purpose of election infallibly ensures that the elect will be granted every saving blessing in Christ, including the blessing of free justification, and that they will be preserved in this salvation by God's steadfast love and faithfulness. According to the CD, God eternally determined to give his people to Christ. In order to accomplish this purpose, God in time redeems, effectually calls, justifies, and glorifies them.[1] Therefore, the CD expressly repudiate the error of those who teach that Christ has purchased any temporal saving benefits for the nonelect, even those who may be members of the church for a time, as though they were temporally justified.[2] The simple identification of covenant, election, and salvation, which is a principal theme of several FV proponents, can only leave the impression that there is a kind of covenant election that depends upon the covenant member's faithfulness and obedience. Such covenant election does not ensure anything more than a "temporary salvation" and can be subsequently lost through covenant apostasy. Though some FV authors insist that the covenant of grace is tantamount to election unto salvation in Christ, they are compelled to equivocate in their use of the language of "election," "justification," and "salvation," since by their own admission not all of the elect or justified persevere in the way of an obedient faith. In this FV teaching, elect and justified persons can cease to enjoy a salvation they once possessed.

There are at least two ways in which FV authors diverge at this point from the teaching of the Three Forms of Unity. In the first place, the CD are quite explicit in rejecting the teaching of various "kinds of election," as though some are elected only to grace but not to glory, or to salvation but not to "the way of salvation, which he [God] prepared in advance for us to walk in."[3] According to the CD, all the fruits of election, which include "[f]aith, holiness, and the other saving gifts," are included within God's purpose of election and are granted in time to those whom he elects.[4] The formulation of some FV authors that allows for an election to salvation "for

1. CD 1.7: "And so he decided to give the chosen ones to Christ to be saved, and to call and draw them effectively into Christ's fellowship through his Word and Spirit. In other words, he decided to grant them true faith in Christ, to justify them, to sanctify them, and finally, after powerfully preserving them in the fellowship of his Son, to glorify them"; 2.8: "it was God's will that Christ through the blood of the cross (by which he confirmed the new covenant) should effectively redeem from every people, tribe, nation, and language all those and only those who were chosen from eternity to salvation and given to him by the Father; that he should grant them faith . . . that he should faithfully preserve them to the very end."

2. Ibid., Rejection 1:2.

3. Ibid., 1:8.

4. Ibid., 1:9.

a time," which can then be lost through subsequent disobedience and apostasy, is expressly included among the views that the Canons reject.[5] In my survey of FV emphases in the previous chapter, I noted how some authors speak of an election to a temporary salvation and nonpersevering faith. As it stands, this FV emphasis is incompatible with the express language of the CD, when they reject the position of those

> [w]ho teach that God's election to eternal life is of many kinds: one general and indefinite, the other particular and definite; and the latter in turn either incomplete, revocable, nonperemptory (or conditional), or else complete, irrevocable, and peremptory (or absolute). Likewise, who teach that there is one election to faith and another to salvation, so that there can be an election to justifying faith apart from a peremptory election to salvation.[6]

Contrary to the teaching of a temporary salvation and a nonpersevering faith, the last main point of doctrine set forth in the CD deals with the believer's perseverance in the way of faith and salvation. The teaching of the perseverance of the saints follows properly from the other main points of doctrine that the Canons summarize. Since God's purpose of election will be infallibly accomplished, believers may be assured that God will preserve them in the way of faith and salvation. In the beautiful language of the Canons, God's "plan cannot be changed, his promise cannot fail, the calling according to his purpose cannot be revoked, the merit of Christ as well as his interceding and preserving cannot be nullified, and the sealing of the Holy Spirit can neither be invalidated nor wiped out."[7]

5. Ibid., Rejection 1:6: "Who teach that not every election to salvation is unchangeable, but that some of the chosen can perish and do in fact perish eternally, with no decision of God to prevent it."

6. Ibid., Rejection 1:2.

7. Ibid., 5.8. Cf. Rejection 5.3: "Who teach that those who truly believe and have been born again not only can forfeit justifying faith as well as grace and salvation totally and to the end, but also in actual fact do often forfeit them and are lost forever. For this opinion nullifies the very grace of justification and regeneration as well as the continual preservation by Christ."

In the second place, the FV tendency to equate election and membership in the covenant of grace compromises the CD's teaching of *unconditional* election. Though FV writers maintain that all covenant members are elect in Christ, they also want to stress the *conditionality* of the covenant relationship. If those with whom God covenants do not meet the conditions of the covenant, namely, persevering faith and repentance, they can lose their salvation and become subject to God's covenant wrath. Since the covenant obliges believers and their children to embrace the promise of the gospel in the way of a living faith, it is possible that some covenant members can lose the grace of communion with God in Christ that was once theirs. The problem with the FV formulation at this point is not that it emphasizes the "conditionality" of the covenant relationship. It is undoubtedly true that the covenant promise demands the response of faith and repentance. The Reformed confessions consistently maintain that believers and their children are ordinarily saved in Christ in the way of faith and repentance.[8] However, the FV tendency to identify election and covenant in an unqualified manner renders saving election losable, election being conditional upon covenant faithfulness. In this way, faith and repentance, as conditions of the covenant, cease to be the fruits of God's gracious purpose of election (cf. Phil. 2:12–13; Eph. 2:10; Titus 3:4–8; Rom. 8:1–4). It is proper to emphasize, as FV authors do, the decisive importance of persevering faith and obedience within the covenant relationship. However, it is improper to formulate the relation between election and covenant so that persevering faith and obedience are not themselves the fruits of God's gracious election and work on behalf of his own through the ministry of the Spirit. From the standpoint of the Reformed confessions, it must always be emphasized that what the Lord requires in the way of faith and repentance, he also gives by the operations of the Holy Spirit through the gospel Word and its accompanying sacraments. Even the so-called "conditions" of the covenant of grace are graciously met in accordance with God's purpose of election.[9]

8. HC 20–23, 53–56, 65–68, 86–91; BC 22–24; CD 1.4, 7; 2.6–8; 3/4.10–17.

9. See, e.g., CD Rejection 5.1: "Who teach that the perseverance of true believers is not an effect of election or a gift of God produced by Christ's death, but a condition of the

The Prefall Covenant

One of the most significant features of FV teaching, and one that directly bears upon the doctrine of justification, is its position on the prefall covenant relationship between God and all human beings in Adam. FV proponents do not approve the Reformed language of a prefall "covenant of works" and reject the idea that Adam's obedience within this covenant relationship would in any sense "merit" the reward of eternal life that was promised to him. Furthermore, since there is a close biblical parallel between the fall and disobedience of the first Adam, which is the basis for the condemnation and death of all men, and the obedience of Christ, which is the basis for the justification and life of all who are members of Christ by faith, FV authors oppose some features of the historic Reformed view of Christ's saving work. In the Reformed tradition, the obedience of Christ in its entirety (active and passive) is viewed as an obedience that justly "merits" eternal life for believers. Christ's righteousness is viewed in terms of his fulfillment of all the obligations "under the law" that Adam failed to meet, but that Christ met on behalf of his own for their justification. The manner in which FV writers reject the doctrine of a prefall "covenant of works" compels them to reject the teaching that the believer's justification is based upon Christ's entire obedience under the law, which "merits" righteousness and eternal life for his people.

When evaluated by the standard of the Three Forms of Unity, this FV denial of a prefall covenant of works raises two crucial questions: (1) do the Three Forms of Unity teach a doctrine of a prefall "covenant of works," as is evidently the case in WCF 7; and (2) do the Three Forms of Unity affirm the teaching that Christ "merited" righteousness and life for his people? Both questions are of special importance to an evaluation of the FV and its doctrine of justification.

With respect to the first question—do the Three Forms of Unity teach a prefall "covenant of works" doctrine?—the answer might appear at first glance to be relatively easy. Since the confessions

new covenant which man, before what they call his 'peremptory' election and justification, must fulfill by his free will."

nowhere use the language of a prefall "covenant" or "covenant of works," it appears that this is a confessional teaching that belongs only to the Presbyterian tradition. The negative answer to this question, however, is too hasty. Though the language of "covenant" or "covenant of works" may not be used in the Three Forms of Unity, what matters is whether the components of a "covenant of works" doctrine are present. No one who subscribes to the Three Forms of Unity is obliged to use the language of a prefall "covenant of works." Nor is a subscriber to the Three Forms of Unity obliged to agree with every formulation or view of the prefall relationship between God and (all men in) Adam. Such persons are obliged, however, to subscribe to the confessional descriptions of the prefall relationship, and to do so particularly in terms of the way they inform the confessional understanding of Christ's saving work as the Mediator of the covenant of grace.

There are several key elements that belong to the confessions' summary of the relationship between God and Adam in the prefall state. First, the confessions teach that Adam's obedience to God's holy law was indispensable to his life in blessed fellowship with God. The life promised Adam (cf. Gen. 3:22) in this fellowship is not viewed as a "free gift" of God's *saving grace*, but as an inheritance that depends upon Adam's perfect obedience to the law of God. If Adam were to have perfectly obeyed the holy law of his triune Creator, he would have continued to enjoy fellowship with God and received the reward of eternal life. The reward of eternal life promised Adam would have been granted Adam in full harmony with God's truth and justice.[10] Second, in the confessional view of the prefall relationship between God and Adam, Adam's status of favor and acceptance with God was not based upon the righteousness of Another, but upon a righteousness that was his own (though his by virtue of

10. See BC 14: "We believe that God created man out of the dust of the earth, and made and formed him after His own image and likeness, good, righteous, and holy, capable in all things to will agreeably to the will of God. But *being in honor, he understood it not,* neither knew his excellency, but wilfully subjected himself to sin and consequently to death and the curse, giving ear to the words of the devil. For the commandment of life, which he had received, he transgressed; and by sin separated himself from God, who was his true life"; HC 6: "so that [aus dass] he might live with Him in eternal blessedness"; HC 40.

God's gracious enablement and provision). Prior to Adam's fall into sin, he was properly reckoned to be righteous by God, and this was not an act of God's saving grace in Christ (cf. Rom. 5:12–21). Even though the confessions do not say that Adam's acceptance with God and eternal life would have been "merited" through his obedience, they do insist that Adam's inheritance of eternal life and blessedness was dependent upon his obedience to the "commandment of life."[11] And third, the confessions view the work of Christ, as Mediator of the covenant of grace, within the framework of their understanding of the prefall relationship between God and (all men in) Adam.[12] In the covenant of grace, Christ, the "last Adam," fulfills all the requirements of God's holy law on behalf of his people. In this way, Christ's work of redemption obtains eternal life for his people in a way that upholds God's truth and justice.

11. BC 14. Since the Reformed confessions do not use the term "merit" in their descriptions of the obedience Adam was obliged to render to God in order to enjoy life, subscribers to these confessions are not required to do so. However, subscribers to the confessions are required to recognize that Adam's obedience was the stipulated condition for his enjoyment of God's favor and eternal life, and that his disobedience justly forfeited (demerited) God's favor. Reformed theologians who have used the language of "merit" in the prefall covenant context typically recognize that the language is being used "improperly," and merely expresses the "connection" between God's covenant promise and the reward of eternal life. It is a kind of "covenantal merit" (*meritum ex pacto*) that accords with divine truth and justice, but ultimately originates with God's unmerited favor in conferring upon Adam a "right" to eternal life that surpasses anything he "deserved" as a creature in the presence of his Creator. Since God promises to bless human obedience to his will, God's bestowal or granting a blessing to Adam for obedience to his will is a matter of being true to himself (that is, his promise) and therefore a matter of covenanted justice. Contrary to the claims of some FV writers, this understanding of the connection between Adam's obedience and the promised reward of eternal life does not represent a Reformed appropriation of the Roman Catholic doctrine of human "merit," whether "condign" (full) merit or "congruent" (half) merit. In the Roman Catholic view, "condign" merit is the intrinsic merit or worth of human obedience as it is prompted by God's grace and Spirit; "congruent" merit is the "half-merit" of human works that receive a reward that exceeds their intrinsic worth. For classic Reformed treatments of this question, see *IET*, 2:710–23; *RD*, 2:569–71; and *CCT*, 112–19, 196–202, 326–28. The following observation of Turretin is of particular significance to an understanding of the Reformed view: "Hence also it appears that there is no merit properly so called of man before God, in whatever state he is placed. Thus Adam himself, if he had persevered, would not have merited life in strict justice, although (through a certain condescension [*synchatabasin*]) God promised him by a covenant life under the condition of perfect obedience (which is called meritorious from that covenant in a broader sense. . . .)" (*IET*, 2:712). See also chap. 1 of this volume.

12. HC 6–19.

Therefore, the absence of the terminology of a "covenant of works" in the confessions does not alter the fact that all the elements of the Reformed doctrine are materially present in them.[13] The Three Forms of Unity clearly affirm the original state of integrity in Adam, the obligation of perfect obedience to the law of God, the promise of life upon condition of such obedience, and the consequence of Adam's sin and fall for the whole human race. Because Adam transgressed the law of God and broke fellowship with his Creator, he forfeited for himself and all his posterity any possibility of eternal life in unbreakable communion with God in the way of obedience to God's holy law. After the fall and disobedience of Adam, the only way to obtain eternal life is through faith in Christ, the last Adam, who alone is able to grant the fullness of life and glory to those who belong to him. Consequently, though the language of a "covenant of works" may be disputed, the substance of the historical Reformed understanding of this covenant is present in the Three Forms of Unity.[14]

Consistent with the FV denial of the teaching of a prefall covenant that required obedience to the law as a condition for obtaining eternal life, FV writers reject the language of "merit" even when it is applied to the work of Christ. However, the confessions often speak of Christ's "merits" to refer to his entire obedience under the law on behalf of his people. Just as the disobedience of the first Adam brings condemnation and death to the whole human race whom he represented, so the obedience of Christ brings justification and life to those whom he represented as Mediator of the covenant of grace. Christ satisfied the justice and truth of God in his active obedience to all the requirements of his Father's holy will and his passive obedience

13. BC 14, 15; HC 6–11; CD 3/4.

14. See *RD*, 2:569, which notes that "one may doubt the word, provided the matter is safe" (*de vocabulo dubitetur, re salva*). In the history of Reformed theology, the prefall covenant between God and humanity in Adam has been variously designated. Sometimes it is termed a "covenant of nature," since this covenant required obedience to the moral law of God that man knew by nature and was able to obey by virtue of the created gifts and integrity with which he was originally endowed. However, it is most commonly designated a "covenant of works," since the eternal life promised in the covenant was only able to be obtained in the way of works, that is, in the way of keeping God's commandments.

to the penalty due those who transgress God's holy law. For this reason, the confessions expressly use the language of Christ's "merits" or "meriting" eternal life for his people.[15]

Contrary to the claims of many FV authors, therefore, the Three Forms of Unity clearly teach that the entire obedience of Christ under the law was performed in his office as Mediator and that this obedience remedies the failure of Adam to live in obedience to God. With respect to the doctrine of justification, the confessions take the righteousness of Christ, which is granted and imputed to believers for their justification, to include "all His merits, and so many holy works which He has done for us and in our stead" under the law.[16] This means that what some FV authors disparage as a "works-merit" paradigm is expressly set forth in the confessions, particularly in their description of Christ's saving *work* on behalf of his people.

Law and Gospel in the Covenant

In my summary of the FV, I noted that FV proponents oppose a sharp distinction between the law and the gospel in their understanding of the covenant of grace, and even in their understanding of the difference between the prefall and postfall relationship between God and his people. Just as Adam was required to respond to God's grace in the way of an obedient faith in order to obtain what was promised to him, so believers are required to respond to the gospel of Christ in the way of an obedient faith in order to secure their inheritance of eternal life. Though the language of "gospel" is appropriately

15. See, e.g., BC 20–23; HC 3–23, 59–64; and CD Rejection 2.3–4. When the confessions speak of the "merit" of Christ's work, they affirm that the work of Christ, though entirely the fruit of God's gracious purpose to provide for the redemption of the elect through the work of the Mediator, *truly and properly merits*, in full conformity to the requirements of God's exact justice, eternal life and favor for his people. Unlike the improper use of "merit" to describe the connection between Adam's stipulated obedience and the promised reward of eternal life, the language of "merit" is entirely appropriate in respect to the perfect righteousness of Christ, who fulfills all the obligations of the law in his person as true God and true man on behalf of his people (cf. Rom. 3:26; 8:1–4; Gal. 3:10–14). See HC 9–19; and *Institutes*, 2.17, "Christ Rightly and Properly Said to Have Merited God's Grace and Salvation for Us."

16. BC 22. See also BC 14, 20, 23, 24; HC 6–19, 37–45, 59–64; CD Rejection 2.3–4.

used only with respect to the covenant of grace, it remains true that the "way" to covenant blessing is always "by grace" through an obedient faith, whether before or after the fall into sin.

The problem with this FV tendency to blur the difference between Adam's obligations of obedience under the law in the prefall state and the believer's obligations to the law in the postfall covenant of grace is that it undermines the biblical and confessional view of justification. When it comes to the justification of believers, it is imperative that a sharp distinction be drawn between the "law" and the "gospel." As a result of the sin and disobedience of Adam, no one is able to obey the law perfectly, not even the believer who enjoys the grace of the Spirit's work in sanctification. According to the Reformed confessions, the believer's obedience to the law of God plays no role whatsoever in obtaining the grace of free justification.[17] Under the conditions of human sinfulness, the holy and good law of God can only expose our sin and misery.[18] The only way back for sinners to renewed fellowship with God is through faith in Jesus Christ, who fulfilled all the obligations of the law on behalf of his people.[19] So far as the believer's justification is concerned, the radical contrast between the "righteousness of faith" and the "righteousness of the law" cannot be overstated. No human works, not even the good works of believers that are prompted by the Holy Spirit and performed in gratitude for God's grace in Christ, can contribute anything to the believer's acceptance with God.[20] Of course, this does not mean that the confessions deny the believer's obligation to live before God in grateful devotion and conformity to the holy requirements of his law. However, such obedience is itself a gift of God's grace in Christ, who renews his own by the working of the Holy Spirit, and is performed out of gratitude for a salvation that is a free

17. HC 59–64, esp. 62: "But why cannot our good works be the whole or part of our righteousness before God? Because the righteousness which can stand before the tribunal of God must be absolutely perfect and wholly conformable to the divine law, while even our best works in this life are all imperfect and defiled with sin"; BC 21–24.

18. HC 3–5.

19. Ibid., 9–23; and 60: "God, without any merit of mine, of mere grace, grants and imputes to me the perfect satisfaction, righteousness, and holiness of Christ."

20. Ibid., 62–64; BC 22–24.

gift of God's grace.[21] Therefore, believers are not "under the law" in the sense in which Adam was obliged to live in obedience to its requirements. Since Christ has discharged all of the obligations of the law in the place of his own, the obedience of believers is a free response to God's grace and can only be pleasing to God upon the basis of a prior acceptance with him.[22] Contrary to the FV claim that believers are obliged to secure their inheritance in the covenant in the same way as Adam, namely, in the way of an obedient faith, the confessions teach that Christ has secured this inheritance for them through his perfect obedience and atonement.[23]

It should be noted that, though the confessions insist upon a sharp distinction between the law and the gospel when it comes to the justification of believers, they also maintain the perpetual validity of God's holy law in their understanding of Christ's saving work. Though Adam (and all men in him) failed to keep the law of God perfectly, and thereby brought himself and all his posterity under the curse and judgment of God, Christ assumed our human nature in order, as Mediator, to perform on behalf of his people all that the law required.[24] The difference between man's fellowship (or covenant) with God before and after the fall does not mitigate the fact that in both circumstances the law of God is fully upheld. Because God is unchangeably holy and righteous, the demand of his holy law is maintained not only before the fall under the covenant of works but after the fall in the administration of the covenant of grace. No human being can find favor with God without doing what the law of

21. HC 64: "[I]t is impossible that those who are implanted into Christ by a true faith should not bring forth fruits of thankfulness"; 86: "Christ, having redeemed us by His blood, also renews us by His Holy Spirit after His own image, that with our whole life we may show ourselves thankful to God for His benefits"; 91: "But what are good works? Only those which are done from true faith, according to the law of God, and to His glory; and not such as are based on our opinions or the precepts of men."

22. Ibid., 91; BC 24: "These works, as they proceed from the good root of faith, are good and acceptable in the sight of God, forasmuch as they are all sanctified by His grace. Nevertheless they are of no account towards our justification, for it is by faith in Christ that we are justified, even before we do good works; otherwise they could not be good works, any more than the fruit of a tree can be good before the tree itself is good."

23. HC 52; and 59: "But what does it profit you now that you believe all this? That I am righteous in Christ before God, and an heir to eternal life."

24. Ibid., 3–4, 54–56, 59–64, 113–115; BC 20–23.

God requires. This is as true in the covenant of grace as it was in the covenant of works. Therefore, in the covenant of grace, God does not act capriciously or arbitrarily. He always acts in a way that maintains and upholds the righteous requirements of his holy law (cf. Rom. 3:21–26). Indeed, after the fall into sin, the whole human race comes to stand "under the law" in two respects: first, all remain obligated to do what the law requires in order to be pleasing to God; and second, all now come under the law in terms of its liability and penalty. After the fall into sin, the requirement of perfect obedience in order to obtain eternal life remains, but it has now been complicated by the additional requirement that payment be made for the debts that disobedient sinners now owe God for their sins.

The Doctrine of the Church and Sacraments (Baptism)

In my summary of some of the characteristic features of the FV, I called special attention to three aspects of its doctrine of the church and sacraments: (1) a repudiation of the Reformed distinction between the "visible" and the "invisible" church; (2) a strong doctrine of the efficacy of the sacraments; and (3) a common advocacy of admitting children to the sacrament of the Lord's Supper. On each of these aspects, there are elements of the FV that are out of accord with the teaching of the confessions.

While it is true that the Three Forms of Unity do not explicitly distinguish between what some Reformed confessions term the "visible" and "invisible" church,[25] the most important elements of this distinction are present in them. The primary use of this distinction in the history of the Reformed churches is to observe that not all members of the covenant community, the church of Jesus Christ, are "elect" persons and therefore truly and savingly joined to Christ by faith. God alone knows those who are his (2 Tim. 2:19), and some of those who are embraced under the covenant of grace in time do not genuinely belong to God. The church is comprised of genuine believers and hypocrites, persons who do not have a true faith and who do

25. See WCF 25.1–2; BC 29.

not persevere in the way of faith and obedience. It is inappropriate, therefore, to affirm the election and salvation of all who belong to the covenant community, and to do so in an unqualified and undifferentiated manner.

Perhaps the clearest statement in the Three Forms of Unity that has a direct bearing upon this question is found in BC 29. In this Article, which identifies the "marks of the true church" and the "marks of Christians," the church is said to include "hypocrites, who are mixed in the Church with the good, yet are not of the Church, though externally in it." This language coincides with the usual way in which the "visible" church is distinguished from the "invisible" church in the history of the Reformed churches. It reflects the common teaching of Scripture (and, for that matter, of Christian experience) that not all who fall under the administration of the covenant of grace in time (professed believers and their children) are genuine members of Christ by faith. Remarkably, this Article also goes on to note, with respect to the "marks of Christians," that the primary mark is faith: "With respect to those who are members of the Church, they may be known by the marks of Christians; namely, by faith, and when, having received Jesus Christ the only Savior, they avoid sin, follow after righteousness, love the true God and their neighbor, neither turn aside to the right or left, and crucify the flesh with the works thereof." This language clearly implies that those who are properly members of the church are only those who receive the gospel promise in the way of persevering faith. Though this acknowledgment that not all who belong to the church "externally" are genuinely "of" the church is explicit in the BC, it is also clearly implied in the HC and the CD. In the HC, those who are savingly joined to Christ are joined to him by a "true faith."[26] This faith, which is produced by the Holy Spirit and confirmed by the sacraments, is a persevering faith.[27] It is not a faith that grants a temporary salvation, but a faith that confidently professes God will preserve his own and make all things subservient to their salvation.[28] Throughout the HC, a strong

26. HC 20–23.
27. Ibid., 53–56, 65–68.
28. Ibid., 1–2.

emphasis is placed upon membership in the covenant community or church of Christ and upon the use of the Word and the sacraments in the communication of the gospel. But such membership and reception of the "means of grace" do not automatically confer salvation in Christ, since the "means of grace" are only effective when the Spirit of God accompanies them and produces the kind of faith that confidently believes the gospel promise.

The necessity of true faith, which the Holy Spirit works through the gospel, for possessing Christ and his saving benefits, is also evident in the confessions' treatment of the sacraments. Though the FV emphasis upon the importance of the sacraments is laudable and not out of accord with the confessions, it often leads FV authors to neglect the indispensability of faith to the appropriation or reception of the grace communicated in the sacraments. However, in the Three Forms of Unity, the sacraments are consistently defined as visible signs and seals of the promise of the gospel that require the same response of faith as does the Word. It is only when and as the Spirit authors faith through the Word of God, to which the sacraments are appended as confirmatory signs and seals, that the grace of Jesus Christ is communicated.[29] Consequently, in all the confessional statements about the sacraments as means of grace, the necessity of faith to the right use and efficacy of the sacrament as a means of grace is affirmed.

Contrary to the FV conception of sacramental efficacy, the Three Forms of Unity do not countenance any view of the sacrament of baptism, for example, that would ascribe to the sacrament the power to "regenerate" its recipient. Nor do they teach that all recipients of baptism are savingly incorporated into Christ. The HC speaks of the sacraments in general, including baptism, as a means that the Holy Spirit uses to "confirm" faith. Just as is true of the preached Word, the visible Word of the sacrament requires that it be received in the way of faith. It is especially important to observe the way the HC distinguishes between the "sign" of baptism and the

29. Ibid., 65: "Since, then, we are made partakers of Christ and all His benefits by faith only, whence comes this faith? From the Holy Spirit, who works it in our hearts by the preaching of the holy gospel, and confirms it by the use of the holy sacraments."

"reality" to which it points. Without diminishing the importance of the sacrament of baptism to the confirmation and strengthening of faith in its recipient, the Catechism rejects the idea that the water of baptism itself washes away the sin of the person baptized. Only the blood of Jesus Christ and the work of the Holy Spirit are able to cleanse believers from their sins.[30] Any doctrine of sacramental efficacy, therefore, that ascribes to the sacrament in its administration the power to effect what it signifies, without clearly emphasizing the necessary appropriation of God's grace in Christ by faith, is not in harmony with the Three Forms of Unity. But this is precisely the emphasis that can be found in the writings of FV advocates. Because the FV wants to stress the objectivity of the covenant and its sacraments, it often neglects to emphasize equally the necessity of the Spirit's work in the application of redemption, particularly in authoring the faith necessary to benefit from the Word and its accompanying sacraments.

The FV advocacy of admitting children to the Lord's Table is of one piece with its tendency to identify covenant membership with election and saving communion with Christ. Since children are truly and savingly united to Christ, possessing all the benefits of such union, they ought to be received at the Table of the Lord to be further nourished in Christ. Failure to admit covenant children to the Table of the Lord is an intolerable act of "excommunication," since it excludes them from partaking of Christ even though they are full members of him. As noted in the foregoing, the sacrament of the Lord's Supper, because it is a visible representation and confirmation of the gospel promise in Christ, *requires faith* on the part of its participants. Because the sacrament visibly signifies and seals the promises of the gospel, it demands the same response as the gospel. Neither the gospel Word nor the sacrament work merely by virtue of their administration (*ex opera operato*). The sacrament communicates Christ to his people only by a spiritual eating and drinking with the mouth of faith. Therefore, the Roman Catholic teaching of an

30. Ibid., 72: "Is, then, the outward washing with water itself the washing away of sin? No, for only the blood of Jesus Christ and the Holy Spirit cleanse us from all sins."

objective presence of Christ in the sacramental elements, irrespective of a believing response to the gospel Word that the sacrament confirms, is rejected. Not only does this Roman Catholic view improperly identify the sacramental sign and the spiritual reality it signifies, but it also maintains that Christ is objectively present before, during, and even after the administration of the elements whether or not those participating (or not participating) actively accept the gospel in faith and repentance.

In the Reformed confessions, moreover, the kind of faith that is competent to remember, proclaim, and receive Christ through the Lord's Supper is carefully defined. Before members of the church may receive the sacrament, they have a biblical mandate to engage in self-examination. This requires that believers test their faith against the normative requirements of God's Word. Essential to such faith are the acknowledgment of the believer's sin and unworthiness, the recognition that Christ alone by his mediatorial work has made atonement for the sins of his people, and a resolution to live in holiness and obedience to his will. In this way believers are called actively to embrace the gospel promises that the sacrament visibly confirms in the same way they respond to gospel preaching. Furthermore, it is the duty of the ministers and elders of the church to oversee the sacrament's administration, preventing from participating—so far as they are able—those who are unbelieving or living an ungodly life. Since Christ has instituted the sacrament for the purpose of nourishing the faith of believers, it would violate the sacrament's nature to invite the unbelieving or the impenitent to partake. Unworthy participation, that is, participation on the part of those who have not properly examined themselves or who are unbelieving, would profane the Lord's Table and be contemptuous of its ordained purpose.

Since this feature of the Reformed confessions' teaching touches directly upon the propriety of paedocommunion, we need to take particular note of the confessions' teaching regarding the proper recipients of the sacrament. The BC, after noting that the recipient of the Lord's Supper receives the body and blood of the Lord "by faith (which is the hand and mouth of our soul)," speaks directly to this subject.

> [W]e receive this holy sacrament in the assembly of the people of God, with humility and reverence, keeping up among us a holy remembrance of the death of Christ our Savior, with thanksgiving, making there confession of our faith and of the Christian religion. Therefore no one ought to come to this table without having previously rightly examined himself, lest by eating of this bread and drinking of this cup he eat and drink judgment to himself. In a word, we are moved by the use of this holy sacrament to a fervent love towards God and our neighbor.[31]

According to the language of this article, the sacrament of the Lord's Supper requires the active engagement of its recipients. Only believers, who are capable of remembering the faith and the Christian religion, may come to the table in order to be nourished and fortified in the way of faith and love. With an obvious allusion to the apostle Paul's teaching in 1 Corinthians 11, this Confession also insists upon a proper preparation on the part of believers for the reception of the sacrament. Only those who have previously examined themselves should partake of the bread and the cup, lest they should eat and drink judgment unto themselves.

In its extensive treatment of the Lord's Supper, the HC also expressly addresses the question of those for whom the sacrament is instituted.

> Q. For whom is the Lord's supper instituted? A. For those who are truly displeased with themselves for their sins and yet trust that these are forgiven them for the sake of Christ, and that their remaining infirmity is covered by His passion and death; who also desire more and more to strengthen their faith and amend their life. But hypocrites and such as turn not to God with sincere hearts eat and drink judgment to themselves.[32]

31. BC 35.

32. HC 81. See also ibid., 82. It should be noted that the Scripture proofs cited for these answers include 1 Cor. 10:19–22; 11:20, 34. In earlier questions and answers, additional passages are cited to show that faith is required on the part of the recipient of the sacrament (e.g., John 6:35, 40, 47, 48, 50, 51, 53, 54).

It is important to observe that the three marks of true faith, which are identified in this question and answer, are the same as the three general headings of the HC. This is not accidental, since the purpose of the Catechism is to provide an instrument for the instruction in the Christian faith. True faith always includes three elements: (1) a conscious awareness of the believer's sin and misery; (2) an understanding of the person and work of Christ, who satisfied for the believer's sins by his cross and passion; and (3) a Spirit-worked readiness on the part of the believer to live in gratitude to God. When children of believing parents, who have received the sign and seal of incorporation into Christ through the sacrament of baptism, are instructed in these principal elements of the Christian religion, they are being invited to respond in faith to their baptism and to come believingly to the Lord's Supper. Though this is not the place to answer the objections of paedocommunion proponents, the teaching of the HC does not seem to create an artificial and unnecessary barrier before children might be received at the Lord's Table. All believers who are received at the Lord's Table come in the same way and with the same obligations. Consistent with the nature of true faith, all believers who come to the Lord's Table in order to be nourished in faith are expected to come believingly. If the sacrament is used to strengthen faith, it is only appropriate that those who receive the sacrament do so as professing believers.

Assurance, Perseverance, and Apostasy

Though a number of the emphases of the FV seek to resolve the problem of assurance, it is likely that the FV aggravates this problem by its particular understanding of assurance in relation to perseverance and apostasy.

On the one hand, the FV places a great deal of emphasis upon the "objectivity" of the covenant. All who are embraced within the covenant of grace, and who receive its sacraments, especially baptism, may conclude that they are elect and saved in Christ and in possession of all the saving benefits of this union. From this point of view, the FV claims to have provided a sure and reliable basis for confidence and assurance of salvation. If someone has been baptized and incorporated thereby into the covenant community, there is no need to look inward or to engage in any form of self-examination to determine whether he or she is in the faith or saved. On the basis of covenant membership, and on the basis of an appeal to what has been communicated through baptism, all believers and their children ought to be convinced of their election and salvation, including the benefit of free justification. On the other hand, however, the FV view of the obligations of the covenant tends to undermine whatever assurance is gained through membership in the covenant with its sacraments. Since election and salvation, at least in terms of covenantal membership, may only be election and salvation for a time, it is possible for covenant members to lose what was once theirs. Covenant election and salvation can be lost. Unless the covenant member perseveres in obedient faith, there remains the fearful prospect of falling away irrevocably and forfeiting salvation. To put the matter in rather blunt terms: the FV attempt to solve the problem of assurance ends up making the believer's assurance hang by the thin thread of an obedient and persevering faith. The believer is cast upon his own persevering faithfulness instead of upon Christ and his saving work.

Though FV proponents often claim that their understanding of the covenant resolves the alleged problem of assurance in the Reformed churches, it actually undermines the basis for assurance highlighted in the Three Forms of Unity. In the Three Forms of Unity, faith, worked by the Holy Spirit through the gospel and strengthened by the accompanying sacraments, produces a strong assurance of favor with God. Because the promise of the gospel is especially the promise of free justification and acceptance with God, which is based upon the perfect obedience, righteousness, and satisfaction of Christ, believers ought to enjoy a heartfelt confidence in God's mercy and grace.[33] The absolute exclusion of good works from playing any role instrumental to the believer's justification before God

33. Ibid., 21: "True faith is not only a sure knowledge . . . but also a firm confidence which the Holy Spirit works in my heart by the gospel, that not only to others, but to me also, remission of sins, everlasting righteousness and salvation are freely given by God, merely of grace, only for the sake of Christ's merits"; ibid., 60.

and inheritance of eternal life is decisive to the confessions' insistence that such assurance belongs ordinarily to true faith. In the HC, the believer's comfort is founded upon the conviction that Jesus Christ, to whom the believer belongs body and soul, "has fully satisfied for all my sins" (HC 1). In the BC, the close link between justification through faith alone and the believer's confidence with God is particularly emphasized:

> And therefore we always hold fast this foundation, ascribing all the glory to God, humbling ourselves before Him, and acknowledging ourselves to be such as we really are, without presuming to trust in any thing in ourselves, or in any merit of ours, relying and resting upon the obedience of Christ crucified alone, which becomes ours when we believe in Him. This is sufficient to cover all our iniquities, and to give us confidence in approaching to God; freeing the conscience of fear, terror, and dread, without following the example of our first father, Adam, who, trembling, attempted to cover himself with fig-leaves.[34]

The confessions consistently link the doctrine of justification by grace alone through faith alone to the joyful confidence it grants believers. When faith rests in Christ's perfect work, it finds a solid basis for assurance before God. However, when believers seek to base assurance upon their own righteousness or good works, the consequence is loss of confidence before God.

Now it should be noted that the confessions do draw a connection between the believer's assurance of salvation and the good works that genuine faith produces by the Holy Spirit's renewing work. The HC, for example, affirms that good works serve to "assure" believers of the genuineness of their faith.[35] Just as a good tree is known from the fruits that it produces, so genuine faith is confirmed by the good works that such faith necessarily produces. Even though the Catechism ascribes this confirmatory role to good works in relation to the

34. BC 23.

35. HC 86: "that each of us may be assured in himself of his faith by the fruits thereof."

genuineness of faith, it must be observed that this role is not foundational to the believer's assurance of salvation. Since the good works of believers stem from true faith, which is a necessary precondition for them to be good works,[36] they can hardly constitute the basis for the believer's confidence before God. In the CD, the assurance of salvation and perseverance is likewise based, firstly, upon the gospel promise and the Holy Spirit's testimony with the Word, and only secondarily, upon the good works that true faith produces.

> Accordingly, this assurance [of perseverance] does not derive from some private revelation beyond or outside the Word, but from faith in the promises of God which he has very plentifully revealed in his Word for our comfort, from the testimony of *the Holy Spirit testifying with our spirit that we are God's children and heirs* (Rom. 8:16–17), and finally from a serious and holy pursuit of a good conscience and of good works.[37]

Unlike the FV, the Three Forms of Unity present a carefully balanced view of the basis for the believer's assurance of salvation. On the one hand, this assurance is born out of faith's confidence in the perfection and sufficiency of Christ's work as Mediator. Nothing tends to buttress the believer's assurance more than the gospel promise of free justification on the basis of Christ's righteousness and the solid conviction that God's saving purpose of election will preserve the believer in the way of salvation until its completion. Contrary to the covenantal objectivism of the FV that appeals to covenant

36. Ibid., 91: "But what are good works? Only those which are done from true faith."

37. CD 5.10, emphasis original. The balance of the confessions is evident in their treatment of the role of good works in the believer's confidence before God. Though good works may confirm the genuineness of faith and provide confirmation of salvation, they may never become the principal foundation for the assurance of salvation. The believer's assurance rests upon the fullness and perfection of Christ's work for free justification. Cf. BC 24: "Moreover, though we do good works, we do not found our salvation upon them; for we can do no work but what is polluted by our flesh, and also punishable; and although we could perform such works, still the remembrance of one sin is sufficient to make God reject them. Thus, then, we would always be in doubt, tossed to and fro without any certainty, and our poor consciences would be continually vexed if they relied not on the merits of the suffering and death of our Savior."

membership and baptism as a sufficient basis for such assurance, the confessions always emphasize the necessity of faith as the means whereby the gospel promise and its sacramental confirmation are received. Furthermore, when the confessions acknowledge the legitimate role of self-examination and good works to the confirmation of the genuineness of the believer's faith, they do not do so in a way that undermines the assurance of salvation. The confessions base their confidence on the scriptural teaching that perseverance itself is one of the "better things . . . that belong to salvation" (Heb. 6:9). From the perspective of the Three Forms of Unity, nothing could be more harmful to the cultivation of assurance of salvation than the teaching that believers can be saved or elect "for a time," but not preserved in this salvation. Unlike the FV attempt to resolve the alleged problem of assurance, the confessions offer a careful and balanced view that provides a sure basis for assurance, but without giving any place to presumptuousness or complacency.

11

Covenant, Justification, and the "Federal Vision" (3): *Covenant and Justification*

The central point of doctrine in the present controversy regarding the FV and related views is, undoubtedly, the doctrine of justification. Were it not for the way various writers within the orbit of the FV have reformulated this doctrine, it is hard to imagine that the FV would have provoked as much concern as it has. Since the grace of free justification is a principal theme of the gospel of Jesus Christ, uncertainty regarding what this grace entails must be a matter of grave concern to any Reformed believer or church. In order to evaluate the way in which FV authors have compromised the biblical and Reformed understanding of this doctrine, I will begin this chapter with a brief statement of the historic Reformed understanding of justification. After this review, I will identify and evaluate several revisions of the doctrine that have been proposed by FV authors. In the last section of this chapter, I will offer an assessment of the seriousness of these FV departures from the biblical and confessional understanding of justification.

The Biblical and Confessional Doctrine of Justification

When considering justification, we must always be careful to formulate the doctrine as clearly as possible. Saying merely that believers are "justified by grace through faith" does not adequately state biblical teaching. In the biblical and confessional view, believers are said to be justified before God *by grace alone* (*sola gratia*) on account of the work of *Christ alone* (*solo Christo*), and this free justification becomes theirs *by faith alone* (*sola fide*). Each of these expressions is an essential part of the Reformed understanding of justification. In my summary, therefore, I will successively treat each of these phrases. The questions we must answer are: (1) what the confessions mean when they speak of the believer's "justification"; (2) why the confessions insist that this justification is "by grace alone" on account of the work of "Christ alone"; and (3) why they also emphasize that the gracious justification of believers is "by faith alone."

Justification: A Judicial Declaration of Acceptance with God

One common way of expressing the Reformed understanding of justification is that it views justification as a *judicial* declaration of God. Unlike the classic Roman Catholic doctrine, which regards justification as including a *moral transformation* of believers, the Protestant conception identifies justification with the pronouncement of the believer's innocence in God's court. According to the Reformation view, justification is a legal declaration by God, which declares the justified person righteous and acceptable to him.[1] For this reason, the apostle Paul contrasts "justification" with "condemnation" in Romans 8:33–34. The Roman Catholic view maintains

1. The descriptions of justification in the HC and BC confirm that it refers to the judgment God pronounces regarding believers who entrust themselves to Jesus Christ. Cf. HC 60: "How are you righteous before God? Only by a true faith in Jesus Christ; that is, though my conscience accuse me that I have grievously sinned against all the commandments of God and kept none of them, and am still inclined to all evil, yet God, without any merit of mine, of mere grace, grants and imputes to me the perfect satisfaction, righteousness, and holiness of Christ, as if I had never had nor committed any sin, and myself had accomplished all the obedience which Christ has rendered for me; if only I accept such benefit with a believing heart"; BC 22: " we *are justified by faith* alone, or *by faith apart from works*. However, to speak more clearly, we do not mean that faith itself justifies us, for it is only an instrument with which we embrace Christ our righteousness. But Jesus Christ, imputing to us all His merits, and so many holy works which He has done for us and in our stead, is our righteousness. And faith is an instrument that keeps us in communion with Him in all His benefits, which, when they become ours, are more than sufficient to acquit us of our sins." Cf. HC 62: "But why cannot our good works be the whole or part of our righteousness before God? Because the righteousness which can stand *before the tribunal of God* must be absolutely perfect and wholly conformable to the divine law." (Emphases added.)

that justification includes a process of moral transformation equivalent to what in the Reformed conception is regarded as the work of sanctification.[2] Essentially the Roman Church's view confuses the two distinct graces of justification and sanctification.

Though the courtroom image of justification is metaphorical, depicting sinners in legal terms as persons called to appear before God as their Judge, this language represents the real circumstance of sinners in relation to God. As creatures originally created in God's image, but now fallen into sin in Adam, all human beings are accountable before God and deserve condemnation and death (Rom. 2–3).[3] Consequently, the problem that justification addresses can hardly be exaggerated. To be judged innocent or guilty by a human court is a matter of some importance. But to be judged in God's court is a matter of ultimate religious importance. Everything finally depends upon the sinner's "reputation" in God's judgment. The question of justification is not merely one question among many, but *the* religious question, the paramount question in life and death. The justification of believers is a definitive act, which declares the forgiveness of their sins and righteousness before God. It anticipates the final judgment and proclaims that "all the curse" of the law has been removed for believers.[4] Therefore, in the biblical and confessional understanding of the gospel, justification is the principal benefit of Christ's saving work, revealing God's grace toward undeserving sinners whom he saves from condemnation and death (Rom. 5:12–21).[5]

2. Cf. the definition of justification in *The Canons and Decrees of the Council of Trent*, Sixth Session, chap. 7 (quoted from Philip Schaff, *The Creeds of Christendom*, 3 vols. [1931; repr., Grand Rapids, MI: Baker, 1985], 3:94): "This disposition, or preparation, is followed by Justification itself, which is not remission of sins merely, but also the sanctification and renewal of the inward man, through the voluntary reception of the grace, and of the gifts, whereby man of unjust becomes just [*fit iustus*]."

3. HC 10.

4. Ibid., 52: "What comfort is it to you that Christ *shall come to judge the living and the dead*? That in all my sorrows and persecutions, with uplifted head I look for the very same Person who before has offered Himself for my sake to the tribunal of God, and has removed all curse from me, to come as Judge from heaven" (emphasis added).

5. Ibid., 59: "But what does it profit you now that you believe all this? That I am righteous in Christ before God, and an heir to eternal life"; BC 23.

The Basis for Free Justification: "By Grace Alone," "On Account of Christ Alone"

Though the Reformed confessions reject the traditional Roman Catholic view that confuses justification and sanctification, treating justification as though it involved a process of moral renewal, this is not their basic objection to it. According to the confessions, the basic error of Roman Catholicism resides in its wrong conception of *the basis* of the verdict of innocence and righteousness that justification declares. In Roman Catholic teaching, God justifies believers in part based on their own righteousness. Because justification includes a process of moral renewal, the righteousness that justifies believers is said to be an inherent righteousness.[6] In other words God does not justify believers solely upon the basis of the work and merits of Christ, which are granted and imputed to believers by grace, but partly upon the basis of the work and merits of believers, which are the fruit of God's grace at work in them.[7]

In the Reformed confessions' rejection of this Roman Catholic understanding of the basis for justification, they affirm that justification is wholly a free gift of God's grace. Grace alone—not grace plus the working of believers prompted by grace—is the exclusive basis for justification. When it comes to acceptance with God, believers rest their confidence, not in anything they might do in obedience to God, but only in God's gracious favor demonstrated in the free provision of redemption through Jesus Christ. Consequently, the confessions emphasize that the righteousness of believers is an "imputed" righteousness, not a personal or inherent righteousness.[8]

6. Cf. Schaff, *Creeds*, 2:95–96: "For, although no one can be just, but he to whom the merits of the Passion of our Lord Jesus Christ are communicated, yet is this done in the said justification of the impious, when by the merit of that same most holy Passion, *the charity of God is poured forth*, by the Holy Spirit, *in the hearts* of those that are justified, and is inherent therein [*atque ipsis inhaeret*]."

7. *Council of Trent*, Sixth Session, chap. 10 (Schaff, *Creeds*, 2:99). This has two serious and acknowledged consequences: first, Christ alone is no longer the believer's righteousness before God; and second, the believer cannot have any assurance of salvation (unless by special dispensation and revelation) since his own righteousness can scarcely provide any sure footing in the presence of God.

8. HC 60: "[God] grants and imputes to me the perfect satisfaction, righteousness, and holiness of Christ"; ibid., 62; BC 22: "But Jesus Christ, imputing to us all his merits."

Though this language is frequently criticized for suggesting that justification involves a kind of "legal fiction," the confessions use it on the basis of scriptural teaching that the believer's justification rests upon the righteousness of Another, namely, Jesus Christ (Rom. 5:12–21; Phil. 3:9; 2 Cor. 5:18–21). By means of his suffering and death, Christ bore the penalty and curse of the law on behalf of his people (Rom. 3:21–26; 4:25; Gal. 3:13; 1 Peter 3:18). Christ satisfied God's justice by his endurance of the condemnation and death due those who violate the law of God. Furthermore, by means of his obedience and fulfillment of all the requirements of the law, Christ met all the demands of righteousness on their behalf. Christ alone, upon the basis of "all his merits, and so many holy works which he has done for us and in our stead," secures the justification of his people before God.[9]

Consistent with this understanding of the basis for justification, the confessions sharply distinguish between the law and the gospel in relation to justification. In this context, the law of God refers to the righteous requirements that God imposes upon human beings as his image-bearers. Whether Jews, who received the law of God in written form through Moses, or Gentiles, who have the works of the law written upon their consciences, all human beings fail to live in perfect conformity to the law's demands (Rom. 2–3).[10] By the standard of God's perfect law, all human beings stand condemned and deserve death as the wages of sin (Rom. 6:23). Though the law of God is good and holy, it can only demand from believers

9. BC 22. Cf. Berkhof's definition of justification in *ST*, 513: "Justification is a judicial act of God, in which He declares, on the basis of the righteousness of Jesus Christ, that all the claims of the law are satisfied with respect to the sinner." Reformed theology distinguished in this connection between the "active" and "passive" obedience of Christ. The purpose of this distinction was not to divide Christ's obedience into two chronological stages (the first being his earthly ministry, the second being his sacrificial death upon the cross) or even into two parts, but to distinguish two facets of the one obedience of Christ. Christ's active obedience refers to his life of conformity to the precepts of the law; Christ's passive obedience refers to his life of suffering under the penalty of the law, especially in his crucifixion (Rom. 5:12–21; Phil. 2:5–11; Gal. 4:4). For presentations of this distinction and its significance for justification, see *ST*, 379–82, 513–16; *IET*, 2:646–59; and James Buchanan, *The Doctrine of Justification* (1867; repr., Edinburgh: Banner of Truth, 1997), 314–38.

10. HC 3–5.

what they cannot do.[11] No one can be justified by the works of the law because no one perfectly performs what the whole law requires. Contrary to the law's function to expose human sin and guilt, the gospel proclaims the good news that God freely grants to believers what the law could never achieve: acceptance and favor with himself on account of the righteousness of Christ.

The Instrument of Justification: "Through Faith Alone"

The confessions' insistence that believers are justified by faith alone obviously conveys their firm belief in justification as God's free gift of grace in Christ. A free gift, based upon a righteousness graciously imputed to believers, is most emphatically not by works. "Grace alone," "Christ alone," and "faith alone" are interrelated expressions. To say the one is to say the other. To deny the one is to deny the other. If we are saved by grace alone, then works must be excluded as a necessary condition for our being accepted into favor with God. If we are saved by the person and work of Christ alone, then nothing believers do in obedience to the law could possibly complete or compensate for anything lacking in God's righteousness. This is precisely why the confessions proclaim "faith alone" as the instrument whereby believers receive the free gift of justification upon the basis of the righteousness of Christ alone.[12]

The Reformers used a variety of expressions to express the unique role of faith in the reception of free justification. Calvin, for example, spoke of faith as an "empty vessel" in order to stress its character as a receptacle that brings nothing to God but receives all things from him.[13] Luther used the striking analogy of a ring that

11. Ibid., 62: "while even our best works in this life are all imperfect and defiled with sin."

12. Ibid., 61: "Why do you say that you are righteous only by faith? Not that I am acceptable to God on account of the worthiness of my faith, but because only the satisfaction, righteousness, and holiness of Christ is my righteousness before God, and I can receive the same and make it my own in no other way than by faith only"; BC 22. The Scriptures speak of faith as the instrument or occasion of the believer's justification, but never speak of faith as that "on account of which" believers are justified. See, e.g., Gal. 2:16 ("through faith"); 3:24 ("by faith"); and Rom. 5:1 ("by faith").

13. *Institutes*, 3.11.7.

holds a jewel; faith has no value in itself, but clasps the gem that is Christ and his righteousness.[14] Calvin also remarked that, in a manner of speaking, faith is a "passive thing," because all working and striving to obtain favor and acceptance with God must cease, resting only in the favor freely given in Christ.[15] Faith becomes a suitable instrument for the reception of justification when marked by a humble acknowledgment that all honor in salvation belongs to God. As a receptive and passive acknowledgment of the sheer graciousness of free justification, faith is an act of trustful acceptance of what God freely grants believers in Christ. When believers accept the free gift of justification by faith, they look away from themselves and focus their attention upon Christ who is their righteousness. Faith is the antithesis of any boasting in human achievement before God. Because such faith finds its sufficiency in Christ's saving work, it also produces a confident assurance of his favor.[16]

Faith and Works (Justification and Sanctification)

Before turning to how the FV revises the confessional doctrine of justification, I need to note briefly two additional features of the confessions' doctrine of justification. The first is the confessional understanding of the relation between faith as the alone instrument of justification and the good works that justifying faith necessarily produces.

The confessions draw a clear distinction between faith, which is the alone instrument of justification, and the works that faith produces in the way of sanctification. Though the confessions, echoing

14. Martin Luther, *Lectures on Galatians, 1535, Chapters 1–4*, vol. 26 of *Luther's Works*, ed. Jaroslav Pelikan and Helmut T. Lehmann, American ed. (St. Louis: Concordia, 1963), 89, 134.

15. *Institutes*, 3.13.5.

16. The formulation "faith alone" does not mean to imply that faith, which is the exclusive instrument of justification, is a lonely or workless faith. According to the Reformers, true faith always produces fruits in good works. Cf. Calvin's well-known comment in his "Canons and Decrees of the Council of Trent, with the Antidote," in *Selected Works of John Calvin: Tracts and Letters*, ed. Henry Beveridge and Jules Bonnet, 7 vols. (1851; repr., Grand Rapids, MI: Baker, 1983), 3:152: "It is therefore faith alone which justifies, and yet the faith which justifies is not alone; just as it is the heat alone of the sun which warms the earth, and yet in the sun it is not alone, because it is constantly conjoined with light."

scriptural teaching (Gal. 5:6), insist that true faith always and necessarily produces good works, they are careful to exclude the works that are the fruits of faith from faith's instrumentality in justification.[17] For example, the HC notes that "good works" are only those that flow from true faith, are conformed to the standard of the law of God, and are performed in order to glorify God.[18] The BC clearly affirms that faith justifies believers "before [they] do good works; otherwise they could not be good works, any more than the fruit of a tree can be good before the tree itself is good."[19] This language should not be understood to imply a temporal relationship between faith and good works, as though believers could first be justified and sometime later begin to be sanctified. The precedence of faith here is a theological precedence. Only believers, who are acceptable to God and dearly loved for the sake of Christ's work alone, can please God, even though the works that flow from faith are never perfect and cannot contribute anything to their justification.[20] The inseparability of faith and works, of justification and sanctification, is based upon the fullness of Christ's work for and in believers. Christ, whose righteousness alone is the basis for the believer's justification, also renews the believer after his own image by the Holy Spirit.[21] However, the necessity and obligation of new obedience in the life of the believer is not motivated by any suggestion that good works play a role in the believer's justification. Rather, the believer's new obedience is a "free" and "grateful" response to the gracious provision of redemption through the work of Christ and is not motivated fundamentally by the prospect of reward or obtaining final salvation.

Justification and the Sacraments

Another feature of the confessions' understanding of justification concerns the role of the sacraments in confirming and nourishing faith. In traditional Roman Catholic teaching, the sacraments

17. HC 64, 86, 91; BC 24.
18. HC 91.
19. BC 24.
20. HC 62.
21. Ibid., 86.

confer grace to their recipients by their administration, provided no obstacle nullifies their efficacy. The sacraments "infuse" grace in an *ex opera operato* ("by the work performed") fashion. Furthermore, the grace infused by the sacraments, when the recipient freely concurs with this grace and performs good works, makes the believer a righteous or holy person. So far as the doctrine of justification is concerned, the Roman Catholic view is that baptism entirely removes original sin and makes the baptized person inherently righteous.[22] For this reason, the "instrumental" cause of "first justification" is the sacrament of baptism. So long as those who are baptized do not commit "mortal sin" and fall out of a state of grace, the use of the other sacraments provides a continual infusion of grace whereby the faithful are able to enjoy "further" or "second" justification as they increase in good works and "merit" further grace and, finally, the grace of eternal blessedness. In this conception of the sacraments, justification, as a process of renewal in righteousness, is first given and then increased by means of the sacraments.[23]

According to the Reformed confessions, the Holy Spirit produces the response of faith by means of the holy gospel and confirms or strengthens faith by the proper use of the sacraments.[24] As visible signs and seals, which the Lord has appointed in view of the weakness of believers, the sacraments do not add anything to the Word but rather serve as visible tokens of the gospel promise of salvation.[25] Faith alone is the instrument of justification, and the sacrament strengthens faith by confirming the gospel promise of free justification on the basis of the merits of Christ. Though the sacraments are a means of grace, they serve to communicate Christ and his saving benefits only in the way of faith and never apart from the preceding Word to which the sacraments are added. To ascribe to the sacrament by itself the power to effect a saving union with Christ, which imparts all of the benefits of his work as Mediator, including

22. BC 15 has in mind this view of the sacrament, when it notes that original sin is not "altogether abolished or wholly eradicated even by baptism."

23. *Council of Trent*, Sixth Session, chap. 10 (Schaff, *Creeds*, 2:89–118).

24. HC 65.

25. Ibid., 66; BC 33.

justification, is contrary to the biblical and confessional understanding of the sacrament.

An Evaluation of the FV Revisions of the Doctrine of Justification

Though FV authors hold diverse positions on the doctrine of justification, some have proposed several significant revisions to the confessional view I have outlined. These revisions are the consequence of a number of key themes in the FV reformulation of covenantal doctrine, particularly the obligation of obedience to God's law in the prefall covenant between the triune God and Adam, humanity's representative head. Because FV proponents reject the teaching that Adam's wholehearted obedience to the law of God was the only way whereby he could justly inherit, and in that sense merit, the blessing (promise) of everlasting life in unbreakable communion with God, they also reject the teaching that Christ's entire obedience to God's law (all his holy works or "merits") is the exclusive basis for the believer's inheritance of eternal life. Thus, the serious errors present in the FV reformulations of the doctrine of justification are symptoms of an erroneous understanding of the covenants between the triune God and his people before and after the fall into sin. These errors are the inevitable result of a failure to acknowledge the implications of God's "righteousness" in the administration of the covenants before and after the fall, including the obligation of perfect obedience to his righteous law.

Justification as the "Forgiveness of Sins"

Proponents of the FV often define justification in a way that conforms to the historic Reformed view, or appears to conform to it. Though at least one author has suggested enlarging the language of justification to include the idea of "definitive sanctification,"[26] most FV proponents acknowledge that justification is a judicial declaration

26. Peter Leithart, "'Judge Me, O God': Biblical Perspectives on Justification," in *TFV*, 203–36.

of the believer's right standing (or status) before God and that it ought to be clearly distinguished from sanctification. Justification does not refer to the process of renewal in righteousness that occurs by the working of the Holy Spirit in the believer's heart and life. Rather, it refers to God's gracious acquittal of believing sinners on account of the righteousness of Jesus Christ.

Despite the acknowledgment among FV proponents that justification is a judicial act of God (declaring the believer's innocence), however, there is a tendency to define this act as consisting only in the "forgiveness of sins" or the nonimputation (reckoning) of sin's guilt to believers. Norman Shepherd, an influential figure among those associated with the FV, explicitly asserts that justification consists only in the forgiveness of sins and does not include the imputation of the entire righteousness of Christ to believers.[27] Though I will return to this subject more directly later, it should be noted that this identification of justification with the forgiveness of sins represents a significant change in the usual Reformed doctrine of justification. It is one thing to say that justified believers are not regarded by God as guilty sinners who are obliged to suffer the penalty due them for their sins. It is another thing to say that justified believers are regarded by God as holy and righteous, even as Christ is holy and righteous.[28] When justification is defined simply as the forgiveness of sins, it cannot grant title to eternal life. The forgiveness of sins removes the guilt of sin, but it does not declare that the forgiven sinner has met the full requirement of the law in order to obtain the inheritance of eternal life. Since the implications of this difference will become clearer in what follows, I will refrain from further evaluation of this reduction in the meaning of justification at this point. The most serious

27. Norman Shepherd, "Justification by Faith in Pauline Theology," in P. Andrew Sandlin, ed., *Backbone of the Bible: Covenant in Contemporary Perspective* (Nacogdoches, TX: Covenant Media Press, 2004), 89; Shepherd, "Justification by Works in Reformed Theology," in Sandlin, ed., *Backbone of the Bible*, 103–20; Shepherd, "The Imputation of Active Obedience," in P. Andrew Sandlin, ed., *A Faith That Is Never Alone: A Response to Westminster Seminary California* (La Grange, CA: Kerygma, 2007), 249–78.

28. HC 60: "as if I had never had nor committed any sin, and myself had accomplished all the obedience which Christ has rendered for me; if only I accept such benefit with a believing heart"; ibid., 61.

problems with the FV reformulation of the doctrine of justification relate to the critical questions of the basis for the believer's acquittal before God and the instrumentality of faith in receiving the grace of justification.

The Basis for Justification: Christ's "Passive Obedience" Alone

That FV writers reduce the meaning of justification to the forgiveness of sins is not accidental. This becomes especially evident when we consider the basis for the justification of believers. The FV authors sometimes argue that the basis for the justification is not the imputation of Christ's entire obedience to the law. Some authors will acknowledge the importance of the act of imputation for justification. However, the "righteousness" imputed to believers is solely the righteousness of Christ's so-called "passive obedience" or substitutionary endurance of the penalty of the law. Christ's so-called "active obedience," namely, his lifelong obedience to the Father's will and voluntary subjection to the requirements of God's holy law, may "qualify" Christ to offer himself as an unblemished sacrifice for the sins of his people.[29] But FV proponents deny that Christ's entire obedience to the law is attributed to believers and removes their obligation to obey the law in order to be justified before God. Provided the works of faith are "nonmeritorious" works, they belong to faith as the proper instrument of justification and are necessary in order for believers to obtain final justification.[30] Furthermore, among other authors of the FV, it is sometimes suggested that the believer's "union with" or "incorporation" into Christ through faith is a sufficient basis for justification.[31]

29. See, e.g., Norman Shepherd, "Justification by Works," in Sandlin, ed., *Backbone of the Bible*, 103–20.

30. Norman Shepherd, "Thirty-Four Theses on Justification in Relation to Faith, Repentance, and Good Works," Thesis 24, http://www.hornes.org/theologia/norman-shepherd/the-34-theses.

31. E.g., Richard Lusk, "A Response to 'The Biblical Plan of Salvation,'" in *TAAT*, 141–43; Don Garlington, "Imputation or Union with Christ? A Response to John Piper," *R&R* 12, 4 (2003): 45–113; and Michael F. Bird, "Incorporated Righteousness: A Response to Recent Evangelical Discussion concerning the Imputation of Christ's Righteousness in Justification," *JETS* 47, 2 (2004): 253–75.

The idea of imputation is said to become superfluous by virtue of the believer's union with Christ.

In my summary of the confessional understanding of justification, I have already noted that Christ's righteousness, granted and imputed to believers by sheer grace, includes his entire obedience. The language of the confessions, though it does not use the theological distinction between Christ's "active" and "passive" obedience, strongly affirms that the entirety of Christ's obedience "under the law" is imputed to believers as the basis for their justification. This could not be more clear than in BC 22 and HC 59–61.[32] Therefore, the claim of FV writers that the active obedience of Christ plays no direct role in God's declaration of the righteousness of believers is contrary to the explicit teaching of the confessions.[33]

32. See N. H. Gootjes, "Christ's Obedience and Covenant Obedience," *Koinōnia* 19, 2 (2002): 6–10. Gootjes provides evidence that the language of BC 22 was slightly edited and revised at the Synod of Dort from its original form in order to express explicitly the imputation of Christ's active obedience. These changes were made in order to refute some in the late sixteenth and early seventeenth centuries who denied the imputation of Christ's active obedience. Contrary to the FV tendency to deny that Christ's entire obedience to the law "merits," in accordance with God's truth and justice, the believer's acceptance before God, the confessions often speak of Christ's "merits" or his "meriting" of the grace of free justification, or of his fully "satisfying" the requirements of God's justice. See, e.g., HC 12–14, 16, 21, 40, 50, 60–61; BC 22–24, 29; CD Rejection 1.3; 2.8; Rejection 2.1, 3, 4; Rejection 5.1. Objections to the idea of "merit" among FV authors are common. See, e.g., Lusk, "A Response to 'The Biblical Plan of Salvation," in *TAAT*, 118–48; James B. Jordan, "Merit versus Maturity: What Did Jesus Do for Us?," in *TFV*, 151–202; P. Andrew Sandlin, "Covenant in Redemptive History: 'Gospel and Law' or 'Trust and Obey,'" in Sandlin, ed., *Backbone of the Bible*, 63–84; Norman Shepherd, *The Call of Grace: How the Covenant Illuminates Salvation and Evangelism* (Phillipsburg, NJ: P&R Publishing, 2000), 25–26; Shepherd, "Justification by Works," in Sandlin, ed., *Backbone of the Bible*, 111–18.

33. It is disingenuous to insist that HC 60 does not teach the imputation of Christ's entire obedience, when you consider how Ursinus, one of its principal authors, interpreted its teaching. Ursinus, in his *Larger Catechism* (which was written as a basis for his university lectures on the Catechism), Q. & A. 135, makes this clear: "Why is it necessary that the satisfaction and righteousness of Christ be imputed to us in order for us to be righteous before God? Because God, who is immutably righteous and true, wants to receive us into his covenant of grace in such a way that he does not go against the covenant established at creation, that is, that he neither treats us as just nor gives us eternal life unless his law has been perfectly satisfied, either by ourselves or, since that cannot happen, by someone in our place" (as quoted and translated in Lyle D. Bierma et al., *An Introduction to the Heidelberg Catechism: Sources, History, and Theology* [Grand Rapids, MI: Baker Academic, 2005], 188).

Biblical and Confessional Evidence for the Imputation of Christ's Entire Obedience

Since some FV writers argue that the Bible nowhere teaches the imputation of the "active obedience" of Christ to believers, it is necessary that we consider several biblical and confessional reasons why the basis for the believer's justification includes the entire obedience of Christ.

Christ's Obedience Is Comprehensive

First, the biblical descriptions of Christ's relation to God's law in his state of humiliation are comprehensive. Throughout the whole course of Christ's life, from his conception in the Virgin Mary's womb to his sacrifice upon the cross, he was lovingly obedient to his Father's will and devoted to his people for whom he laid down his life. The obedience of Christ is a "seamless" garment of active conformity to the requirements of the law of God. In Galatians 4:4, for example, the apostle Paul declares that "when the fullness of time had come, God sent forth his Son, born of woman, born *under the law*." In this pivotal verse, the expression "under the law" refers to the state from which believers in Christ have been redeemed or set free (cf. Gal. 4:21; Rom. 6:14–15). In the first instance, this freedom from the law is a freedom from the "curse" of the law, since Christ voluntarily subjected himself to this curse even though he continued in all things written in the book of the law to do them (Gal. 3:13; cf. Rom. 3:21–24). But in the second instance, this freedom from the law refers to a freedom from the obligation to obtain life on the basis of doing perfectly what the law requires (Gal. 3:11–12; 4:5; 5:3–4; Rom. 9:30–10:10). Christ assumed our flesh and was born "under the law" in order that he might "fulfill all righteousness" and meet all the obligations of the law on behalf of his own (Matt. 3:15; Rom. 8:1–4).

Another passage of particular importance is Romans 5:12–19, which closes Paul's summary treatment of the doctrine of justification in Romans 3–5. This passage remarkably compares and contrasts the first Adam and the last Adam, Christ. Just as all who are "in Adam" are subject to condemnation on account of his one trespass, so all who are "in Christ" receive justification and life on account of his "one act of righteousness." Though this passage bristles with difficult questions of interpretation, it is crucially important to our understanding of the obedience of Christ, which is imputed to believers for their justification.[34] The burden of Paul's argument in this passage is that there is an *immediate link* between *the one trespass of the one man, Adam*, on the one hand, and the reign of death *and the judgment that brings condemnation upon the many*, on the other. For this reason, he emphasizes that death reigned from Adam to Moses, "even over those whose sinning was not like the transgression of Adam, who was a type of the one who was to come" (v. 14). Even though the trespass was Adam's, and Adam's alone, the consequence of this trespass, death, reigned over all. Accordingly, the apostle insists that the "one trespass led to condemnation for all men" and "the many were made sinners" (vv. 18–19). Because of the union of all with Adam in his one trespass, God imputes or reckons to all men the guilt of this trespass and its judicial consequence, death. This is the sense in which we may say that "all sinned" in Adam, and all bear, as a consequence, the judicial liability of condemnation and death.

In a similar way, the apostle links the one man's obedience (lit., "the act of righteousness of one") with the making righteous of the many. Just as death reigned through the disobedience of the first Adam, so "the free gift of righteousness reign[s] in life through the one man Jesus Christ." So far as the doctrine of imputation is concerned, the important phrase in these verses is "the free gift of righteousness." The many who receive justification and life through the work of Christ are not made righteous through their own deed or deeds. Nothing believers do in obedience to the law constitutes them righteous or beneficiaries of God's favorable verdict and acceptance. Rather, God's grace "superabounds" toward the many who become, through union with Christ, partakers of his righteousness.

34. For a more extensive treatment of Romans 5:12–21 and its implications for the imputation of Christ's righteousness, see John Piper, *Counted Righteous in Christ: Should We Abandon the Imputation of Christ's Righteousness?* (Wheaton, IL: Crossway, 2002), 90–114; John Murray, *The Imputation of Adam's Sin* (Philadelphia: Presbyterian and Reformed, 1959); and Cornelis P. Venema, "N. T. Wright on Romans 5:12–21 and Justification," *MAJT* 16 (2005): 29–81.

For understanding the doctrine of imputation, the decisive point in Paul's argument is his insistence upon the direct (or immediate) participation of all who are united with Christ in his one act of obedience. Just as Adam's sin (and not the sins of all men) constitutes all as sinners under the judicial sentence of condemnation and death, so Christ's obedience (and not the obedience of the many) constitutes the many as righteous under the judicial sentence of justification and life. The dominant thread in Paul's argument is the *judicial implication* of our union with the first and second Adams. God reckons as guilty all who are in Adam; and he reckons as innocent all who are in the second Adam, Christ.

A critical question in this connection relates to the meaning of Paul's expression, "the one act of obedience/righteousness." Does this refer to Christ's passive obedience alone (his cross)? Or does it refer to Christ's active and passive obedience, using the language of "one act" to summarize the whole of his life of obedience? John Murray provides a helpful answer to this question:

> If the question be asked how the righteousness of Christ could be defined as "one righteous act," the answer is that the righteousness of Christ is regarded in its compact unity in parallelism with the one trespass, and there is good reason for speaking of it as the one righteous act because, as the one trespass is the trespass of the one, so that one righteousness is the righteousness of the one and the unity of the person and his accomplishment must always be assumed.[35]

Christ's obedience upon the cross epitomizes his whole life of obedience. The cross does not exhaust Christ's obedience but reveals it in its most striking form (cf. Phil. 2:8, "becoming obedient to the point of death, even death on a cross"). Indeed, were it not for the entirety of Christ's obedience from the beginning to the end of his ministry, it would not be possible to speak of his having died "*the*

35. John Murray, *The Epistle to the Romans*, 2 vols., NICNT (Grand Rapids, MI: Eerdmans, 1959, 1965), 1:201–2. Cf. Piper, *Counted Righteous*, 110–14.

righteous for the unrighteous, that he might bring us to God" (1 Peter 3:18). Even though the reference to the "one act of righteousness" in Romans 5 describes Christ's death upon the cross, it is not possible to separate this act of obedience from his entire life "under the law" (cf. Gal. 4:4). To distinguish between Christ's "active" and "passive" obedience in this way is artificial. The so-called "passive obedience" of Christ cannot be restricted to a single act or event. The cross of Christ represents the culmination of a life marked by suffering under the consequence of human sinfulness (Rom. 8:1–4).[36] The passive obedience of Christ may not be reduced to a "point," namely, the cross. It should rather be regarded as a "line" that took him from conception to death. Furthermore, in all of his suffering, Christ actively offered himself in obedience to the Father and on behalf of his people. It should also be observed that, whereas the "one act of disobedience" on the part of the first Adam was sufficient to constitute him and his posterity liable to condemnation and death, only the entire "curriculum" of Christ's perfect and constant obedience sufficed to restore his people to righteousness and life. Christ's seamless obedience in all its fullness under the law was alone sufficient to procure everlasting life for believers.

Another important passage for understanding the imputation of Christ's righteousness as the basis for the believer's justification is Philippians 3:8–9.

> Indeed, I count everything as loss because of the surpassing worth of knowing Christ Jesus my Lord. For his sake I have suffered the loss of all things and count them as rubbish, in order that I may gain Christ and be found in him, not having a righteousness of my own that comes from the law, but that which comes through faith in Christ, the righteousness from God that depends on faith.

Paul wrote this remarkable testimony in the context of his fierce and unyielding opposition to certain persons who placed their

36. See HC 37: "That all the time He lived on earth, but especially at the end of His life, He bore, in body and soul, the wrath of God against the sin of the whole human race."

confidence in their own flesh (v. 3). Though the apostle does not explicitly identify his opponents, it appears they were boasting of their own religious pedigree and credentials, particularly circumcision, on the basis of which they sought to commend themselves before God. In his initial reply to these opponents, the apostle engages in an extended *ad hominem* argument. If his opponents would place their confidence in such things, Paul has even more right to do so (vv. 5–6): "circumcised on the eighth day, of the people of Israel, of the tribe of Benjamin, a Hebrew of Hebrews; as to the law, a Pharisee; as to zeal, a persecutor of the church; as to righteousness, under the law blameless."

Unlike these opponents, however, Paul's boast or confidence is not in "a righteousness of my own that comes from the law." His boast, rather, is in "the righteousness from God that depends on faith." This righteousness comes "through faith" to those who are "found in Christ." Though Paul does not explicitly speak of God imputing or reckoning the righteousness of Christ in these verses, the idea is certainly present. Those who are *united with Christ through faith* receive, *on that account*, a righteousness from God. This righteousness, Paul insists in the most emphatic terms, is not his own righteousness but a righteousness that comes from outside of himself as God grants it to him. Paul's righteousness, as is true of any believer's, consists in the free bestowal of an "alien" righteousness by God to all who are in union with Christ.

The final passage I consider is 2 Corinthians 5:19–21.

> [I]n Christ God was reconciling the world to himself, not counting their trespasses against them, and entrusting to us the message of reconciliation. Therefore, we are ambassadors for Christ, God making his appeal through us. We implore you on behalf of Christ, be reconciled to God. For our sake he made him to be sin who knew no sin, so that in him we might become the righteousness of God.

Perhaps no passage in Scripture more clearly teaches the doctrine of imputation than this one. The reconciling work of God in

Christ took place when Christ, who "knew no sin," was "made to be sin." In an inscrutable manner, God regarded the sinless Christ as though he were sin. On the other hand, God did not count our "trespasses against [us]"; He did not regard us in a manner consistent with our condition and circumstance as sinners. By these means—not counting our sins against us, making and treating Christ as though he were sin—we "become the righteousness of God *in him*." In this passage, as in those previously considered, Paul does not expressly speak of the imputing of Christ's righteousness to believers. However, no other interpretation can legitimately claim to do justice to this passage. It is only by virtue of our union and participation in Christ that we benefit from his saving and reconciling work. Charles Hodge's comments on this passage express this truth well:

> Our sins were imputed to Christ, and his righteousness is imputed to us. He bore our sins; we are clothed in his righteousness. . . . Christ bearing our sins did not make him morally a sinner . . . nor does Christ's righteousness become subjectively ours, it is not the moral quality of our souls. . . . Our sins were the judicial ground of the sufferings of Christ, so that they were a satisfaction of justice; and his righteousness is the judicial ground of our acceptance with God, so that our pardon is an act of justice. . . . It is not mere pardon, but justification alone, that gives us peace with God.[37]

According to this reading of 2 Corinthians 5:19, the justification of believers on account of the work of Christ involves a great transaction: the sins of believers are imputed to Christ and the righteousness of Christ is imputed to believers.

The Substitutionary Nature of Christ's Obedience

Second, the FV denial of the imputation of Christ's active obedience to believers for their justification also fails to do justice to the

37. Charles Hodge, *An Exposition of the Second Letter to the Corinthians* (1872; repr., Grand Rapids, MI: Eerdmans, 1965), 150–51.

biblical teaching that Christ's work as Mediator was a comprehensive work of substitution. Even as imputation corresponds to what is expressed by the language of "faith alone" and "Christ alone," it also expresses what is implicit in the biblical themes of Christ's substitutionary atonement and the believer's union with Christ. If Christ's life, death, and resurrection occurred by God's design for or in the place of his people, then it follows that all he accomplished counts as theirs. How could Christ's work on their behalf and for their benefit not be reckoned to their account, if indeed it is just as though they had performed it?[38] Furthermore, when believers become united to Christ through faith, they participate in all the benefits of his saving work. Faith is the "empty hand" by which believers receive all Christ has accomplished for them. To say that God grants and imputes the righteousness of Christ to believers is, accordingly, to acknowledge what is required by the doctrines of Christ's substitutionary atonement and the believer's union with Christ through faith.

The link between the themes of Christ's substitutionary work, union with Christ, and the imputation of Christ's righteousness to believers, sheds light on recent claims that Paul has no doctrine of imputation but only of incorporation into Christ. It has been argued, for example, that the "modality" for the believer's becoming the "righteousness of God" is union with Christ, not the imputation of Christ's righteousness to believers.[39] The element of truth in this

38. D. A. Carson, "Atonement in Romans 3:21–26," in *The Glory of the Atonement: Biblical, Historical & Practical Perspectives*, ed. Charles E. Hill and Frank A. James III (Downers Grove, IL: InterVarsity, 2004), 134n53, makes an important observation regarding the connection between substitution and imputation: "Part of the contemporary (and frequently sterile) debate over whether or not Paul teaches 'imputation,' it seems to me, turns on a failure to recognize distinct domains of discourse. Strictly speaking, Paul never uses the verb *logizomai* to say, explicitly, that Christ's righteousness is imputed to the sinner or that the sinner's righteousness is imputed to Christ. So if one remains in the domain of narrow exegesis, one can say that Paul does not explicitly teach 'imputation,' except to say slightly different things (e.g., that Abraham's faith was 'imputed' to him for righteousness). But if one extends the discussion into the domain of constructive theology, and observes that *the Pauline texts themselves* (despite the critics' contentions) teach penal substitution, then 'imputation' is merely another way of saying much the same thing" (emphasis original).

39. Cf. Garlington, "Imputation or Union," 97: "Hand in hand with the preeminence of the person of Christ is that union with him bespeaks a personal (covenant) relationship

claim is certainly that the believer's justification by faith only occurs by virtue of his or her incorporation into Christ. Nothing that God does for believers in Christ can benefit them, unless they are joined to him by faith. So far as the justification of believers is concerned, the governing theme of Paul's gospel is that Christ was put to death on account of their sins and raised on account of their justification (Rom. 4:25). However, if justification refers to the believer's status in union with Christ, which is based upon the judicial verdict that God first declared in raising Christ from the dead, then imputation precisely corresponds to the nature of the justifying verdict itself. In justification, God declares the believer to be in the same judicial circumstance before him as Christ is. This declaration presumes that all Christ is and has done is equally the believer's by virtue of his or her faith-union with Christ.[40] To deny that this transaction involves a legal component, equivalent to the declaration of a person's innocence in a court of law, would expunge the theme of justification from the gospel. Imputation language functions to express the believer's status before God on the basis of Christ's work on his or her behalf. To argue that the theme of incorporation into Christ offers an alternative explanation of how believers become righteous makes no sense, if justification essentially refers to the believer's standing in God's court. For the believer's justification on the basis of the imputation of Christ's righteousness is but a way of saying that the believer is justified by virtue of his or her judicial connection with the work of Christ. Imputation is a corollary of union with Christ and not an alternative to it.[41]

---

that is obscured when legal and transactional matters are given as much prominence as they are in Reformed thought. 'Imputation' is the transferal of a commodity from one person to another; but 'union' means that we take up residence, as it were, within the sphere of the other's existence."

40. Cf. Richard B. Gaffin Jr., *Resurrection and Redemption: A Study in Paul's Soteriology*, 2nd ed. (Phillipsburg, NJ: Presbyterian and Reformed, 1987), 123: "Jesus' being delivered up (his death) on account of our transgressions identified him with us in the condemnation inevitably attendant on our transgressions; in fact his death is the pointed manifestation of this solidarity in condemnation. Consequently, his being raised on account of our justification identifies him with us in the justifying verdict inevitably attendant on the righteousness which he himself established for us (better, which he established for himself as he was one with us) by his obedience unto death; his resurrection is the pointed manifestation of this solidarity in justification."

41. Cf. John Murray, *Select Lectures in Systematic Theology*, vol. 2 of *Collected Writings*

Justification Declares the Believer Righteous

Third, unless believers are granted the righteousness of Christ in his obedience to the law as well as in his suffering of its curse, they could not, strictly speaking, be justified in the proper sense of being "declared righteous" before God. The justification of believers upon the basis of the righteousness of Christ involves a favorable verdict that goes beyond the mere forgiveness or nonimputation of sin's guilt to believers. When God justifies the ungodly for the sake of Christ's saving work, he declares believers to be in a positive state of innocence or righteousness. Justified believers are not simply declared to be without sin; they are declared to be positively righteous before God. In Christ the justified person enjoys a righteous standing before God that properly belongs to someone who has not only borne the curse of the law but also met all of its demands.[42] In the resurrection of Jesus Christ, the ground for the believer's justification, God vindicates his own righteousness and establishes the believer's right to be received into his favor as a righteous person. Not only is there now no condemnation for those who are in Christ Jesus, but there also is no longer any possible basis for a charge to be brought against them (Rom. 8:33–34). As those crucified and raised with Christ, believers enjoy the privileged status of full acceptance with God. As John Murray observes,

> [I]t is prejudicial to the grace and nature of justification to construe it merely in terms of remission. This is so to such an extent that the bare notion of remission does not express, nor does it of itself imply, the concept of justification. The latter means not sim-

of John Murray (Carlisle, PA: Banner of Truth, 1977), 214: "In reality the concept is richer than that of imputation; it is not simply reckoned as ours, but it is reckoned to us and we are identified with it. Christ is ours, and therefore all that is his is ours in union with him and we cannot think of him in his vicarious capacity or of anything that is his in this capacity except in union and communion with his people. . . . These are not legal fictions. They are the indispensable implicates of what union with Christ entails."

42. In this connection, appeal may be made to passages like Rom. 10:5 and Gal. 3:12, which enunciate the principle that the law as such promises life only to those who do what it requires. Christ's active and passive obedience, accordingly, are understood to have met all the claims (preceptive and penal) of the law on behalf of his people. In this way, the law is upheld in the gospel of Christ, and God is both just and the one who justifies those who believe in him (cf. Rom. 3:26).

> ply that the person is free from guilt but is accepted as righteous; he is declared to be just. In the judicially constitutive and in the declarative sense he is righteous in God's sight. In other words, it is the positive judgment on God's part that gives to justification its specific character.[43]

God's Justice and the Believer's Justification

A fourth biblical and confessional consideration that argues for the imputation of the entire obedience of Christ in justification, is the doctrine of Christ's mediatorial work as a complete *satisfaction of all the demands of God's righteousness.* If justification involves *God's* pronouncement of the believer's righteousness, this pronouncement must surely accord with the dictates of God's own truth and righteousness. God will not declare righteous and an heir of eternal life human beings who have not met the demands of his righteousness, either in their own person or in the person of Jesus Christ. If Christ as Mediator "satisfied" all the requirements of God's justice on behalf of believers, then believers must fully share through imputation in the fullness of his righteousness. This follows from the scriptural teaching that God, in the justification of believers, demonstrates his own justice or righteousness (Rom. 3:26).

This consideration can be illustrated by a simple analogy. Suppose a father promises to give his son an inheritance, provided his son fulfills certain filial obligations of obedience. Failure to fulfill these obligations would nullify the son's right to receive the promised inheritance. Suppose further that this son should forfeit his inheritance through disobedience and become worthy of punishment instead. Suppose still further that, in a remarkable and undeserved display of fatherly mercy, the father assumes the burden of suffering the punishment that was due to his son. Would the father's substitutionary endurance of his son's just punishment be sufficient to support the son's insistence that he receive his promised inheritance? Not at all. Though the son would not be liable to punishment, he would scarcely have a right to the promised inheritance, since he had

43. Murray, *Select Lectures*, 218.

not fulfilled his filial obligations of obedience. This simple analogy's point is that the grace of justification, based upon the imputation of Christ's entire obedience and satisfaction, "entitles" the believer to eternal life. No obligation of obedience under the law of God has been left unfulfilled, since Christ has undertaken to fulfill all righteousness on behalf of his own.[44] In this way, the glorious inheritance of eternal life, which is the believer's through faith in Christ, is secured in a manner that fully accords with God's truth and justice.

Justification by the Instrument of an "Obedient Faith"

One characteristic feature of the FV view of the role of faith in justification is a persistent ambiguity of definition. In the confessions and the Scriptures, justifying faith is viewed as a "receptive" instrument that rests in the perfect work of Christ alone for justification. Believers are not justified "on account of" their faith but "through faith." As the apostle Paul insists in Romans 4:16, justification is by faith "in order that the promise may rest on grace." What distinguishes faith in its role as the instrument of justification is that it receives and rests alone in the righteousness of Christ. Faith is not a human work in lieu of obedience to the law of God. Faith is the cessation of all human work or effort, and a confident resting in the work and merits of Jesus Christ.

In the writings of FV authors, however, faith, even in respect to its instrumentality for justification, is defined differently. Norman Shepherd, for example, persistently speaks of the instrument of justification as a "living," "obedient" faith (or "faithfulness").[45] Rather than distinguishing between faith as instrument of justification and the works that such faith produces, Shepherd insists that faith justifies by virtue of the obedience it produces. The "works" that are excluded, when we speak of justification "by faith alone," are only

44. Cf. Robert L. Dabney, *Systematic Theology* (1871; repr., Edinburgh: Banner of Truth, 1985), 624–25. Dabney observes that "[p]ardon would release from the punishment of its [the law's] breach, but would not entitle to the reward of its performance."

45. Norman Shepherd, "Law and Gospel in Covenantal Perspective," *R&R* 14, 1 (2005): 76. See also Shepherd, *Call of Grace*, 50; Shepherd, "Justification by Faith Alone," *R&R* 11, 2 (2002): 82; Shepherd, "Faith and Faithfulness," in Sandlin, ed., *A Faith That Is Never Alone*, 53–72.

those works that are performed in order to "merit" acceptance and favor with God. Once the whole idea of "merit" or "meritorious" works is rejected, we may speak of *one* "method of justification" that holds for Adam (and all men in Adam) before the fall, for Christ himself, and for all believers.[46] The one method of justification in the covenant relationship before the fall and after the fall involves God's crediting the believer's obedient faith for righteousness. Though Shepherd acknowledges that there is an additional factor in the post-fall state, namely, the provision for the believer's forgiveness on the basis of Christ's sacrifice on the cross, he maintains that justification always is obtained by way of an active, obedient faith. By obedience of faith, the believer finds, maintains, and ultimately enjoys acceptance and favor with God.[47]

This understanding of faith in relation to justification commits what Ursinus in his commentary on the HC calls a "fallacy of composition."[48] Though it may be true that justifying faith is "not alone," it is not true that the works of faith belong to faith as an instrument of justification. The contrast between faith and works in respect to the believer's justification is absolute (Rom. 3:27; 4:6, 13; 9:11; 11:6; Gal. 2:16; Titus 3:5; Eph. 2:9). No human works, not even those "fruits of thankfulness" that God graciously rewards in the believer, play any role instrumental to justification. All of our works are unable to meet the standard of perfect righteousness that is revealed in the holy law of God. Such works cannot be the whole or any part of our righteousness before God. They merit nothing

46. Shepherd, "Covenantal Perspective," 76. Shepherd even ascribes this "method of justification" to Christ himself whose "living, active, and obedient faith" took him all the way to the cross (*Call of Grace*, 19). For a careful critique of Shepherd's formulations, see Wesley White, "Saying 'Justification by Faith Alone' Isn't Enough," *MAJT* 17 (2006): 239–65.

47. Shepherd, "Thirty-Four Theses," Theses 20–25. Cf. Rich Lusk, "Future Justification: Some Theological and Exegetical Proposals," in Sandlin, ed., *A Faith That Is Never Alone*, 309–56.

48. Zacharias Ursinus, *The Commentary of Dr. Zacharias Ursinus on the Heidelberg Catechism*, trans. G. W. Williard (1852; repr., Grand Rapids, MI: Eerdmans, 1954), 337. Unlike Shepherd, whose chapter, "Faith and Faithfulness" (in Sandlin, ed., *A Faith That Is Never Alone*) trades upon this "fallacy of composition," Ursinus treats the relation of faith and works in a wonderfully clear manner. For example, Ursinus notes that "good works, although they are necessarily connected with faith, are nevertheless not necessary for the apprehension of the merits of Christ" (*Heidelberg Catechism*, 337).

so far as our righteousness before God is concerned. The persistent and studied ambiguity of FV authors like Norman Shepherd compromises this truth in the most fundamental manner. By redefining faith in its instrumental role for justification to include the nonmeritorious works that true faith produces, human works are made constitutive of the way believers are justified.

The Role of Baptism as an Instrument of Justification

One of the recurring themes in the writings of FV authors is an emphasis upon the efficacy of the sacraments, particularly the sacrament of baptism, in the communication of the grace of Christ to his people. Some authors even use the language of "baptismal regeneration" or "baptismal efficacy" to underscore its constitutive significance, not only as a sign and seal of the covenant promise in Christ, but also as the instrument that actually effects saving union with Christ and communicates all his benefits.[49] All those who are baptized, head-for-head, are not merely to be regarded as recipients of the gospel promise in an "objective" sense; they actually possess immediately, on account of their baptism, all that the sacrament visibly declares and confirms. The consequence of this unqualified and exaggerated view of baptismal efficacy for the doctrine of justification is not difficult to ascertain. Because baptized believers and their children are savingly united to Christ and therefore in possession of the grace that the sacrament attests, the grace of justification may also be viewed as conferred by the sacrament itself. The writings of FV authors sometimes assert that all those embraced by the administration of the covenant should be regarded as already possessing the fullness of salvation in Christ.[50]

49. See, e.g., Douglas Wilson, *"Reformed" Is Not Enough: Recovering the Objectivity of the Covenant* (Moscow, ID: Canon Press, 2002), 103–4; Rich Lusk, "Some Thoughts on the Means of Grace: A Few Proposals," http://www.hornes.org/theologia/rich-lusk/some-thoughts-on-the-means-of-grace; Lusk, "Paedobaptism and Baptismal Efficacy," in *TFV*, 89–97.

50. E.g., John Barach, "Covenant and Election," in *TAAT*, 15–44; Rich Lusk, "Paedobaptism and Baptismal Efficacy: Historic Trends and Current Controversies," in *TFV*, 71–126; Steve Wilkins, "Covenant, Baptism, and Salvation," in *TFV*, 47–70; and Douglas Wilson, "Sacramental Efficacy in the Westminster Standards," in *TAAT*, 233–44.

The FV emphasis upon the efficacy of baptism is difficult to distinguish from the traditional Roman Catholic view. Like the Roman Catholic doctrine, it distorts the relation between the Word and sacraments as "means of grace." In the biblical and Reformed view, the Holy Spirit uses principally the preaching of the Word and promise of the gospel to produce faith and thereby savingly join believers with Christ. The sacraments are appointed as a means whereby the Spirit strengthens faith. However, ordinarily neither the Word nor the sacraments work effectively as "means of grace" apart from the response of faith that they produce and confirm. Without the response of faith, which the Holy Spirit authors through these means, we may not say that every recipient of the gospel promise or sacramental sign and seal of that promise possesses the grace of Christ. Though the sacraments are not to be disparaged in their importance as a means of grace, we may not ascribe to baptism an instrumental efficacy apart from the proper use of the sacrament in the way of faith. The inevitable fruit of the FV emphasis upon baptism's efficacy is the advocacy of a quasi-Roman Catholic doctrine of baptism as an instrument of justification. However, the biblical and confessional doctrine of justification ascribes such instrumentality to faith alone. Baptism does not confer the grace of justification apart from faith in the gospel promise, which is produced by the Spirit through the Word.

Summary and Conclusion

Throughout my summary of the distinctive emphases of the FV movement, I have especially focused upon its reformulation of the doctrine of justification. For this reason, I attempted, even in my summary of the distinctive themes of the FV, to bear in mind the way these themes relate to our understanding of the believer's justification before God. To conclude my evaluation of the FV, I wish to identify those features of the FV that have special significance to its understanding of the doctrine of justification. I will then offer a few comments on the doctrine's importance and the seriousness of the FV reformulations of it.

In my summary of distinctive themes in the FV movement, I identified several of particular significance for the doctrine of justification. The following FV themes have implications that are inconsistent with the scriptural and confessional view of justification:

- The FV insistence upon the close connection, even coincidence, between election and covenant, which leads to the unqualified claim that all members of the covenant community enjoy the gospel blessing of justification in Christ.
- The FV claim that all members of the church are savingly united to Christ, even though some do not persevere in the way of faith and obedience and lose the grace of justification through apostasy.
- The FV emphasis that the obligations of believers in the covenant of grace parallel the obligations of Adam in his fellowship with God before the fall, thereby undermining the sheer graciousness of the believer's justification and salvation in Christ.
- The FV denial of the meritorious character of Christ's work as Mediator, who fulfills all the obligations of the law on behalf of his people and secures their inheritance of eternal life.
- The FV tendency to reduce justification to the forgiveness of sins, which is based upon the imputation of Christ's passive obedience alone.
- The FV emphasis upon a "living" or "obedient" faith in the definition of its role as the instrument for receiving the grace of justification in Christ.
- The FV teaching that the sacrament of baptism effectively incorporates all of its recipients into Christ and puts them in possession of all the benefits of his saving work, including justification.
- The FV insistence that all covenant children be admitted to the Lord's Supper without having professed the kind of faith that is able to discern the body of Christ, remember his sacrifice upon the cross, and proclaim his death until he comes again.

- The FV attempt to resolve the problem of assurance by an appeal to the "objectivity" of church membership and the sacrament of baptism, while insisting that some believers may lose their salvation because of a nonpersevering faith.

In my judgment, these features of the FV formulation of the doctrine of justification are among the most serious errors in the FV movement as a whole. Though it is never satisfactory when views are formulated in a confusing manner or in a way that seems inconsistent with the confessional summary of scriptural teaching, confusion and inconsistency on the doctrine of justification by those who hold to the Reformed confessions are inexcusable. On the doctrine of justification, the FV movement has not only contributed to confusion in the churches but also failed to guard from serious error the gospel of free justification on the basis of Christ's work alone. I concur, therefore, with those Presbyterian and Reformed churches that have come to similar conclusions and have called FV proponents to reconsider their formulations, urging them to proclaim clearly the Reformational teaching of justification.

The doctrine of justification is more than simply one biblical teaching among many. It is "the article of the standing and falling of the church" (*articulus stantis et cadentis ecclesiae*). Though the grace of free justification does not encompass the whole message of the gospel, it lies at its core. Unless sinners are restored to favor with God upon the basis of the works and merits of Christ alone, they will ever remain liable to condemnation and death. Guilty, disobedient sinners have no hope for restored communion with the living God apart from the perfect work of Christ as Mediator. The glory of Christ's work on behalf of his people is that he has "fully satisfied for all their sins." Every obligation "under the law" has been met for believers by the obedience, satisfaction, and righteousness of Christ. The gospel promise of free justification in Christ is, indeed, what Calvin termed the "main hinge" of the Christian religion. Consequently, when the HC asks, "What profit is there now that you believe all this?" (that is, the Christian faith as it is summarized in the words of the Apostles' Creed), the answer is,

"I am righteous before God in Christ, and an heir of eternal life."[51] For Reformed believers and churches, no truth is more precious or worthy of more ardent defense. In the words of John Calvin, "For this is the key which openeth whatsoever is requisite to our salvation; this is the means to decide all controversies; this is the foundation of all true religion; to be short, this is that setteth open the heavens unto us."[52]

In my survey of the revisions to the doctrine of justification advocated by writers of the FV, I identified several themes that imperil this gospel of free acceptance in Christ. The justification of believers is diminished to refer only to the forgiveness of sins. Rather than a rich and fulsome pronouncement of the believer's positive righteousness before God, justification is reduced to the pronouncement that the believer is no longer regarded to be guilty. Because justification means only the forgiveness of sins, it does not include the glorious pronouncement that *all the requirements of obedience to the law have been met in Christ and are the believer's through gracious imputation*. The denial of the imputation of Christ's entire obedience for justification, an inevitable consequence of this reductionistic view of justification, has a most undesirable, yet unsurprising, consequence: believers must maintain and secure their justification before God by means of a living, obedient faith. The good works that faith produces by the Holy Spirit are inserted into faith as the instrument of justification. Therefore, by denying the imputation of Christ's active obedience, believers are merely restored to the position Adam, the original representative head of the human race, possessed before the fall into sin. In order to secure and maintain their justification before God, believers find themselves under the same obligation that obtained in the covenant relationship between God and man before the fall. The irony of the FV denial of Christ's fulfillment of all the law's requirements on behalf of his people is that it turns the gospel into a restored form of the original covenant between the triune God and his people.

51. HC 59–61.

52. John Calvin, *Sermons on Melchizedek & Abraham* (Willow Street, PA: Old Paths Publications, 2000), 95.

To use the language of the Reformed tradition, the covenant of grace becomes a "covenant of works," and the gospel is transformed into a new "law."

By the standard of biblical and confessional teaching, this reformulation of the doctrine of justification by FV writers is erroneous. Contrary to the biblical teaching, which ascribes everything necessary for justification to the works and merits of Christ, the unwillingness of some FV writers to affirm the imputation of Christ's entire obedience for justification appears to leave believers "under the law" so far as their justification before God is concerned. Rather than a radical contrast between justification by grace alone through faith alone, apart from works of any kind, a distinction is drawn between "meritorious" works, which play no role in justification, and "nonmeritorious" works, which do play a role in justification. To the degree that Christ's works and merits in their entirety are excluded from the basis for the believer's justification, to that degree the works of faith are included within faith as an instrument for justification. It is impossible to avoid the conclusion that this reformulation of the doctrine of justification diminishes the work of Christ and enlarges the role played by the works of believers (cf. Gal. 2:21b, "[F]or if justification were through the law, then Christ died for no purpose").[53] Furthermore, the assurance of favor and acceptance with God, which the confessional teaching undergirds, is undermined in the formulations of FV proponents. Rather than resting entirely in the perfect righteousness of Christ, believers are encouraged to think that their covenantal faithfulness plays some role in their justification before God. This weakens the gospel's testimony and undermines the confident assurance of believers in God's

53. Cf. J. Gresham Machen, *Machen's Notes on Galatians* (Nutley, NJ: Presbyterian and Reformed, 1972), 161: "This verse is the key verse of the Epistle to the Galatians; it expresses the central thought of the Epistle. The Judaizers attempted to supplement the saving work of Christ by the merit of their own obedience to the law. 'That,' says Paul, 'is impossible; Christ will do everything or nothing; earn your salvation if your obedience to the law is perfect, or else trust wholly to Christ's completed work; you cannot do both; you cannot combine merit and grace; if justification even in slightest measure is through human merit, then Christ died in vain."

justifying verdict. Contrary to these tendencies within the FV, evangelical and Reformed churches must continue to proclaim clearly that justification is "by grace alone through faith alone," for only then will they truly give glory "to God alone."

12

Covenant and Justification in N. T. Wright's Interpretation of Romans 5:12–21

In the history of Reformed theology, Romans 5:12–21 served as one of the principal *sedes doctrinae* for understanding Christ's work as Mediator of the covenant of grace. The interpretation of this passage, which draws a sustained comparison between the first Adam and Christ, played a pivotal role in the development of Reformed thought on the relation between the prelapsarian "covenant of works" and the postlapsarian "covenant of grace."[1] It would not be an exaggeration to say that Romans 5:12–21 constitutes a linchpin in the biblical case for the Reformed view of the way Christ's saving work redresses the problem bequeathed to Adam's descendants.

The importance of this passage to Reformed theology can be illustrated from the WCF, which presents a classic exposition of covenant theology. The WCF understands Christ's work as fulfilling all obligations stipulated by God since the creation of man as God's image-bearer. To paraphrase the language of WCF 7, the original covenant relationship between God and man required that Adam obey God perfectly and thereby enjoy life and blessedness in communion with him.[2] Although the covenant relationship was initiated through

1. I am using the traditional language for these covenants, though I am aware of the objection that the language of "covenant of works" may downplay the element of God's sovereign favor and initiative in the prelapsarian covenant. For a discussion of this issue, see chap. 1 of this volume.

2. WCF 7.2: "The first covenant made with man was a *covenant of works*, wherein life

a "voluntary condescension" on God's part, it stipulated "perfect and personal obedience" on Adam's part. By virtue of Adam's sin, the life and blessedness promised to him upon condition of obedience was closed to him and his posterity. However, in the covenant of grace, God graciously provides a Mediator, Christ as the "second Adam," who fulfills all the obligations of God's law on behalf of his people. Upon the basis of Christ's righteousness, which consists in his active obedience to the law's requirements and his substitutionary endurance of the law's sanctions, believers are justified. Christ's work as the second Adam, accordingly, fulfills the law of God and restores believers to life and blessedness. In this traditional understanding of Reformed theology, Romans 5:12–21 constitutes a key biblical testimony to the nature of Christ's saving work, particularly in the justification of believers through the imputation of Christ's righteousness. Whereas condemnation and death come to all men through the sin and disobedience of Adam, righteousness and life come to believers who benefit from the obedience and cross of Christ in their place.

During the last several decades, however, this long-standing consensus in Reformed theology regarding the significance of Romans 5:12–21 for our understanding of the work of Christ has been challenged from a number of directions. One of the more significant challenges has surfaced within the orbit of what is commonly termed the "new perspective on Paul." N. T. Wright, perhaps the most influential advocate of a form of this new perspective, has offered an interpretation of Romans 5:12–21 that illustrates some principal differences between the older, Reformation view and the newer view.[3]

---

was promised to Adam; and in him to his posterity, upon condition of perfect and personal obedience."

3. Wright, who formerly served as the Bishop of Durham in the Church of England and now teaches at St. Mary's College, St. Andrews, in Scotland, has written a number of substantial volumes in NT studies and in the contemporary "third quest" for the historical Jesus: N. T. Wright, *Christian Origins and the Question of God*, 3 vols. (Minneapolis: Fortress, 1992, 1996, 2003); Wright, *The Climax of the Covenant: Christ and the Law in Pauline Theology* (Minneapolis: Fortress, 1991); Wright, *Who Was Jesus?* (Grand Rapids, MI: Eerdmans, 1992). Among Wright's works that most directly represent his understanding of Paul and the doctrine of justification are the following: N. T. Wright, *Justification: God's Plan & Paul's Vision* (Downers Grove, IL: IVP Academic, 2009); Wright, "New Perspectives on Paul." http://ntwrightpage.com/Wright_New_Perspectives.htm; Wright,

Wright's treatment of this text provides an interesting case study in the contemporary debate regarding the apostle Paul's understanding of the gospel of Jesus Christ, particularly his understanding of the doctrine of justification. In Wright's estimation, the traditional Reformed treatment of this passage requires considerable modification.

Wright's revisionist reading illuminates the present debates swirling about regarding the doctrine of justification. My aim in this chapter will be to examine Wright's handling of this passage to highlight some key differences between the historic Reformed view and some emphases of new perspective authors. I will also consider how Wright's explanation of this passage reflects a number of important features of his exegetical and theological method.

My approach will be to begin with an exposition of Wright's interpretation of Romans 5:12–21. After I summarize his handling of this passage, I will offer a series of observations illustrating the differences between his reading and that of more traditional Reformed theology.

N. T. Wright's Interpretation of Romans 5:12–21

Before plunging into an exposition of Wright's reading of Romans 5:12–21, we need to prepare the way by noting how Wright understands the theme of Romans and the place of this passage in the flow of the narrative. Wright insists this text must be interpreted, not in isolation from what precedes and follows it, but in terms of its contribution to the overall argument of the epistle. Furthermore, Wright also maintains that an important key to this passage's interpretation

---

Paul for Everyone: Romans Part 1, Chapters 1–8 (Louisville: Westminster John Knox Press, 2004); *Romans*; Wright, "The Law in Romans 2," in *Paul and the Mosaic Law*, ed. James D. G. Dunn (Grand Rapids, MI: Eerdmans, 1996), 131–50; Wright, "The Paul of History and the Apostle of Faith," *Tyndale Bulletin* 29 (1978): 61–88; Wright, "The Shape of Justification," http://www.thepaulpage.com/the-shape-of-justification; and Wright, *What Saint Paul Really Said: Was Paul of Tarsus the Real Founder of Christianity?* (Grand Rapids, MI: Eerdmans, 1997). For critical assessments of Wright's reformulation of the doctrine of justification, see John Piper, *The Future of Justification: A Response to N. T. Wright* (Wheaton, IL: Crossway, 2007); Guy Prentiss Waters, *Justification and the New Perspectives on Paul: A Review and Response* (Phillipsburg, NJ: P&R Publishing, 2004), esp. 119–50; and *GFA*.

lies in the traditional understanding of Adam and Israel within Judaism. Biblical theology requires that the Pauline texts be read within the context of their historical setting and Paul's background within the period of Second Temple Judaism. If we are to avoid an unduly abstract and decontextualized reading of Paul's argument in this passage, these considerations must be borne in mind.

The Theme of Romans: God's Faithfulness to His Covenant with Israel

Wright assumes a view of the main theme and narrative structure of Romans that differs considerably from the traditional Reformation view. In the Reformation reading of Romans, the theme of the believer's justification by grace alone is typically thought to be its main emphasis. Shaped by Luther's discovery that the "righteousness of God" is not the demand of the law but the free gift of being received into God's favor for the sake of Christ, this reading of the epistle often treats it as a kind of general theological treatise on justification and related themes.[4] The opening chapters of the book (Rom. 1–3) describe in general terms the predicament of all human beings who have transgressed God's law and stand under its condemnation. The subsequent section on the doctrine of justification (Rom. 4–5) provides an account of how believers receive the free gift of justification in Christ by faith. The apostle Paul then moves to a treatment of sanctification (Rom. 6–8). The epistle moves on to an excursus on the subject of election and God's purpose for the salvation of Israel (Rom. 9–11) and concludes with an extended series of exhortations regarding the Christian life (Rom. 12–16). The governing motif throughout the epistle, however, is the great question as to how an individual sinner can obtain right standing before God.

A very different picture emerges in Wright's analysis of the theme and structure of Romans. Though Wright grants that the

4. *Romans*, 403: "Romans has suffered for centuries from being made to produce vital statements on questions it was not written to answer. All that has been said thus far by way of historical and theological introduction will seem strange to those traditions of reading the letter that assume its central question to be that of Martin Luther: 'How can I find a gracious God?'"

"righteousness of God" is the book's theme (1:17), he argues that the Reformers misunderstood this language. When Paul speaks of the "righteousness of God," he is speaking the language of a first-century Jew who would understand it to refer to God's faithfulness to his covenant promise to his people Israel. Rather than referring abstractly to God granting individual sinners a status of acceptance, this language announces the theme of Romans as the way in which God has in Christ fulfilled his promises to Abraham.[5] God's promises to his covenant people Israel gave birth to the expectation of a blessing after their exile. In the day of that promised fulfillment, God would demonstrate his loyalty to the covenant by restoring his people from exile and "setting the world to rights" in demonstration of his justice.[6] The language of the "righteousness of God" combines these themes of covenant loyalty and restorative justice in a way that, according to Wright, has not often been appreciated in the interpretation of Romans. On the one hand, it speaks of God's faithfulness to his covenant promises to Israel; on the other hand, it speaks of a "vindication" of the cause of God's righteous people in a world that is being corrupted and ruined through human sin and disobedience. Summarizing his understanding of the theme of Romans, Wright notes that

> [c]ovenant and lawcourt are far more closely linked than often imagined. Behind both categories there stands a fundamental Jewish self-perception, which, if we grasp it, will enable us to understand things Paul holds together in many passages in Romans, but which interpreters have consistently separated. Through many and various expressions of covenant theology in the biblical and postbiblical periods, a theme emerges that, though by no means central in all Second Temple Judaism, has a claim to represent a deep-rooted and biblical viewpoint. It can be stated thus: The covenant between God and Israel was established in the first place in order to deal with the problem of the world as

5. Ibid., 398.
6. Ibid., 400.

> a whole. Or, as one rabbi put it, God decided to make Adam first, knowing that if he went to the bad God would send Abraham to sort things out. The covenant, in other words, was established so that the creator God could rescue the creation from evil, corruption, and disintegration and in particular could rescue humans from sin and death.[7]

This comprehensive understanding of the theme of Romans forms the background to, and interpretive matrix for, a proper reading of Paul's teaching about the work of Christ in Romans 5:12–21.

Romans 5:12–21 in the Narrative Structure of Romans

In Wright's analysis of the structure of the book of Romans, the theme of God's righteousness is proclaimed through a narrative that recounts how Christ, the Messiah, fulfills Israel's history. Romans tells the story of the way Christ represents Israel and fulfills the covenant promises of salvation for God's covenant people. These promises include not only the vindication of God's people, but also the restoration of justice within the whole creation, which has suffered the consequence of sinful injustice and disorder. The challenge Paul faces in Romans and in his other epistles is to demonstrate how Christ, who suffered the unexpected destiny of crucifixion at the hands of the Roman authorities, fulfills the expectations of Israel and realizes God's covenant purposes through her. Since the life, death, and resurrection of Jesus Christ broke the pattern of Israel's common expectation for the triumph of the Messiah and the coming of his kingdom, Paul seeks to demonstrate that this apparent reversal reveals God's covenant faithfulness, though in a surprising and unanticipated manner.

Once a clear picture emerges of the broad theme of the book of Romans, it is not difficult to recognize the place of Romans 5:12–21 within its narrative structure. Wright, like many commentators on the book of Romans, recognizes that the epistle rather easily divides

7. Ibid., 399.

into four sections: chapters 1–4, 5–8, 9–11, and 12–16.[8] However, the more pressing question concerns how each of these sections contributes to the elaboration of Paul's primary theme, namely, the demonstration of God's faithfulness to his covenant in the work of Jesus Christ. Wright answers this question by claiming that the narrative structure of Romans is patterned after the history of God's prior dealings with his people Israel. Indeed, the book of Romans recapitulates the grand narrative of biblical history that is recorded in the OT. This narrative begins with the introduction of human sin and disobedience through the first human being, Adam. It then moves to the decisive moment of God's covenanting with Abraham and his descendants, which grants to Israel the role of a new Adam through whom God will bring blessing to humanity and restore the world in righteousness. The great redemptive event in this covenant story is the exodus, the paradigmatic act whereby God constituted Israel a people and liberated her from all her enemies. After the exodus and the giving of the law (Torah), Israel failed to live appropriately before God and eventually suffered the covenant judgment of exile. Within the context of her exile, Israel's future, which was often described in the language of "apocalyptic," held the promise of a restoration to favor with God, vindication in the presence of her enemies, and an entrance into the fullness of her inheritance as a people in a world that has experienced a restoration in righteousness.

According to Wright, this broad pattern of redemptive history is mirrored in the narrative sequences of the book of Romans.[9]

8. Ibid., 397.

9. For a brief summary of Wright's view of the structure of the epistle as a whole, see *Romans*, 4–5; and his "New Exodus, New Inheritance: The Narrative Substructure of Romans 3–8," in *Romans and the People of God: Essays in Honor of Gordon D. Fee on the Occasion of His 65th Birthday*, ed. S. Soderlund and N. T. Wright (Grand Rapids, MI: Eerdmans, 1999), 26–35. In his article on the structure of Romans 5–8, Wright acknowledges his indebtedness to the following authors who have suggested a similar view: Frank Thielman, "The Story of Israel and the Theology of Romans 5–8," in *Romans*, vol. 3 of *Pauline Theology*, ed. David M. May and E. Elizabeth Johnson (Minneapolis: Fortress, 1995), 169–95; Sylvia C. Keesmaat, *Paul and His Story: (Re)Interpreting the Exodus Tradition* (Sheffield: Sheffield Academic, 1999); and Ignace de la Potterie, "Le Chrétien conduit par l'Esprit dans son cheminement eschatologique (Rom. 8.14)," in *The Law of the Spirit in Rom 7 and 8*, ed. L. de Lorenzi (Rome: St. Paul's Abbey, 1976), 209–41.

Chapters 1–4 describe the world in sin and rebellion before God, and the work of Christ, the Messiah of Israel, who has kept the covenant God made with Abraham and brought salvation to the whole world. Chapters 5–8 recount how God has fulfilled the covenant with Abraham through Christ. The "latent" substructure of this portion of the epistle is the story of Israel's exodus: just as Abraham's descendants were delivered from enslavement to sin in Egypt, so God delivers his people from the power of human sin (Adam) through the work of Christ and leads them "through the wilderness of the present life by the Spirit (not by the Torah)."[10] This section of the epistle closes with the promise that the new community of Christ's people will inherit a renewed creation (Rom. 8). Chapters 9–11, which are often read as though they interrupt the flow of the argument of Romans, highlight the particular problem of the failure of Israel to receive the Messiah. Within the overarching purposes of God, however, this failure becomes the occasion for the blessing of the covenant to extend not only to the Gentiles but eventually also to the Paul's fellow Jews. Chapters 12–16 describe the new life in the Spirit to which the community of believers in Jesus Christ is called through the gospel.

Within this architectonic structure of the epistle, Romans 5:12–21 forms part of a narrative sequence governed by the theme of exodus. This passage serves as an introduction to a section that follows the sequence of liberation from exile through the crossing of the Red Sea (baptism in Rom. 6), the arrival at Sinai and the giving of the Torah (Rom. 7:1–8:11), and the ultimate reception of the whole earth as a covenant inheritance (Rom. 8:12–25). In this passage, the apostle Paul sums up the preceding sections of Romans and anticipates what is to follow. As Wright understands the place of this text in Romans,

> 5:12–21 can then take its place as the overarching narrative through which the whole of 1:18–8:39 is comprehended, summing up what has gone before and laying foundations for what is to come. By means of the faithful obedience of Israel's

10. *Romans*, 405.

> representative, the Messiah, not only has all the glory, all the inheritance, of Adam accrued to the people of God, as the Qumran sect already claimed for themselves; all the evils that accrued from Adam's disobedience are undone. Within this large-scale historical story, the arrival of the Torah strikes a negative, not a positive, note (5:20, pointing ahead to 7:7–12); the new Exodus is not simply to be a repeat performance of the old, but must itself undo the extra problems that arose through Israel's being "under the law." Through his faithful obedience, the Messiah has brought with him out of the Egypt of sin and death a great multitude who now live under the rule, and in the hope, of grace, righteousness, and life (5:21).[11]

Rather than focusing upon the particular question of individual participation in Christ in Romans 5:12–21, this understanding of the narrative structure of Romans indicates that Paul's interest is in the "large scale" story. The narrative of Romans 5:12–21 is the narrative of the history of redemption, and not that of the way individual believers become beneficiaries of the saving work of Jesus Christ.

The Background in Jewish Literature

The preceding summary of Wright's view of the theme and structure of the Epistle to the Romans illustrates an important feature of his approach. Unlike the traditional reading of Romans, which tends to abstract its teaching from its setting within the context of Judaism and the history of redemption, Wright's reading proceeds from the conviction that Paul writes as a first-century Jew. The gospel, which is to be preached first to the Jews and then to the Gentiles (1:16), tells the story of how the God of Israel has demonstrated his covenant faithfulness and set the world to rights by means of the obedience and cross of Jesus Christ, crucified and risen from the dead. The Jewish background of Paul's articulation of the gospel is especially significant with respect to Romans 5:12–21 and its sustained comparison between the first Adam and Christ. If

11. "New Exodus," 34.

we are to understand Paul's view of the role of Adam in the history of redemption, the only relevant background must be found in the literature of Judaism.

In his assessment of this literature, Wright argues that it tends to cluster around one principal theme:

> God's purposes for the human race in general have devolved on to, and will be fulfilled in, Israel in particular. Israel is, or will become, God's true humanity. What God intended for Adam will be given to the seed of Abraham. They will inherit the second Eden, the restored primeval glory. If there is a "last Adam" in the relevant Jewish literature, he is not an individual, whether messianic or otherwise. He is the whole eschatological people of God. If we take "Adam" language out of this context we do not merely distort it; we empty it of its basic content.[12]

Both the OT and the intertestamental literature of Israel represent the covenant people as the new humanity, the people through whom God aims to undo the sin of Adam. Corporately, Israel assumes the place of Adam and is granted the blessing originally bestowed upon Adam and Eve in the primal state. The promise that Abraham's descendants will be multiplied echoes the original creation mandate to Adam and Eve. Furthermore, Israel's reception of a land of plenty and her subjection of her enemies fulfill the original circumstance in which God granted Adam dominion over the creatures of the earth. Even Israel's exile, which represented a crisis in her history, became the occasion for the drawing together in "apocalyptic" language of a future time of blessing, when these purposes for Israel as the new Adam would be fulfilled.

In Wright's estimation, this understanding of Adam and Israel within traditional Judaism shapes Paul's treatment in Romans 5:12–21 of the respective roles of Adam and Christ. The role assigned by God to Israel in the history of redemption, namely, to reverse the

12. "Adam, Israel, and the Messiah," in *Climax of the Covenant*, 20–21. For an extended treatment of Wright's understanding of Second Temple Judaism's conception of Israel as the "new humanity," see *Romans and the People of God*, 262–79.

consequences of Adam's sin and constitute a new humanity through the restoration of all things, is now assigned by Paul, the Christian, to Christ. As the Messiah of Israel, Christ representatively fulfills all that was traditionally believed would be accomplished through his covenant people Israel.

Wright's Exegesis of Romans 5:12–21

Now that we have considered Wright's view of Romans 5:12–21 in the narrative sequence of Romans, as well as the background for Paul's understanding of Christ as the second Adam in the literature of Judaism, we are in a position to take up directly Wright's exegesis of this passage. Like many commentators before him, Wright observes that this passage has a clear shape or structure. Verse 12, which introduces a central point of the passage, is followed by a lengthy parenthetical explanation in verses 13–17, which is itself broken into two parts (vv. 13–14, 15–17). Only in verse 18 does the apostle return to and begin to conclude the point begun in verse 12. One great theme runs throughout the passage like a thread: the contrast between Adam, whose disobedience resulted in the reign of sin and death over humanity, and Christ, whose obedience has brought righteousness and life. Five times Paul uses the verb βασιλεύω ("to rule as a king") to emphasize how the kingdom of God prevails through the work of Christ over the principalities and powers of the world, especially those of sin and death. Against the background of the common expectations of Second Temple Judaism, Paul is asserting that Christ, the Messiah of Israel, has representatively fulfilled God's ultimate intention for the human race. The role of Israel within the plan and purpose of God, which as we have seen is that of the new Adam or humanity, has been assumed by Christ and is now being shared with those who belong to Christ.

> This paragraph, then, demonstrates that, by fulfilling the covenant promises to Abraham, the creator God has addressed and dealt with the problem of Adam; a new humanity has come into being for whom sin and death have been conquered. "The age to come" has arrived in the present with the death and resurrection

> of the Messiah; those who belong to the Messiah already share in its benefits. That which Israel, or groups within Israel, thought to gain has been appropriately attained by the true Israelite, the Messiah, the obedient one.[13]

In order to give an accurate presentation of Wright's handling of this passage, we will provide a verse-by-verse or section-by-section summary of its most important features.

> Verse 12: Therefore, just as sin came into the world through one man, and death through sin, and so death spread to all men because all men sinned.[14]

The apostle Paul introduces this passage with Διὰ τοῦτο ("therefore"). Wright notes this introductory particle shows that Paul is now going to draw a conclusion from what has been said in the opening section of Romans 5 (vv. 1–11). This particle joins the paragraph with Paul's preceding description of Christ's death on behalf of the unrighteous. It also points forward to Paul's subsequent elaboration of God's deliverance of his people from exile through their participation in Christ. After having detailed the problem of sin and death in Romans 1:18–3:20, and the solution of justification and life that come through the work of Christ in Romans 3:21–5:11, Paul is now going to draw some broad and sweeping conclusions regarding the course of redemption's history.

The statement of verse 12 introduces the sustained comparison that Paul draws in this passage between Adam and Christ. Following the general consensus of the Judaism of his day, Paul treats the story of Adam and Eve in Genesis 2–3 in a straightforwardly historical and literal manner. Having violated the specific commandment of God, Adam became the occasion for introducing the "alien powers" of sin and death into God's good creation. Subsequent to Adam's

13. *Romans*, 524.

14. Διὰ τοῦτο ὥσπερ δι' ἑνὸς ἀνθρώπου ἡ ἁμαρτία εἰς τὸν κόσμον εἰσῆλθεν καὶ διὰ τῆς ἁμαρτίας ὁ θάνατος, καὶ οὕτως εἰς πάντας ἀνθρώπους ὁ θάνατος διῆλθεν, ἐφ' ᾧ πάντες ἥμαρτον. . . .

sin, the powers of sin and death have held sway, exercising a kind of tyrannical dominion over human history. In his interpretation of this verse, Wright acknowledges that it "has created huge problems of interpretation for subsequent readers, not least those eager to press Paul for solutions to problems he was not addressing."[15] Two problems in particular stand out: first, the problem of the character of the history recorded in Genesis; and second, the theological problem of the connection between Adam's sin and the sin of all humanity.

Regarding the first of these problems, Wright observes that Paul clearly believed "there had been a single first pair, whose male, Adam, had been given a commandment and had broken it."[16] Though Paul was undoubtedly aware of the "mythical and metaphorical" dimensions of this history, he would not have regarded these as inimical to the affirmation of the existence of Adam and Eve as the primal pair in the history of the human race. In Wright's estimation, however difficult it might be to define the meaning of "sin" in the "early dawn of the human race," it is plausible to imagine a turning away on the part of humanity "at any stage of anthropoid development" from an earlier "open and obedient relationship with the loving creator."[17] Nothing that is now known by biblical theology or science prevents this kind of understanding of the introduction of sin and death into God's good creation through the fall of humanity in Adam. Indeed, the biblical story of redemption requires the affirmation of an original state of integrity enjoyed by the creation as a whole and by humanity in particular. It is helpful to remember, when seeking to explain how this can be, that "death" in Paul's understanding refers to something "more than simply the natural decay and corruption of all the created order."[18] The created order was undoubtedly subject to decay and death prior to the introduction of sin through Adam's disobedience. However, the "death" threatened in the case of human disobedience carries a deeper and richer significance. "This death is a darker force, opposed to creation itself, unmaking that which was

15. *Romans*, 525.
16. Ibid., 526.
17. Ibid.
18. Ibid.

good, always threatening to drag the world back toward chaos."[19] When Adam sinned, what once was a kind of natural sleep of death was transmuted under God's judgment into something that acquired the further significance of shame and threat.

In Wright's judgment, the second of these problems is more intractable. In the history of Christian theology, the expression ἐφ' ᾧ πάντες ἥμαρτον ("because all sinned") has occasioned ongoing controversy. The principal question regarding this expression is, does Paul have in mind the actual sins of all people? Or, is he referring to the one sin of the one person, Adam, which was in some sense the sin of all people? Wright tilts slightly toward the second view, namely, that Paul refers to Adam's particular sin as somehow the sin of all people. One exegetical argument for this view is Paul's use of the aorist tense ("because all sinned"), which implies a particular act in the past, rather than the perfect tense ("because all have sinned"), which would suggest the sins of all people in the past and the present. Even though Wright leans toward the first of these views, he also cites the context, in which Paul speaks of the actual sins of all humans (cf. Rom. 1:18–3:20; 5:16, "many trespasses"), and concludes that we probably do not need to affirm one or the other view exclusively. In Romans 3:23 ("all have sinned and fall short of the glory of God"), Paul also uses the aorist tense, though he certainly means to refer to the actual sins of all people. The same could be true in Romans 5:12. Without taking a position on the question, Wright also notes that there has been a long-standing discussion regarding the "mode by which sin is then transmitted," if we assume that the emphasis of this verse is upon the primal sin of Adam, not the particular actual sins of all people.[20]

19. Ibid.

20. Ibid. Wright concludes his treatment of this verse by commenting unfavorably upon a recent translation of this phrase offered by Joseph A. Fitzmyer ("The Consecutive Meaning of ἐφ' ᾧ in Romans 5.12," *New Testament Studies* 39, 3 [1993]: 321–39). Fitzmyer suggests that it be translated "with the result that" rather than "because," a translation that allows for a kind of "secondary causality" for the actual sins of all people and their consequent liability to death. Wright judges this suggestion to be "at best not proven" and adds that "Paul's meaning must in any case be both that an entail of sinfulness has spread throughout the human race from its first beginnings and that each individual has contributed their own share to it. Paul offers no further clue as to how the first of these actually works or how the two interrelate" (*Romans*, 527). We will return to this claim in

> Verses 13–14: for sin indeed was in the world before the law was given, but sin is not counted where there is no law. Yet death reigned from Adam to Moses, even over those whose sinning was not like the transgression of Adam, who was a type of the one who was to come.[21]

With these verses Paul offers the first of two parenthetical statements that elaborate upon the opening statement of verse 12. In this first part of his extended parenthesis, Paul addresses the question concerning the generations of human beings between the time of Adam and Moses. In this period, which antedates the giving of the Torah or law through Moses at Mt. Sinai, there would not be any law by which to measure human obedience or disobedience. Though this might appear, Wright acknowledges, to be a kind of "abstruse question"—after all, the patriarchal generations seem to have had little difficulty knowing right from wrong—Paul may be addressing it in order to avoid the implication that sin is tied too closely to the Torah or law. Since the Jews typically thought of sin in terms of any violation of the Torah, Paul wishes to offer an explanation as to how even the Gentiles, who were not the recipients of the Torah of Moses, could nonetheless be regarded as sinners. Paul answers this question simply by noting that, because death was there, sin must also have been present. Even though these generations did not sin after the likeness of Adam's trespass, they were subject to the rule of death. The implications of this, according to Wright, are evident in a negative and a positive manner. Negatively, Paul denies that the generations between Adam and Moses were sinless, even though they were without the law. Positively, Paul implies that those who came after Moses, and to whom the law was given, were in some sense imitating Adam by sinning against a known commandment of God (cf. 5:20; 6:14–15; and chap. 7).

One important feature of this parenthetical statement is the

---

our critical evaluation of Wright's exegesis of this passage.

21. ἄχρι γὰρ νόμου ἁμαρτία ἦν ἐν κόσμῳ, ἁμαρτία δὲ οὐκ ἐλλογεῖται μὴ ὄντος νόμου, ἀλλ᾽ ἐβασίλευσεν ὁ θάνατος ἀπὸ Ἀδὰμ μέχρι Μωϋσέως καὶ ἐπὶ τοὺς μὴ ἁμαρτήσαντας ἐπὶ τῷ ὁμοιώματι τῆς παραβάσεως Ἀδὰμ ὅς ἐστιν τύπος τοῦ μέλλοντος.

introduction of a comparison between Adam and Christ. Noting that this is one of only two places where the apostle Paul uses the term τύπος ("type") in a technical sense, Wright observes that Paul is underscoring that Adam "prefigured the Messiah in certain respects . . . notably in this, that he founded a family that would bear his characteristics."[22] Christ is introduced for the first time in this passage, the remainder of which will develop a sustained comparison and contrast between him and Adam.

> Verses 15–17: But the free gift is not like the trespass. For if many died through one man's trespass, much more have the grace of God and the free gift by the grace of that one man Jesus Christ abounded for many. And the free gift is not like the result of that one man's sin. For the judgment following one trespass brought condemnation, but the free gift following many trespasses brought justification. If, because of one man's trespass, death reigned through that one man, much more will those who receive the abundance of grace and the free gift of righteousness reign in life through the one man Jesus Christ.[23]

These verses introduce a second explanatory aside. After addressing the question how sin can be acknowledged where there is no law, Paul offers an extended comparison between the reign of sin on account of the disobedience of Adam and the reign of grace on account of the obedience of Christ. The main point of this aside is that there is a dissimilarity and an "imbalance" between God's gift of grace in Christ and the trespass of Adam.

Wright notes that this imbalance between sin and grace is

22. *Romans*, 527.

23. Ἀλλ᾽ οὐχ ὡς τὸ παράπτωμα, οὕτως καὶ τὸ χάρισμα• εἰ γὰρ τῷ τοῦ ἑνὸς παραπτώματι οἱ πολλοὶ ἀπέθανον, πολλῷ μᾶλλον ἡ χάρις τοῦ θεοῦ καὶ ἡ δωρεὰ ἐν χάριτι τῇ τοῦ ἑνὸς ἀνθρώπου Ἰησοῦ Χριστοῦ εἰς τοὺς πολλοὺς ἐπερίσσευσεν. καὶ οὐχ ὡς δι᾽ ἑνὸς ἁμαρτήσαντος τὸ δώρημα• τὸ μὲν γὰρ κρίμα ἐξ ἑνὸς εἰς κατάκριμα, τὸ δὲ χάρισμα ἐκ πολλῶν παραπτωμάτων εἰς δικαίωμα. εἰ γὰρ τῷ τοῦ ἑνὸς παραπτώματι ὁ θάνατος ἐβασίλευσεν διὰ τοῦ ἑνός, πολλῷ μᾶλλον οἱ τὴν περισσείαν τῆς χάριτος καὶ τῆς δωρεᾶς τῆς δικαιοσύνης λαμβάνοντες ἐν ζωῇ βασιλεύσουσιν διὰ τοῦ ἑνὸς Ἰησοῦ Χριστοῦ.

illustrated in three distinct ways in these verses. First, there is an imbalance between the progression from sin to death and the "astonishing reversal" in which the grace of God in Christ "flourishes in what had seemed a hopeless situation."[24] Second, in a "torturous" sentence, the apostle Paul declares, "and not 'as through the one man sinning, the gift'" (καὶ οὐχ ὡς δι' ἑνὸς ἁμαρτήσαντος τὸ δώρημα). By means of this language and its subsequent elaboration, the apostle aims to underscore the imbalance in the "judicial result" of the disobedience of Adam and the obedience of Christ. This imbalance is that between sin that brings condemnation and death, and grace that brings righteousness and life. Though these two consequences may appear to be simple opposites, the language Paul uses intends to underscore the radical implications of the imbalance between them in the lives of the people concerned: "the one a denial and ending of life itself, the other an affirmation, opening up new possibilities."[25] And third, in the closing part of these verses, Paul offers a striking picture of the imbalance between the two "reigns" of sin and death, on the one hand, and of believers who reign in life, on the other. The imbalance Paul describes at this juncture is not between two abstract realities: sin and grace. Rather, the imbalance is between the reign of sin and death in the lives of all humans and the reign of righteousness and life in the lives of all believers who acknowledge the gospel of Jesus the Messiah. When the apostle Paul speaks of the believers' reign in life, he is thinking in terms of the apocalyptic tradition that promised "God's final rule would be exercised through God's people." He writes, "Here, as throughout this passage, Paul is thinking in terms of the promised blessings that Israel hoped for in the age to come being achieved by the Messiah and shared with his people."[26]

> Verses 18–19: Therefore, as one trespass led to condemnation for all men, so one act of righteousness leads to justification and life for all men. For as by the one man's disobedience the many were

24. *Romans*, 528.
25. Ibid.
26. Ibid.

> made sinners, so by the one man's obedience the many will be made righteous.[27]

After the extended parenthesis of verses 13–17, Paul returns to the argument that he introduced in verse 12. This is evident from the opening phrase, Ἄρα οὖν ("so then," not simply, "therefore"). By this phrase, Paul indicates that he is resuming the argument where he left it off, and at the same time is drawing the consequence that follows from what he had previously stated regarding the sin of Adam. Just as the disobedience of Adam brought sin and death upon all, so the obedience of Christ brings righteousness and life to all who benefit from it.

Whereas the previous verses stressed the imbalance between the respective "reigns" of death and life, these verses begin with an emphasis upon the balance between the "universality" of the condemnation that falls upon all on account of the disobedience of Adam and of the righteousness that is extended to all on account of the obedience of Christ. For the apostle Paul, the only way of escaping the condemnation and consequence of sin is through faith in Christ. The themes of "condemnation" and "judgment" that play such important roles in the comparison of these verses apply to the whole argument of the opening chapters of Romans. "Paul here, as usual, refers to the final coming judgment, the time when there will be wrath for some and life for others (2:5–11). The theme remains central in the coming chapters, reaching its dramatic climax in 8:1 . . . and 8:33–34."[28] In the middle of history, Christ's δικαίωμα ("act of righteousness/acquittal") constitutes the basis for God's eschatological verdict of "righteous," which he pronounces with respect to all who are in Christ. With "audible overtones of Isa 53:11," Paul is announcing that "as Adam's disobedience gave 'the many' the status

27. Ἄρα οὖν ὡς δι' ἑνὸς παραπτώματος εἰς πάντας ἀνθρώπους εἰς κατάκριμα, οὕτως καὶ δι' ἑνὸς δικαιώματος εἰς πάντας ἀνθρώπους εἰς δικαίωσιν ζωῆς· ὥσπερ γὰρ διὰ τῆς παρακοῆς τοῦ ἑνὸς ἀνθρώπου ἁμαρτωλοὶ κατεστάθησαν οἱ πολλοί, οὕτως καὶ διὰ τῆς ὑπακοῆς τοῦ ἑνὸς δίκαιοι κατασταθήσονται οἱ πολλοί.

28. *Romans*, 529.

of being 'sinners' . . . so Christ's obedience has given 'the many' the status of being 'righteous.'"[29] Even though what Paul means by "sinner" extends beyond the notion of "mere status," clearly this is the point of emphasis in these verses: through the disobedience of Adam, the many are regarded to be in the status of sinner. On the other hand, what Paul means by "righteous" is also governed by the notion of a person's status: "[j]ustification, rooted in the cross and anticipating the verdict of the last day, gives people a new status, ahead of the performance of appropriate deeds."[30]

In his closing comments on these verses, Wright addresses the way in which the "obedience" of Christ is understood within "one strand of Reformation thought."[31] According to this understanding, the obedience of Christ, which constitutes the basis for God's declaration of the believer's right standing before him, consists of Jesus' perfect obedience to the law. Wright regards this understanding, however, to be mistaken.

> Powerful though this thought is, and influential though it has been (even in liturgy, where "the merits and death of Christ" are sometime mentioned in this double sense), it is almost certainly not what Paul has in mind here. The Isaianic servant, to whom reference is being made, was obedient to the saving purpose of YHWH, the plan marked out for Israel from the beginning but that, through Israel's disobedience, only the servant, as an individual, can now accomplish. The "obedience" of the Messiah in 5:19 therefore corresponds closely to the "faithfulness" of the Messiah in 3:22. It refers to his obedience to God's commission (as in 3:2), to the plan to bring salvation to the world, rather than his amassing a treasury of merit through Torah obedience.[32]

The obedience of Christ, which was effected by means of his cross, was an obedience to God's particular plan and purpose to

29. Ibid.
30. Ibid.
31. Ibid.
32. Ibid.

bless all through the Messiah of Israel. It does not refer to a general or abstract obedience to the law of God, which is then granted or imputed to those who believe.

> Verses 20–21: Now the law came in to increase the trespass, but where sin increased, grace abounded all the more, so that, as sin reigned in death, grace also might reign through righteousness leading to eternal life through Jesus Christ our Lord.[33]

In these verses, Paul concludes with a remarkable interpretation of the work of the Messiah in fulfilling God's purposes for Israel. Contrary to the expectations of many fellow Jews, Paul declares that the Torah or law of God, far from serving as a means of blessing and salvation for his people, served to "increase the trespass" (πλεονάσῃ τὸ παράπτωμα). Indeed, Paul goes so far as to declare that this was God's purpose in granting the Torah (ἵνα is used to express purpose, and not simply result). In the traditional Jewish narrative of redemption, the Torah was thought to be the means whereby God would enable his people Israel "to escape the entail of Adam's sin, to be different from the pagan world around."[34] Israel's role as the new Adam, as a people through whom the sin of Adam and its consequence would be reversed, would be fulfilled by means of her obedience to the Torah. Paul's Christian reinterpretation, however, teaches that Christ has assumed the role of Israel's representative. By means of his obedience to God on the cross, Christ "offered to Israel's God the faithful obedience that Israel had not. In Christ, God has come to where the Torah has magnified sin, and has dealt with it."[35]

In the climactic closing statement of these verses, the apostle Paul summarizes once more the great contrast between the two kingdoms of sin and grace. Though death reigned through sin on

33. νόμος δὲ παρεισῆλθεν, ἵνα πλεονάσῃ τὸ παράπτωμα· οὗ δὲ ἐπλεόνασεν ἡ ἁμαρτία, ὑπερεπερίσσευσεν ἡ χάρις, ἵνα ὥσπερ ἐβασίλευσεν ἡ ἁμαρτία ἐν τῷ θανάτῳ, οὕτως καὶ ἡ χάρις βασιλεύσῃ διὰ δικαιοσύνης εἰς ζωὴν αἰώνιον διὰ Ἰησοῦ Χριστοῦ τοῦ κυρίου ἡμῶν.

34. *Romans*, 530.

35. Ibid.

account of the trespass of Adam, grace reigns through righteousness on account of the obedience of Christ. When Paul speaks of the "righteousness" of Christ, he is referring to the "covenant faithfulness of God," who has fulfilled his promise to Abraham that he would be the source of blessing for all the peoples of the families of the earth. "Eternal life" or the "life of the age to come," which had long been anticipated by God's people Israel, has now come through the obedience of the Messiah, Israel's representative. The traditional expectation that Israel would be the new humanity, whose obedience would reverse the consequence of Adam's sin and bring the blessings of the age to come, is now being realized through Christ.

An Assessment of Wright's Interpretation of Romans 5:12–21

Though there are undoubtedly features of Wright's handling of Romans 5:12–21 that we have overlooked or treated inadequately in the foregoing, our summary of his interpretation of this passage should provide sufficient basis for raising a number of questions regarding his exegesis and theological method, particularly its significance for his understanding of justification. Like other authors within the field of biblical studies who advocate a new perspective on Paul, Wright offers a reading of this passage that is, as we noted at the outset, at considerable variance from the traditional reading of Reformed theology. To use language borrowed from the title of a popular presentation of his views, Wright is not bashful in claiming that his reading of this passage within the framework of the narrative structure of Romans as a whole offers a more contextualized and exegetically warranted interpretation of "what Saint Paul really said" than the one offered in the tradition of the Reformation. The boldness and sweeping nature of this claim challenge Reformed theologians to examine carefully Wright's arguments.

In the following assessment of Wright's reading of this passage, I will evaluate his interpretation at three distinct levels. First, I will make several preliminary observations about general aspects of Wright's approach to and exegesis of the passage. Second, I will examine critically especially those aspects of Wright's understanding of this passage that relate to the doctrine of justification. And third, I will briefly explore the way Wright's theological method is illumined by his handling of this passage.

Some Preliminary Observations

Before I consider directly the significance of Wright's handling of Romans 5:12–21 for his understanding of justification, I wish to begin with some observations regarding general features of his exegesis of this passage that are open to dispute. Much of Wright's exegesis of this passage is not objectionable, nor does it directly relate to our interest in what it tells us about his understanding of justification. This holds true especially for his observations regarding the structure of the passage (v. 12 states the first part of the argument; vv. 13–17 form an extended parenthesis; vv. 18–21 resume and conclude the argument), and its place within the outline of the book of Romans. However, there are some features of Wright's treatment of this passage that require comment before we turn to the question of its implications for the doctrine of justification.

When I make these observations, it should be understood that I am not taking exception to a fundamental assumption of Wright's reading of Romans 5:12–21, namely, that the biblical text must have priority over the exegetical conclusions of the past. I do not raise questions about Wright's exegetical conclusions simply because they are at variance with a more traditional reading of this passage. Despite Wright's disagreement with the more usual Reformed reading of Romans 5:12–21, he does regard himself to be a true heir of the Reformation in his commitment to the principle of *sola Scriptura*. The final determination of the meaning of a passage may not rest upon a simple acceptance of the interpretations of the past, even those sanctioned by a long history and consensus of opinion. An attractive feature of Wright's theological work is his deep interest in a fresh interpretation of the Scriptures that will undergird a contemporary proclamation of the gospel of Jesus Christ. Even though Wright clearly believes that the older, Reformation reading of the apostle Paul is in need of significant revision, he considers himself to be in the line of the Reformation by virtue of his deep commitment to the principle of the authority of Scripture for Christian theology.

Misconstruing the "Righteousness of God"

The premise for Wright's reading of Romans 5:12–21 is his understanding of the main theme of the book of Romans. In the tradition of exegesis stemming from the Reformation and particularly from Luther, Romans has been read as an extended theological exposition of how individual sinners can obtain favor with God. This Reformation reading of Romans treats the theme of the "righteousness of God," which is announced in the prologue of Romans (1:17), to refer to the way God grants the righteousness of Christ to individual believers in order that they may be justified. Wright, as we have seen, challenges this reading of Romans and argues that the "righteousness of God" refers comprehensively to God's covenant faithfulness to his people Israel. The gospel of Jesus Christ, articulated in the narrative of Romans, is all about how through Christ the promise originally made to Abraham (and through him to Israel as a people) is being fulfilled. Even though Wright derives this understanding from other parts of the epistle and Paul's writings generally, it shapes his reading of Romans 5:12–21.[36]

Due to the influence of Wright's understanding of the "righteousness of God" for his reading of Romans 5:12–21, it is necessary to question whether it is an adequate representation of the epistle's theme. In my judgment, it is not. Wright's understanding of the language of the "righteousness of God" is much too general and vague to capture some important levels of meaning of this language in the Epistle to the Romans. That the "righteousness of God," which is revealed in the gospel of Jesus Christ, has something to do with God's work of salvation in faithfulness to his covenant with

36. Wright is actually reflecting a widespread opinion among biblical scholars regarding the meaning of the language of the "righteousness of God." This view is associated with prominent biblical theologians of the OT (Gerhard von Rad) and the NT (Ernst Käsemann) and has become a kind of working assumption among contemporary biblical scholars. For a fine summary of the discussion, which includes some pointed criticisms of this view, see Douglas J. Moo, *The Epistle to the Romans*, NICNT (Grand Rapids, MI: Eerdmans, 1996), 79–89.

Israel, seems too obvious and general a point to require emphasis. Nothing in traditional Protestant exegesis would deny it. The writings of the apostle Paul, not to mention the claims of the NT writings generally, confirm how all the promises of God have their "yes and amen" in Christ (2 Cor. 1:20). What remains to be seen is whether the "righteousness of God" speaks of something more specific with respect to the way God's saving work is accomplished.

Mark Seifrid and other critics of the new perspective have recently addressed this question.[37] Contrary to Wright's claim that the "righteousness of God" refers simply to God's covenant faithfulness in granting salvation to his people, Seifrid has demonstrated that this language more closely conforms to the claims of traditional Reformation exegesis. In the writings of the OT, the terms "covenant" (בְּרִית) and "righteousness" (צְדָקָה) seldom occur together. The particular nuance of the term "righteous" (צַדִּיק) and its cognates, as most traditional lexica will confirm, is the idea of conformity to a norm or law (cf. Lev. 19:36). When this term or a cognate is used verbally, it most commonly refers to the exercise of judgment by those in positions of authority. A ruler in Israel is primarily someone who renders judgments and secures the rule of law by punishing the wicked and vindicating the righteous. A basic substratum of meaning in many passages that speak of an earthly judge or of God, the divine Judge and Lord of all creation, is the concept of retribution that must fall upon those who disobey the Creator. One of the most frequently met themes in the OT is the theme of God's just punishment for those who sin against him.[38] The same Lord who upholds the cause of those who do right is the One who puts down those who do wrong. In conformity to the pattern of the divine Judge, it is the duty of human judges to execute justice by condemning the guilty and declaring innocent the righteous. Within the context of

37. Mark A. Seifrid, "Righteousness Language in the Hebrew Scriptures and Early Judaism," in *JVN1*, 415–42. See also Peter O'Brien, "Was Paul a Covenantal Nomist?," in *JVN2*, 249–96, esp. 274–76; and Henri Blocher, "Justification of the Ungodly (*Sola Fide*)," in *JVN2*, 465–500, esp. 473–78.

38. Blocher, "Justification of the Ungodly," cites the following passages as a sampling: Deut. 32:35; 2 Sam. 3:39; Job 34:11; Pss. 31:23; 91:8; 94:2; Isa. 34:8; 35:4; 40:10; 62:11; 65:6; 66:6; Jer. 16:18; 25:14; 50:29; 51:6; Ezek. 7:2–9; Hos. 12:2; Obad. 15.

this kind of understanding, the "justification" of the righteous is an act of vindication on the part of a judge, who declares the righteous to be innocent of a charge of wrongdoing and thereby upholds the cause of righteousness.[39]

When Wright maintains that Paul identifies the "righteousness of God" with his covenant faithfulness, he fails to do justice to this OT background and usage. For our purpose, it is especially noteworthy that he does not appreciate the extent to which this biblical idea of the righteousness of God, which especially emphasizes God's just retribution upon those who disobey his law, informs the argument of Romans 5:12–21.[40] Because of his prior commitment to the notion that the "righteousness of God" means God's faithfulness, Wright cannot adequately address the way this passage deals with such broad themes as the obligation of all human beings to obey the norms of God's law; the just consequence of disobedience to the law of God in the way of condemnation and death; the provision for the satisfaction of God's justice through the obedience of Christ, especially his death upon the cross on behalf of believers; and the granting of the gift of righteousness to those who belong to Christ, which enables them to enter into the blessing of righteousness and life. Later sections will illustrate how Wright's treatment of this passage, because of his assumptions about the meaning of the "righteousness of God," do not adequately represent what it teaches about the doctrine of justification.

An Imbalance between Historia Salutis *and* Ordo Salutis

One striking characteristic of Wright's interpretation of Romans 5:12–21 is his emphasis upon its place within the epistle's narrative sequences. This letter is usually read as the most theological of Paul's writings, and the broad framework of his argument throughout is seldom given its due. Wright, who considers Paul's epistle against the background of his acquaintance with Judaism and the OT, insists

39. See Ex. 23:7; Deut. 25:1; Prov. 17:15; Isa. 5:23; 53:11.

40. In his *What Saint Paul Really Said*, 103, Wright dismisses the idea that retributive justice belongs to the meaning of "the righteousness of God" by calling it a "Latin irrelevance."

that Romans be read as an extended retelling of the story of God's dealings with Israel. This story, now told from Paul's vantage point as a preacher of the gospel, is all about how God has fulfilled his covenant with Israel by means of the representative life, death, and resurrection of the Messiah. As we noted in our summary of Wright's treatment of Romans 5:12–21, Wright views it as a kind of summary narrative, which recapitulates the preceding narrative of Romans 1–4 and anticipates the subsequent narrative of Romans 6–8. Paul structures the sequence in Romans according to the historical pattern of redemption in general. He initially rehearses the story of creation and the fall in the opening section of Romans, especially beginning at 1:18. He then moves to the covenant with Abraham and his descendants, the children of Israel, through whom God purposed to bring salvation for the human race and reverse sin's adverse consequences within the whole creation. By means of Israel's history, her exodus from captivity and the giving of the law at Sinai through Moses, God had revealed his covenant purpose to defeat the powers of sin and death and to grant to a new humanity an inheritance that encompasses the whole world, the creation renewed in righteousness. This pattern of redemptive history with its conception of Israel's role as the "new humanity" (second Adam) shapes the story line of Romans. Moreover, in the section that encompasses Romans 5:12–21, Paul is especially keen to show how Christ's death and resurrection constitute the basis for the church's exodus from her bondage to sin and entrance into the promised inheritance of a new creation.

Wright's emphasis upon the importance of redemptive history to our reading of Romans is a commendable reminder that *historia salutis* (the history of redemption) is basic to *ordo salutis* (the order of redemption, as it applies to the believer). However, though Wright properly emphasizes the importance of *historia salutis* to the structure and themes of the book of Romans, he tends to overstate its importance and to downplay those elements of Paul's argument that address more directly the traditional topics of *ordo salutis*. Throughout his commentary on Romans, including his treatment of Romans 5:12–21, Wright consistently focuses upon the broad panorama of God's purpose for and through Israel within the scope of the history of redemption. The big theme of the book is that God keeps his covenant promise to Abraham and brings redemption through Israel's Messiah to Jews and Gentiles alike. The actors on the stage of the history of redemption are not individuals, whether Jews or Gentiles, who believe or do not believe. They are not particular sinners who know personally that they have sinned and fallen short of God's glory and who can only be restored to favor with God through faith in Jesus Christ. These customary and directly *ordo salutis* implications of the story of salvation are diminished in Wright's commentary.

Admittedly, Wright's almost exclusive focus upon the broad themes of *historia salutis* rather than of *ordo salutis* does not create, when applied to a passage like Romans 5:12–21, the kind of obvious problems that it does with respect to other parts of the epistle. After all, in Romans 5:12–21 Paul deliberately summarizes the whole history of redemption in terms of two respective heads, Adam and Christ, and in terms of two humanities, the old and the new. This passage provides a summary sketch of the great developments in the unfolding plot of redemptive history. In other parts of the argument of Romans, however, Wright's emphasis upon historical aspects compels him to downplay a number of rather transparently personal dimensions of God's work of redemption through Jesus Christ.[41] Though Wright's view of the historical-redemptive structure and underpinnings of the book of Romans may be closer to the truth of the matter than the popular "Romans road" approach of evangelical piety, it does seem that the proverbial pendulum swings too far in his case in an overreaction to traditional Protestant exegesis. This kind of

41. A remarkable example of this tendency is the way Wright treats the first person pronoun, "I," in Romans 7:7–25. Throughout this passage, Paul is employing "I" as a "rhetorical device" to refer to the people of Israel corporately. Though Wright acknowledges that contemporary biblical commentators on Romans, including such noteworthy figures as C. E. B. Cranfield (*A Critical and Exegetical Commentary on the Epistle to the Romans* [Edinburgh: T. & T. Clark, 1975], 342–47) and James D. G. Dunn (*Romans 1–8*, Word Biblical Commentary 38A [Dallas: Word, 1988], 387–99), take a different view, he insists that we must "rule out any possibility that Paul might here [Rom. 7:7–25] be referring to the 'normal Christian'" (*Romans*, 551). Though this is not the place to engage Wright's treatment of this passage, his exclusion of the personal dimensions of Paul's argument illustrates the point: he plays the history of redemption off against the personal appropriation of redemption in an unnecessary and unhelpful way.

exaggerated emphasis upon the history of redemption skews Wright's interpretation of justification.

Adam, Christ, and the Question of History

One of the more significant components of the narrative that is assumed in Romans 5:12–21 is the historical identity of the two key figures whom the apostle Paul compares and contrasts. The argument of Romans 5:12–21, as Wright acknowledges, focuses upon the comparison/contrast between the first Adam whose disobedience is associated with the tyranny of the powers of sin and death over the human race and creation, and the Messiah of Israel whose obedience is associated with the liberating powers of righteousness and life over those who share in his victory. These two figures, representing fallen and redeemed humanities respectively, are determinative for the whole course of the narrative of redemptive history detailed throughout Romans.

An irony of Wright's interpretation of Romans 5:12–21 is that, in spite of the determinative role of these two figures, he leaves the question of the identity and historicity of the first Adam somewhat obscure. In his comments on the important question of the "historical nature" of the narrative in Genesis that Paul obviously references in this passage, Wright properly notes that Paul would have assumed the essential historicity of the Genesis narrative. As a first-century Jew, Paul undoubtedly believed that God had created a first human pair, Adam and Eve, and that the sin of Adam (and Eve) introduced sin and death into the human race (and, for that matter, brought chaos into the creation itself) for the first time. Moreover, Wright insists that the transition from an original state of integrity to one of fallenness belongs necessarily to the biblical story, and is not contradicted by any theological or scientific axiom. Death in the human sphere, for example, has come by virtue of human sin to refer not only to the natural process of decay and dissolution that is an ordinary feature of human creatureliness, but also to a situation of being-under-the-judgment of God. Wright affirms a kind of "historical fall" into sin at an earlier stage of "anthropoid development." But, in spite of these positive affirmations about a historical fall into sin and of an integral connection between human sin and (spiritual) death, Wright stops short of an unequivocal affirmation of what, as he himself acknowledges, belongs to the apostle Paul's teaching in this passage. Unlike the traditional reading of Romans 5:12–21, which affirms the original creation of Adam in a state of integrity and his subsequent fall into sin, Wright equivocates on the identity and historical nature of the first figure in the passage. What seems to belong integrally to the history Paul recites, namely, the real existence of a particular person, Adam, in whom the whole human race was organically joined, is left open to reinterpretation in Wright's exegesis. Though Paul may have understood the narrative of creation in Genesis in a way that was characteristic of a first-century Jew, the meaning of the story he recounts does not necessarily require that we embrace the same understanding.

"In That All Sinned": An Exegetical Crux

A disappointing aspect of Wright's comments on Romans 5:12–21 concerns his handling of the phrase, "in that all sinned," with which Paul concludes verse 12. The meaning of this phrase within the larger context of Paul's argument in Romans 5:12–21 has compelled Christian (especially Reformed) theologians to address the question of the union between Adam and his posterity and the implications of this union for the way Paul connects Adam's sin with its consequences for all human beings. Wright's exegesis of this passage hardly begins to address some of its most important features so far as the subject of "original sin" is concerned. As I observed in our summary of his exegesis, Wright glosses over some important questions this passage raises by suggesting that they are not Paul's questions, but the "abstract" questions of traditional theology. Though space limits me from providing a full treatment of this phrase in verse 12 or adequately exploring the implications of the broader context for an understanding of the connection between Adam's sin and his posterity's guilt, I do want to summarize what seems to be the most likely reading of the passage.[42] The key question that needs to be answered

42. For a more fulsome statement of the position I will summarize in what follows, see

is, what does Paul mean when he says, "death passed upon all men, for that all have sinned?"

Though Wright does not name any theologians in his comments on this phrase, he acknowledges that there are, broadly speaking, two ways theologians have historically interpreted it. One way is to take the "all have sinned" as a reference to the actual sins of all human beings who have repeated the original sin of Adam. This way of interpreting the phrase, which has historically been associated with the name of the British monk Pelagius, denies that Paul speaks of Adam's particular (primal) sin, on account of which death reigns over all his posterity. Paul uses the language, "all have sinned," in a manner that parallels the language of Romans 3:23; "all have sinned" means simply that all human beings, starting with Adam, have committed transgressions that render them culpable and liable to condemnation. Advocates of this interpretation maintain that it not only adequately explains the meaning of Paul's phrase and its parallel in Romans 3:23, but it also resolves a difficult theological problem, namely, how all human beings could be regarded by God as guilty for a sin that they did not commit. A second way of interpreting this phrase maintains that Paul is referring to the direct participation of all human beings in the original sin of Adam. This way of interpreting the phrase, which is historically linked with the name of Augustine (Pelagius's arch-opponent), appeals to Paul's use of the aorist tense.[43] That tense suggests a particular act of Adam in the past, not the actual sins of all his posterity. As we have seen in our summary of Wright's comments on this verse, Wright admits that the second of these two interpretations is the more likely, but he

Charles Hodge, *Commentary on the Epistle to the Romans* (1886; repr., Grand Rapids, MI: Eerdmans, 1950), 142–91; John Murray, *The Epistle to the Romans*, 2 vols., NICNT (Grand Rapids, MI: Eerdmans, 1959, 1965), 1:178–210; Murray, *The Imputation of Adam's Sin* (Philadelphia: Presbyterian and Reformed, 1959); John Stott, *Romans: God's Good News for the World* (Downers Grove, IL: InterVarsity Press, 1994), 148–62; and John Piper, *Counted Righteous in Christ: Should We Abandon the Imputation of Christ's Righteousness?* (Wheaton, IL: Crossway, 2002), 90–114.

43. Augustine's understanding of the final phrase of verse 12, ἐφ' ᾧ πάντες ἥμαρτον, was influenced by the Vulgate's (mis)translation, *in quo omnes peccaverunt* ("in whom all sinned"). See Murray, *Imputation*, 9.

nonetheless declines to rule the first out altogether or to explore further the implications of these divergent interpretations for an understanding of the broader argument in Romans 5:12–21. By declining to do so, Wright's handling of Romans 5:12–21 neglects to examine a pivotal part of Paul's argument, which is of special importance, as we shall see below, to the issue of Paul's understanding of justification and the imputation of the righteousness of Christ to believers.

If Paul's language in verse 12 is interpreted in the light of the broader context of the concise argument of Romans 5:12–21, Wright's caution at this point appears unnecessary.[44] There are, broadly speaking, at least three important considerations that contribute to a more definite interpretation of Paul's language, "because all sinned." These considerations demonstrate that Paul is not referring to the actual sins of all men, but to Adam's original sin. They also show that Paul views Adam on analogy to Christ as the covenant representative of his posterity.

The first consideration relates to Paul's parenthesis in verses 13–15, which is appended to the statement of verse 12 as a kind of elaboration or, as Wright terms it, an "explanatory aside." In these verses, Paul makes three distinct but related points, each of which argues for an interpretation of "all have sinned" as a reference to Adam's original sin and the participation of all humans in that sin. First, Paul observes in verse 13a that "for sin indeed was in the world until the law was given" (ἄχρι γὰρ νόμου ἁμαρτία ἦν ἐν κόσμῳ). Long before God gave the Torah to his people Israel through Moses, indeed from the time of Adam onward, disobedience to God as Creator was an incorrigible feature of human life. Second, Paul also notes in verse 13b that "sin is not counted where there is no law" (ἁμαρτία δὲ οὐκ ἐλλογεῖται μὴ ὄντος νόμου). So long as the law had not been given in the specific form in which God gave it through Moses at Sinai, the "counting" of sin did not occur by the measure of God's revealed law. And third, Paul utilizes

44. The context is decisive to the interpretation of the concluding phrase in verse 12. As Murray observes (*Romans*, 1:182–83), "verse 12 of itself is compatible with a Pelagian interpretation, and if Paul had entertained the Pelagian view he could have stated it admirably well in these terms."

these two points in a remarkable statement about Adam's sin and its consequence for his descendants: "Yet death reigned from Adam to Moses, even over those whose sinning was not like the transgression of Adam, who was a type of the one who was to come" (ἀλλ' ἐβασίλευσεν ὁ θάνατος ἀπὸ Ἀδὰμ μέχρι Μωϋσέως καὶ ἐπὶ τοὺς μὴ ἁμαρτήσαντας ἐπὶ τῷ ὁμοιώματι τῆς παραβάσεως Ἀδὰμ ὅς ἐστιν τύπος τοῦ μέλλοντος). The force of this third point is that the reign of death held universal sway over all human beings, not by virtue of their actual sins against the law of God, but by virtue of Adam's transgression. The language Paul uses to describe those subject to death's reign might be translated, "those who did not sin by breaking a specific/explicit command, as did Adam." Whatever difficulties this may present for Christian theology and its understanding of Adam's original sin, the language Paul uses in this "explanatory aside" seems undeniably to point in the direction of direct connection between Adam's sin and the reign of death over all his descendants.

The second consideration is the larger context of verse 12, especially verses 15–19. In these verses, Paul states on five distinct occasions that the trespass of the one man, Adam, brought condemnation and death upon all human beings. The implication of this context for the interpretation of verse 12 seems clear: all are subject to condemnation and death *on account of the sin of Adam, the head and representative of fallen humanity*, not on account of their actual sins. Though it is certainly true that all human beings disobey the law of God—a point Paul labors to make throughout the early chapters of Romans—the specific burden of Paul's understanding of Adam's role in Romans 5:12–21 points in a different direction. Paul directly connects Adam's sin and its consequence for his posterity. Though Wright declines to appeal to this context when he dismisses the connection between Adam's sin and the guilt of his posterity, the language Paul uses in verses 15–19 clearly points to an understanding of Adam as the representative head of the human race.

The third consideration has to do with the sustained comparison that Paul draws throughout this passage between the respective roles of Adam and Christ, particularly the implications of these roles for those who are joined with them. Later sections will return to this consideration, when we take up the subject of this passage's implications for an understanding of justification and the idea of "imputation" that it entails. What is remarkable about Wright's handling of Romans 5:12–21 is how he studiously avoids discussing what Paul's argument presupposes regarding the similarity in relationship between Adam and his posterity and between Christ and his beneficiaries. If we interpreted Paul to be teaching that death reigns over all human beings because they all have sinned, we would seem to be compelled by Paul's argument to say that life reigns over all believers because they all have obeyed like Christ. Nothing is more obvious in this passage than that there is a similar *modus operandi* in the way human beings become guilty by virtue of the disobedience of the one man, Adam, and the way believers become righteous by virtue of the obedience of the one, Christ. The apostle Paul maintains that the justification of those who belong to Christ is based, not upon their own obedience, but upon the obedience of Christ. The analogy that this passage assumes between Adam and Christ would be violated were the condemnation of those who are in Adam based, not upon the disobedience of Adam, but upon their own works of disobedience. To quote an apt summary by Charles Hodge of the nature of Paul's argument in this passage,

> Paul has been engaged from the beginning of the Epistle in inculcating one main idea, viz. that the ground of the sinner's acceptance with God is not in himself, but the merit of Christ. And the correspondence between Christ and Adam must preserve, not destroy this truth. It should read, therefore: "As we are condemned on account of what Adam did, (so) we are justified on account of what Christ did."[45]

Wright's unwillingness to enter into a more full discussion of the implications of Paul's argument in Romans 5:12–21 for our understanding of original sin and its consequence, as well as the connection

45. Hodge, *Romans*, 142.

between Christ's obedience and the believer's justification, constitutes an important reason for his failure to do justice to what this passage teaches about justification. Now that we have offered these preliminary observations about general aspects of Wright's interpretation of Romans 5:12–21, the time has come to address directly the way he handles the subject of justification in his comments on this passage.

Wright, Romans 5:12–21, and Justification

In my chapter introduction, I noted that Romans 5:12–21 has played an important role in the formulation of traditional Reformed theology and its understanding of the doctrine of justification. In Reformed theology, this passage provides a comprehensive statement of the comparison/contrast between the first Adam, whose one act of disobedience resulted in the condemnation and death of all men, and the second Adam, Christ, whose act of obedience resulted in righteousness and life for all believers.[46] In the covenant or "federal" theology of the WCF, Romans 5:12–21 is a key biblical testimony to the doctrine of justification through the imputation of the righteousness of Christ to those who are united to him by faith. In the construction of covenant theology, this passage depicts two humanities in terms of their judicial relationship to God: fallen humanity, which lies under the sentence of condemnation and death on account of the disobedience of the first Adam as its covenant head or representative; and redeemed humanity, which has been constituted righteous and heir of eternal life on account of the obedience of Christ, the second Adam and the covenant head of all who share in him through faith. With respect to the doctrine of justification, this passage comprehensively witnesses to the acceptance of all believers who are recipients by faith of the free gift of righteousness in Christ. The traditional reading of Romans 5:12–21 clearly testifies to several key

46. Paul uses the language of "all" in v. 18, which might be interpreted to teach a "universalism" in which all human beings are now saved in Christ as they once perished in Adam. There are contextual considerations, however, in the book of Romans that clearly show that only believers, that is, those who are united to Christ by faith, are saved. It should not be overlooked that Paul speaks in this passage of the "many" who will be made righteous (v. 19) and insists in Rom. 6 that baptism into Christ is necessary to participate in the benefit of his death and resurrection.

elements of the Reformation doctrine of justification. Among these elements Romans 5:12–21 especially illustrates the nature of God's righteousness as that which is freely imputed to believers and the nature of justification as a judicial act whereby sinners are declared acceptable to God on the basis of Christ's work on their behalf.

Wright's handling of this passage, especially with respect to the doctrine of justification, is quite different. Because the "righteousness of God" refers to God's covenant faithfulness, Wright rejects any idea of the imputing of this righteousness to believers. The righteousness of God is simply his faithfulness in fulfilling his covenant promise to Israel through the death of the Messiah. When Paul speaks of the granting of righteousness to those who share in the work of Christ, he is identifying those who are now recognized by God to be members of his covenant family, whether Jews or Gentiles. Wright gives little or no consideration to the "imputation" of Adam's guilt to his posterity or of Christ's righteousness to believers. The legal transaction that was so integral a part of the historic Reformed reading of this passage is reduced to a declaration that those who share in Christ are in favor with God and acknowledged members of his covenant people (their status). However, the righteousness of God is not something that can be granted or imputed by God to believers. Wright also expressly repudiates the older Reformed view that the obedience of Christ comprehensively includes his positive fulfillment of the demands of God's law and his endurance of the law's sanction, granted and imputed to believers as a free gift of God's grace. Wright summarily rejects this older view, which he characterizes as a doctrine of accruing a "treasury of merit" that is apportioned to believers. In its place, Wright argues that the obedience of Christ is his "faithfulness" in fulfilling the calling of Israel in the history of redemption, namely, to secure the blessing of salvation for the new humanity and to obtain its inheritance of a renewed cosmos.

Three significant weaknesses in Wright's approach become apparent in the way he interprets Romans 5:12–21 (although many other facets could be addressed). These weaknesses have already surfaced in part in the preceding, but now require more direct comment in terms of their significance for the doctrine of justification.

The "Righteousness of God" Revisited

In an earlier section of this chapter, we noted how Wright's understanding of the theme of Romans, "the righteousness of God," follows an emphasis in more recent Pauline studies that identifies it with God's faithfulness to his covenant. Wright treats as largely "irrelevant" to biblical usage the older themes of God's righteousness as his conformity to and administration of his own law, both in terms of its demand upon humans and its sanctions in the case of disobedience. Unlike the older view, which took the "righteousness of God" revealed in the gospel to refer to Christ's work in obeying the law and suffering its curse, Wright stresses the motif of God's acting to secure the promise to Abraham and his descendants. In his view, since the "righteousness of God" refers to God's saving action in Christ, which calls a worldwide covenant community into existence (composed of Jews and Gentiles alike), it does not refer to the demands or sanctions of the law of God, who as the Creator and Judge rules and judges all creatures. Because the "righteousness of God" means something like God's faithfulness in action, it can hardly be said to be imputed or transferred from Christ to those joined to him by faith.

If we consider the argument of the apostle Paul in Romans 5:12–21, however, it seems undeniable that the older view more closely captures Paul's understanding of the "righteousness of God" than Wright's view. Remarkably, Wright's exposition of this passage utilizes language that frequently belies his own claims regarding the meaning of God's righteousness. The thrust of Paul's argument in this passage seems transparently to be that all human beings are regarded by God as sinners because of the disobedience of the first man, Adam. The reign of sin and death over human life throughout history—from the time of Adam's transgression until the present, even in the case of generations not given the law of God as it was proclaimed to Israel through Moses—testifies to the fact that God holds all accountable and liable for their sin *in Adam*. Paul's emphasis throughout is upon the *one* man, Adam, whose *one* act of disobedience has brought the judgment and wrath of God upon all his posterity. What is particularly important to our interest is that Paul focuses especially upon *the explicitly legal* or *judicial consequences of*

Adam's sin: all human beings are subject, he declares, to "condemnation" and "death." Within the opening chapters of Romans, especially the preliminary conclusion in Romans 3:19–20 (all human beings are accountable before God for their sin and have nothing to present in their own defense that would exonerate them in God's court), the implications of this focus are clear. Paul speaks about the human situation in the court of heaven (*coram Deo*), and he insists that all human beings are liable to the exposure and sanction of the law of God, the Creator and Judge of all creatures. Though there are undoubtedly other facets of the human predicament in sin, particularly the inheritance of what Christian theologians have called a "sinfully depraved or corrupted nature," Paul's interest in this passage remains fixed upon the explicitly *legal* dimension of human sinfulness to which the doctrine of justification alone provides a remedy.

In a similar way, Paul's description of Christ's work in this passage particularly addresses the legal dimension of the problem of sin. Just as the sin, condemnation, and death came through the transgression of the one man, Adam, so righteousness, acceptance with God, and life have come through the obedience of the one man, Christ. All who have a share in Christ, who are *judicially implicated* in his saving work of obedience, now are granted a new status of being acceptable to God and in right standing before him. Paul, in other words, concisely elaborates on the respective relationship of all human beings to Adam and to Christ, in a comprehensive account of how the gospel provides the only remedy for the radical predicament of all human beings before God, whether Jews or Gentiles. It doesn't matter whether the Gentiles were given the law through Moses or not; they are still subject to the law, have violated its demands, and stand liable to its sanction. Nor does it matter that the Jews have apparently enjoyed a distinguishing privilege as recipients of the law through Moses; the law of Moses, which the Jews thought would serve them instrumentally as a means of maintaining favor with God, only aggravates the problem by exposing and increasing their sinfulness. Only through the person and work of Christ, whose obedience contrasts with the disobedience of Adam, can Jews and

Gentiles alike be constituted righteous and become heirs of life in communion with God.

A brief rehearsal such as this of the argument of Romans 5:12–21 confirms that it presupposes Paul's (and the Scriptures') understanding of the "righteousness of God." That understanding cannot be reduced to something like God's faithfulness to his promise. To be sure, the gospel of Jesus Christ reveals God's faithfulness and confirms his promise to Abraham. But if we consider how it particularly reveals God's righteousness, then we are left with the older Reformed view. What commends the love of God in the gospel is not only that it displays God's undeserved goodness to sinners who are altogether unworthy (cf. Rom. 5:1–11), but also that it answers to and fulfills all the demands and sanctions of God's holy law. God, who is just and the One who justifies *the ungodly* (Rom. 4:5), has provided for the salvation of his people in a way that wondrously illumines both his love and his justice, his grace and his holiness. In all of this, the conception of the "righteousness of God" that seems to leap from the page is precisely the conception historically associated with the Reformation doctrine of justification.

One element of this view remains to be considered, namely, the gracious granting and imputing of what Christ has accomplished to those who belong to him by faith. We will reserve our consideration of this element, however, to our discussion below of the theme of "imputation" in Romans 5:12–21. What seems clear enough at this point is how Wright's definition of the "righteousness of God" misses key elements that belong to it and are present in the argument of Romans 5:12–21.

The Nature of Justification

In Wright's conception of Paul's doctrine of justification, he admits that the idea of justification finds its home in the legal sphere. According to Wright, the language of justification for Paul and Judaism plays upon a legal metaphor with three principal figures: a judge, a plaintiff, and a defendant. What matters in the court is that the judge declares in favor of, or vindicates, a defendant against charges. To be justified in this context is simply to be in favor with the court, to be in the status of innocence or without guilt. Justification is not a process of moral transformation or renewal, as in some traditional Roman Catholic formulations, but it is a verdict the judge pronounces in court that vindicates a defendant. Within the setting of the gospel's revelation of the "righteousness of God," Wright consistently argues that justification therefore refers to God's identification of those who belong properly to his covenant family. To be justified within the context of God's faithfulness to his promise to Abraham and his descendants is tantamount to being numbered among the people of God. To be righteous is to be acknowledged a member of God's people, a beneficiary of God's covenant promise to Abraham. Justification by faith, which Wright terms the "badge" of such covenant membership, is Paul's doctrine of how God's worldwide covenant family is to be identified. Justification, though not the principal theme of the gospel, is an ecclesiological doctrine answering the problem as to whether Gentiles are also to be included within God's covenant people, even though they were not recipients of the Torah through Moses or obedient to its particular "markers of identity" that distinguish God's people, Israel, from others. Because justification is all about the status of those whom God identifies as properly members of the covenant community, it should be not regarded, as in the older Reformation view, as how believers "enter into" favor with God. When Paul speaks of entry into the company of God's covenant family, he identifies this with baptism (Rom. 6) or "calling" (Rom. 8:29).[47]

When this conception of what Paul means by justification is compared to the argument of Romans 5:12–21, it appears to be unnecessarily reductionistic, perhaps even misguided. Though Paul undoubtedly affirms the evident ecclesiological implications of the doctrine of justification—that Jews and Gentiles alike belong to God's covenant family through faith in Jesus Christ, apart from the works of the law—this is not the way justification is primarily defined in this passage. Though Paul does not expressly use the verb

47. This summary of Wright's understanding of Paul's doctrine of justification in Romans and the other Pauline Epistles reflects his discussion in *What Saint Paul Really Said*, 113–33.

"to justify" in this passage, he does use the noun "justification" and obviously speaks in terms directly relevant to and explanatory of what it is to be justified. The antonym of justification is "condemnation" (vv. 16, 18; cf. Rom. 8:33–34). All who are "in Adam" stand under the condemnation of God and are liable to the consequence of their sin in the way of death. All who are "in Christ," however, are now the recipients of "justification and life." Those who have a share in Christ are, according to the apostle Paul, "made righteous" (δίκαιοι κατασταθήσονται).[48] To return to the distinction between *historia salutis* and *ordo salutis*, which we have discussed above, Paul seems to undeniably address the theme of salvation at both levels. Undoubtedly, the broad comparison/contrast between Adam and Christ that dominates the argument of Romans 5:12–21 represents an all-embracing panorama. The history of redemption is dominated by these two figures and the two humanities whom they represent. The question of justification, therefore, can be expressed in redemptive-historical terms as the question of the identity of the covenant people of God. But this question also comes to its sharpest expression in terms of the patently *ordo salutis* question: do I belong by faith to Christ and accordingly have a share in the benefits of his saving obedience? Even though Paul does not expressly address the *ordo salutis* question in his argument in Romans 5:12–21, one can hardly read the book of Romans without noticing that the question of faith and unbelief is a matter of supreme interest to the apostle throughout. For example, whatever one makes of the place of Romans 9–11 in the overall structure of the Epistle to the Romans, it clearly addresses the problem of unbelief on the part of some, but not all, of Paul's kinsmen according to the flesh.

To put the matter in bold relief, Wright's insistence that justification is primarily an ecclesiological issue for Paul shipwrecks rather patently upon the hard rock of a passage like Romans 5:12–21. It is neither exegetically defensible nor theologically necessary to play

48. For a brief discussion of the "forensic" meaning of Paul's language in v. 18, see Albrecht Oepke, s.v. καθίστημι, in *Theological Dictionary of the New Testament*, ed. Gerhard Kittel (Grand Rapids, MI: Eerdmans, 1965), 3:445–46. Paul is speaking of a declaration or pronouncement of innocence that properly takes place in a court of law.

off ecclesiology against soteriology in Paul's understanding of justification. Justification, among other things, undoubtedly identifies those who properly belong to the number of God's covenant people through faith in Christ. But it does so because justification has everything to do with the soteriological question of how any sinner can stand before God in spite of his or her evident sinfulness. Justification answers the profound *ordo salutis* question that played such an important role at the time of the Reformation; namely, how can I find a gracious God when I am clearly exposed by the law of God as someone who is worthy of condemnation and death? No useful purpose, certainly no exegetically necessary purpose, is served by opposing *historia salutis* to *ordo salutis*, or ecclesiology to soteriology, in the manner Wright does. Romans 5:12–21 constitutes a strong argument for the older view of justification, which emphasized its forensic nature as a judicial act in which God declares sinners to be righteous before him. This view, which was compelled to address the issue of justification in terms of the *ordo salutis* questions posed by medieval Roman Catholic teaching, did not fail at the same time to recognize the basis of salvation in the objective history of God's action on behalf of his people in Christ.[49] No Reformation theologian, including the much-maligned Luther, would have denied the priority of the history of redemption and the objective work of Christ *extra nos*, when it comes to the subjective benefit of this history for the believer in Jesus Christ.

What about "Imputation"?

In his treatment of Romans 5:12–21, Wright gives short shrift to the subject of "imputation" and the manner in which believers have a share in Christ and his righteousness. Though he acknowledges the essential place of the idea of imputation in the older Reformation view of this passage and the doctrine of justification, Wright strongly denies that Paul, here or elsewhere, ever teaches that imputation occurs in the act of justification. Since Wright is quite emphatic

49. This is the significance of such traditional distinctions as that between Christ's work *pro nobis* ("for us") or *extra nos* ("outside of us") and *in nobis* ("in us").

in his rejection of the idea of imputation, it is disappointing how he largely glosses over those elements of Paul's argument in Romans 5:12–21 that speak directly to the subject. The closest Wright comes to addressing the question is his backhanded repudiation of any attempt to explain "the mode by which . . . sin is transmitted" from Adam to all human beings. The "primal sin" of Adam, Wright acknowledges, "somehow" involves "all subsequent humanity," but how this is so lies outside the purview of Paul's argument in Romans 5:12–21. When it comes to the parallel question as to how believers come to have a share in the "representative" work of Christ, Wright is just as noncommittal. Though he emphatically rejects the idea of imputation as explaining this participation in the representative work of Christ, he does acknowledge that believers do "share" in the work of Christ and enjoy a new status on this account.[50]

At the risk of repeating some points that we have previously argued, the failure on Wright's part to address directly the question that imputation historically answered must be judged untenable. Readers of Romans 5:12–21 can scarcely gloss over how Paul seems to argue that all human beings are guilty before God on account of the one act of the one man, Adam. Nor can they overlook the evident connection Paul makes between Adam's sin, on the one hand, and the universal reign of condemnation and death over all human beings, on the other. Similarly, Paul parallels this argument concerning the first Adam with a comparable argument concerning Christ. Perhaps the most important point in Romans 5:12–21 is Paul's claim that all who have a share in Christ are righteous by virtue of his one act of obedience on their behalf. There is an immediate connection

50. Due to my focus in this chapter upon Wright's handling of Romans 5:12–21, I am not able to evaluate critically his understanding of the role of faith in justification. Wright generally rejects the idea of faith as an "instrument" by which the righteousness of God is received for justification, despite Paul's association of the righteousness of God or justification by grace with its reception "by faith" and "not by works" (see e.g., Rom. 1:17; 3:22, 25, 28; 4:16; 5:1; 9:30, 32; 10:6; Gal. 2:16, 20). Consistent with his understanding of the righteousness of God, Wright also argues that passages like Romans 3:22 (διὰ πίστεως Ἰησοῦ Χριστοῦ) and Galatians 2:16 (διὰ πίστεως Ἰησοῦ Χριστοῦ) be translated "by the faithfulness of Christ." For a recent critical assessment of this translation, which enjoys considerable popularity among contemporary biblical scholars, see Moisés Silva, "Faith versus Works of Law in Galatians," in *JVN2*, 217–48, esp. 227–34.

between Christ's obedience on the one hand and the justification and life that come to believers on the other. The judicial implications Paul maintains (whether of condemnation or of justification) are entailed by the actions of the first Adam and of Christ, suggesting that the verdict pronounced in God's court requires the constitutive acts of granting/imputing the guilt of Adam or granting/imputing the righteousness of Christ to their respective beneficiaries.

Perhaps to appreciate this more, we need to revisit the idea of imputation, not as Wright and others sometimes misrepresent it,[51] but as it has been understood historically by Reformed theologians. In the instance of the imputation of the guilt of Adam's sin to his posterity, the older view understood this to mean that, though Adam personally disobeyed the commandment of God, God reckoned or attributed the guilt of this offence to his posterity or those whom he represented. In terms of the consequence of this imputation or reckoning, all Adam's descendants are thereby guilty, under condemnation and subject to death. The great objection, of course, to this explanation of Paul's argument in Romans 5:12–21 is that it attributes guilt to human beings who were not personally culpable for a sin committed by another. This is what is known in theological shorthand as the problem of "alien guilt." On the other side of the comparison, this problem is alleviated somewhat by the awareness that something similar happens in the case of Christ's obedience and the share others have in it. In the language of the traditional view, God attributes—or put in the terms of Romans 5:19, "constitutes the many righteous"—the obedience of Christ to believers so that it is truly their own. What distinguishes the act of imputation is that it maintains the *judicial* emphasis essential to Paul's argument in Romans 5:12–21 and to his understanding of justification in this and

51. In one of the few places where Wright offers a definition of "imputation," he clearly seems to confuse it with what theologians historically termed "infused" righteousness. Cf. *What Saint Paul Really Said*, 98: "If we use the language of the law court, it makes no sense whatever to say that the judge imputes, imparts, bequeaths, conveys or otherwise transfers his righteousness to either the plaintiff or the defendant. Righteousness is not an object, a substance or a gas which can be passed across the courtroom." This statement not only misrepresents the idea of imputation, but it also leaves unanswered the corollary question, by what means do human beings become guilty of the transgression Adam committed?

other passages. If justification has everything to do with what God pronounces or declares persons to be in his court, then imputation is precisely the proper category to account for the respective judgments God makes regarding all sinners in Adam and all believers in Christ. When God declares a person guilty in Adam and liable to condemnation, he does not do so by a procedure that makes him or her an actual perpetrator of the transgression of Adam. Rather, Adam's guilt is reckoned to those whom he represented within the ordinance and purpose of God as Creator. Because God (presumably) ordered his relationship with all human beings by constituting Adam the head of humanity in its original state, the act of imputing the guilt and liability of his sin to his posterity expresses the Creator's administration of this relationship in a manner that accords with his own righteousness.[52]

The importance of the idea of imputation becomes most apparent in terms of the way believers benefit from Christ's obedience. Though Wright caricatures the idea of the imputation of the righteousness of Christ to believers, Paul's explanation of the justification of believers in Romans 5:12–21 seems clearly to affirm it. What else could be entailed by Paul's language that Christ's "free gift came upon all men unto justification of life" (KJV)? Or by his language that by "the obedience of one shall many be made righteous" (KJV)? Isn't this language affirming an act of God, a free bestowal upon believers of a gift of righteousness received by faith and the basis for their justification? In a way that strikingly parallels God's reckoning of guilt to all human beings on account of the transgression of

52. Since Paul does not explicitly use the language of "reckoning" or "accounting" in Romans 5:12–21, I will not address directly the significance of this language (or its OT background). Clearly this language belongs properly within the framework of a courtroom where a judicial pronouncement is the most important thing that occurs. Such a pronouncement tells its recipients what the court "reputes" a person to be, whether innocent or guilty. For a more extended discussion of the explicit language of "imputation" in Paul's epistles, see D. A. Carson, "The Vindication of Imputation: On Fields of Discourse and Semantic Fields," in *Justification: What's at Stake in the Current Debates?*, ed. Mark Husbands and Daniel J. Treier (Downers Grove, IL: IVP, 2004): 46–78; Piper, *Counted Righteous in Christ*; James R. White, *The God Who Justifies* (Minneapolis: Bethany House, 2001), 111–18; and James Buchanan, *The Doctrine of Justification* (1867; repr., Grand Rapids, MI: Baker, 1959), 314–38.

Adam, Paul affirms God's granting and reckoning of righteousness to believers on account of the obedience of Christ. Believers are justified, not because they have become righteous in themselves or by their own act of obedience, but because God has attributed to them the righteousness of Christ. In the court of heaven, the obedience of Christ, which is manifestly not an obedience rendered by believers themselves, is reckoned to believers so that it becomes truly their own. Though this idea of imputation may often have had to suffer the complaint that it is a kind of "legal fiction," Paul's argument amounts to the claim that it is anything but fictional. It may be an "imputed" righteousness, but it is a real righteousness that really justifies.

The obscurity and inadequacy of Wright's handling of the connection between the work of Christ and believers who come to share in it is illustrated by his preference for the language of "representative" to describe Christ's obedience and death. By this language, Wright seems to want to affirm that Christ's work is also somehow the work of believers. Because Christ is Israel's representative, all who believe in him can be said to obey and suffer "in" and "with" him. Christ's obedience and death are, in some sense, truly theirs as much as his. This is all well and good, of course, but it leaves some questions unanswered, most specifically the question to which imputation historically provided an answer. How do we get from Christ's work "outside of us" to ourselves in such a way that we can meaningfully say "what he did, we have done"? Here Reformed theology has insisted that the language of "representation" can only be adequately employed, when it includes and rests upon the idea of a *genuine substitution*.[53] Because Christ acts as a representative

53. It is not clear why Wright prefers to speak of Christ's work for his people as a "representative" work. Whether he wishes to exclude the idea of substitution by doing so is open to debate, though there is a tendency in modern theology that prefers the language of "representation" to "substitution" for this very reason. See e.g., James D. G. Dunn, *The Theology of Paul the Apostle* (Grand Rapids, MI: Eerdmans, 1998), 386. For a critical discussion of this tendency in modern theology, see Leon Morris, *The Cross in the New Testament* (Grand Rapids, MI: Eerdmans, 1965), 407–19. For a recent discussion of the necessary connection between the themes of substitution and imputation in Paul's understanding of justification, see Carson, "Vindication of Imputation," 46–78. Cf. D. A. Carson, "Atonement in Romans 3:21–26," in *The Glory of the Atonement: Biblical, Historical & Practical*

substitute in all his atoning work, his work is in the most profound sense our work. Because Christ died in the place of his own people, God accepts his death in lieu of theirs. Because Christ obeyed in the place of his own people, God accepts his obedience in lieu of theirs. *This is the exact meaning of the language of "imputation" in traditional Reformed theology: believers who are united to Christ, their substitute, are reckoned by God to have performed all that he performed in their place.* On account of Christ's obedience and death, God regards believers to have fulfilled all righteousness. For this reason, believers who are in Christ are the recipients of justification and life. To put the matter in a backhanded fashion, any denial of the reality of Christ's substitution and representation on behalf of believers will necessarily and inevitably entail a denial of imputation. Or to put the matter straightforwardly, only an affirmation of imputation can do justice to Paul's teaching that believers are "constituted righteous" on account of the obedience of Christ.[54]

Perspectives, ed. Charles E. Hill and Frank A. James III (Downers Grove, IL: InterVarsity, 2004), 134n53, who makes an apt observation regarding the connection between substitution and imputation: "Part of the contemporary (and frequently sterile) debate over whether or not Paul teaches 'imputation,' it seems to me, turns on a failure to recognize distinct domains of discourse. Strictly speaking, Paul never uses the verb λογίζομαι to say, explicitly, that Christ's righteousness is imputed to the sinner or that the sinner's righteousness is imputed to Christ. So if one remains in the domain of narrow exegesis, one can say that Paul does not explicitly teach 'imputation,' except to say slightly different things (e.g., that Abraham's faith was 'imputed' to him for righteousness). But if one extends the discussion into the domain of constructive theology, and observes that *the Pauline texts themselves* (despite the critics' contentions) teach penal substitution, then 'imputation' is merely another way of saying much the same thing."

54. It may be admitted that Romans 5:12–21 does not offer a complete answer to some of the questions that have arisen in the history of theology regarding the nature of the righteousness that God grants and imputes to believers. Even though I am convinced that there are good exegetical and theological arguments for insisting that the righteousness imputed consists of both the "active" and "passive" obedience of Christ, to use the traditional categories of theology, I will not seek to make that case here. However, even were I to grant a minimalist view of Paul's language in this passage regarding Christ's "one act of obedience" (the "passive" obedience of Christ upon the cross), we would still have a fairly clear statement of imputation as the *constitutive act* whereby believers are justified. For an exegetical and theological case for the idea in this passage of an imputation of Christ's righteousness, which comprehensively includes all of his (active and passive) obedience, see Murray, *Romans*, 1:200–202; and Piper, *Counted Righteous in Christ*, 110–15. See also chap. 11 of this volume.

An Excursus on Wright's Theological Method

A critical assessment of Wright's interpretation of Romans 5:12–21 can hardly remain within the parameters of exegesis and biblical theology. Some readers of our evaluation of Wright's exegesis of Romans 5:12–21 and its implications for Paul's doctrine of justification might be tempted, for example, to ascribe it simply to the fact that I am writing as a systematic theologian. If I were to limit my comments to what can be determined from the passage within the constraints of biblical studies, then many of the more explicitly theological aspects of my evaluation would be seen as an illegitimately "abstract" and "dehistoricizing" handling of the text. As I noted in my introduction to Wright's interpretation of this passage, he insists as a biblical theologian that the passage be read in its first-century context and from the conviction that Paul writes as a Jew convinced of Jesus Christ as Israel's Messiah. The problem with the traditional Reformation handling of Romans 5:12–21 and related passages is that the concerns of a later period in the history of Christian theology are often imported into the text. In the traditional interpretation, questions are asked and answered that are not the apostle Paul's. A historically contextualized exegesis of Romans 5:12–21 will seek to understand Paul's argument as that of a Christian apostle, who writes as a first-century Jew from within the framework and in terms of the categories of Second Temple Judaism.

At the risk of taking this evaluation of Wright's position too far afield of its appropriate limits, I would like to close with a comment regarding Wright's theological method, especially as it comes to expression in his reading of Romans 5:12–21. In the introduction to this chapter, I noted that Wright's handling of this passage may be viewed as a kind of "test case," not only for the exegetical conclusions he draws regarding Paul's doctrine of justification, but also for some of the methodological strictures he advocates in his approach to the Pauline Epistles and other biblical texts. Though some students of the new perspective are tempted to view Wright's work as a simple matter of straightforward exegesis of the biblical texts, it is apparent that much more is at stake in the discussions regarding his claims and those of other authors of the new perspective. Without attempting to be exhaustive or to do much more than take note of some issues requiring further exploration, I wish to identify several important elements of Wright's theological method. If these components are clearly recognized and evaluated in terms of their implications for Christian theology, it should become apparent that they largely preclude the possibility of any legitimate movement from exegesis to the traditional topics of systematic theology. Indeed, Wright's theological method would seem to rule out from the beginning the kinds of questions and answers traditional Christian theology has addressed in the context of passages like Romans 5:12–21.

The three components that form an important methodological basis for Wright's work as a biblical theologian are a theological epistemology that he labels "critical realism," the primary role of narratives in mediating worldviews, and the authority of scriptural narratives for Christian theology.

In the most extended statement of his theological method and epistemology, Wright describes his theological epistemology as a form of "critical realism."[55] The task of Christian theology is to seek to know something of the reality of what it describes and interprets. In this respect, Christian theology aims to describe "what is known" in a way that genuinely conforms to the nature and character of what it describes. The knowledge that theology mediates is not subjective in the sense that it says more about the knower or theologian than it does about what is known. The term "realism" indicates that the task of theology is to ascertain what is genuinely the case in respect to its peculiar subject matter. There is a true correspondence in theological knowledge between the knowledge of reality and the reality that is known. At the same time, Wright acknowledges that there is an element of the knower's interpretation of reality that contributes to the enterprise of theology. Theologians do not simply describe the "brute facts" or the simple, objective reality of what they claim to know about God, the world, and the relations between them. Theologians must recognize that they enter into a conversation with other theologians when they are engaged in the task of theological inquiry.

55. *Romans and the People of God*, 32–35.

They also recognize that there is a measure of "provisionality" to their conclusions and descriptions of this or that theological topic. Wright employs the language of "critical realism" to describe theological knowledge in order to steer a course between the extremes of "naïve realism" or objectivism on the one hand, and "subjectivism" on the other. Theology is a disciplined academic exercise in which the theologian, who studies the scriptural texts, aims to reflect in his or her critical knowledge a measure of conformity to what can be known of theology's object.[56]

A second component of Wright's theological method is his assertion that narrative or story is the primary medium for the articulation and expression of distinctive worldviews. Though we have a tendency to disparage stories as an inadequate means to express our basic convictions about the world, about ourselves, and about those things that are of greatest value to us, Wright insists that the distinct worldviews of diverse faith communities are principally (and invariably) represented in the form of narratives or stories. Indeed, the more articulate a worldview becomes, the more sophisticated and complete its "metanarrative" becomes. Such a metanarrative is a story that embraces the totality of the world in a coherent and all-inclusive manner. The preeminence of narrative as a means to communicate a worldview is of particular importance to Christian theology. The Scriptures, which constitute a kind of authoritative telling-the-story that expresses a Christian worldview, are cast largely in the form of narrative or story. The literary and theological reading of the Scripture narrative, accordingly, is the basic task of Christian theology. By following the narrative of Scripture, the Christian theologian seeks to uncover the answers to such questions as: Who are we? Where are we? What is wrong? What is the solution?[57] The answers to these worldview questions are not provided by means of a

56. Ibid., 35: "I propose a form of *critical realism*. This is a way of describing the process of 'knowing' that acknowledges the *reality of the thing known, as something other than the knower* (hence 'realism'), while also fully acknowledging that the only access we have to this reality lies along the spiraling path of *appropriate dialogue or conversation between the knower and the thing known* (hence 'critical')" (emphasis original).

57. Ibid., 132–33.

systematic distinguishing between and defining of theological topics or subjects. Rather, they are provided by means of a careful study of the biblical texts in their own historical context, a study whose aim is to uncover the worldview that is mediated by the scriptural narrative.

A third component of Wright's theological method is his claim that the Scriptures, which articulate the grand narrative that mediates the distinctives of a Christian worldview, must be acknowledged as the primary norm or authority for Christian theology. As a biblical theologian in the Protestant tradition, Wright wishes to uphold the classic principle of *sola Scriptura*. The Christian theologian's great task is to engage in a careful historically and literarily contextualized reading of the biblical tests. The scriptural narrative or narratives have a normative authority for Christian theology, even though Wright recognizes that the reading of Scripture inescapably occurs within the framework of our present world and its presuppositions. Though Wright sounds almost "precritical" at times in his assertion of the normativity and authority of the scriptural narratives, he hastens to note that a "critical" realist reading of Scripture is not to be confused with a "precritical" one. As he describes his approach, "[t]his is not to go back to pre-modernism. We have abandoned biblicistic proof texting, as inconsistent with the nature of the texts that we have."[58] If we are to grant the proper place to scriptural authority in contemporary theology, we must do so in a way that honors the historical context in which they emerged and the narrative structure of its literary forms. Any reading of the Scriptures that treats them as a collection of timeless theological doctrines, which are cast in the form of the topics that are grist for the mill of systematic theology, will inappropriately diminish the story-form of the biblical texts. Additionally, any reading of the biblical texts that superimposes upon them the questions and answers of a different period in the history of theology will risk the temptation to wrest the scriptural texts from their original historical context and their distinctive narrative structures.

Much more needs to be said about these and other characteristics of Wright's understanding of the proper method for contemporary

58. Ibid., 139–40.

Christian theology. Our brief synopsis of these important components of his method, however, should be sufficient to establish a connection between Wright's underlying theological and methodological principles and his interpretation of a passage like Romans 5:12–21. Each of these components of Wright's method is not difficult to detect in the way he reads this passage. In conformity to his commitment to "critical realism," Wright does not read this passage naively or precritically. He recognizes that Paul writes as a first-century Jew, and that he tells the story of the gospel from within the framework of the scriptural narrative he has inherited, which includes elements of a "mythical and metaphorical" nature. Though the aim of the Christian theologian is to know the reality that is mediated by means of the biblical text, Wright acknowledges that the elements of the worldview that are reflected in the text are not given in the form of an "objective" presentation of the facts. Furthermore, Wright, consistent with his understanding of the nature of narrative and the scriptural texts, regards the book of Romans in general, and this passage in particular, to form part of a narrative sequence that constitutes a kind of substratum or deep structure for the epistle. Contrary to the tendency of Christian theology to treat Romans as the most "theological" of Paul's epistles, Wright treats it as a narrative that mediates Paul's worldview. In his handling of Romans 5:12–21, Wright resists the temptation to cast its narrative into the forms of systematic theology, or to treat its argument as an occasion for exploring its implications for the traditional topics or categories of systematic theology. Many of the topics of theology that historically have occupied the attention of readers of Romans 5:12–21 are simply bypassed or shunted aside in his interpretation. These topics include the historicity of the first human being, Adam, and the importance of the organic unity of the human race to Paul's argument; the debate regarding the nature of the union between Adam and his posterity, and between Christ and those who are united to him; the manner in which the guilt of Adam is communicated to his descendants; the "imputation" or granting of the righteousness of God to those who are justified; etc.

Though Wright's theological method requires more careful and thorough study than we can give it here, we would observe that it necessarily undermines and calls into question the enterprise of systematic theology, at least as it has historically been conducted in the Christian tradition. Though I would not wish to quarrel unduly with Wright's argument for what he calls "critical realism," I believe he seriously misunderstands the significance of the importance of narrative for the enterprise of Christian theology. The obvious fact that the Scriptures consist primarily of narratives or stories does not preclude the legitimacy of a systematic and coherent treatment of the distinct topics or subjects that interpret the meaning of these stories. Nor does it preclude a consideration of the universal and categorical significance of the theological topics that interpret the biblical stories. Not only do we find many instances in the Scriptures themselves where a rudimentary form of Christian doctrine or teaching is present, but we also are inescapably constrained to ask questions of a systematic and universal nature when we read the Scriptures. Any coherent or systematic explanation of the history of redemption, which is narrated for us in the Scriptures, will have to "connect the dots" between the various parts of Scripture. Indeed, the possibility of Christian theology depends upon convictions, not only about the authority of the scriptural narratives, but also about the coherence and consistency of its teaching. Reading the biblical texts is more than a biblical and historical exercise in seeking to discover the worldview of first-century Christians, for example, who happen to have cast their views on great questions in the form of a grand narrative. Inevitably, the biblical texts will prompt questions of a systematic nature. These questions have preoccupied exegetes and theologians throughout the history of the church. The task of theology, if we assume that the biblical texts do cohere and present a consistent set of teachings regarding God, the world, sin, Christ, etc., cannot be restricted to a biblical-historical investigation of what Paul, a first-century Jew and Christian, for example, communicates to us by means of the story he inherited and reinterpreted.

Another way of making this point would be note that there is something profoundly "biblicistic" about Wright's method. Wright's reading of Romans 5:12–21 largely ignores, as we have seen, the usual questions and answers of historic Christian theology. In the name of biblical theology, Wright frequently caricatures the concerns of systematic theology as being "abstract" and "dehistoricizing." He is also very critical of any interpretation of the biblical text that approaches it from the standpoint of the history of Christian doctrine and the implications—inferentially, deductively, inductively, or adductively—of the biblical texts that are in view. Perhaps Wright thinks it is possible to leave aside the questions that theology has historically addressed in the context of reading a passage like Romans 5:12–21. But, unless one stays within the guild of biblical scholars who are primarily interested in what Paul expresses in his retelling of the narrative he inherited from his Jewish past, it does not seem that his handling of the text goes far enough. Christian theology, at least in its usual historical practice, asks questions that move from the text to its implications for an articulate and coherent statement of Christian teaching. A passage like Romans 5:12–21 naturally prompts a treatment of a variety of topics that express, in a categorical and universal form, what is to be believed by all regarding such themes as the creation of Adam and Eve in God's image; the obligations of the creature to serve the Creator in accord with the norms of God's righteous law; the universal sway of sin and death on account of the one act of Adam; the inability of the law of Moses, which in its peculiar historical form reiterated the righteous obligations of God's image-bearers to their Creator and Redeemer, to provide for the justification and life of its recipients; the obedience of Christ, the second Adam, that is the sole basis for the justification of believers to whom it is granted as a free gift, etc. The limitations and inadequacies of Wright's interpretation of Romans 5:12–21 are the direct result of deficiencies in his theological method, particularly the relation between biblical and systematic theology.[59]

59. For two helpful discussions of the relation between biblical and systematic theology, one an older, the other a more recent contribution, see D. A. Carson, "Unity and Diversity in the New Testament: The Possibility of Systematic Theology," in *Scripture and Truth*, ed. D. A. Carson and John D. Woodbridge (Grand Rapids, MI: Zondervan, 1983), 65–95; and David VanDrunen, "A System of Theology? The Centrality of Covenant for Westminster Systematics," in *The Pattern of Sound Doctrine: Systematic Theology at the Westminster Seminaries*, ed. David VanDrunen (Phillipsburg, NJ: P&R Publishing, 2004), 195–220.

Conclusion

In my treatment of Wright's interpretation of Romans 5:12–21, particularly in terms of its significance for the way he understands Paul's doctrine of justification, I have argued that Wright's view is considerably at odds with traditional Reformed theology. Though I have not attempted anything like a comprehensive study of Wright's contribution to the new perspectives on Paul, I have noted that Romans 5:12–21 constitutes an important testimony to his approach and theological method.

Wright's claims regarding Romans 5:12–21 and its relationship to the doctrine of justification do less justice to this passage than the traditional view. Though Wright wants to view the "righteousness of God" in Paul's epistle to the Romans as God's covenant faithfulness, he neglects to give proper due to the specific manner in which Paul emphasizes God's just vindication of his holy law. The righteousness of God that is revealed in the gospel includes the elements of God's maintenance of the law's requirements for all human beings and the consequence of condemnation and death upon all who have transgressed the law of God in Adam. The most disappointing feature of Wright's treatment of Romans 5:12–21 is his failure to do justice to the force of Paul's comparison between Adam and Christ as the respective covenant heads of two distinct humanities, the old and the new. I have argued that the older, Reformation tradition of exegesis not only properly insists upon the full historical character of the trespass of the one man, Adam, in which all human beings participate by virtue of God's ordinance, but also offers a more exegetically credible account of the judicial implications of Adam's disobedience for the imputation of guilt to his posterity.

Similarly, the older view, which has usually been articulated in terms of a doctrine of a prelapsarian covenant of works and a postlapsarian covenant of grace, better accounts for the way Paul understands the connection between Christ's obedience and the way believers are constituted righteous and become heirs of life in communion with God. Contrary to Wright's redefinition of justification as identity language, which declares Jews and Gentiles alike to be members of God's covenant people, Paul assumes an understanding of justification that explains how otherwise guilty human beings can be restored to right standing before God. In this connection, Paul, though he does not expressly use the language of "imputation" in this passage, teaches clearly that believers are granted the free gift of righteousness in Christ in order that they may rightly be received into favor with God. Romans 5:12–21 provides an obvious testimony to the Reformed view of justification as a soteriological as well as an ecclesiological theme in Paul's writings. It also confirms the theological appropriateness, even necessity, of the idea of imputation. Adam's sin is attributed or imputed to his posterity, just as Christ's obedience is attributed or imputed to believers. Imputation is not a kind of theological addendum to Paul's argument in Romans 5:12–21, but a necessary implication of the basic argument of this passage.

Before contemporary Reformed theologians embrace Wright's doctrine of justification over the view articulated in the confessions of the Reformed churches, they need to evaluate critically his exegetical and theological method, which is illustrated by his handling of a passage like Romans 5:12–21. More is at stake than simply the exegesis of this passage and others. Wright's interpretation of this passage reflects as much his theological methodology as it does the straightforward findings of exegesis. This theological method is one that proscribes the kinds of theological questions that inevitably arise out of a consideration of a passage like Romans 5:12–21.

Conclusion

In the preface to the essays in this volume, I noted that they were written to address several recurring issues in Reformed covenant theology. Some of these issues are contemporary expressions of older debates in the history of Reformed theology. Others represent newer debates and controversies in the articulation of the doctrine of the covenant. As I have observed throughout this volume, in recent history a number of theologians have sought to revise aspects of the doctrine of the covenant in order to achieve a better understanding of the way the triune God grants and administers his gracious purpose to enjoy covenant fellowship with human beings. Whether in the context of the prefall covenant of works or the postfall covenant of grace, the doctrine of the covenant provides a comprehensive and synthetic account of how the divine-human relationship is effected throughout history, from the original relationship in Adam in the state of integrity until the restored relationship in Christ in the consummation of God's redemptive purposes. Covenant doctrine has served Reformed theology as a biblical-theological account of the nature of God's communion with the human race in creation and in redemption. Despite Reformed unanimity on the central importance of the covenants to God's purposes in redeeming a people for himself through Christ, and enjoying unbreakable communion with them, a cluster of issues have surfaced in recent discussion that require careful reflection upon and formulation of the nature of the biblical covenants.

Though I do not wish to rehearse again many of the arguments of the diverse chapters that comprise this volume, I believe it will be helpful to offer a synthetic account of the conclusions with respect to several issues that have been the focus of controversy in the recent history of Reformed theology, especially in the North American context. Consequently, a brief synopsis of the main themes of these essays will serve to provide a synthesis of the book.

In the following summary, I will follow the sequence of issues identified in the preface. Since the arguments for these conclusions are given in the essays themselves, my summary will not repeat those. Rather, I will simply restate as briefly as possible the way these essays contribute to a resolution of the more important issues in recent discussion.

The Covenant of Works

Perhaps the most pressing issue in contemporary discussion concerns the legitimacy of speaking of the prefall relationship between God and the human race in Adam as a covenant relationship, and one that may be properly denominated a "covenant of works." Due to the foundational significance of the theological understanding of the prefall covenant, the features of this covenant have far-reaching significance for an understanding of the postfall covenant, and particularly the work of Christ as Mediator of the covenant of grace. Consequently, in the history of Reformed theology, the doctrine of the prefall covenant of works ultimately served to illumine particular aspects of Christ's work as Redeemer in the covenant of grace.

While it is always possible to quibble over terminology, I believe it is biblically and theologically appropriate to speak of the prefall relationship between the triune God and the human race in Adam as a "covenant of works." Several arguments cumulatively support the language of "covenant" to describe this relationship: (1) the use of the covenant name of God in the Genesis account of God's relationship with the human race in Adam; (2) a number of elements that belong to a covenant relationship in the biblical presentation of the fellowship between God and the human race in Adam—e.g., the special providence of God described in Genesis 2, which includes a divinely revealed stipulation of obedience that tests Adam's devotion to God and obedience to his holy law; the explicit sanction of eternal death and separation from God that would follow upon Adam's failure to obey the stipulated obedience; the implicit promise of eternal life in the event of Adam's continued obedience to God's revealed will; (3) the parallels in language descriptive of the prefall relationship between God and the human race in Adam and the postfall relationship between God as Redeemer and his people in Christ; (4) and the apparent allusion in Hosea 6:7 to the parallel between the covenant disobedience of Adam before the fall and the covenant disobedience of Israel after the fall.

In addition to all these indicators of a covenant relationship in the prefall state, the formulation of the covenant of works in Reformed history stemmed from theological convictions first expressed by the biblical doctrine of the covenant of grace. Since the work of Christ as the last Adam redresses the consequences of the first Adam's sin, and since this work secures the promise of eternal life that was first extended to Adam (and the human race in him) before the fall, it seems most appropriate that covenant terminology, describing the way God initiates and regulates the communion he desires to enjoy with his people, be employed to describe the prefall circumstance. For these reasons, it is quite appropriate that Reformed theology employs the biblical language of "covenant" to describe this relationship, despite the fact that the express terminology of covenant is not used in the biblical account of God's special providence in the initiation and administration of his fellowship with his image-bearers before the fall. To use the Latin expression, *De vocabulo dubitetur, re salva* ("the word may be in doubt, but the matter is certain"), there is ample biblical and theological warrant for denominating the prefall relationship between God and the human race in Adam as a covenant relationship.

Admittedly, in the history of Reformed theology, a variety of expressions have been employed to describe the prefall relationship. The prefall covenant is most frequently termed a "covenant of works," but it has also been termed a "covenant of nature" to express the truth that human beings as creatures were first created for a communion of life with the living God. Sometimes it has been called a "covenant of life" to highlight the promised inheritance of life in indefectible relationship with God that would ensue from the fruition of the covenant relationship. It has also been termed a "covenant of favor" to emphasize God's sovereign and undeserved initiative in granting the human race in Adam the privilege of life in communion with himself. All these expressions express different aspects of the prefall covenant relationship, and are needed to capture the fullness of the covenant relationship. However, the most common designation of this relationship as a "covenant of works" emphasizes one of its most integral and distinctive features: the promise of an unbroken communion of life in fellowship with God demands that the human race in Adam offer God a personal and perfect obedience to his holy law. What distinguishes the prefall covenant of works from the postfall covenant of grace is the stipulated condition of perfect obedience to God's law on Adam's part, aside from which the life promised in the covenant would neither be retained nor advanced to a perfected fullness of eternal life. The prefall covenant relationship involved elements of a "voluntary condescension" on God's part, the stipulation of perfect obedience that was tested by a divinely instituted probationary command, the promise of eternal life that was sacramentally signified by the "tree of life" (cf. Gen. 3:24), and the sanction of eternal death in Adam's disobedience to the revealed will of his covenant Lord. But the central point of emphasis in the biblical depiction of this covenant is an obligation of obedience as the indispensable requirement for the realization of perfected communion with God in the state of glory.

Grace and Merit in the Covenants

Throughout the history of Reformed theology, a recurring issue in the doctrine of the covenants of works and of grace focuses upon the legitimacy of the language of "merit" in the divine-human relationship that the covenant articulates. Since the covenant of works required personal and perfect obedience on the part of the human race in Adam, the nature of the connection between Adam's obligatory obedience and the promised reward of eternal life has provoked vigorous controversy. Does the prefall covenant relationship imply that Adam would have "deserved" the inheritance of eternal life, were he to meet the condition of personal and perfect obedience? Or does the divine initiative and undeserved favor that undergirds the covenant relationship before the fall militate against the language of merit in any description of the prefall communion between God and the human race in Adam? In recent discussions of the covenant of works, some Reformed theologians have followed the lead of John Murray and emphasized the "elements of grace" in the prefall covenant of works, shying away from formulations that speak of any "merit" on Adam's part in securing the promised inheritance of eternal life. On the other end of the spectrum of opinion, Meredith Kline and theologians who follow his lead have insisted that Adam's obedience to the demands of God's law in the prefall covenant of works would properly merit this reward in accordance with strict justice.

According to Kline and Reformed theologians influenced by him, the covenant of works enunciates a strict works-inheritance principle in which Adam's obedience would justly secure his covenant inheritance. Any failure to formulate the doctrine of the covenant of works in its alleged works-inheritance principle creates difficulties for a proper understanding of Christ's work in the covenant of grace. Since Christ's work involves a substitutionary obedience and satisfaction of all requirements of the law of God, first disclosed through the administration of the covenant of works, Reformed theology has properly insisted upon the "meritorious" nature of Christ's obedience. In order to secure the promise of eternal life and favor with God, Christ's "entire obedience" under the law, his active fulfillment of the law's precepts, and his passive endurance of the law's penalties, justly secures the title of eternal life in covenant with God for the elect who are beneficiaries of this saving work. For Reformed theologians influenced by Kline, it is even necessary to insist upon the republication in some sense of the covenant of works during the Mosaic economy in order to provide a solid basis for the articulation of Christ's saving and meritorious obedience in the covenant of grace.

Throughout the essays in this volume, I have argued that the topic of the meritoriousness of Adam's obedience in the prefall covenant of works has been inadequately treated in the formulations of some recent Reformed theologians. Although John Murray properly emphasizes the gracious or undeserved elements in the prefall covenant of works, he tends to overlook the careful way in which the best Reformed theologians of the orthodox period spoke of "merit" in the prefall covenant. Francis Turretin, who offers one of the most helpful formulations of the nature of Adam's stipulated works of obedience, notes that Adam's obedience would not have "merited" the reward of eternal life in the "proper" sense of this language. In what Turretin terms its "proper" use, the language of "merit" describes *the strict proportion or commensurateness* that obtains between a work performed and the reward granted for its performance. Therefore, Turretin argues that in this proper sense of the term, no true merit obtains in the relation between the work Adam was obliged to perform and the reward that he was promised for its performance. Rather, in the "voluntary condescension" of the covenant of works, God granted to the human race in Adam a promised reward that was disproportionate with the obedience required. According to Turretin, had Adam obeyed God perfectly, his obedience would have been nothing more that the legitimate fruit of a right use of God's free bestowal of the original righteousness with which he was furnished. As a mere creature, Adam's perfect obedience would constitute him no more than "an unworthy servant." Such obedience would never have constituted, according to the principle of strict justice (granting what is due, and nothing more), the basis for a reward that consisted in the promise of glorified and perfected life in unbreakable communion with God. And yet, in the covenant of works God freely promised Adam the reward of *eternal, glorified* life in unbreakable communion with himself.

Consequently, when I defend the qualified use of "merit" in the prefall covenant of works, I do so in the sense of an "improper" merit that is in virtue of God's covenant promise. Because God freely promised to grant Adam eternal life for an obedience he was obliged to render to God as a creature, he joined Adam's obedience to a reward graciously, because undeservedly, promised. Following Turretin and others in the history of Reformed theology, I believe it is permissible to speak of a sort of "covenanted merit" (*meritum ex pacto*) in the precise sense in which God joined Adam's obedience to the promise of eternal life. Within the terms of the covenant God initiated by an act of voluntary condescension, it would accord with the covenanted justice of God to grant Adam the reward of eternal life upon the condition of his perfect and personal obedience. From the perspective of this understanding of the connection between Adam's obedience and the promised reward of eternal life, it is possible to affirm both the elements of God's undeserved favor and covenanted justice in the prefall covenant of works. On the one hand, the covenant of works was freely and undeservedly granted to the human race in Adam by virtue of God's voluntary condescension. And on the other hand, the covenant of works stipulated and tested Adam in respect to his obedience to the holy law of God. Only in the way of Adam's personal and perfect obedience would the promised reward of eternal life be justly granted to him by virtue of the covenant's stipulation and promise.

While the obedience of Adam in the covenant of works could be said to "merit" the reward of eternal life in an improper sense, it must be observed that the obedience of Christ as Mediator of the covenant of grace *properly merits* the gift of eternal life. Due to the unique identity of the Mediator of the covenant of grace, it is not possible to infer from the strict sense in which Christ's obedience secured the inheritance of eternal life for his people to the conclusion that Adam's obedience, were it perfect and personal, would be meritorious in the same way. Whereas Adam's obedience as a mere creature could never strictly merit the reward of eternal life, the obedience of Christ, as the incarnate Son of God, was a just basis for his procuring the gift of eternal life for his own. However, even in the case of the merits of Jesus Christ, who discharged all the obligations of the law on behalf of his elect people, the surpassing greatness of God's grace is manifest in his willingness to provide such a Mediator to accomplish the redemption of the people whom he is pleased to give to him. Thus, in the redemptive work of Christ as Mediator of the covenant of grace, both the free grace and the exact justice of God are upheld.

Covenant and Election, Distinct Yet Inseparable

Contrary to the claim of some interpreters of Reformed theology, the doctrines of the covenant and of election are not two disparate ways of summarizing what is central to the Scripture's teaching regarding God's purposes of redemption. Neither the doctrine of the covenant nor the doctrine of election serves Reformed theology as an abstract principle from which all of its subordinate parts are derived. The formulation of covenant doctrine in the Reformed tradition does not represent a deliberate attempt to soften the sharp edges of the doctrine of election, or to give Reformed theology a greater sensitivity to the exercise of human responsibility in the relationship between God and his people.

In the history of Reformed theology, the doctrines of election and covenant, each in their own way, disclose the nature and manner of the triune God's sovereign purposes of redemption in Christ. Whereas the doctrine of election emphasizes the sheer graciousness of God's unconditional choice to grant salvation to his elect people in and on account of the work of Christ, the doctrine of the covenant emphasizes the manner in which the triune God chooses to realize this electing purpose. While election manifests God's purpose to save his beloved people in Christ, covenant manifests his intention to do so by means of the mutual operations of the Father, the Son, and the Holy Spirit. In the covenant of redemption, each of the persons of the Trinity acts in a mode corresponding to his incommunicable property and in a fashion exhibiting perfect harmony of divine will and purpose. In this way, the doctrines of election and covenant exalt God's sovereign initiative and appointed means for the accomplishment of his saving purposes on behalf of his people. When Reformed theology roots the historical administration of the covenant of grace in an eternal "covenant of redemption," it confirms the intimate relation between election and covenant as *corollary* ways of articulating the doctrine of salvation. The administration of the covenant of grace in all its diversity throughout redemption's history—from the time of its first pronouncement in the mother promise of Genesis 3:15 until the coming of Christ in the fullness of time and the subsequent outpouring of the Holy Spirit at Pentecost—represents nothing less than the fulfillment in time of God's covenant of redemption. From that vantage point, the covenant of grace is the divinely appointed instrument whereby the triune God saves his elect people.

While it is true that the doctrine of the covenant accents the mutuality of the relationship between God and his people in the course of redemptive history, Reformed theology at its best always insists that the requirements of the covenant are only realized in the elect by the working of Christ's Spirit. Viewed from the perspective of election, the so-called "conditions" of the covenant of grace, faith and repentance, are sovereignly granted to believers in a way that accords with God's sovereign counsel. Though faith and repentance are worked by the Spirit of Christ through the ordinary means of administering the covenant of grace, preaching and sacraments, they are genuine graces God grants only to his elect people. For this reason, it is not permissible to simply identify God's purpose of election with the historical administration of the covenant of grace in time, as is attempted by advocates of the "Federal Vision." The circle of the covenant in its historical expression does not exactly coincide—at least not on this side of the consummation of history—with the circle of election. When this distinction between covenant and election is respected, the danger of an objectivism that prematurely identifies the covenant community with God's sovereign purpose of election can be avoided. At the same time, when the covenant in its historical administration is viewed in close association with the manner in which God realizes his electing purpose—though election and covenant do not coincide, they do overlap considerably—it is possible to avoid the danger of emptying the covenant of its significance as the divinely appointed instrument to accomplish God's electing purpose. The doctrines of covenant and election are distinct, yet inseparable, as corollary ways of describing God's great work of redemption.

The Stability of the Law as a Perpetual Rule of Righteousness

Several disputed issues in the formulation of the doctrine of the covenant in the Reformed tradition can be expressed in terms of the way the holy law of God functions in the administration of the covenants of works and of grace. The issue of the permissibility and usefulness of the language of "merit" in the covenant of works, for example, stems from the fact that the law of God functions differently in the prefall covenant of works than in the postfall covenant of grace. When God attached the promise of eternal life to the requirement of personal and perfect obedience in the prefall covenant of works, he gave the law a particular function that did not belong to it intrinsically. In the covenant of works, God condescended to human beings in Adam and promised eternal life upon condition of perfect and personal obedience to the law's requirements. Detached from its divinely appointed function in the covenant of works, however, God's holy law consists simply of the disclosure of God's will for the moral conduct of his image-bearers. To use the language of chapter 19 in the WCF, the law is a "perfect rule of righteousness" that—however variously it be revealed or function at different times and places throughout the course of history—reveals the duty of human beings toward God and neighbor. Because the law of God expresses God's essential attributes of holiness and righteousness, it can only reveal the perfect standard of righteousness that ought to govern the conduct of any moral creature, whether redeemed or unredeemed.[1] Whether in the state of integrity, the state of fallenness, or the state of redemption, the law ever reveals the form of conduct that pleases God and answers to his holiness. The law of God by itself can only make known what behavior pleases the holy Creator of all things and Redeemer of his people in Christ. But the law can never give human beings the capacity or will to do what it requires.

Though God's law remains a perpetual rule of righteousness, it functions differently in the covenant of grace than in the covenant of works. Consistent with God's redemptive purpose, the law of God subserves the gospel within the divine intention by fulfilling three distinct functions, each of which is in keeping with the nature of the

1. WCF 19: "This law, after his [Adam's] fall, continued to be a perfect rule of righteousness; and, as such, was delivered by God upon Mount Sinai, in ten commandments, and written in two tables; the four first commandments containing our duty towards God; and the other six, our duty to man."

law. In Reformed theology historically, these three uses are ordinarily defined as: (1) a "theological use" in which the law condemns all fallen sinners as lawbreakers, worthy of condemnation that brings death; (2) a "civil use," in which the law constrains outwardly the sinful conduct of human beings, particularly through the civil magistrate's wielding of the power of the sword; and (3) a "normative use," in which the law discloses the moral will of God for the grateful obedience of his redeemed people. It is particularly important to observe that these three uses are consistent with the redemptive intention of the covenant of grace, and are present throughout the entire history of the covenant of grace in all of its diverse administrations. The law subserves the gospel of Jesus Christ in each of its distinct uses.

While some authors have argued recently that the Mosaic economy within the administration of the covenant of grace was a republication in some sense of the covenant of works, this view does not comport with the traditional three uses of the law. Though the "theological use" of the law within the covenant of grace includes the revelation of what the law required in the prefall covenant of works, it does not include the reinstitution of a relationship between God and his redeemed people which promises (even temporal) life upon condition of personal and perfect obedience. While it is true that the law in its pedagogical use requires perfect obedience (the law never requires less, however it functions), it was not given throughout the course of redemptive history to place the people of God in a position analogous to that of the human race in Adam before the fall. Rather, the law was given to remind God's people that they are sinners worthy of condemnation and death, who can only hope to be restored to favor with God upon the basis of the perfect obedience by the Mediator, Jesus Christ. Furthermore, though believers are not justified by works of obedience, they are obliged to obey God's law as a "rule of gratitude." So far as the believer's justification before God is concerned, the law is powerless to secure eternal life. But so far as the believer's new life in Christ is concerned, the law reveals the kind of life that pleases God. In respect to justification, the law and gospel are antithetical. But in respect to sanctification, the law belongs to the gospel as it is enlivened by the Spirit who sanctifies believers in the way of obedience.

Renewed Obedience to the Law: A Covenant Grace

In recent treatments of the doctrine of the covenants of works and of grace, the primary interest of many theologians has been upon the implications of the covenant for justification. Because the covenant of works emphasizes the obligation of obedience to the law of God, it reminds believers of the importance of Christ's work of obedience as the last Adam "under" the obligations of the law (Rom. 5:12–21; Gal. 4:4–5). For believers to be restored to favor and right standing with God, they require a Mediator who assumes all their obligations under the law, both preceptive and penal, to be justified. The entire obedience of Christ, which includes his passive endurance of the law's penalty and his active fulfillment of the law's requirements, constitutes the righteousness imputed to believers. By virtue of obedience and satisfaction, Christ merited the gift of justification and eternal life for his people, and thereby redressed the demerit of Adam's (and their own) sin. The doctrine of the covenant of works provides the biblical framework for a proper understanding of the work of Christ, especially as it relates to the foremost benefit of the gospel, free justification before God. In the covenant of grace, Christ obtains the inheritance of life for his people in a manner that simultaneously magnifies the surpassing richness of God's mercy and his exact justice. In the work of Christ for his people, God demonstrates his love and reveals himself to be both just and the one who justifies (Rom. 3:26). The truth first revealed in the covenant of works—that fellowship with God requires perfect obedience on the part of his covenant people—is upheld in the covenant of grace.

While this emphasis upon the obedience and sacrifice of Christ, which is the only basis for forgiveness and acceptance with God, is a key note of the gospel, it is important to highlight that the law of God is affirmed in the covenant of grace in a further fashion. God not only upholds his own law in the obedience and sacrifice of Christ for his people, but he also upholds his law through the work of Christ's

Spirit, who writes the law upon the hearts of his redeemed people and begins to renew them in the way of obedience to the law's obligations (Heb. 10:16). It must always be remembered that in the covenant of grace Christ's redeeming work includes not only the grace of free justification but also the grace of repentance and renewal after the image of Christ. The obligations of the covenant of grace include a believing and empty-handed (apart from works, Rom. 3:28) reception of the promise of acceptance with God upon the basis of the merits of Christ alone, to be sure. But the obligations of the covenant of grace also include a penitent turning from sin and to the service of the living God, who continues to declare what pleases him in his holy law. In the covenant of grace, Christ, the last Adam, discharges all the law's obligations on behalf of his people to secure their inheritance of eternal life. But the destiny of the new humanity in Christ includes, in addition to the grace of free justification or acceptance with God, the grace of sanctification in renewed obedience to the law of God. This too belongs to the gracious work of Christ as Mediator of the covenant of grace. As Calvin often noted, when discussing the inseparable connection between the graces of justification and sanctification through Christ, Paul speaks of Christ as having been given to us for "righteousness and sanctification" (1 Cor. 1:30).

Christ and Covenant Theology

The title of this book, *Christ and Covenant Theology*, deliberately places special emphasis upon the person and work of Christ in the formulation of the doctrine of the covenant of works and the covenant of grace. When Reformed theology seeks to articulate the doctrine of the covenants upon the basis of biblical teaching, it does so in order to magnify the person and work of Christ in the realization of God's purpose for human life in fellowship with himself.

Contrary to the oft-repeated claim that the doctrine of the covenant of works serves to mischaracterize the covenant between God and his people as a species of legalism, thereby corrupting the fundamentally gracious character of the divine-human relationship, the covenant of works ultimately testifies to God's grace in Christ.

Even though the covenant of works precedes the covenant of grace in history—the history of redemption is typically represented in an "infralapsarian" fashion, grace perfecting nature and redressing the consequences of the fall in Adam—it ultimately reveals the truth that the destiny of human life in fellowship with God can ever be obtained only through Christ. When the apostle Paul contrasts Adam and Christ in Romans 5:12–21 and 1 Corinthians 15:42–49, he contrasts the first, earthly head of the human race with the last, heavenly head. While Adam stands at the beginning of the history of God's fellowship with the human race, Christ stands at the end. In the person and work of Christ, the divinely intended destiny of the human race in unbreakable communion with God is finally accomplished. The realization of that destiny in Christ brings the ultimate blessedness of the state of glorified human life that could not be accomplished through the work of the first Adam, who was a "type" of the one to come. Christ alone brings the new humanity into life-communion with God, world without end, in a manner that fulfills every obligation of the law for and in the elect people whom he justifies and sanctifies through and through.

To use the language of the apostle John in the book of Revelation, Christ is the Alpha and the Omega, the origin and the end of God's loving and gracious purpose to dwell in everlasting communion with his covenant people. The covenant relationship with Adam, which was only a provisional and temporary beginning, has now become reality through the work of Christ in whom all the promises of God have their Amen. In and through Christ, believers now enjoy the beginning of the blessedness first promised to the human race in Adam, but obtained only through the work of the One greater than Adam. While the story of redemption recounted in Scripture is infralapsarian in form, since the state of integrity precedes the fall and the subsequent work of redemption—this story is in a profound sense supralapsarian. From the beginning, that is, from the perspective of God's ultimate redemptive purpose within his eternal counsel, the blessedness of human life in communion with God was always to be realized in and through Christ. All the ways of God find their beginning and their fulfillment in the person and work of Christ, and this is most powerfully testified through the history of the covenants.

Nowhere in Scripture is the truth of Christ and the covenants more beautifully celebrated than in Revelation 22:1–5, which portrays the consummation in language echoing the promise first announced to Adam in paradise:

> Then the angel showed me the river of the water of life, bright as crystal, flowing from the throne of God and of the Lamb through the middle of the street of the city; also, on either side of the river, the tree of life with its twelve kinds of fruit, yielding its fruit each month. The leaves of the tree were for the healing of the nations. No longer will there be anything accursed, but the throne of God and of the Lamb will be in it, and his servants will worship him. They will see his face, and his name will be on their foreheads. And night will be no more. They will need no light of lamp or sun, for the Lord God will be their light, and they will reign forever and ever.

Select Bibliography

à Brakel, Wilhelmus. *The Christian's Reasonable Service*. 4 vols. Edited by Joel R. Beeke. Translated by Bartel Elshout. Grand Rapids, MI: Reformation Heritage, 1992.

Acta of Handelingen der Nationale Synode. Edited by J. H. Donner and S. A. van den Hoorn. Leiden: J. H. Donner, n.d.

Acts of Synod London 2010: Seventh Synod of the United Reformed Churches in North America, July 26–30, 2010. London, ON: Cornerstone United Reformed Church, 2010.

"A Joint Federal Vision Statement." http://www.federal-vision.com/.

Aquinas, Thomas. *Summa Theologiae*. Rev. ed. 5 vols. 1920. Reprint, Allen, TX: Christian Classics, 1981.

Baker, J. Wayne. *Heinrich Bullinger and the Covenant: The Other Reformed Tradition*. Athens, OH: Ohio University Press, 1980.

Bakhuizen van den Brink, J. N. *De Nederlandse Belijdenisgeschriften*. 2nd ed. Amsterdam: Bolland, 1976.

Ball, John. *A Treatise on the Covenant of Grace*. London, 1645.

Barach, John. "Baptism and Election." Lecture, Auburn Avenue Presbyterian Church Pastor's Conference, 2002.

———. "Covenant and Election." Lecture, Auburn Avenue Presbyterian Church Pastor's Conference, 2002.

———. "Covenant and History." Lecture, Auburn Avenue Presbyterian Church Pastor's Conference, 2002.

Barth, Karl. *The Doctrine of Creation*. Vol. 3.1 of *Church Dogmatics*. Edinburgh: T. & T. Clark, 1958.

———. *The Doctrine of God*. Vol. 2.1 of *Church Dogmatics*. Edinburgh: T. & T. Clark, 1957.

Bavinck, Herman. *Our Reasonable Faith: A Survey of Christian Doctrine*.

Translated by Henry Zylstra. 1960. Reprint, Grand Rapids, MI: Baker, 1977.

———. *Reformed Dogmatics.* Edited by John Bolt. Translated by John Vriend. 4 vols. Grand Rapids, MI: Baker Academic, 2003, 2004, 2006, 2008.

———. *Roeping en Wedergeboorte.* Kampen: Ph. Zalsman, 1903.

———. *Saved by Grace: The Holy Spirit's Work in Calling and Regeneration.* Edited by J. Mark Beach. Translated by Nelson D. Kloosterman. Grand Rapids, MI: Reformation Heritage, 2008.

Beach, J. Mark. "Abraham Kuyper, Herman Bavinck, and 'The Conclusions of Utrecht 1905.'" *MAJT* 19 (2008): 11–68.

———. *Christ and the Covenant: Francis Turretin's Federal Theology as a Defense of the Doctrine of Grace.* Göttingen: Vandenhoeck & Ruprecht, 2007.

———. "The Doctrine of the *Pactum Salutis* in the Covenant Theology of Herman Witsius." *MAJT* 13 (2002): 101–42.

———. "Introductory Essay." In *Saved by Grace: The Holy Spirit's Work in Calling and Regeneration,* by Herman Bavinck, ix–lvi. Edited by J. Mark Beach. Translated by Nelson D. Kloosterman. Grand Rapids, MI: Reformation Heritage, 2008.

Beeke, J. R. "Children Dying in Infancy: Young People Ask (9)." *Banner of Truth,* 54, 1 (1988): 22–23.

Beisner, E. Calvin, ed. *The Auburn Avenue Theology: Pros & Cons: Debating the Federal Vision. The Knox Theological Seminary Colloquium on the Federal Vision, August 11–13, 2003.* Ft. Lauderdale, FL: Knox Theological Seminary, 2004.

Berkhof, L. *Systematic Theology.* 4th ed. Grand Rapids, MI: Eerdmans, 1939, 1941.

Berkouwer, G. C. *Divine Election.* Translated by Hugo Bekker. Studies in Dogmatics. Grand Rapids, MI: Eerdmans, 1960.

———. *Sin.* Translated by Philip C. Holtrop. Studies in Dogmatics. Grand Rapids, MI: Eerdmans, 1971.

Bierma, Lyle D. "Covenant or Covenants in the Theology of Olevianus." *CTJ* 22, 2 (1987): 228–50.

———. *The Covenant Theology of Caspar Olevianus.* Grand Rapids, MI: Baker, 1996.

———. "Federal Theology in the Sixteenth Century: Two Traditions?" *WTJ* 45, 2 (1983): 304–21.

———. "The Role of Covenant Theology in Early Reformed Orthodoxy." *Sixteenth Century Journal* 21, 3 (1990): 453–62

Beirma, Lyle D., with Charles D. Gunnoe Jr., Karin Maag, and Paul W. Fields. *An Introduction to the Heidelberg Catechism: Sources, History, and Theology*. Grand Rapids, MI: Baker Academic, 2005.

Bird, Michael F. "Incorporated Righteousness: A Response to Recent Evangelical Discussion concerning the Imputation of Christ's Righteousness in Justification." *JETS* 47, 2 (2004): 253–75.

Bos, T. *De Dordtsche Leerregelen*. Kampen: J. H. Kok, 1915.

Bremmer, R. H. *Herman Bavinck als Dogmaticus*. Kampen: J. H. Kok, 1961.

Brown, Michael. *Christ and the Condition: The Covenant Theology of Samuel Petto (1624–1711)*. Grand Rapids, MI: Reformation Heritage, 2012.

Buchanan, James. *The Doctrine of Justification*. 1867. Reprint, Edinburgh: Banner of Truth, 1997.

———. *The Doctrine of Justification*. 1867. Reprint, Grand Rapids, MI: Baker, 1959.

Bullinger, Heinrich. *The Decades of Heinrich Bullinger*. 1849–52. Lithographic reprint of 4 volumes in 2. Grand Rapids, MI: Reformation Heritage, 2004.

Calvin, John. *Calvin's New Testament Commentaries*. Edited by David W. Torrance and Thomas F. Torrance. 12 vols. Grand Rapids, MI: Eerdmans, 1960.

———. "Canons and Decrees of the Council of Trent, with the Antidote." In *Selected Works of John Calvin: Tracts and Letters*, edited by Henry Beveridge and Jules Bonnet, 3:17–188. 7 vols. 1851. Reprint, Grand Rapids, MI: Baker, 1983.

———. *Commentaries on the Four Last Books of Moses Arranged in the Form of a Harmony*. Grand Rapids, MI: Baker, 1979.

———. *Ioannis Calvini opera quae supersunt omnia*. Edited by G. Baum, E. Cunitz, E. Reuss, et al. 59 vols. *Corpus Reformatorum*. Brunsvigae, Ger.: Schwetschke, 1862–1900.

———. *Institutes of the Christian Religion*. Edited by John T. McNeill. Translated by Ford Lewis Battles. 2 vols. Library of Christian Classics. Philadelphia: Westminster, 1960.

———. *Opera Selecta*. Edited by P. Barth and G. Niesel. 5 vols. Munchen: Kaiser, 1926–52.

———. *Sermons on Melchizedek & Abraham*. Willow Street, PA: Old Paths Publications, 2000.

Carson, D. A. "Atonement in Romans 3:21–26." In *The Glory of the Atonement: Biblical, Historical & Practical Perspectives*, edited by Charles E. Hill and Frank A. James III, 119–39. Downers Grove, IL: InterVarsity, 2004.

———. "Unity and Diversity in the New Testament: The Possibility of Systematic Theology." In *Scripture and Truth*, edited by D. A. Carson and John D. Woodbridge, 65–95. Grand Rapids, MI: Zondervan, 1983.

———. "The Vindication of Imputation: On Fields of Discourse and Semantic Fields." In *Justification: What's at Stake in the Current Debates?*, edited by Mark Husbands and Daniel J. Treier, 46–78. Downers Grove, IL: IVP, 2004.

Carson, D. A., Peter T. O'Brien, and Mark A. Seifrid, eds. *Justification and Variegated Nomism*. 2 vols. Grand Rapids, MI: Baker Academic, 2001, 2004.

Clark, R. Scott., ed. *Covenant, Justification, and Pastoral Ministry: Essays by the Faculty of Westminster Seminary California*. Phillipsburg, NJ: P&R Publishing, 2007.

Clarkson, L. *Death, Disease and Famine in Pre-industrial England*. Dublin: Gil and MacMillan, 1975.

Cocceius, Johannes. *Summa Doctrinae de Foedere et Testamento Dei*. 1648.

———. *Summa Theologiae ex Scripturis repetita*. 1662.

Cranfield, C. E. B. *A Critical and Exegetical Commentary on the Epistle to the Romans*. International Critical Commentary. Edinburgh: T. & T. Clark, 1975.

Dabney, Robert L. *Systematic Theology*. 1871. Reprint, Edinburgh: Banner of Truth, 1985.

De Graaf, S. G. "De Genade Gods en de Structuur Der Gansche Schepping." *Philosophia Reformata* 1 (1936): 17–29.

———. *Het Ware Geloof.* Kampen: J. H. Kok, 1954.

de la Potterie, Ignace. "Le Chrétien conduit par l'Esprit dans son cheminement eschatologique (Rom. 8.14)." In *The Law of the Spirit in Rom 7 and 8*, edited by L. de Lorenzi, 209–41. Rome: St. Paul's Abbey, 1976.

den Boer, C. *Om 't Eeuwig Welbehagen*. Utrecht: De Banier, 1974.

Denlinger, Aaron. "Calvin's Understanding of Adam's Relationship to His Posterity: Recent Assertions of the Reformer's 'Federalism' Evaluated." *CTJ* 44, 2 (2009): 226–50.

Dijk, Klaas. *De Strijd over Infra- en Supralapsarisme in de Gereformeerde Kerken van Nederland*. Kampen: J. H. Kok, 1912.

Dunn, James D. G. *Romans 1–8*. Word Bible Commentary 38A. Dallas: Word, 1988.

———. *The Theology of Paul the Apostle*. Grand Rapids, MI: Eerdmans, 1998.

Ecumenical and Reformed Creeds and Confessions. Classroom Edition. Orange City, IA: Mid-America Reformed Seminary, 1991.

Elam, Andrew M., Robert C. Van Kooten and Randall A. Bergquist, *Merit and Moses: A Critique of the Klinean Doctrine of Republication*. Eugene, OR: Wipf & Stock, 2014.

Engelsma, David. "Response." *Standard Bearer*, February 15, 1991, 223–24.

Estelle, Bryan D., J. V. Fesko, and David VanDrunen, eds. *The Law Is Not of Faith: Essays on Works and Grace in the Mosaic Covenant*. Phillipsburg, NJ: P&R Publishing, 2009.

Evans, William B. "'Really Exhibited and Conferred . . . in His Appointed Time': Baptism and the New Reformed Sacramentalism." *Presbyterion* 31, 2 (2005): 72–88.

Faber, J. "American Secession Theologians on Covenant and Baptism," in Klaas Schilder, *Extra-Scriptural Binding: A New Danger*. Neerlandia, AB: Inheritance, 1996, 15–54.

Ferguson, Sinclair. *The Whole Christ: Legalism, Antinomianism, & Gospel Assurance—Why the Marrow Controversy Still Matters*. Wheaton, IL: Crossway, 2016.

Ferry, Brenton C. "Cross-Examining Moses's Defense: An Answer to Ramsey's Critique of Kline and Karlberg." *WTJ* 67, 1 (2005): 163–68.

Fesko, J. V. "The Accommodated Scriptures: A Response to Cornelis Venema." *Confessional Presbyterian* 9 (2013): 178–87.

———. "The Republication of the Covenant of Works." *Confessional Presbyterian* 8 (2012): 197–212.

F[isher], E[dward]. *The Marrow of Modern Divinity, with a Recommendatory Preface by James Hog*. 9th ed., corrected. 2 vols. Edinburgh: John Mosman and William Brown, 1718.

Fitzmyer, Joseph. A. "The Consecutive Meaning of ἐφ' ᾧ in Romans 5.12." *New Testament Studies* 39, 3 (1993): 321–39.

Francke, Joh. "Zijn de Kinderen der Gelovigen, die God in hun Kindsheid uit dit Leven Wegneemt, Wedergeboren?" *De Reformatie* 44, 42 (1969): 330–33.

Fuller, Daniel P. *Gospel and Law, Contrast or Continuum? The Hermeneutics of Dispensationalism and Covenant Theology*. Grand Rapids, MI: Eerdmans, 1980.

———. *The Unity of the Bible*. Grand Rapids, MI: Zondervan, 1992.

Gaffin, Richard B., Jr. *Resurrection and Redemption: A Study in Paul's Soteriology*. 2nd ed. Phillipsburg, NJ: Presbyterian and Reformed, 1987.

Garlington, Don. "Imputation or Union with Christ? A Response to John Piper." *R&R* 12, 4 (2003): 45–113.

Garrett, Duane. *Hosea, Joel*. New American Commentary 19A. Nashville: Broadman and Holman, 1997.

Godfrey, W. Robert. "Tensions within International Calvinism: The Debate on the Atonement at the Synod of Dort, 1618–1619." PhD diss., Stanford University, 1974.

Golding, Peter. *Covenant Theology: The Key of Theology in Reformed Thought and Tradition*. Fearn, Ross-shire: Christian Focus Publications, 2004.

Gootjes, N. H. "Can Parents Be Sure? Background and Meaning of Canons of Dort, I, 17." *Lux Mundi* 15, 4 (1996): 2–6.

———. "Christ's Obedience and Covenant Obedience." *Koinōnia* 19, 2 (2002): 2–22.

Greaves, Richard. "The Origins and Early Development of English Covenant Thought." *Historian* 31, 1 (1968), 21–35.

Griffith, Howard, and Muether, John R., eds. *Creator, Redeemer, Consummator: A Festschrift for Meredith G. Kline*. Greenville, SC: Reformed Academic Press, 2000.

Hall, Joseph H. "The Marrow Controversy: A Defense of Grace and the Free Offer of the Gospel." *MAJT* 10 (1999): 239–57.

Helm, Paul. "Calvin and the Covenant: Unity and Continuity." *Evangelical Quarterly* 55, 2 (1983): 65–81.

———. "Calvin, the 'Two Issues,' and the Structure of the *Institutes*." *CTJ* 42, 2 (2007): 341–48.

Hendriksen, William. *Exposition of Galatians*. Grand Rapids, MI: Baker, 1968.

Hodge, Charles. *Commentary on the Epistle to the Romans*. 1886. Reprint, Grand Rapids, MI: Eerdmans, 1950 .

———. *An Exposition of the Second Letter to the Corinthians*. 1872. Reprint, Grand Rapids, MI: Eerdmans, 1965.

———. *Systematic Theology*. Vol. 2. 1871. Reprint, Grand Rapids, MI: Eerdmans, 1952.

Hoekema, Anthony A. "Herman Bavinck's Doctrine of the Covenant." Th.D. diss., Princeton Theological Seminary, 1953.

Hoeksema, Herman. *Believers and Their Seed*. Translated by Homer Hoeksema. Grand Rapids, MI: Reformed Free Publishing, 1970.

———. *Reformed Dogmatics*. Grand Rapids, MI: Reformed Free Publishing, 1966.

Hoeksema, Homer. *The Voice of Our Fathers: An Exposition of the Canons of Dordrecht*. Grand Rapids, MI: Reformed Free Publishing, 1980.

Horton, Michael. *God of Promise: Introducing Covenant Theology*. Grand Rapids, MI: Baker, 2006.

Irons, Lee. "Redefining Merit: An Examination of Medieval Presuppositions in Covenant Theology." In *Creator, Redeemer, Consummator: A Festschrift for Meredith G. Kline*, edited by Howard Griffith and John R. Muether (Greenville, SC: Reformed Academic Press, 2000), 253–69.

Jeon, Jeong Koo. *Covenant Theology: John Murray's and Meredith G. Kline's Response to the Historical Development of Federal Theology in Reformed Thought*. Lanham, MD: University Press of America, 1999.

Justification: A Report from the Orthodox Presbyterian Church. Willow Grove, PA: Committee on Christian Education of the OPC, 2007.

Kaajan, H. *De Groote Synode van Dordrecht in 1618–1619*. Amsterdam: De Standaard, n.d.

Kamphuis, J. *An Everlasting Covenant*. Australia: Free Reformed Churches, 1985.

Karlberg, Mark W. *Covenant Theology in Reformed Perspective: Collected Essays and Book Reviews in Historical, Biblical, and Systematic Theology*. Eugene, OR: Wipf and Stock, 2000.

———. "The Mosaic Covenant and the Concept of Works in Reformed Hermeneutics: A Historical-Critical Analysis with Particular Attention to Early Covenant Eschatology." Th.D. diss., Westminster Theological Seminary, 1980.

———. "The Original State of Adam: Tensions in Reformed Theology." *Evangelical Quarterly* 59, 4 (1987): 291–309.

———. "Reformed Interpretation of the Mosaic Covenant." *WTJ* 43, 1 (1980), 1–57.

Keesmaat, Sylvia C. *Paul and His Story: (Re)Interpreting the Exodus Tradition*. Sheffield: Sheffield Academic, 1999.

Kevan, Ernest F. *The Grace of Law: A Study in Puritan Theology*. 1964. Reprint, Grand Rapids, MI: Baker, 1976.

Kline, Meredith G. *By Oath Consigned: A Reinterpretation of the Covenant Signs of Circumcision and Baptism*. Grand Rapids, MI: Eerdmans, 1968.

———. "Gospel until the Law: Rom 5:13–14 and the Old Covenant." *JETS* 34, 4 (1991): 433–46.

———. *Kingdom Prologue: Genesis Foundations for a Covenantal Worldview*. Eugene, OR: Wipf & Stock, 2006.

———. *Kingdom Prologue: Genesis Foundations for a Covenantal Worldview*. Overland Park, KS: Two Age Press, 2000.

Kuyper, Abraham. *E Voto Dordraceno: Toelichting op den Heidelbergschen Catechismus*. 4 vols. Amsterdam: J. A. Wormser, 1892–1895.

———. *E Voto Dordraceno: Toelichting op den Heidelbergschen Catechismus*. Vol. 3. Kampen: J. H. Kok, n.d.

Letham, Robert. "'Not a Covenant of Works in Disguise' (Herman Bavinck): The Place of the Mosaic Covenant in Redemptive History." *MAJT* 24 (2013): 143–77.

———. *The Westminster Assembly: Reading Its Theology in Historical Context*. Phillipsburg, NJ: P&R Publishing, 2009.

Lillback, Peter A. *The Binding of God: Calvin's Role in the Development of Covenant Theology*. Texts and Studies in Reformation & Post-Reformation Thought, edited by Richard A. Muller. Grand Rapids, MI: Baker Academic, 2001.

———. "Ursinus' Development of the Covenant of Creation: A Debt to Melanchthon or Calvin?" *WTJ* 43, 1 (1981): 247–88.

Lusk, Rich. "Baptismal Efficacy and Baptismal Latency: A Sacramental Dialogue." *Presbyterion* 32, 1 (2006): 18–37.

———. “Covenant and Election FAQs.” http://www.hornes.org/theologia/rich-lusk/covenant-election-faqs.

———. *Paedofaith: A Primer on the Mystery of Infant Salvation and a Handbook for Covenant Parents*. Monroe, LA: Athanasius, 2005.

———. “Some Thoughts on the Means of Grace: A Few Proposals.” http://www.hornes.org/theologia/rich-lusk/some-thoughts-on-the-means-of-grace.

Luther, Martin. *Lectures on Galatians, 1535: Chapters 1–4*. Vol. 26 of *Luther’s Works*. Edited by Jaroslav Pelikan and Helmut T. Lehmann. American ed. St. Louis: Concordia, 1963.

Machen, J. Gresham. *Machen’s Notes on Galatians*. Nutley, NJ: Presbyterian and Reformed, 1972.

Marcel, Pierre Ch. *The Biblical Doctrine of Infant Baptism*. Translated by Philip E. Hughes. London: James Clarke, 1953.

McGiffert, Michael. “From Moses to Adam: The Making of the Covenant of Works.” *Sixteenth Century Journal* 19, 2 (1988): 131–55.

McGraw, Ryan M. “Review of Michael Brown, *Christ and the Condition*.” MAJT 23 (2012): 152–55.

McIlhenny, Ryan C., ed. *Kingdoms Apart: Engaging the Two Kingdoms Perspective*. Phillipsburg, NJ: P&R Publishing, 2012.

Meijering, M. *De Dordtsche Leerregels*. Groningen: Jan Haan, 1924.

Mid-America Reformed Seminary Faculty and Board. *Doctrinal Testimony regarding Recent Errors*. Dyer, IN: Mid-America Reformed Seminary, 2007.

Moo, Douglas J. *The Epistle to the Romans*. NICNT. Grand Rapids, MI: Eerdmans, 1996.

Morris, Leon. *The Cross in the New Testament*. Grand Rapids, MI: Eerdmans, 1965.

Muller, Richard A. *After Calvin: Studies in the Development of a Theological Tradition*. Oxford Studies in Historical Theology. New York: Oxford University Press, 2003.

———. “The Covenant of Works and the Stability of Divine Law in Seventeenth-Century Reformed Orthodoxy: A Study in the Theology of Herman Witsius and Wilhelmus à Brakel.” *CTJ* 29, 1 (1994): 75–100.

———. *Dictionary of Latin and Greek Theological Terms: Drawn Principally from Protestant Scholastic Theology*. Grand Rapids, MI: Baker, 1985.

———. "The Placement of Predestination in Reformed Theology: Issue or Non-Issue?" *CTJ* 40, 2 (2005): 184–210.

———. *Prolegomena to Theology*. Vol. 1 of *Post-Reformation Reformed Dogmatics*, Grand Rapids, MI: Baker Academic, 1987.

———. "Toward the *Pactum* Salutis: Locating the Origins of a Concept." *MAJT* 18 (2007): 11–66.

———. *The Unaccommodated Calvin: Studies in the Foundation of a Theological Tradition*. New York: Oxford University Press, 2000.

Murray, John. *Christian Baptism*. 1952. Reprint, Phillipsburg, NJ: Presbyterian and Reformed, 1980.

———. *The Covenant of Grace: A Biblico-Theological Study*. London: Tyndale, 1954.

———. *The Covenant of Grace: A Biblico-Theological Study*. 1954. Reprint, Phillipsburg, NJ: Presbyterian and Reformed, 1988.

———. "Covenant Theology." In *The Encyclopedia of Christianity*, 3:199–216. Marshallton, DE: National Foundation for Christian Education, 1972.

———. *The Epistle to the Romans*. 2 vols. NICNT. Grand Rapids, MI: Eerdmans, 1959, 1965.

———. *The Imputation of Adam's Sin*. Philadelphia: Presbyterian and Reformed, 1959.

———. *Redemption Accomplished and Applied*. Grand Rapids, MI: Eerdmans, 1955.

———. *Select Lectures in Systematic Theology*. Vol. 2 of *Collected Writings of John Murray*. Carlisle, PA: Banner of Truth, 1977.

O'Donnell, Laurence R., III. "Not Subtle Enough: An Assessment of Modern Scholarship on Herman Bavinck's Reformulation of the *Pactum Salutis* Contra 'Scholastic Subtlety.'" *MAJT* 22 (2011): 89–106.

Oepke, Albrecht. s.v. καθίστημι. In *Theological Dictionary of the New Testament*, edited by Gerhard Kittel, 3:445–46. Grand Rapids, MI: Eerdmans, 1965.

Olevianus, Caspar. *De Substantia foederis gratuiti inter Deum et electos. . . .* Geneva: Eustathius Vignon, 1585.

———. *A Firm Foundation: An Aid to Interpreting the Heidelberg Catechism*. Edited and translated by Lyle D. Bierma. Texts & Studies in Reformation & Post-Reformation Thought, edited by Richard A. Muller. Grand Rapids, MI: Baker Academic, 1995.

Otis, John M. *Danger in the Camp: An Analysis and Refutation of the Heresies of the Federal Vision*. Corpus Christi, TX: Triumphant Publications, 2005.

Pieters, K. J., and J. R. Kreulen. *De Kinderdoop volgens de Beginselen der Gereformeerde Kerk, in haar Gronden, Toedieningen en Praktijk*. Franeker, Neth.: T. Telenga, 1861.

Piper, John. *Counted Righteous in Christ: Should We Abandon the Imputation of Christ's Righteousness?* Wheaton, IL: Crossway, 2002.

———. *The Future of Justification: A Response to N. T. Wright*. Wheaton, IL: Crossway, 2007.

Polanus, Amandus. *The Substance of the Christian Religion*. London: W. Apsley, 1608.

Praamsma, Louis. "The Background of the Arminian Controversy (1586–1618)." In *Crisis in the Reformed Churches*, edited by Peter Y. De Jong, 22–38. Grand Rapids, MI: Reformed Fellowship, 1968.

Preston, John. *The New Covenant, or, the Saints Portion*. London, 1629.

Ramsey, D. Patrick. "In Defense of Moses: A Confessional Critique of Kline and Karlberg." *WTJ* 66, 2 (2004): 373–400.

Ridderbos, Herman. *Paul: An Outline of His Theology*. Translated by John R. De Witt. Grand Rapids, MI: Eerdmans, 1975.

Robertson, O. Palmer. *The Christ of the Covenants*. Phillipsburg, NJ: Presbyterian and Reformed, 1980.

———. *The Christ of the Prophets*. Phillipsburg, NJ: P&R Publishing, 2004.

Rolston, Holmes, III. *John Calvin versus the Westminster Confession*. Richmond, VA: John Knox, 1972.

———. "Responsible Man in Reformed Theology: Calvin versus the Westminster Confession." *Scottish Journal of Theology* 23, 2 (1970): 129–56.

Sandlin, P. Andrew, ed. *Backbone of the Bible: Covenant in Contemporary Perspective*. Nacogdoches, TX: Covenant Media Press, 2004.

_____, ed. *A Faith That Is Never Alone: A Response to Westminster Seminary California*. La Grange, CA: Kerygma, 2007.

Schaff, Philip. *The Creeds of Christendom*. 3 vols. 1931. Reprint, Grand Rapids, MI: Baker, 1993.

Schreiner, Thomas R. *The Law and Its Fulfillment: A Pauline Theology of Law*. Grand Rapids, MI: Baker, 1993.

———. *Romans*. Grand Rapids, MI: Baker, 1998.

Scott, Thomas. *The Articles of the Synod of Dort, Translated from the Latin, with Notes*. 1818. Reprint, Harrisburg, PA: Sprinkle Publications, 1993.

Shepherd, Norman. *The Call of Grace: How the Covenant Illuminates Salvation and Evangelism*. Phillipsburg, NJ: P&R Publishing, 2000.

———. "The Covenant Context for Evangelism." In *The New Testament Student and Theology*, 51–75. Vol. 3 of *The New Testament Student*. Edited by John H. Skilton. Nutley, NJ: Presbyterian and Reformed, 1976.

———. "Justification by Faith Alone." *R&R* 11, 2 (2002): 75–90.

———. "Law and Gospel in Covenantal Perspective." Lecture presented on March 11, 2004, at a symposium titled *Trust and Obey: A Symposium on Law and Gospel*, Warrenville, IL.

———. "Law and Gospel in Covenantal Perspective." Pamphlet published by Norman Shepherd, 2004.

———. "Law and Gospel in Covenantal Perspective." *R&R* 14, 1 (2005): 73–88.

———. "Thirty-Four Theses on Justification in Relation to Faith, Repentance, and Good Works." www.hornes.org/theologia/norman-shepherd/the-34-theses.

Silva, Moisés. "Abraham, Faith, and Works: Paul's Use of Scripture in Galatians 3:6–14." *WTJ* 63, 2 (2001): 251–67.

———. *Interpreting Galatians: Explorations in Exegetical Method*. 2nd ed. Grand Rapids, MI: Baker Academic, 2001.

Sinnema, Donald. "The Issue of Reprobation at the Synod of Dort (1618–19) in Light of the History of This Doctrine." Ph.D. diss., University of St. Michael's College, 1985.

Smilde, E. *Een Eeuw van Strijd over Verbond en Doop*. Kampen: J. H. Kok, 1946.

Stam, Clarence. *The Covenant of Love: Exploring Our Relationship with God*. Winnipeg, MB: Premier, 1999.

Stanglin, Keith D. "'Arminius *avant la lettre*': Peter Baro, Jacob Arminius, and the Bond of Predestinarian Polemic." *WTJ* 67, 1 (2005): 51–74.

Stek, John H. "Covenant Overload in Reformed Theology." *CTJ* 29, 1 (1994): 12–41.

Stone, L. *The Family, Sex and Marriage in England 1500–1800*. Rev. ed. Mammondsworth, U.K.: Penguin, 1985.

Stott, John. *Romans: God's Good News for the World*. Downers Grove, IL: InterVarsity Press, 1994.

Street, T. Norton. *How to Understand Your Bible*. Rev. ed. Downers Grove, IL: InterVarsity, 1974.

Strawbridge, Gregg, ed. *The Case for Covenant Communion*. Monroe, LA: Athanasius, 2006.

"Summary Statement of AAPC's Position on the Covenant, Baptism, and Salvation." www.auburnavenue.org.

Thielman, Frank. "The Story of Israel and the Theology of Romans 5–8," in *Romans*, 169–95. Vol. 3 of *Pauline Theology*. Edited by David M. May and E. Elizabeth Johnson. Minneapolis: Fortress, 1995.

Torrance, James B. "Calvin and Puritanism in England and Scotland—Some Basic Concepts in the Development of 'Federal Theology.'" In *Calvinus Reformator: His Contribution to Theology, Church and Society*, 264–77. Potchefstroom, South Africa: Potchefstroom University for Christian Higher Education, 1982.

———. "Covenant or Contract? A Study of the Theological Background of Worship in Seventeenth-Century Scotland." *Scottish Journal of Theology* 23, 1 (1970): 51–76.

———. "Strengths and Weaknesses of the Westminster Theology." In *The Westminster Confession*, edited by Alisdair Heron, 40–53. Edinburgh: St. Andrews, 1982.

Trigland, J. *Kerckelycke Geschiedenissne*. Leiden: Adriaen Wyngaerden, 1650.

Trinterud, Leonard. "The Origins of Puritanism." *Church History* 20, 1 (1951): 37–57.

Turretin, Francis. *Institutes of Elenctic Theology*. Edited by James T. Dennison Jr. Translated by George M. Giger. 3 vols. Phillipsburg, NJ: P&R Publishing, 1992, 1994, 1997.

Ursinus, Zacharias. *The Commentary of Dr. Zacharias Ursinus on the Heidelberg Catechism*. Translated by G. W. Williard. 1852. Reprint, Grand Rapids, MI: Eerdmans, 1954.

van Asselt, Willem J. *The Federal Theology of Johannes Cocceius (1603–*

1669). Translated by Raymond A. Blacketer. Studies in the History of Christian Thought, edited by Robert J. Bast. Leiden: Brill, 2001.

Van Der Waal, C. *The Covenantal Gospel.* Neerlandia, AB: Inheritance, 1990.

VanDrunen, David. *A Biblical Case for Natural Law.* Grand Rapids, MI: Acton Institute, 2006.

———. "Israel's Recapitulation of Adam's Probation under the Law of Moses." *WTJ* 73, 2 (2011): 303–24.

———. *Natural Law and the Two Kingdoms: A Study in the Development of Reformed Social Thought.* Grand Rapids, MI: Eerdmans, 2010.

———. "A System of Theology? The Centrality of Covenant for Westminster Systematics." In *The Pattern of Sound Doctrine: Systematic Theology at the Westminster Seminaries*, edited by David VanDrunen, 195–220. Phillipsburg, NJ: P&R Publishing, 2004.

Vander Hart, Mark. "Creation and Covenant Part One: A Survey of the Dominion Mandate in the Noahic and Abrahamic Covenants." *MAJT* 6, 1 (1990): 3–18.

Van Genderen, J. *Covenant and Election.* Translated by C. Pronk. Neerlandia, AB: Inheritance, 1995.

Venema, Cornelis P. *Accepted and Renewed in Christ: The "Twofold Grace of God" and the Interpretation of Calvin's Theology.* Göttingen: Vandenhoeck & Ruprecht, 2007.

———. "Calvin's Doctrine of the Imputation of Christ's Righteousness: Another Example of 'Calvin Against the Calvinists'?" *MAJT* 20 (2009): 37–44.

———. *Children at the Lord's Table? Assessing the Case for Paedocommunion.* Grand Rapids, MI: Reformation Heritage, 2009.

———. "Covenant Theology and Baptism." In *The Case for Covenantal Infant Baptism*, edited by Gregg Strawbridge, 201–29. Phillipsburg, NJ: P&R Publishing, 2003.

———. "The Doctrine of the Sacraments and Baptism according to the Reformed Confessions." *MAJT* 11 (2000): 21–86.

———. "The Election and Salvation of the Children of Believers Who Die in Infancy: A Study of Article I/17 of the Canons of Dort." *MAJT 17* (2006): 57–100.

———. *The Gospel of Free Acceptance in Christ: An Assessment of the*

Reformation and New Perspectives on Paul. Carlisle, PA: Banner of Truth, 2006.

———. *Heinrich Bullinger and the Doctrine of Predestination: Author of "the Other Reformed Tradition"?* Texts and Studies in Reformation and Post-Reformation Thought, edited by Richard A. Muller. Grand Rapids, MI: Baker Academic, 2002.

———. "The Law of Moses: Not a Disguised Covenant of Works." *Confessional Presbyterian* 8 (2012): 212–27.

———. "The Mosaic Economy and the Covenant of Grace." *Confessional Presbyterian* 9 (2013): 157–78.

———. "N. T. Wright on Romans 5:12–21 and Justification." *MAJT* 16 (2005): 29–81.

———. "One Kingdom or Two? An Evaluation of the 'Two Kingdoms' Doctrine as an Alternative to Neo-Calvinism." *MAJT* 23 (2012): 77–129.

———. "Recent Criticisms of the 'Covenant of Works' in the *Westminster Confession of Faith*." *MAJT* 9, 2 (1993): 165–98.

Vos, Geerhardus. *Biblical Theology: Old and New Testaments.* Grand Rapids, MI: Eerdmans, 1948.

———. "The Doctrine of the Covenant in Reformed Theology." In *Redemptive History and Biblical Interpretation: The Shorter Writings of Geerhardus Vos*, edited by Richard B. Gaffin Jr., 234–67. Phillipsburg, NJ: Presbyterian and Reformed, 1980.

———. *Dogmatiek.* Vol. 1, part 1. Grand Rapids, MI: mimeographed, 1910.

Vos, J. G. *The Covenant of Grace.* Pittsburgh, PA: Crown and Covenant Publications, n.d.

Wagenaar, L. H. *Van Strijd en Overwinning: De Groote Synode van 1618 op '19 en Wat aan Haar Voorafging.* Utrecht: G. J. A. Ruys, 1909.

Ward, Rowland S. *God & Adam: Reformed Theology and the Creation Covenant.* Wantirna, Australia: New Melbourne Press, 2003.

Warfield, Benjamin Breckinridge. *Selected Shorter Writings of Benjamin B. Warfield.* Edited by John E. Meeter. 2 vols. Nutley, NJ: Presbyterian and Reformed, 1970.

———. *Studies in Theology.* 1932. Reprint, Grand Rapids, MI: Baker, 1981.

———. *The Westminster Assembly and Its Work.* New York: Oxford University Press, 1931.

Waters, Guy Prentiss. *The Federal Vision and Covenant Theology: A Comparative Analysis*. Phillipsburg, NJ: P&R Publishing, 2006.

———. *Justification and the New Perspectives on Paul: A Review and Response*. Phillipsburg, NJ: P&R Publishing, 2004.

Weir, David A. *The Origins of the Federal Theology in Sixteenth-Century Reformation Thought*. Oxford: Clarendon, 1990.

White, James R. *The God Who Justifies*. Minneapolis: Bethany House, 2001.

White, Wesley. "Saying 'Justification by Faith Alone' Isn't Enough." *MAJT* 17 (2006): 239–65.

Wilkins, Steve. "Apostasy and the Covenant II." Lecture, Auburn Avenue Presbyterian Church Pastor's Conference, 2002.

Wilkins, Steve, and Duane Garner, eds. *The Federal Vision*. Monroe, LA: Athanasius, 2004.

Wilson, Douglas. "The Objectivity of the Covenant." *Credenda/Agenda* 15, 1 (2012): 4–5.

———. *"Reformed" Is Not Enough: Recovering the Objectivity of the Covenant*. Moscow, ID: Canon Press, 2002.

Witsius, Herman. *The Economy of the Covenants between God and Man: Comprehending a Complete Body of Divinity*. Translated by William Crookshank. 2 vols. 1822. Reprint, Escondido, CA: Den Dulk Foundation, 1990.

Woolsey, Andrew. *Unity and Continuity in Covenantal Thought: A Study in the Reformed Tradition to the Westminster Assembly*. Grand Rapids, MI: Reformation Heritage, 2012.

Wright, N. T. *The Climax of the Covenant: Christ and the Law in Pauline Theology*. Minneapolis: Fortress, 1991.

———. *Christian Origins and the Question of God*. 3 vols. Minneapolis: Fortress, 1992, 1996, 2003.

———. *Justification: God's Plan & Paul's Vision*. Downers Grove, IL: IVP Academic, 2009.

———. "The Law in Romans 2." In *Paul and the Mosaic Law*, edited by James D. G. Dunn, 131–50. Grand Rapids, MI: Eerdmans, 1996.

———. *The Letter to the Romans*. Vol. 10 of *The New Interpreter's Bible*. Nashville: Abingdon, 2002.

———. "New Exodus, New Inheritance: The Narrative Substructure of Romans 3–8." In *Romans and the People of God: Essays in Honor of*

Gordon D. Fee on the Occasion of His 65th Birthday, edited by S. Soderlund and N. T. Wright, 26–35. Grand Rapids, MI: Eerdmans, 1999.

———. "New Perspectives on Paul." http://ntwrightpage.com/Wright_New_Perspectives.htm.

———. *Paul for Everyone: Romans Part 1, Chapters 1–8*. Louisville: Westminster John Knox Press, 2004.

———. "The Paul of History and the Apostle of Faith." *Tyndale Bulletin* 29 (1978): 61–88.

———. "The Shape of Justification." http://www.thepaulpage.com/the-shape-of-justification/.

———. *What Saint Paul Really Said: Was Paul of Tarsus the Real Founder of Christianity?* Grand Rapids, MI: Eerdmans, 1997.

———. *Who Was Jesus?* Grand Rapids, MI: Eerdmans, 1992.

Index of Scripture

Index of Subjects and Names

More from P&R

"It is clear from Waters's critique that the new Federal Vision theologians desire to be biblical, a goal all of us gladly share. What we most earnestly want is not victory in theological debate but unity in biblical understanding. We are indebted to Waters for advancing the discussion along biblical lines 'in the bond of peace.'"

—**David Calhoun,** Professor Emeritus of Church History, Covenant Theological Seminary

"Preferring light to heat, Waters has done an admirable job of allowing his interlocutors to speak for themselves. He offers clear-headed, exegetically grounded responses."

—**Michael S. Horton**, J. Gresham Machen Professor of Systematic Theology and Apologetics, Westminster Seminary California

More from P&R

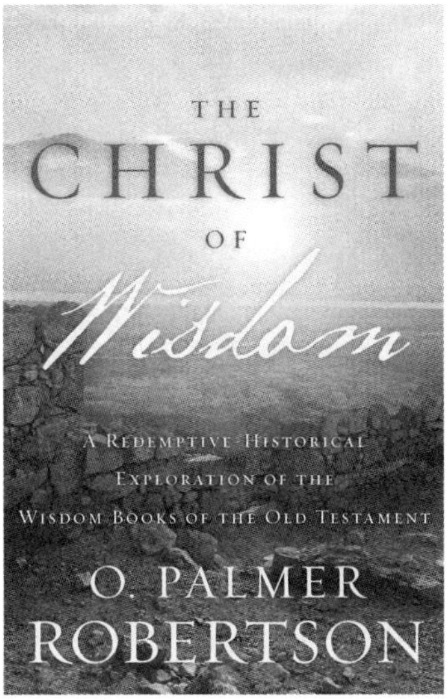

"Robertson's book is the best I know of on this subject. It focuses on what the Bible itself says about wisdom, particularly in the wisdom literature. I have learned much from it, and I hope that many others will as well."

—**John M. Frame**, Professor Emeritus of Systematic Theology and Philosophy, Reformed Theological Seminary, Orlando

"A major contribution to Christian understanding of wisdom in the Old Testament. As always, Palmer Robertson's work is firmly rooted in the full authority of Scripture and in the supremacy of Christ over all creation. . . . He not only addresses academic issues, but also provides enormously helpful insights into the practical application of biblical wisdom to modern life."

—**Richard L. Pratt Jr.**, President, Third Millennium Ministries